Maximum Performance: The Dow Jones-Irwin Complete Guide to Practical Business Management

Volume II

Joseph Shetzen

DOW JONES-IRWIN
Homewood, IL 60430
Boston, MA 02116

TO MY MOTHER, Alichen Shetzen, who instilled in me
decency, diligence, optimism, and the desire to help others.

TO MY FATHER, Benno Shetzen, who taught me that in order to succeed,
one needs to persevere and remain strong and calm.

This publication is designed to provide accurate and
authoritative information in regard to the subject matter
covered. It is sold with the understanding that neither the
author nor the publisher is engaged in rendering legal, accounting,
or other professional service. If legal advice or other expert
assistance is required, the services of a competent
professional person should be sought.

*From a Declaration of Principles jointly adopted by a Committee
of the American Bar Association and a Committee of Publishers.*

Sponsoring editor: Jim Childs
Project editor: Joan A. Hopkins
Production manager: Diane Palmer
Compositor: Publication Services
Typeface: 11/13 Times Roman
Printer: The Maple-Vail Book Manufacturing Group

Library of Congress Cataloging-in-Publication Data
Shetzen, Joseph.
    Maximum performance: The Dow Jones-Irwin
    complete guide to practical business
    management, Volumes I and II
      1. Industrial management. I. Dow Jones-Irwin.
II. Title.
HD31.S453 1990   658   89–25848
ISBN 1–55623–111–3 (v. 1)
ISBN 1–55623–112–1 (v. 2)

Printed in the United States of America

1 2 3 4 5 6 7 8 9 0 MP 7 6 5 4 3 2 1 0

Preface

If you are a business owner, accountant, or management consultant, this book is definitely for you. The primary purpose of this book (Volumes I and II) is to provide you with essential, practical knowledge and the ability to solve problems in business management. Although numerous books have been written by various experts on this subject, most are designed to meet the needs of students and therefore present complex theoretical concepts coupled with little practical knowledge.

This book, however, contains substantial practical information and is designed as a highly effective business management tool. Just like a builder who uses tools in erecting a house, you need tools to plan, develop, and manage your business or to provide sound professional advice to your clients. Your task is particularly difficult since your success or failure depends primarily upon your personal knowledge and experience in various areas of business management.

As a co-owner of a small manufacturing company and later as a management consultant, I have engaged in an extensive search for the "magic formula" for successful business management. While gaining experience, I found that many business owners have limited management skills and fail to see the "big picture." Some employ experts in various management areas but then cannot coordinate the activities of their management teams effectively.

This brings to mind the story about Swan, Pike, and Crayfish written by a Russian fabulist, Ivan Krilov. These three friends wanted to move a cart together. They tried very hard but could not succeed because Swan wanted to fly, Pike wanted to swim, and Crayfish wanted to crawl. In the end they failed in their efforts, and the cart was never moved. In business terms this is called "mismanagement."

A business owner's inability to see the "big picture" and the resulting mismanagement are among the major causes of failure for thousands of businesses every year. This is particularly unfortunate because starting a new business requires tremendous internal strength and motivation, significant financial resources and sacrifices, and a total commitment to working 25 hours a day to become the master of one's destiny.

Since lack of managerial knowledge and experience is so widespread in the business community, I felt compelled to continue the search for the "magic formula" for successful business management. The discovery took place unexpectedly one evening during a symphony concert. While I was listening to the beautiful music and watching the conductor leading his orchestra, something struck me. I suddenly realized that every business should operate precisely like an orchestra; the conductor knows what each musician should play and when it should be played. In business terms this means that every entrepreneur, company president, or CEO must know what each member of the management team should do and when it should be done. Only then will the business produce "beautiful music" or perform to the satisfaction of its shareholders and employees.

This simple discovery led me to devise a new business management method, which I hope will break the vicious cycle of incompetence, ignorance, mismanagement, and ultimate failure. The method represents a "be-your-own-management-consultant" guide for business owners. It is designed to enable entrepreneurs, company presidents, and CEOs to identify, analyze, and solve various management problems. This method also teaches business people to delegate effectively a wide range of responsibilities to subordinates and to control their performances. Finally, it is designed to help accountants and management consultants render effective management advice to their clients.

I termed it the "Business Engineering Method" because it is based on an integrated multidisciplinary approach to business management and it uses engineering principles of solving problems. The six parts to this method are described in two volumes as follows:

Volume I

Part 1   General Management Guide
Part 2   Personnel Management Guide
Part 3   Financial Management Guide

Volume II

Part 4   Production and Operations Management Guide
Part 5   Marketing and Sales Management Guide
Part 6   Business Analysis and Action Guide

Each part is written in simple language, and, together they highlight all the major elements of practical business management. In addition, each part contains a detailed set of working instructions and self-explanatory standard forms. These have been designed for and successfully used in various small and medium-sized companies.

When you complete the management tasks according to the guidelines in both volumes, you should be able to:

1. Understand all major elements of operational business management.
2. Assess personal knowledge and evaluate your company's performance in each management area.
3. Evaluate your company's financial performance, interpret results, and prepare a consolidated plan of action.
4. Implement the most effective business solutions by following the prescribed guidelines.
5. Assess action taken and adjust such action where necessary.

Business Management Club

If you experience difficulty in accomplishing any of these tasks, additional management assistance can be yours through membership in Business Management Club. This organization represents a network of licensed and highly skilled business experts who are professors in various business schools, accountants, and management consultants. Since Business Management Club is being developed on a countrywide basis, you will soon have an opportunity to obtain additional assistance locally.

Business Management Club has a number of important purposes:

• To provide business owners with a wide range of practical management methods, systems, and solutions.

- To enable business owners to act as management consultants to their own organizations.
- To enable business owners to coordinate the work of their management teams in the most efficient manner.
- To keep business owners abreast of all the latest developments in operational business management.
- To provide business owners with low-cost management consulting service when necessary.
- To provide training for business owners, accountants, and management consultants in various areas of operational business management.

Business Management Club is totally committed to the promotion of interests of all small and medium-sized organizations. This commitment will always remain the most important single factor in the process of development, distribution, and implementation of sound, effective management solutions on a do-it-yourself basis or through low-cost services of licensed management consultants.

Since additional management assistance is provided solely to members of Business Management Club, you are invited to apply for your free membership. Once your application is accepted, you will be contacted by the local representative of Business Management Club's network, who will then give you additional details about the management assistance you can expect in the future. Hopefully, this will be the beginning of a most productive and mutually beneficial association.

Joseph Shetzen

Santa Monica, California
April 1, 1990

Acknowledgements

Just as a long distance runner feels tremendous appreciation of his supporters, I am filled with deep gratitude to a few very special people who helped me complete this project.

First, I want to thank my parents, Alichen and Benno Shetzen, for their devotion and continual support throughout my life and particularly during the tought times we endured together. They served as a constant source of inspiration to me from the very beginning of the project.

I also want to thank Dr. Bruce A. Samuelson, Chairman of Accounting, Law and Finance at the School of Business and Management, Pepperdine University. Dr. Samuelson's generous contribution of knowledge, time, and moral support played a significant role in the completion of this project.

Further, thanks go to the following contributing editors for their valuable input to this project:

- Dr. Richard E. Gunther, Professor of Management Science at California State University, Northridge
- Dr. Charles W. Fojtik, Associate Professor of Marketing at the School of Business and Management, Pepperdine University
- Dr. Barry R. Nathan, Assistant Professor of Management and Organization at the School of Business Administration, University of Southern California

In addition, I am grateful to the following persons for their generous assistance and cooperation during the development of this project:

- Mr. Anthony Southall, management consultant
- Mr. Brian C. Schiff, partner at Price Waterhouse Associates
- Dr. Zvi Livne, Professor at the Graduate School of Business, Columbia University
- Dr. Richard H. Buskirk, Professor of Marketing and Director of the Entrepreneur Program, University of Southern California
- Dr. William A. Cohen, Professor of Marketing, California State University, Los Angeles

Moreover, I want to thank Jim Childs, Senior Editor with Dow Jones-Irwin, and the staffs of Dow Jones-Irwin, Richard D. Irwin, Inc., and Publication Services, Inc., who worked so hard to make this book a reality. My special thanks go to Shirley Sunn for her support and superb proofreading of my manuscripts. She certainly helped me overcome the fact that English in not my mother tongue. My thanks also to Jeanette Udwin and David D'Albany for their efficiency and patience in typing the manuscripts.

Finally, I would like to express my appreciation to all my clients, who provided me with a variety of management problems and the ultimate challenge of finding the right solutions.

J. S.

About the Author

Joseph Shetzen is the founder and president of the Business Management Club, Inc., a nationwide organization that is committed to promoting self-education of entrepreneurs and professionals in the area of business management. Mr. Shetzen is constantly engaged in developing practical management solutions for organizations in such areas as general administration, human resources, finance and accounting, production and operations, marketing, and sales. One of his major accomplishments is the development of the unique "business engineering" method. This method is designed to enable business owners to become management consultants to their organizations and to solve a broad range of managerial problems on a "do-it-yourself" basis.

Mr. Shetzen is a professional engineer with extensive business management experience. He previously ran a successful management consulting practice and co-owned a small manufacturing company. Mr. Shetzen received his B.S. in engineering from Ben-Gurion University in Israel and is a member of the American Production and Inventory Control Society.

About the Contributing Editors

BRUCE A. SAMUELSON
B.S., M.B.A., Washington State University; C.P.A., State of Washington;
D.B.A., University of Southern California

B. Samuelson is a Professor of Accounting and Chairman of the Department of Accounting, Law and Finance at School of Business and Management, Pepperdine University. Prior to that he served for five years as a Director of the Small Business Institute at the University of California and in that capacity provided a management consutling service to small businesses in Orange County. Dr. Samuelson is also an executive officer of several corporations. Previously he served as an audit supervisor in the U.S. General Accounting Office, an auditor for a public accounting firm, and an accountant for a manufacturing firm. He also taught at University of Southern California, California State University in Long Beach, and the University of California at Irvine. Furthermore, he is an author of several articles that have appeared in *The Accounting Review, The Journal of Accountancy*, and *Organization Studies*.

RICHARD E. GUNTHER
Ph.D. in Operations Management, UCLA

R. Gunther is a Professor of Management Science at California State University in Northridge. His research interests are in production and inventory control. Dr. Gunther also has an extensive management consulting experience providing service to various small and medium-sized companies in California. In addition, he serves as executive officer of several organizations. Dr. Gunther has also taught a number of courses for the Ventura and San Fernando Valley Chapters of the American Production and Inventory Control Society (APICS). He has also published several articles in such professional publications as *Management Science, Decision Sciences,* and the *Journal of Operations Management*.

CHARLES W. FOJTIK
B.A., Northwestern University; M.B.A. and D.B.A., University of Southern California

C. Fojtik is an Associate Professor of Marketing at the School of Business and Management, Pepperdine University. His research interests are in various areas of marketing management. In addition, Dr. Fojtik heads the Delphi Bureau, a consulting operation specializing in forecasting and research for new products and services. He provided management consulting service to numerous small and medium-sized companies in such areas as assessment of sales potential and development of marketing plans.

BARRY R. NATHAN
B.S., University of Maryland; M.A. and Ph.D., University of Akron

B. Nathan is an Assistant Professor of Management and Orgainzation in the School of Business Administration, University of Southern California. He specializes in various areas of human resource management such as employee selection, compensation, performance appraisal, and training. Dr. Nathan is the author of many professional publications—the latest include *Legal and Technical Standards for Performance Assessment* and *Behavior Modeling: Training Principles and Applications*. Furthermore, he is a member of the Academy of Management and the Society of Industrial/Organizational Psychology.

Contents for Volume I

Contents for Volume II

Part 4

Production and Operations Management Guide

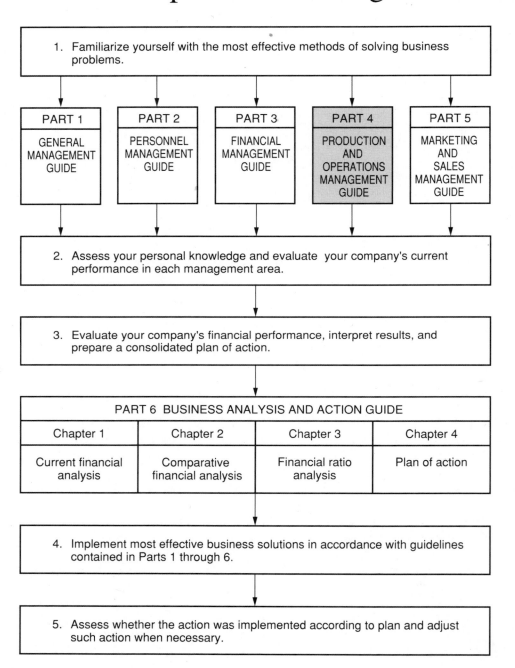

1. Familiarize yourself with the most effective methods of solving business problems.

PART 1	PART 2	PART 3	PART 4	PART 5
GENERAL MANAGEMENT GUIDE	PERSONNEL MANAGEMENT GUIDE	FINANCIAL MANAGEMENT GUIDE	PRODUCTION AND OPERATIONS MANAGEMENT GUIDE	MARKETING AND SALES MANAGEMENT GUIDE

2. Assess your personal knowledge and evaluate your company's current performance in each management area.

3. Evaluate your company's financial performance, interpret results, and prepare a consolidated plan of action.

PART 6 BUSINESS ANALYSIS AND ACTION GUIDE			
Chapter 1	Chapter 2	Chapter 3	Chapter 4
Current financial analysis	Comparative financial analysis	Financial ratio analysis	Plan of action

4. Implement most effective business solutions in accordance with guidelines contained in Parts 1 through 6.

5. Assess whether the action was implemented according to plan and adjust such action when necessary.

- *The 20 elements of practical production and operations management*
- *Working instructions and forms for evaluating your company's production and operations management*
- *Guidelines for implementing effective production and operations management strategies and much more*

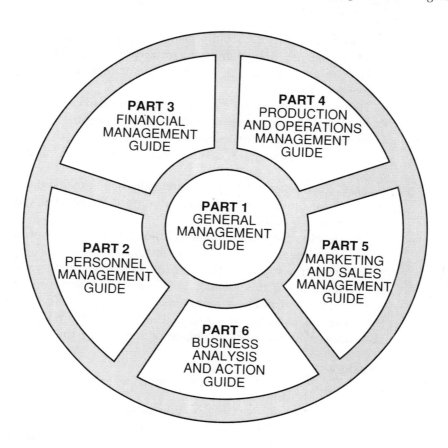

Contents

4.00 Introduction

The prime purpose of the **production and operations management guide** is to identify business problems and implement the most effective solutions in the area of production and operations management. This guide highlights a variety of issues, such as:

- How to design, locate and organize a manufacturing facility
- How to select, design and standardize products and manufacturing processes
- How to evaluate, select, position, maintain, and replace machinery, equipment, and tools
- How to prepare accurate cost estimates prior to obtaining production orders
- How to plan and control production and operations in manufacturing and nonmanufacturing environments
- How to plan, purchase, control, store, and dispatch materials

These and other related issues are addressed in the production and operations management guide. All issues are described in **20 checkpoints** presented in **Sections 4.01—4.20.**

To develop the most suitable solutions in the area of production and operations management, it is necessary to understand the issues discussed in this part. Thorough self-assessment by company executives and evaluation of company performance in the aforementioned area will indicate the effectiveness of current production and operations management principles. This, in turn, will help to formulate a sound plan of action and implement the most effective solutions in accordance with the **work program** presented in Exhibit 4–1.

Exhibit 4–1

Work Program for Part 4

Work Program	
Planned Action	**Objective**
1. Study of production and operations management principles	To attain an adequate level of knowledge in the area of production and operations management
2. Self-evaluation of knowledge by members of the management team in the area of production and operations management	To identify individual strengths and weaknesses of members of the management team in the area of production and operations management
3. Evaluation of company performance in the area of production and operations management	To identify the level of company performance in the area of production and operations management and to establish the average evaluation level
4. Formulation of a plan of action in the area of production and operations management	To summarize the range of activities that must be undertaken in the area of production and operations management
5. Implementation of the most effective business solutions in the area of production and operations management	To develop a set of the most suitable solutions in accordance with guidelines presented in this part
6. Evaluation and control of actions in the area of production and operations management	To assess whether the action was implemented according to plan and to adjust such action when necessary

Note: Please familiarize yourself with relevant working instructions prior to completing forms at the end of this part. Additional information on these forms is available from Business Management Club, Inc. upon request

4.01 The Production and Operations Management Process

The main purpose of production and operations management is to plan, organize, direct, and control the process of bringing together people, equipment, and materials to manufacture products or provide services. It is essential, therefore, that top managers pay serious attention to these activities and develop, implement, and maintain the **production and operations management process**.

The term "production management" has been associated with various product manufacturing activities for many years. A broader term "production and operations management" has been popularized in recent years and covers manufacturing and nonmanufacturing activities alike. Since each term addresses similar management issues, both are used interchangeably throughout this volume.

The most important task of the production or operations manager is to initiate the production and operations management process within the organization. Planning and control of the production and operations management process entails a number of steps outlined in Exhibit 4–2.

The production and operations management process requires familiarization with various types of operational activities. These activities are generally classified as manufacturing activities, nonmanufacturing activities, contracts, and special projects. Manufacturing activities, for example, entail conversion of raw materials into finished products in a job shop, batch production, or flow production environment. Nonmanufacturing activities, on the other hand, include rendition of custom or standard services and sale of merchandise on a wholesale or retail basis. These activities, as well as contracts and special projects, are discussed further in this part.

Once a particular type of operations is identified, a suitable facility needs to be designed, located, and organized. Facility design entails consideration of a broad range of factors such as present and future accommodation needs, manufacturing or operational requirements, budget limitations, and time parameters. Selection of a suitable location for the new facility is also an important managerial responsibility. The selection process is usually based on such considerations as intercompany integration; availability and cost of labor, services, materials, and transportation; expansion potential; zoning and legal regulations; cost of land; and living conditions. Finally, the process of facility organization entails building a working structure and developing an efficient framework for relationships within the production department.

Another aspect of production and operations management entails selection, design, and standardization of products or services offered to customers. The product selection process, for example, represents the combined and continuous effort of production and marketing executives. Product design, on the other hand, is carried out by production personnel and involves several stages. These stages generally include product conception, feasibility study, preliminary design, prototype construction and testing, final design, and pre-production testing. Sound production management also requires continuous simplification and standardization of the product range to maximize overall operational efficiency.

Selection, design, and standardization of products and services are meaningless without a comprehensive set of procedures for manufacturing such products or providing such services. Hence, one of the major responsibilities of the production manager is to develop efficient manufacturing or operational processes to satisfy customer needs. Process design requires consideration of several important factors including company financial resources, specific design requirements, equipment and manpower availability, and demand in the marketplace.

Exhibit 4–2

The Production and Operations Management Process

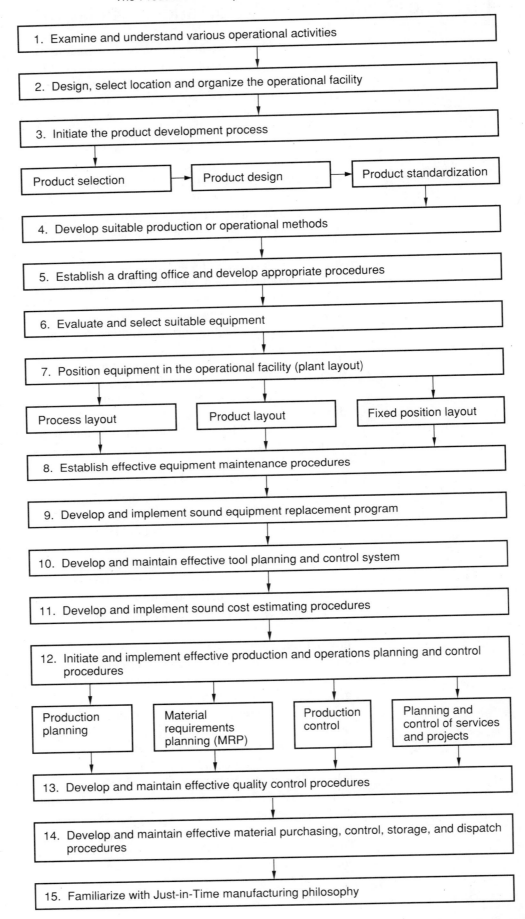

1. Examine and understand various operational activities

2. Design, select location and organize the operational facility

3. Initiate the product development process

| Product selection | → | Product design | → | Product standardization |

4. Develop suitable production or operational methods

5. Establish a drafting office and develop appropriate procedures

6. Evaluate and select suitable equipment

7. Position equipment in the operational facility (plant layout)

| Process layout | Product layout | Fixed position layout |

8. Establish effective equipment maintenance procedures

9. Develop and implement sound equipment replacement program

10. Develop and maintain effective tool planning and control system

11. Develop and implement sound cost estimating procedures

12. Initiate and implement effective production and operations planning and control procedures

| Production planning | Material requirements planning (MRP) | Production control | Planning and control of services and projects |

13. Develop and maintain effective quality control procedures

14. Develop and maintain effective material purchasing, control, storage, and dispatch procedures

15. Familiarize with Just-in-Time manufacturing philosophy

Design of products and processes represents an important function within the design department or in the drafting office. This function is normally carried out by a designer or a design engineer, depending upon the company's organizational structure. The drafting office is responsible for the timely issue of all new and revised drawings related to product and process design and modification. It is necessary, therefore, to develop effective working procedures within the drafting office to meet various manufacturing and operational requirements.

Another important function of the production manager relates to evaluation and selection of suitable equipment. This process requires consideration of factors such as equipment operational capacity, versatility, reliability, maintenance, safety, and compatibility. Additional factors may include equipment availability, installation, design, ancillary equipment, and overall effect on the organization. The final selection of equipment also demands comprehensive evaluation of anticipated fixed and operating costs associated with the utilization of equipment in the production department.

Once suitable equipment is selected it needs to be properly positioned within the production facility to ensure most effective performance. Hence, facility layout, or plant* layout, represents another important responsibility of the production or operations manager. Good plant layout involves consideration of several factors such as operational flexibility, coordination, accessibility and visibility, movement and handling of materials, personnel comfort, safety, and operational security. Depending upon the specific technological requirements, three different types of plant layout may be selected. These include process layout, product layout, and fixed position layout.

Effective performance of the operational facility strongly depends upon the standard and frequency of equipment maintenance. This function may also include design, construction, modification, installation, and removal of machinery. Equipment maintenance in a small or medium-sized company is usually handled by the service section within the production department or by a specially designated maintenance person. Moreover, many companies develop and adhere to preventive maintenance programs to secure high standards of operational performance.

Since equipment does not last forever, it is necessary to develop and implement a sound equipment replacement program. Some of the major objectives of this program include reduction of operational and repair costs, increase in operational capacity, and simplification of manufacturing operations and processes. Subsequently, the development of an equipment replacement program requires consideration of several technical and cost-related factors associated with the use of equipment in the production department.

Another important responsibility of the production or operations manager is the development and implementation of an effective tool planning and control system. Such a system relates to standard, special, and perishable tools as well as jigs and fixtures used in the production facility. The planning of tooling requirements represents an integral part of the effective production planning process. Although some companies have their own toolroom, the bulk of tools is still being purchased from tooling specialists.

Once the production facility becomes functional the routine operational activities may begin. One of the first elements of these activities is preparation of

---

*"Plant" is defined by Webster as "the tools, machinery, fixtures, buildings, grounds, etc. of a factory or business."

accurate cost estimates of products or services and specification of delivery or completion dates. The cost estimating procedure requires identification of all labor, material, and plant overhead costs involved in a particular operational process. Moreover, cost estimating provides the foundation for controlling manufacturing or nonmanufacturing expenses and determining the final selling price of products or services.

One of the most important functional responsibilities imposed on the production manager is effective planning of operations within the production department. This entails systematic predetermination of methods and procedures for the completion of products or services in the most economical manner. Effective production plans aim to accommodate manufacturing output, manpower, and equipment utilization requirements as well as to maintain sufficient inventory levels. The two basic functions of production planning are scheduling manufacturing activities into acceptable timetables and loading various machines and operations in accordance with specific operational needs.

The material requirements planning (MRP) system is an integral element of the overall production planning process. The prime purpose of the MRP system is to calculate the quantity and determine the timing of materials, parts, and components required to complete a particular manufacturing task. Some small and medium-sized companies use a computerized version of the MRP system to maximize the efficiency of the production planning process. Among the main sources of information used by the MRP system are the master production schedule, the bill of materials file, and the inventory status file.

Production control represents one of the most critical functional responsibilities of the production manager. The main purposes of production control are to authorize operational activities, to secure effective implementation of production plans, and to maintain control over manufacturing costs within the production department. The two basic functions of production control are dispatching and expediting work in accordance with the production planning requirements. Dispatching entails authorization and initiation of manufacturing activities. The main purpose of work expediting, on the other hand, is to maintain overall control of all manufacturing activities once production has begun.

Effective production planning and control are also critical in a nonmanufacturing environment. This managerial responsibility relates specifically to planning and control of services, contracts, and long-term projects. The prime purpose of operational planning in a nonmanufacturing environment is to formulate methods and procedures required for completion of various services, contracts, or long-term projects. Operational control in a nonmanufacturing environment, on the other hand, aims at authorizing and monitoring appropriate activities to ensure the fulfillment of operational plans.

The effectiveness of manufacturing and nonmanufacturing organizations also depends upon quality control standards established and maintained within the production or operations department. The major purpose of a sound quality control procedure is to develop a suitable quality assurance program within the production facility. The quality assurance program generally aims at ensuring the quality of design, conformance, and performance of products and services offered by the company. Moreover, quality control entails evaluation and continuous improvement of manufacturing processes, identification of defects, and prevention of their occurrence in products or services.

Another important element of production and operations management relates to purchasing, control, storage, and dispatch of materials. The prime purpose of material purchasing, for example, is to ascertain that the "right" quality and quantity of materials are purchased at the "right" time, and at the "right" price from the "right" source. Upon their purchase and delivery, all materials must be properly inspected and stored in an appropriate storage place. The storage and control of materials is particularly important to manufacturing organizations where a variety of inventories is used. Finally, materials dispatch entails developing sound procedures to ensure timely delivery of products to customers.

Familiarization with modern production and operations management principles cannot be completed without understanding a highly successful Japanese approach to solving manufacturing problems. This approach, embodied in the Just-in-Time (JIT) manufacturing philosophy, is discussed at the end of this part. The prime objective of the JIT philosophy is to eliminate waste in the total manufacturing process, from purchasing of raw materials through distribution of finished goods. The JIT philosophy also incorporates the concepts of total quality throughout the manufacturing process, uniform loading of equipment, overlapping of operations, reduced setup times, pull system, JIT purchasing, employee participation, and teamwork.

4.02 Classification of Operational Activities

Effective managerial performance in production and operations management requires an in-depth understanding of all operational activities. These activities, illustrated in Exhibit 4–3, can be classified as follows:

- Manufacturing activities
- Nonmanufacturing activities
- Contractors and special projects

Manufacturing activity entails the process of converting raw materials into finished products through the utilization of equipment, tools, labor, and other production facilities. This process is known as the **manufacturing process**. There are three basic production methods used in the manufacturing process, namely job shop production, batch production, and flow production. Comparative evaluation of these methods is presented in Exhibit 4–4.

Job shop production, or **open job shop**, is the intermittent manufacturing process in which each assignment is performed in accordance with a specific customer's order. This process is characterized by manufacturing a broad range of nonstandard products, high capital investment and setup costs, general purpose equipment, and highly skilled labor requirements. A job shop operation, such as a general engineering shop or a custom-designed furniture manufacturer, maintains production capability but does not offer a particular product for sale. Consequently, such an operation is generally only required to carry raw materials inventory and supplies that are frequently used.

The job shop, in essence, offers manufacturing facilities and skilled labor to customers at short notice. Products are usually manufactured in small quantities, often on a one-off basis, according to specific customer requirements. Job shop production is characterized by irregularity of work-flow and necessitates effective implementation of production planning and control procedures.

Batch production, or **closed job shop**, is another intermittent manufacturing process whereby various customers' requirements are grouped into batches

Exhibit 4–3

Classification of Operational Activities

Manufacturing Activities

Job Shop Production	**Batch Production***	**Flow Production**
Custom-designed products	Bakery	Appliances
Special purpose machinery	Clothing	Brewery
Toolmaking manufacturing	Electrical products	Brick and tile
General engineering shop	Fasteners	Cable and wire
Model manufacturing	Footwear	Chemicals
Handmade products	Furniture	Cement
	Jewelry	Cosmetics
	Machinery	Food
	Metal products	Glass
	Plastic products	Newspapers
	Printing	Paint
	Sheet metal products	Paper Mill
		Pharmaceutical
		Refinery
		Soft drinks
		Textile mill
		Tobacco products
		Vehicles

Nonmanufacturing Activities

Service		**Merchandising**	
Custom	**Standard**	**Wholesale**	**Retail**
Health care	Banking	Product wholesaler	Shop
Professional consulting	Child day care	Import agency	Gas station
Accounting	Education	Export agency	Market
Financial	Electroplating		Supermarket
Engineering	Entertainment		
Legal	Insurance		
Psychotherapy	Rental of equipment		
Architectural	Restaurants		
Plumbing	Telecommunications		
Electrical	Transportation		
Maintenance	Traveling		
Repair shop			
Photography			
Musicians			
Catering			
Secretarial			
Cleaning			

Contractors and Special Projects

Contractors	**Special Projects**
Building contractors	Writers, Publishers
Civil contractors (roads, bridges)	Artists, Film producers
	Designers, Engineering design firm
	Scientists, Science research

* Larger quantities of these products may be manufactured in flow production environment.

on a similar product basis. This process is characterized by a broad range of standard and nonstandard products manufactured, high capital investment and average setup costs, general and special purpose machinery, and skilled labor requirements. A batch production operation, such as a bakery or clothing manufacturer, is geared to produce small and average quantities of products on

Exhibit 4–4

Comparative Evaluation of Manufacturing Methods

Description	Job Shop	Batch Production	Flow Production
		Manufacturing Methods	
Manufacturing	To customers' orders only	To customers' orders and stock	To stock and sometimes to order
Type of Order	Most orders are unique and non-repetitive	Most orders are not unique and repetitive	All orders are standard and repetitive
Product Range	There is no standard range of products	There is a broad range of standard and nonstandard products	There is a limited range of standard products
Product Unit Cost	Very high	Average	Very low
Production Volume	Very low, usually one or few items	Average, in batches of tens, hundreds, or even, thousands	Very high
Production Method	Very diversified and sometimes repetitive	Diversified but usually repetitive	Standardized and repetitive (e.g., conveyor line)
Equipment Application	Very general application to various manufacturing processes	General and semi-specialized application to various manufacturing processes	Very specialized application to a limited number of manufacturing processes
Operational Capacity Planning	Can be scheduled at short notice only	Can be planned and scheduled approximately one week in advance	Must be planned and scheduled well in advance
Raw Material Inventory	Should be purchased for every order on an individual basis	Should be purchased in advance in optimal quantities	Must be prepurchased in advance in optimal quantities
Work-in-Process and Components Inventory	No need	Buffer stocks should be kept in optimal quantities for selected products	Buffer stocks should be kept in optimal quantities for all products
Finished Goods Inventory	No need	Optimal quantities should be kept for selected products	Optimal quantities should be kept for all finished goods
Subcontracting Services	Should be used on an individual order basis	Should be preplanned and used on an individual batch basis	Must be planned well in advance for every production run
Personnel Skills Requirements	Very high level for a general application	Average level for semistandardized application	Average level for a highly standardized application

repetitive and nonrepetitive basis. This production method requires that specific raw materials are purchased in advance, and certain components and finished goods are kept in stock in optimal quantities.

Batch production combines versatile manufacturing capabilities and offers operational capacity and skilled labor to customers at a reasonable notice period. Products are manufactured in batches of tens, hundreds, thousands, or more depending upon the specific production requirements. The length of production runs fluctuates in relation to the quantities manufactured and the cost per product-unit varies accordingly. Batch production is decidedly the most popular method utilized by the majority of small and medium-sized manufacturing companies. This method requires a flexible approach and effective planning and control of the manufacturing operations.

Flow production, also known as **continuous production** or **mass production**, is the manufacturing process during which the work content of the product continually increases with time. It means that, as the work on each operation is completed, the work-in-process is passed to the next manufacturing stage without waiting for completion of the entire batch. Smooth performance of flow production necessitates that all manufacturing operations last the same period of time and that no deviation from the standard manufacturing cycle is allowed. A typical example of flow production is a conveyor line or an assembly line. This method is characterized by a large volume of identical products that undergo repetitive and highly mechanized manufacturing processes. Flow production is also characterized by specialized equipment, long production runs, and average labor skill requirements.

Large companies frequently utilize flow production methods to manufacture standard products in a make-to-stock operation. The flow production method requires detailed planning of all operations well in advance. Production control, however, remains relatively simple since all operational instructions are incorporated into the manufacturing process at the planning stage.

The job shop, batch production, and flow production methods are not necessarily associated with any particular manufacturing volume. However, many companies often start the manufacturing process as a job shop, and proceed to batch production methods as volume increases. Finally, upon further increase of the production demand, they introduce flow production techniques.

Nonmanufacturing activity, includes a variety of service and merchandising operations. **Service operation** is a nonmanufacturing activity in which each assignment results in completing a specific type of work or, simply, satisfying a customer's need. All service operations, in turn, can be classified as **custom services**, also known as **specialized services**, or **standard services**. The custom service, similar to the job shop, is characterized by a specialized service-to-order operation. This includes such services as secretarial, plumbing, electrical, repairs, maintenance, photography, catering, medical, legal, consulting, and accounting. Each of these services is provided in accordance with the particular customer's requirements.

The majority of small and medium-sized companies provide custom service to their customers. Standard services, conversely, entail rendition of services on a continuous process basis irrespective of a specific customer's order. Such services include banking, entertainment, communication, education, insurance, and transportation. These services are generally provided by larger organizations. Comparative evaluation of both service methods is summarized in Exhibit 4–5. Additional details pertaining to service companies are discussed further in this part.

Merchandising operation represents another type of a nonmanufacturing activity. Merchandising operation, in essence, is based on buying and selling of products or merchandise at a profit. There are two basic types of merchandising operations, namely wholesale and retail trade. **Wholesale operation** entails the purchase of large quantities of materials and goods and resale to the retail trade. Wholesale companies usually carry a limited number of product lines and sell a high volume of products at a reasonable profit markup. **Retail operation**, on the other hand, entails the purchase of average quantities of products and resale to the general public. Retailers often specialize in particular product lines such as food, appliances, clothing, or furniture and normally carry a large variety of products in that line. These products are sold to individual customers in small quantities at higher profit markups. Comparative evaluation of both merchandising methods is summarized in Exhibit 4–6.

Contractors and **special projects** represent another category of operational activities. These activities are performed in accordance with particular contrac-

Exhibit 4–5

Comparative Evaluation of Service Methods

Description	Service Methods	
	Custom Service	**Standard Service**
Service is Rendered	On an intermittent basis to customers' requirements only	On a continuous flow basis
Type of Order	Most orders are unique and nonrepetitive	All orders are standard and repetitive
Service Range	There is a broad but very specialized range of services	There is a limited range of standard services
Service Unit Cost	Very high	Very low to medium
Service Volume	Low to medium	Medium to high
Service Method	Very diversified and sometimes repetitive	Standardized and always repetitive
Equipment Application	Very general application to various types of service processes	Very specialized application to a limited number of services
Operational Capacity Planning	Can be scheduled at a short notice only	Must be planned and scheduled well in advance
Inventory Requirements	No need except for consumable items	No need except for consumable items
Personnel Skill Requirements	Very high level for a general application	Average level for a highly standardized application

tual obligations undertaken by certain companies or individuals. Building and civil contractors, for example, are engaged in erecting houses, building roads, and constructing bridges. Each project entails a large number of operations and requires heavy planning and equipment, substantial volume of material, and a large number of employees. In addition, special projects may involve such activities as writing a book, designing new product, or conducting scientific research. These projects usually require special types of skills and may last for long periods of time.

Exhibit 4–6

Comparative Evaluation of Merchandising Methods

Description	Merchandising Methods	
	Wholesale	**Retail**
Selling	To retail trade	To general public
Type of Order	Most orders are standard and repetitive	Most orders are unique and nonrepetitive
Product Range	Standard and limited	Broad and specialized
Product Volume	High	Low-medium
Product Cost Markup	Low-medium	High
Inventory Requirements	Large quantity per product type	Small or medium quantity per product type
Personnel Skill Requirements	Average level for a standardized application	High level for a specialized application

4.03 Facility Design, Location, and Organization

The production or operations process takes place in a specially allocated part of the organization called a **work facility** or, simply, **facility**. A facility provides industrial premises where production personnel are employed to convert materials into finished goods or services using equipment, machinery, and tools. The facility represents a major part of any industrial enterprise and provides the necessary environment for various manufacturing and nonmanufacturing processes. It requires the bulk of the financial resources, utilizes most of the physical assets, and often employs the majority of the company's personnel. Furthermore, the facility represents a special system which has to operate continuously within a larger organizational structure and in conjunction with such essential functions as general administration, personnel, finance and accounting, marketing, and sales.

At times operational activity starts with **facility design** and selection of a suitable location. One important aspect of facility design is determining the size of industrial organization. A common approach to the determination of size is to establish what size of organization, using existing resources, operational methods, and organizational ability, will produce goods or services at the lowest unit cost. A preliminary study of facility design requirements should include, among others, the following details:

- Accommodation required at present
- Accommodation required in the future
- Facilities required in the building
- Quality of the building
- Details of the proposed site
- Budgetary limitations
- Final completion date

All of these design details should be evaluated by management and summarized in accordance with the overall long-term objectives of the company. There are a number of essential considerations related to facility design and development which should be accounted for:

- Number of floors
- Access to the facility
- Technological process requirements
- Weight and size of equipment and products
- Material handling requirements
- Services
- Illumination
- Heating and ventilation
- Pollution and waste disposal
- Administrative offices
- Receiving, storage, and distribution of materials

To prepare the final blueprint of the facility design it is necessary to consider and select an appropriate location for the new facility. There are no set rules applicable to selection of **facility location**, but there are a number of factors which may influence the decision and should be taken into consideration. Some of these factors are:

- *Intercompany integration.* If the new facility is a part of a larger group of companies it is essential to ensure sufficient integration of such a facility within the group's total organizational structure.
- *Availability and cost of labor.* It is necessary to assess the availability and cost of labor in the proposed facility location area. Skilled labor is not always available in every location.
- *Availability and cost of services.* It is necessary to examine the availability and cost of such services as electricity, water, gas, canalization, and disposal of waste. Various manufacturing processes may require these services to a greater or lesser extent.
- *Availability and cost of materials.* It is necessary to ensure that all materials are available for timely delivery to the facility. A location near main suppliers may reduce delivery costs and allow more efficient liaison between the company and suppliers.
- *Availability of transport.* It is necessary to ensure that transport is available for company employees to reach the facility at prescribed time. In addition, it is important to have adequate goods transportation facilities to accommodate receiving and shipping requirements.
- *Availability of car parking space.* It is necessary to assess the number of vehicles which may be used by company employees and to ensure that a sufficient space will be available for parking their cars.
- *Expansion potential.* It is necessary to evaluate long-term planning requirements of the organization and to ensure that the size of the site will allow expansion of the facility if it is required in the future.
- *Zoning and legal regulations.* It is essential to examine local zoning regulations which control the types of businesses that are allowed to operate in certain areas. State and federal requirements pertaining to issues such as air and noise pollution, disposal of waste, and effluence should also be examined.
- *The cost of land.* It is necessary to assess the total cost of the industrial land required by the new facility development. This factor plays a particular role in the location selection process and depends substantially on the company's immediate financial resources and future prospects.
- *New development areas.* Federal, state, and local authorities sometimes offer special subsidies, low interest loans, grants, and low rentals in order to develop new industrial areas.
- *Living conditions.* It is necessary to consider existing housing facilities, shops, services, entertainment, and safety of employees. Availability of acceptable living conditions will enhance the company's ability to attract personnel.[1]

Selection of a facility location requires a comprehensive examination of the aforementioned factors. These factors may have a different degree of influence depending on the specific type of operation. Retailers, wholesalers, and service companies, for example, place higher importance on the external appearance of the facility since their operations involve direct contact with consumers. Manufacturing companies have less contact with customers and therefore place a higher priority on the actual cost of the facility and the related operating costs.

Location factors may be evaluated in different ways. A simple and practical approach is the **point-rating method**. This method entails an examination of the importance of each factor in the location selection process. Each location factor is assigned a relative weight out of a maximum number of possible points,

Exhibit 4–7

Selection of a Facility Location

Location Factors	Unfavorable 0–33 A	Unfavorable 0–33 B	Average 34–66 A	Average 34–66 B	Favorable 67–100 A	Favorable 67–100 B	Total Points A	Total Points B
Intercompany integration	20					80	20	80
Availability and cost of labor	30			50			30	50
Availability and cost of services			50			70	50	70
Availability and cost of materials			60	40			60	40
Availability of transport		20	40				40	20
Availability of car parking space	30					80	30	80
Expansion potential			40			90	40	90
Zoning and legal regulations			60			80	60	80
The cost of land			40			90	40	90
New development areas			50			80	50	80
Living conditions		20			90		90	20
Total							**510**	**700**

usually 100. Thereafter, a potential location is evaluated according to every factor considered by management. A number of points is assigned to each factor and the location which scores the highest number of points is subsequently selected as the most suitable one. This is illustrated in Exhibit 4–7.

It is apparent in the example that Location B is more suitable than Location A. It is important, however, for management to consider all location factors before making a final decision.

The next stage in the facility development process necessitates creation of a comprehensive organizational structure in accordance with the overall objectives of the company. The process of **facility organization**, therefore, represents an important task of production management and entails formulation of the following issues:

- Nature of facility organizational activities
- Functions under which these activities are to be carried out
- Positions and titles assigned to these functions
- Production personnel who occupy positions indicated by the assigned titles
- Range of individual authority and responsibility of production personnel
- Framework of relations among production personnel
- Coordination of activities and timing performance of production personnel.[2]

Industrial organizations usually start small and undergo gradual expansion. In the beginning, one person generally has all the authority and responsibility for production. The entire operation centers in and around that individual. As the company grows, this centralization of operations and control becomes ineffective and duties must be delegated. The organization and management are expanded to handle the increased coordinating and directive decisions.

The process of facility organizational development entails determination of authority, responsibility, and duties of production managers, supervisors, and their subordinates. Authority, responsibility, and accountability should be assigned to employees in an orderly manner and in accordance with principles of sound industrial organization. These principles have been discussed in Part 1, (Volume I) and are summarized as follows:

Exhibit 4–8

Work Division in the Facility

Degree of Responsibility	First	Second	Third	Fourth
Position	President	Production Manager	Foreman	Laborer
Range of Duties	General management	General control of production	Detailed control of production	Execution of an allocated job
	Administration policies and managerial control	Operating control of performance	Operating control of performance	

- Separation of functions within the facility; for example, production manager, foreman, laborer
- Setting these functions up in a logical manner to avoid overlapping or conflict and to ensure that no employee receives an order from anyone but his superior
- Clear distinction between line and staff functions
- Clear descriptions and specifications of each job to avoid divided responsibility
- Appropriate allocation of authority and responsibility to each employee
- Competent selection of suitable employees to perform various tasks within the facility

Authority, responsibility, and accountability should be allocated to employees to ensure a **functional work division** within the facility. Work division represents a foundation of the approach to determine the relation of duties to be performed and the selection of personnel to whom duties are to be assigned in the industrial organization. Allocation of separate duties in the facility is essential because of the following reasons:

- High volume of work
- Broad range of experience and knowledge required
- Difference in skill, capability and nature of personnel

A typical example describing various degrees of responsibility and corresponding duties in a facility is illustrated in Exhibit 4–8.

4.04 Product Selection, Design, and Standardization

The major outcome of the company's activities is represented by means of products and services provided to satisfy the needs of consumers in the marketplace. Naturally, such needs vary at all times, creating a continuous demand for new products. These products differ in their design, quality, price, and lifespan, but their main and common purpose is to perform effectively in accordance with the requirements of users. It is thus necessary to constantly search for and select new products to meet the ever-changing market needs at competitive prices.

The process of **product selection** represents the combined effort of the marketing and production executives and contributes toward the future survival, growth, and success of the company. The source of the product selection usually originates from opportunities which may arise as a result of a careful examination of market conditions, existing product range, and special skills and resources of the organization. The process of product selection necessitates investigation of various organizational issues, and deals, with the financial, manufacturing, and marketing aspects. Some of the important manufacturing considerations, for example, are as follows:

- Is additional equipment required?
- How adequate are the labor resources?
- Will the present workload be affected?
- Is the raw material available?
- How reliable are existing suppliers?
- Is there any previous or existing experience?

A new product can be presented to the production manager in the form of an idea, sketch, drawing, completely documented project, or a prototype scaled model which will be subsequently converted into a standard item. It is essential, therefore, for the production manager to appreciate various aspects and procedures related to the process of selection and design of new products.

Once a new product has been selected and its nature has been described, the design of the product may begin. **Product design** represents the activity of converting various requirements into a form suitable for the manufacturing process and further use. Product design is based on a combination of creative and practical activities and usually comprises seven stages as outlined in Exhibit 4–9.

Product conception represents the first stage of product design, where the initial draft specifications are formulated and recorded. This is the most important stage of the design activity and it provides the basis for subsequent actions.

Exhibit 4–9
Seven Stages of Product Design

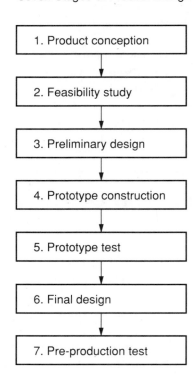

1. Product conception

2. Feasibility study

3. Preliminary design

4. Prototype construction

5. Prototype test

6. Final design

7. Pre-production test

Preliminary specifications should be drawn up in detail by a design engineer in conjunction with information provided by marketing and sales personnel. The prime purpose of the preliminary specifications is to provide basic information related to the exact requirements of the newly developed product. In essence this process entails a translation of sales requirements into a set of technical terms developed by the designer.

As a result of product conception process certain specified information becomes available:

- Product performance and technical requirements
- Product appearance requirements
- Product selling price considerations
- Date by which the product is required
- Quantity in which the product is required
- Product manufacturing cost considerations

Feasibility study represents the second stage of product design. At this stage the new product viability should be investigated and first draft specifications evaluated. As a result of the feasibility study the product draft specifications will have to satisfy the following:

- Marketing requirements
- Legal requirements
- Manufacturing requirements
- Financial requirements
- Distribution requirements

Preliminary design represents the third stage of product design and is carried out by designers and draftsmen in the engineering department. It is generally initiated by the work order specifying the preliminary design parameters of the new product. During the process of preliminary design, all necessary drawings should be prepared and finalized in accordance with the basic specifications and other design requirements. In addition, all design and manufacturing costs of the new product should be identified and calculated. As a result of the preliminary design, the basic specification data will have to be tested to conclude the product's acceptance or rejection. This specification data will have to be used in the process of preparing working drawings to enable the construction of the first prototype.

Prototype construction represents the fourth stage of product design and is carried out by production personnel in conjunction with the engineering department. The main objective of this stage is to translate the information laid down in specifications and working drawings into a real prototype. It is often impossible to take into account all details during the preliminary design stage. Therefore, only the completion of a working prototype will provide additional information related to product design parameters. Such a prototype should meet as many of the basic design requirements as possible, and any differences should be taken into account. Although cost considerations should not be ignored, the technical requirements and appearance play the most important role at this stage of product development. The prototype should provide a clear indication of the feasibility of the proposed design in meeting all aspects of the required product specifications. The cost requirement of the final product should be viewed in the context of further production considerations. These considerations depend substantially on the manufacturing methods applied during the production process and the necessary quantities of manufactured goods.

Prototype test represents the fifth stage of product design and is carried out in order to evaluate the performance of the newly developed product. At this stage the prototype should be tested in real life conditions, and for this purpose some potential users could be of great assistance. Their comments and feedback may be valuable throughout the product development process. The prototype's performance should be monitored during such tests, and appropriate results should be properly evaluated. In addition, the prototype should be examined by the production department and the design team to establish possible manufacturing problems. All components, subassemblies, and the final assembly should be examined separately and detailed manufacturing cost estimates should be prepared. As a direct result of a prototype test certain parts may have to be redesigned or substituted by other parts in order to meet relevant manufacturing requirements. Sometimes there is a need to redesign a particular product in order to satisfy manufacturing cost considerations. This could be achieved by substituting with cheaper materials or by appropriately altering the manufacturing process itself. Finally, the prototype test results should be confirmed and documentation prepared for the final product design.

Final design represents the sixth stage of product design and is carried out by the design team responsible for the whole project development. Once all the preceding stages have been accomplished it is necessary to summarize all relevant information—material specifications, working drawings, manufacturing data and tooling requirements—and to pass them for a final approval by the chief designer. As a result of the final design procedure, all specifications should be summarized and confirmed and all working drawings approved for the actual manufacturing process.

The pre-production test represents the last stage of product design and is carried out by personnel in the production department and the design team. The main objective of this stage is to summarize all details of the manufacturing process and particularly in the case of large-scale production requirements to carry out a pilot test conducted under real production conditions.

The new product should be tested to customer specification with equipment that will be used in the actual manufacturing process. This test should be undertaken prior to the start of the main production operation in order to identify any further faults and problems. During the process of pre-production testing the following data should undergo final evaluation:

- Product specifications
- Manufacturing drawings
- List of components
- Manufacturing processing data
- List of tools, dies, and jigs
- Material specifications
- Details of equipment
- Details of special labor skills

As a result of the pre-production testing procedure all the products, materials, equipment, and labor specifications should be summarized and finally approved prior to commencement of the actual manufacturing process.

The process of product design must be properly planned and controlled to ensure acceptable results and thorough execution of the specific project. One of the most effective methods for product design, planning, and control is the **critical path method (CPM)**. The main objective of this method is to determine a pre-planned sequence of activities that will provide sufficient guidance throughout

Exhibit 4–10

Critical Path Method for New Product Development

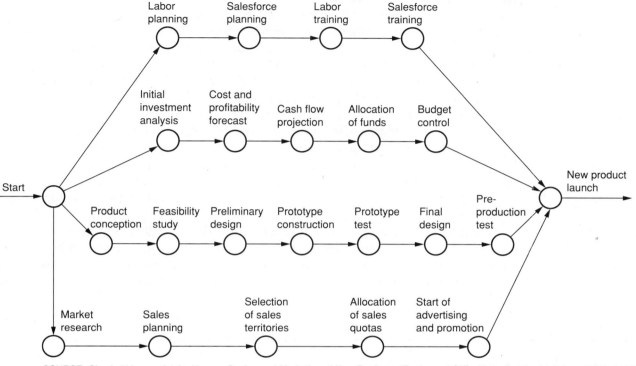

SOURCE: Glen L. Urban and John Hauser, *Design and Marketing of New Products,* (Englewood Cliffs, N. J.: Prentice-Hall, Inc., 1980), p. 469.

the project to achieve its timely completion. Each progressive stage of product design is compared with the **CPM chart** to ensure that all project requirements are met. A typical CPM chart describing various elements of product development and introduction to the market is illustrated in Exhibit 4–10.

Apart from product design procedures it is necessary to establish effective **product standardization** and to determine its influence on various activities of the company. Product variety represents a typical situation within any industrial organization. A range of products is made and different materials are used in conjunction with various manufacturing methods. The degree of product variety differs from one company to another but its control is considered to be an important managerial responsibility.

An increased product range usually requires an additional number of components and enlarged storage facilities. This may subsequently increase the workload in the production department and cause unnecessary difficulties in inventory control. The increased product range may cause problems in many aspects of the company's activities and therefore, it may be necessary to develop a product variety reduction program. This process is known as **product range optimization** and comprises the following:

- *Product range simplification* is the process of identifying the product variety and reducing existing product lines by excluding slow-moving items.
- *Product range standardization* is the product range classification based on a reduced number of product lines.
- *Product range specialization* is the product range classification based on the availability of particular knowledge and skills.

The reduction and optimization of the product range provides greater efficiency in design efforts and increased productivity in the production department. Decreasing the range of products extends the period of production runs and minimizes the unproductive periods of machine setting and breakdown time. The efficiency of production planning, work scheduling, and machine loading will also improve from product range optimization. In addition, a reduction in the product range permits higher equipment and labor utilization in the facility. The decreased product range also allows for reduction in inventory holding and improvement in storage space utilization. Moreover, the efficiency of inventory control and frequent inventory counting procedures will improve and their cost will be minimized.

A decreased product range and larger quantities manufactured simplify the overall production control procedures and reduce the difficulties of the purchasing department because fewer purchase orders are needed, although for larger quantities. Furthermore, reduction and optimization of the product range ensures greater efficiency of the selling efforts and improved results in the marketing department.

The product range optimization program can be initiated at any time and it should proceed in various departments simultaneously. Such a program provides substantial benefits to the company's overall performance and is particularly significant in product design, manufacturing, financial, and selling activities.

4.05 Process Design

Design of products, services, or projects usually raises several difficult questions. Some of these questions relate to **process design** issues and include the following:

- How will the product be manufactured?
- How will the service be provided?
- How will the project be completed?
- Should the item be manufactured, purchased, or subcontracted?

The basic aim of process design is to develop an efficient set of procedures for manufacturing goods, providing services, or completing a project. These procedures must take into account a company's financial resources, specific design requirements, operational and manpower capacity, and demand in the marketplace.

Process design in a manufacturing environment usually starts during product design. The designer, or design engineer, must consider a broad range of operational issues throughout product design. This begins by dividing the product into a number of components, subassemblies, and final assembly. At this stage the product's **explosion chart, parts list**, and **bill of materials** needs to be prepared. The explosion chart and the parts list summarize all details pertaining to components and subassemblies required to complete one product unit. The bill of materials contains detailed specifications, weight, or dimensions of raw materials required to complete the final product assembly.

To illustrate the procedures involved in process design, consider the manufacture of a simple ballpoint pen. The explosion chart, the parts list, and the bill

Exhibit 4–11

Explosion Chart, Parts List and Bill of Materials for Manufacturing a Ballpoint Pen

Explosion Chart
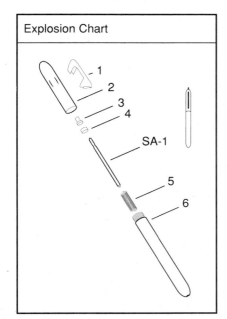

Parts List		
Product: Ballpoint pen		
This parts list is for 1 unit		
No.	Item description	Quantity
1	Clip	1
2	Upper barrel	1
3	Button	1
4	Rotator	1
5	Spring	1
6	Lower barrel	1
7	Tip (SA-1)	1
8	Ball (SA-1)	1
9	Cartridge (SA-1)	1
10	Ink (SA-1)	1 portion

Bill of Materials		
Product: Ballpoint pen		
This bill is for 1,000 units		
No.	Item description	Quantity
1	0.002" st. steel	3 sheets
2	3/8" st. steel tubing	180 ft.
3	1/8" rod	40 ft.
4	Plastic (PVC)	10 lb.
5	0.005" wire	1600 ft.
6	3/8" st. steel tubing	300 ft.
7	Brass tip	1,000
8	Carbide ball	1,000
9	Cartridge	1,000
10	Ink	5 gal.

SOURCE: This example and the following illustrations are adapted from Jack R. Meredith, *The Management of Operations,* 3rd ed. (New York: John Wiley & Sons, Inc., 1987), pp. 281–283. Reprinted with permission.

of materials for this product are summarized in Exhibit 4–11. As described in the product's parts list, the ballpoint pen consists of ten individual components. In order to produce a final assembly it is necessary to prepare a sufficient quantity of all components (items numbered 1,2,3,4,5, and 6) and complete subassembly SA–1 (items numbered 7,8,9, and 10).

A detailed description of manufacturing and operational requirements pertaining to the process design of subassembly SA–1 and final assembly of the product is presented in the **assembly chart** as illustrated in Exhibit 4–12.

The assembly chart helps to clarify the sequence of operations required throughout the product assembly process. Each operation must be examined separately and its estimated time recorded in the **flow process chart**. This chart helps in summarizing a detailed flow of operations pertaining to a specific repetitive task. It is useful, therefore, to prepare a flow process chart for any product which is intended to be manufactured in large quantities.

The flow process chart displays actual or potential movement of materials throughout the manufacturing process. Each activity that may take place during such a process is classified as one of five types, marked with its appropriate symbol, and presented in Exhibit 4–13.

A typical application of a flow process chart provides the details of operations entailed in the subassembly SA–1. This chart is illustrated in Exhibit 4–14. The illustrated flow process chart specifies the time requirement for each operation and provides a summary for the total time of the subassembly. Since each operation is planned in advance throughout process design, it is useful to summarize all details in an **operations process chart**. A typical chart used for ballpoint pen manufacturing operations is illustrated in Exhibit 4–15.

All operational instructions pertaining to a specific manufacturing process must be summarized in a **route sheet**. This document is particularly useful

Exhibit 4–12

Assembly Chart for a Ballpoint Pen

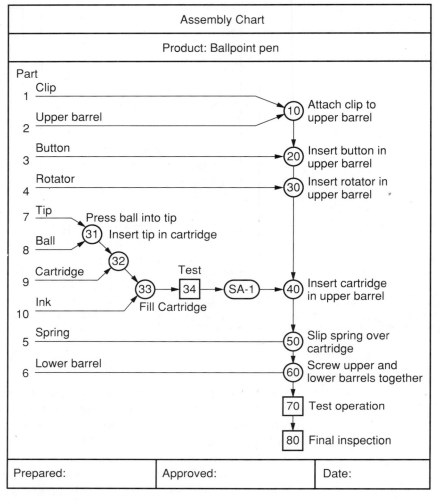

SOURCE: Adapted from Jack R. Meredith. Reprinted with permission.

Exhibit 4–13

Five Types of Activities in a Manufacturing Environment

Symbol	Activity	Description
◯	Operation	Intentional change in the physical or chemical nature of an object
⇨	Transportation	Movement of an object from one location to another
△	Storage	Storage of an object in a protected place
⬭	Delay	Temporary stoppage of the operation
◻	Inspection	Examination of an object's quality or quantity

Exhibit 4–14

Flow Process Chart for SA-1

Flow Process Chart			
Summary	No.	Min.	Operation: Cartridge subassembly
○ Operation	8	2.30	Dept. : _____ Part No. _____
⇨ Transport	5	0.85	Sheet __1__ of __1__ Date: _____
△ Store	1	0.10	Charted by: _____
D Delay	1	0.30	Subject: _____
☐ Inspect	1	0.45	Present method ☒
Total	16	4.00	Proposed method ☐
Feet of travel: 130			

No.	Dist. (ft)	Time (min)	Oper.	Transport	Store	Delay	Inspect	Description
1	30	0.20	○	⇨	△	D	☐	Go to inventory
2		0.35	○	→	△	D	☐	Get tip, ball, cartridge
3	30	0.20	○	⇨	△	D	☐	Return
4		0.40	○	→	△	D	☐	Install on Sheridan press
5		0.10	○	→	△	D	☐	Press ball
6		0.25	○	→	△	D	☐	Remove from press
7		0.50	○	→	△	D	☐	Install on Cummings press
8		0.20	○	→	△	D	☐	Insert tip
9		0.20	○	→	△	D	☐	Remove from press
10	10	0.05	○	⇨	△	D	☐	Go to pump bench
11		0.30	○	→	△	D	☐	Fill cartridge
12		0.45	○	→	△	D	☐	Test pressure
13		0.30	○	→	△	D	☐	Wait for pressure release
14	30	0.20	○	⇨	△	D	☐	Take to inventory
15		0.10	○	→	△	D	☐	Store
16	30	0.20	○	⇨	△	D	☐	Return

SOURCE: Jack R. Meredith. Reprinted with permission.

for production scheduling and for control of manufacturing activities that are discussed later in this part. A typical route sheet for a ballpoint subassembly SA–1 is illustrated in Exhibit 4–16.

The process design procedure is frequently used when products are manufactured in large quantities. Such a procedure usually requires substantial investment in time and should, therefore, remain cost effective when smaller quantities are produced. Process design for services and projects also entails subdivision of the complete operation into separate components and evaluation of each component on an individual basis.

Product and process design procedures have been recently upgraded through the extensive use of modern computer technology. A broad range of **computer aided design (CAD)** equipment became available and is widely utilized by designers and engineers. **Computer-aided engineering (CAE)** software packages use the CAD designs and subject them to additional engineering examination.

Exhibit 4–15

Operations Process Chart for a Ballpoint Pen

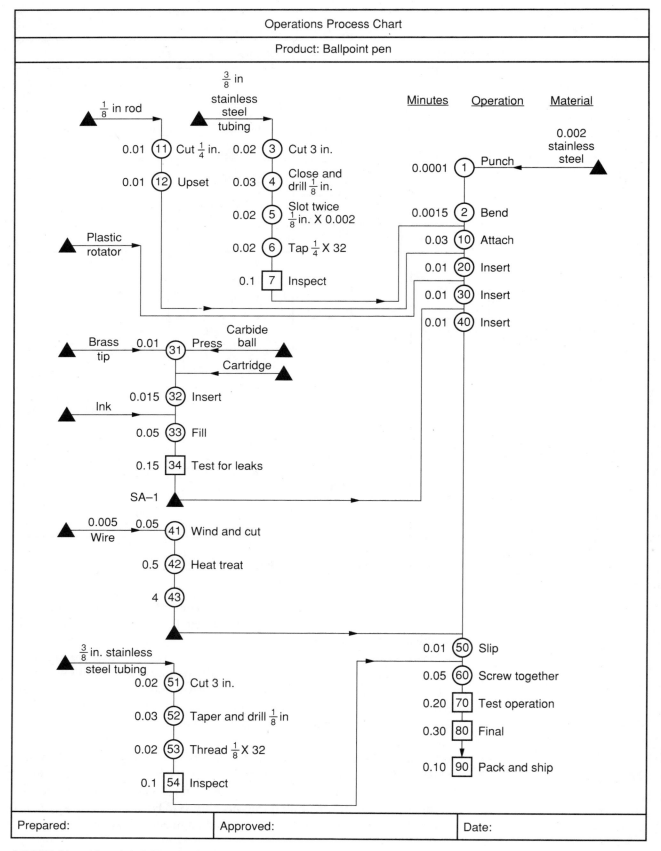

Exhibit 4–16

Route Sheet for Cartridge Subassembly

Route Sheet						
Part Description: Cartridge subassembly				Part No.: SA-1		
Job No.:	Date issued:		Date completed:	Issued by:		
Date	Oper. no.	Operation	Dept.	Setup (min)	Rate/min	Equipment
	—	Tip and ball	Inventory	—	—	—
	31	Press ball into tip, 100psi	Press	30	100	Sheridan press
	—	Cartridge	Inventory	—	—	—
	32	Insert tip into cartridge, 43 psi	Press	30	75	Low volume Cummings press
	33	Fill cartridge, 0.15 each	Paint	45	20	Simms high viscosity pump
	34	Test	Inspection	—	4	No. 1538 pressure tester, Fields Bros.
	—	Subassembly transport	Inventory	—	—	—

SOURCE: Adapted from Jack R. Meredith. Reprinted with permission.

4.06 The Drafting Office

The **drafting office** represents an integral part of any design section or engineering department and provides an essential facility in the process of product development. Technical drawings are commonly used in various industries to transmit specific information from the drafting board to the production department. In certain industries drawings may be replaced by technological process layouts or relevant manufacturing specifications, but they still represent one of the most important descriptive methods used in the process of product design.

The drafting office is responsible for the preparation, issue, and amendment of all the completed drawings prepared by the draftsmen-designers. These drawings should contain relevant details required for the manufacturing process of a particular product or component, such as type of material, physical dimensions, technical specifications, codes, and references to relevant standards.

The efficiency of the drafting office depends on the number of parts per product created by the designers. The productivity of the manufacturing department also starts at the drafting board and depends substantially on the complexity of a specific product design. Often a particular range of products can be designed and manufactured on a more economical basis if the products have a number of interchangeable parts. Sometimes minor modifications of existing parts can also prove useful in the process of item-per-product reduction. It is important, therefore, to ensure that every new product has a minimal number of parts without imposing unnecessary restrictions upon the creative abilities of the designer. It is also advisable to avoid using any special types of raw materials, fasteners, and other commodities, and to use all standard materials and sizes normally obtainable from the appropriate suppliers.

An ordinary product design process usually requires a comprehensive item coding method which could enable the designer to provide the necessary description and identification of various parts designed in the drafting office. Such a method should be based on a logical **numerical coding system**, providing particular code-names for every item of a specific product or product range.

One such coding system is termed the **family name–first name method**. This method is based on classifying products into various groups or families with similar important characteristics. Each group will be given a separate number, the *family name,* and each product belonging to that group will be given a second separate number, the *first name.* The components of each product will be given a third separate number called the *second name.* Thus every group, product, and component may be adequately coded and subsequently identified for design, modification, and manufacturing purposes. This method is very flexible and the numerical coding system can be expanded if necessary. A typical example of products and components coding is illustrated in Exhibit 4–17.

When product design and modification procedures have been established and the appropriate coding system has been developed, the system must be implemented into the drafting office. The drafting office is responsible for the timely issue of all drawings related to product design and modifications. It is essential, therefore, that each drawing is properly checked and authorized by a project leader or an engineer responsible for product development and design. Every inaccuracy on a drawing issued by the drafting office to the production department causes unnecessary expenditure in materials and labor, delays the completion of a particular manufacturing process, and reduces overall efficiency within the production facility.

It is important, therefore, to develop a formalized **product modification procedure** which will ensure control over any change in the existing product design. Such a procedure should include the following four steps:

1. *A product modification proposal.* A modification has been proposed, for example, that would reduce the final assembly cost of the completed product. This proposal should specify the drawing number of the component, the details of the change required, the degree of urgency, and details of potential savings.
2. *Product modification proposal analysis.* Comments on this proposal should be made by relevant departments in order to establish the viability of the product modification. The production department, for example, may establish a need for retooling, the cost of which may exceed the savings in the assembly cost. All comments should be taken into account prior to the acceptance or rejection of the above proposal.
3. *Product modification proposal acceptance.* If the analysis of a proposal indicates the viability of the product modification, that proposal should be accepted and subsequently implemented.
4. *Product modification record.* When the drawing must be amended as a result of the modification, all relevant details should be stated on the new

Exhibit 4–17

Coding of Products and Components

Numerical Coding System

Family Name	First Name	Second Name
01 - office equipment	01 - standard desk	01 - desk-top
02 - office equipment	02 - computer desk	02 - stand
03 - office equipment	03 - board-room desk	03 - draw
04 - office equipment	04 - extra large desk	04 - railing
05 - office equipment	05 - L-shape desk	05 - handles

For example: handles for an extra-large desk (office equipment)—code 01-04-05.

Exhibit 4–18

Drafting Work Progress Report

Drafting Work Progress Report											
Drawing (N-new; R-revised)				Work priority	Name of design engineer or draftsperson	Planned performance			Actual performance		
						Dates		Time	Dates		Time
No.	Description	N	R	1/2/3		Start	Finish	Hour	Start	Finish	Hour
1234	Part A	√		1	A. Jones	9.4.89	9.5.89	4	9.5.89	9.6.89	6
1345	Part B		√	2	B. Stevens	9.5.89	9.6.89	12	9.6.89	9.7.89	15

drawing, providing a brief description of the change made and the date. Old drawings must be removed and destroyed to avoid unnecessary confusion.

Once the product modification procedure has been established, no drawing should be amended without proper maintenance of the above system. Moreover, it is essential to develop and implement effective controlling procedures within the drafting office. All drafting work, for example, should be recorded in a **drafting work progress report**. A typical illustration of such a report is presented in Exhibit 4–18.

Allocation of work in the drafting office should be carried out in accordance with work priority and availability of the drafting staff. It is necessary to ensure

Exhibit 4–19

Drafting Time Allocation Schedule

Drafting Time Allocation Schedule											
Draftsperson: A. Jones						Period: 9.4.89 - 9.8.89					
Monday		Tuesday		Wednesday		Thursday		Friday		Saturday	
Drawing No.	Hr.	Drawing No.	Hr.	Drawing No.	Hr.	Drawing No.	Hr.	Drawing No.	Hr.	Drawing No.	Hr.
1234	4	1288	8	1299	3	1221	4	1680	3	- - - - - - - -	- -
1288	4	- - - - - - - -	- -	1221	5	1388	4	1020	5	- - - - - - - -	- -
Prepared:				Approved:				Date:			

Exhibit 4–20

Drawing Issue and Revision Report

Drawing Issue and Revision Report					
Drawing No.	Work Center Allocation	Dates		Authorized signature	
		Issue	Revision	Issued by	Received by
1234	Machine Shop	9.8.89	------		
1345	Press Shop	------	9.12.89		

that the drafting personnel develop and adhere to a **drafting time allocation schedule** conforming to specific planning requirements in the drafting office. This schedule must be prepared one week in advance in accordance with information summarized in the drafting work progress report. A typical illustration of a drafting time allocation schedule is presented in Exhibit 4–19.

After completing a particular drafting assignment, the actual performance dates and time taken should be recorded in the drafting work progress report. Comparison between the planned and actual performance data helps to identify the source and magnitude of inefficiency in the drafting office.

Another important element of control in the drafting office entails numbering all new and revised drawings and recording them in the **drawing issue and revision report**. The prime purpose of this is to provide an accurate reference for each drawing currently in use. A typical illustration of a drawing issue and revision report is presented in Exhibit 4–20.

In conclusion, the ultimate price and quality of the product as well as the overall productivity and performance of the company start with the design effort in the drafting office. It is vitally important, therefore, to ensure a high standard of product design combined with good housekeeping in the engineering department.

4.07 Equipment Evaluation and Selection

Every industrial organization uses a certain type of equipment to meet its specific objectives. Evaluation, selection, layout, maintenance, and replacement of equipment usually constitute a major managerial task and require a thorough understanding of company needs. Some of the fundamental questions to be considered by the executive and production managers in the process of **equipment evaluation and selection** are:

• Does the equipment perform the work required in the best possible way and with the required level of accuracy?

- Does the equipment have the required operational capacity?
- Does the equipment produce sufficient savings in cost, time, labor, and materials?
- Does the equipment prove itself more viable with regard to operating methods, production control, and quality of work?
- Does the equipment prove itself to be an economically viable proposition?

The process of equipment evaluation and selection usually necessitates that management conducts a thorough investigation into the market of new industrial machinery. Detailed examination of new equipment manufacturers' catalogues; evaluation of technical specifications; visits to showrooms, exhibitions, and companies; and meetings with professionals in allied fields are all essential in the process of selecting new equipment. Some of the important factors which need to be considered at this stage are:

- **Equipment operational capacity.** It is essential to assess the manufacturing capacity of a specific piece of equipment to ensure that it will satisfy not only current production requirements but also the long-term production considerations.
- **Equipment operational versatility.** It is important to analyze the operational functions of a specific piece of equipment and to identify all manufacturing processing requirements that can be satisfied by the functional abilities of the new machinery.
- **Equipment operational reliability.** It is necessary to assess the operational reliability of a specific piece of equipment bearing in mind that unreliable machinery may cause unnecessary and costly breakdowns. This will disrupt production planning and may jeopardize delivery dates promised to customers.
- **Work preparation methods.** It is important to select a piece of equipment that will allow easy work preparation methods. Equipment setting up, breaking down, servicing, and cleaning times are non-productive, and should be kept to a minimum in order to increase the machines' productive running period.
- **Equipment maintenance.** Steady service and maintenance of equipment ensures its continuous and efficient performance. New pieces of equipment should be easy to service in order to keep maintenance costs as low as possible.
- **Equipment operational safety.** A high level of equipment operational safety is necessary to maintain an accident-free production process. Unsafe equipment may cause accidents, decrease production output, lower morale, and cause deterioration in overall labor-management relations.
- **Equipment operational compatibility.** The operational compatibility of the new piece of equipment must be matched with the specific standard of the existing equipment within the facility. Simplification makes it easier to serve and maintain equipment in good operational order and to keep minimum spare parts. From the operational point of view it will be easier to train operators, plan production, and set the machines for production runs.
- **Equipment availability.** It is necessary to inquire about the delivery dates when the new equipment may become available. These dates should be considered and matched with the production requirements of the facility. The identity of the new equipment suppliers and their ability to deliver the equipment in the required time should also be thoroughly examined.
- **Equipment installation.** The new piece of equipment must be examined from the installation point of view. It is necessary to ensure that the equipment can physically fit into the perceived space and that its dimensions or weight do not exceed relevant permissible criteria.
- **Equipment design.** It must be ensured that the new equipment is designed in accordance with the necessary functional requirements and does not repre-

sent a half-completed experimental model. The equipment supplier is, therefore, required to produce all the necessary guarantees and sufficient technological back-up to ensure a high performance and quality functioning of the new machinery.

- **Ancillary equipment.**   The full range of the new ancillary equipment must be identified. This range should be examined and its availability assessed in order to ensure effective utilization of equipment.
- **Effect on the organization.**   Selection, purchase, and installation of new equipment often necessitates specific reorganization within the facility. New equipment may require provision of additional air, electrical, or water installations, or it may necessitate moving certain existent machinery into new positions to provide additional floor space. Computerized equipment and numerically controlled (NC) machines may require additional computer terminal installations. New equipment with additional production capacity will certainly affect product design, production planning, and maintenance procedures. It will necessitate that the company's personnel upgrade their qualifications and readjust their activities in accordance with the technological requirements dictated by the new equipment.

As a direct result of preliminary technical selection, a list of optional machinery should be drawn up, concluding the first part of the new equipment evaluation and selection procedure. This list should thereafter be subjected to the new equipment **economical viability investigation.**

There are several methods of conducting the new equipment economical viability investigation. These methods have been discussed in detail in Part 3 (Volume I) and include the following:

1. **Accounting rate-of-return method.**   This is a simple but not highly accurate method for estimating the possible rate of return on capital investment.
2. **Payback period method.**   This is a simple but crude method for estimating the period of time required to recoup capital investment from anticipated net cash inflow generated by the new equipment.
3. **Discounted cash flow method.**   This is the most accurate but complicated method for measuring the economical viability of a new capital expenditure proposal.

Economical viability investigation of capital equipment is usually carried out by the financial executive, who should be familiar with the appropriate evaluation methods. It takes into account several factors depending upon the method selected by the financial executive. Some of these factors are presented in Exhibit 4–21.

Evaluation of the economical viability of capital equipment also requires detailed knowledge of the proposed operation and understanding of labor, tooling, utilities, services, maintenance, insurance and space requirements. Moreover, the evaluation process entails estimating the anticipated value of the additional production output. If the equipment is to manufacture products for stock it becomes a relatively simple exercise. If, however, the equipment is to be involved in batch production or manufacturing to customer orders, production output cannot be estimated as accurately as previously. The most satisfactory estimation is obtained by forecasting the anticipated production output of *average components* and utilizing this forecast on the basis of running cost calculations.

Evaluation of the economical viability of the new equipment represents a combined effort between financial and production executives. Once the final

Exhibit 4–21

Methods for Evaluating Economical Viability of the Capital Equipment

Accounting Rate-of-Return Method

$$\text{Accounting rate of return (\%)} = \frac{\text{Project's average annual after-tax net income}}{\text{Average investment cost}}$$

$$\begin{matrix}\text{Project's average annual}\\\text{after-tax net income}\end{matrix} = \left[\begin{matrix}\text{Annual}\\\text{cash revenue}\end{matrix} - \begin{matrix}\text{Annual}\\\text{operating cost}\end{matrix}\right] \times \left[1.0 - \begin{matrix}\text{Company's}\\\text{income tax}\\\text{rate}\end{matrix}\right]$$

$$\text{Average investment cost} = \frac{\text{Total investment cost} - \text{Salvage value}}{2} + \text{Salvage value}$$

Payback Period Method

$$\text{Payback period (in years)} = \frac{\text{Total investment cost}}{\text{Annual net cash inflow}}$$

$$\text{Annual net cash inflow} = \begin{matrix}\text{Project's average}\\\text{annual after-tax}\\\text{net income}\end{matrix} + \frac{\text{Total investment cost} - \text{Salvage value}}{\text{Service life period (in years)}}$$

Discounted Cash Flow Method

This method entails the use of present value tables (Tables A-1, A-2, A-3, and A-4) contained at the end of Part 3 (Volume I).

Note: Typical examples explaining the application of each method are provided in Part 3.

selection of the new equipment is completed, an appropriate method of obtaining such equipment needs to be devised. Management may use three different methods to obtain equipment. These methods are as follows:

1. **Cash purchase of equipment.** Here the company outlays its own cash or borrows money from an external source and acquires the asset outright. In this case, the asset and liability are recorded at the amount paid, and the asset is subject to regular depreciation.

2. **Rental of equipment.** Here the company (the *lessee*) enters into a short-term leasing agreement with an equipment rental firm (the *lessor*) and pays a monthly rental fee. A **short-term lease**, also known as an **operating lease**, can be cancelled at any time with a short notice period and all risks of asset ownership lie with the rental firm.

3. **Capital lease.** This is one of the fastest growing ways of financing the acquisition of equipment. This method is also known as a **long-term lease** and has several advantages. First, there is no need for an immediate cash payment. The asset is acquired on a "purchase/sale on installment" basis, whereby the purchaser (the lessee) pays equal monthly installments to the seller (the lessor) for the use of the asset. Hence, the asset remains the property of the lessor. The purchaser, however, is allowed to depreciate the capital asset during its useful service life and thereby receive additional tax benefits. This method can be more cost effective than the first two methods and enables the purchaser to acquire the asset at the end of the lease at a nominal price.[3]

Upon delivery the new equipment needs to be positioned in an appropriate place within the production facility. This represents another important managerial task and is discussed next.

4.08 Plant Layout

Plant was defined earlier as "the tools, machinery, fixtures, buildings, grounds, etc. of a factory or business." **Plant layout**, then, is the process of positioning machinery and equipment within the confines of facility space and is designed to ensure their most effective performance. The process of plant layout represents a fundamental work-study problem and demands a thorough investigation of the product, machinery, and manufacturing process. Although the principles of plant layout are basically similar for different industries, the application may vary substantially, depending upon the nature of the product, size of the facility, type of machinery, and requirements of the manufacturing process.

The ideal plant layout is best designed when a new facility is to be erected. Usually this is not the case, however, and it is often necessary to fit equipment into an existing facility which may not lend itself to the ideal layout. The main objective of plant layout in this case is to ensure improvement in the operating efficiency of the existing manufacturing process or to develop a new product manufacturing line.

Good plant layout is of great importance in any manufacturing organization. It usually provides essential cost saving benefits which can be summarized as follows:

- Work travels in a definite direction.
- Materials are moved over the shortest possible distances.
- The amount and cost of material handling is reduced to a minimum.
- Overall time and volume of work-in-process is reduced.
- The level of inventory in storerooms is decreased.
- Labor and machinery are more efficiently utilized.
- Facility space utilization is improved.
- Work routing is simplified.
- Labor requirements are optimized.
- There is an overall cost reduction of production control procedures.
- Job shop, batch, and flow production environments have increased efficiency.

Plant layout within the facility and relation of various manufacturing sections should be set out correctly to ensure efficient manufacturing operation. The absence of good plant layout may cause deterioration of the production flow so that it becomes difficult to control the progress of work through the facility. Raw materials are no longer prepared on time, components arrive too late, and work interruptions occur more often. The quality of plant layout also affects the ease with which workers operate within the facility, the material handling time, and the space required for the work-in-process. Good plant layout usually contributes substantially to the overall cost decrease of the manufacturing operation and improves the morale of the company's employees. Several factors should be considered by the production manager throughout good plant layout design. Some of these factors are:

- **Operational flexibility.**   Maximum flexibility of plant layout is important to allow further modifications and to accommodate ever-changing working requirements. This necessitates provision of sufficient electrical installations, power, water, and air supply points, depending on the nature of the manufacturing or operational process.
- **Space utilization.**   Maximum space utilization of the facility floor and available height must be ensured. Space utilization is particularly important in the storeroom where raw materials, work-in-process, and finished goods can be

stacked at substantial heights without causing particular inconvenience.

- **Operational coordination.**   Plant layout must provide maximum operational coordination between various departments and activities within the facility. It is essential to ensure the smooth flow of materials and provide for minimum of labor movement during the manufacturing process.
- **Equipment accessibility.**   Maximum accessibility of equipment helps to ensure smooth work flow between various work centers, effective handling of materials, and easy maintenance procedures. For such reasons, equipment should not be placed against a wall or in front of power, water, or air installations.
- **Operational visibility.**   Maximum operational visibility within the facility helps to monitor actions of personnel and movement of materials during the manufacturing process. It is important, therefore, to avoid invisible spots or hiding places and to reduce the number of separate offices and partitions as far as possible.
- **Material movement.**   Minimum material movement within the facility helps to reduce operational times, improve productivity, and minimize overall manufacturing costs. Material movement over extended distances often necessitates the creation of unnecessary intermediate storage places and causes additional delay in production output.
- **Materials handling.**   Simplified material handling procedures help to maintain high production efficiency and reduce overall manufacturing costs. It is essential, therefore, to utilize suitable material-handling equipment to allow for easy handling and movement of materials throughout the facility during the manufacturing process. Such equipment includes conveyors, hoists, cranes, forklifts, and other mechanisms.
- **Personnel comfort.**   Sufficiently comfortable working conditions help to improve the morale of employees and to maximize the overall productivity level. It is important, therefore, to provide good illumination and fresh air at a suitable temperature and to reduce unnecessary noise, heat, dust, vibration, and odors. Certain manufacturing processes may require installation of air control equipment, depending on the degree of discomfort created by such processes.
- **Personnel safety.**   Maximum safety of employees represents a highly important moral obligation. It is essential to install safety guards around all dangerous process points, electrical and compressed air installation units, steam boilers, chemical tanks, and rotating and moving parts of machinery and equipment. Care should be exercised not only in regard to the employees operating such equipment, but also in relation to maintenance personnel and passers-by.
- **Operational security.**   Maximum operational security helps to ensure the safety of employees and prevent possible loss or theft of materials. It is important, therefore, to ensure that plant layout will not cause a potentially hazardous situation and that there will be adequate safeguards against fire, heat, moisture, and other undesirable factors.

The plant layout procedure normally consists of two main stages. First, it is essential to divide the facility into various work centers, and thereafter to provide individual attention to each work center in order to arrange the correct positioning of machinery and equipment. The planning procedure and plant layout design depend primarily on the nature of the manufacturing process. It is important, therefore, to identify the particular parameters of the manufacturing process and to establish the most suitable type of production at the outset of the plant layout planning procedure. Furthermore, there is a need to determine the total capacity of the facility and to evaluate the future requirements of the expansion program. Summarizing all the relevant issues, it becomes possible to:

- Select the suitable type of plant layout.
- Calculate the total movement of materials in the facility.
- Determine the type and number of machinery, equipment and tooling.
- Balance all stages of production.
- List all production inspection facilities.
- Plan all production maintenance requirements.
- Determine material purchasing, storage, and distribution facilities.

In the manufacturing industry there are three distinct methods widely used in the process of plant layout development. These methods are:

- Process layout
- Product layout
- Fixed position layout

Process layout represents a functional layout of the facility where the manufacturing effort is departmentalized in accordance with the processes employed in production. This type of layout, illustrated in Exhibit 4–22, is commonly used in job shop and batch production environments.

This example illustrates plant layout consisting of four operational sections, namely cutting, bending, machining, and welding. Each section has a certain amount of specialized machinery and equipment, similar in their operational application:

Cutting section—cutting machines: 1 — 2 — 3
Bending section—bending brakes: 4 — 5 — 6
Machining section—NC machines: 7 — 8 — 9 — 10
Welding section—arc welders: 11 — 12 — 13

If, for instance, the company is manufacturing three different products, then particular production requirements will necessitate that each item undergoes various operations in accordance with the following sequence:

Product 1—operations: 1 — 4 — 7 — 8 — 11
Product 2—operations: 2 — 5 — 9 — 8 — 12
Product 3—operations: 3 — 6 — 10 — 13

Exhibit 4–22

Process Layout Diagram

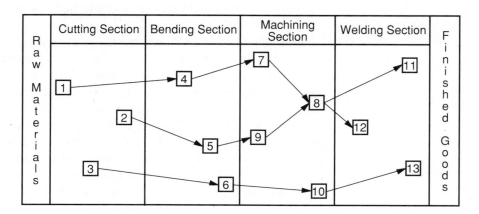

Process layout is usually applied when the product is not or cannot be standardized or when the volume of the identical work is too low. Such an operational condition requires flexibility in the manufacturing sequence and is usually obtainable with this type of plant layout. Process layout has several advantages and disadvantages in its application within the manufacturing environment. Some of the advantages of this type of layout are:

- It requires a lower capital investment in equipment to carry maximum production loads and to handle a number of product lines simultaneously.
- It ensures higher operational capacity utilization.
- It provides improved operational flexibility and allows loading various jobs onto any machine in a similar class available at the time.
- It necessitates that operators maintain a high level of professional skills and requires more universal abilities to operate any size of machinery and equipment in a similar functional operation.
- It enables foremen and supervisors to improve their skills and efficiency in the process of operating machinery and ensures better performance of work.
- It keeps manufacturing costs down. Although labor costs may be higher during the peak production periods, they will be lower during the production slowdown, ensuring minimal expenditure.
- It provides manufacturing process continuity even during the time when certain machinery ceases operating. Workload is merely transferred to another machine, if available, or is rescheduled for a later time.

Some of the disadvantages of the process layout are:

- There is no definite manufacturing process route describing the particular flow of work. The production routing and scheduling is, therefore, more complex.
- There is more material handling and higher costs as a result of the separation of manufacturing operations and the greater distances over which work is travelling.
- There is a need for greater effort during the process of work coordination because of weak control over the manufacturing process sequence and possible delay or loss of work as a result of work traveling longer distances.
- There is an increase in total manufacturing time since work must be prepared in advance and transported to a particular production section to avoid idle machines.
- There is an increased piling-up of work around certain machines because of raw material delivery that can slow work in advance of processing, hold up work for inspection after processing, and cause work to await movement when released.
- There is an absence of compact manufacturing process line layouts and normally larger spacing between machines in various production sections. This results in larger floor area occupation per unit of product.
- There is a need for more inspections, normally one after each operation if work has to go to another production section, instead of one at the end of a specific set of operations within a particular section.
- There is a need for a more complicated system of production planning but no means for visual control. It is necessary to maintain a close check of operations on all components with numerous work-and-inspection orders. This procedure often requires more clerical and non-productive work.
- There is a need to provide more training in order to prepare workers for a wide range of jobs.

Product layout represents a functional layout of the facility where the manufacturing effort concentrates on large quantities of a well-standardized product. This type of layout, illustrated in Exhibit 4–23, is commonly used in a flow production environment.

This example illustrates plant layout consisting of two product sections, Product A and Product B. Each section has a certain number of specialized machinery and equipment which provide all operations required by a particular manufacturing process.

The manufacturing process of Product A, for example, consists of five specialized operations, represented in the following order:

1. Cutting of sheet metal—cutting machine
2. Bending of sheet metal parts—bending brake
3. Welding various components together—spot welder
4. Grinding of the assembled product—grinder
5. Coating of the assembled product—dry powder equipment

Similarly, the manufacturing process of Product B also consists of five specialized operations as follows:

1. Cutting the blank—power saw
2. Turning the shaft—central lathe
3. Milling the key-way—milling machine
4. Hard-chroming the shaft—electroplating equipment
5. Inspecting the shaft—gauging tools and measuring instruments

Product layout is usually applied in manufacturing companies that concentrate on highly-standardized products representing a limited product range and manufactured in fairly large quantities, like in assembly lines. Product layout has certain advantages and disadvantages in its application within the production environment of any industrial organization. Some of the advantages of product layout are:

- It provides a steady flow of work over direct operational routes, minimizing delays in the manufacturing process.
- It requires less material handling because of shorter travel of work between relevant working stations.

Exhibit 4–23

Product Layout Diagram

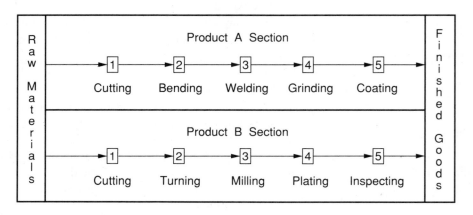

- It provides for closer coordination of the manufacturing process as a result of the preplanned operational sequence.
- It helps to minimize manufacturing time per unit of product.
- It helps to reduce the volume of work-in-process between various working stations.
- It requires smaller floor areas per unit of product within the production facility.
- It simplifies production planning and control procedures since all operations are synchronized well in advance.
- It requires a limited amount of inspection between working stations since quality control becomes an integral part of the manufacturing process.

Some of the disadvantages of product layout are:

- There is a need for higher capital investment in machinery and equipment because of duplication of some manufacturing processes.
- There is an increased potential for machine idleness if certain production lines are not fully loaded to their operational capacity.
- There is less flexibility in the process of work accomplishment because jobs cannot be rerouted to other similar machines as in the process layout arrangement.
- There is little development of workers' operating skills because each operator only learns his or her job at a specific machine or working station. This results in decreased universal abilities of workers in operating a range of machinery and equipment.
- There is no highly efficient supervision because supervisors and foremen become too involved in specific manufacturing processes and neglect the overall in-depth knowledge required to set up and regulate the operation of various machinery and equipment. This process requires skilled setters to prepare specific machines for work in order to meet manufacturing process requirements.
- There is an overall increase in manufacturing costs, although labor costs per unit of product may be lower. This increase is a direct result of high facility overheads on production lines, particularly if there is not full utilization of the operational capacity and if certain machines are idle.
- There is an increased danger of production line shutdown, if certain machinery or equipment fails to perform. It is necessary, therefore, to provide standby equipment or additional manufacturing facilities in order to prevent unnecessary production delays and to keep the work flowing.

Fixed position layout represents a functional layout of the facility based on bringing people and equipment to the item being produced. This type of layout may be used if the work item is too heavy or too bulky to be moved without problems. Typical examples of fixed position layout include airplane or train manufacturers, shipbuilders, and bridge and house construction.

Thorough investigation of manufacturing process requirements will determine the type of plant layout best suited to a particular production environment. Process layout is generally most suitable in a job shop or batch production environment, and the product layout is most useful for the flow production operations. Certain companies, however, employ both types of plant layout within the same facility to ensure maximum flexibility of overall operational abilities. Finally, the fixed position layout is generally used by larger organizations.

4.09 Equipment Maintenance

Effective performance of equipment is essential in meeting the production objectives of the company. This can only be achieved if the machinery is properly maintained during the manufacturing process. The main objective of **equipment maintenance** is, therefore, to ensure that machinery and equipment are always kept in satisfactory condition in accordance with standards set by management. The maintenance function in a small or medium-sized manufacturing company is usually handled by the service section of the production department and the work assigned to it normally includes design, construction, modification, installation, and removal of machinery and equipment. Continuous and preplanned maintenance activity affords the following advantages:

- Continuity of the manufacturing process
- Fewer stoppages and breakdowns of equipment
- Increased mechanization of the manufacturing operations
- Reduction of labor costs per output unit
- Improved level of production planning and control
- Improved reliability of work and quality of manufactured goods
- Lower cost of correcting defective workmanship and providing repair services
- Improved performance of service equipment such as boiler, cooling, and ventilation units
- Lower service expenses for electricity, water, air, and steam
- Lower cost of materials and spares used in the maintenance service
- Improved ability to deliver goods and services on time
- Improved morale of production personnel

To achieve the objectives of equipment maintenance at a reasonable cost, it is necessary to establish some form of organization which will provide all the necessary services related to the specific requirements of the manufacturing operation. It is therefore essential to establish the following:

- Size of the maintenance force
- Method of control over the maintenance force
- Details of routine maintenance requirements
- Details of preventive maintenance requirements
- Daily control of maintenance work
- Standard procedures and instructions related to the maintenance work
- Purchasing requirements and storing of materials, spares, and tools needed for equipment maintenance
- Details of equipment inspection methods and schedules
- Maintenance reports and records

Magnitude of the maintenance force depends mainly upon the physical size of the facility and the quantity of machinery and equipment. The total number of work-hours required to keep equipment in good operational shape under the existing conditions within the facility should be assessed. The work-hour rating of maintenance work should be summarized in accordance with the annual maintenance program and converted into the number of maintenance personnel. If, for example, a particular facility requires 4,300 work-hours per year of maintenance work, the company will have to budget and subsequently to employ two full time maintenance specialists, each working on average:

45 work-hour/week $\times$ 48 weeks/year $= 2,160$ work-hours/year

It is generally more economical to keep a small maintenance team and to use subcontracting services, which are particularly effective in the process of installing, maintaining, or removing specialized equipment. Management in each company, however, should develop its own policy with regard to the maintenance of production equipment. The common objective of the equipment maintenance team is the installation of machinery, aligning it and securing it to a foundation, providing power supply connections, conducting final operating tests, and delivering it to the operator in a functional condition. Another essential duty of the maintenance team is to ensure smooth operation of equipment. This necessitates the following:

- Checking equipment as to foundations, alignment of moving parts, vibrations, bearings, proper functioning of control devices, and safe conditions
- Identifying and repairing all worn parts such as bearings, shafts, blades, gears, bushes, and gaskets
- Replacing all the damaged parts which are worn out beyond repair
- Inspecting the general condition of equipment and summarizing all findings in a relevant maintenance report
- Preparing a cost estimate for all accessory maintenance and repair work
- Specifying and selecting correct lubricants for the machinery and equipment
- Ensuring timely lubrication of equipment in accordance with prescribed servicing frequency and controlling oil consumption
- Ensuring the implementation of preventive maintenance procedures throughout the production facility

The main objective of **preventive maintenance** procedures is to avoid equipment failure and to remedy minor defects before they necessitate major repairs. The effectiveness of preventive maintenance depends substantially upon an adequate equipment inspection and servicing program covering the whole range of machinery in the facility. The frequency of equipment inspection is usually determined in accordance with the general experience related to the particular type of machinery in use. Inspection results and maintenance records normally indicate when the frequency should be changed.

Planning and control of maintenance work in a small or medium-sized company usually entails six steps. These steps are summarized in Exhibit 4–24.

The first task of the maintenance section supervisor is to develop an effective **preventive maintenance program** for every important piece of equipment and machinery in the production facility. The details of all work to be performed in accordance with such a program should be entered into the monthly **preventive maintenance schedule**. The prime purpose of this schedule is to summarize all planned maintenance work requirements in an orderly manner to ensure effective allocation of maintenance tasks. A typical preventive maintenance schedule is illustrated in Exhibit 4–25.

Once preventive maintenance work requirements are identified, all tasks must be scheduled for timely execution. Each planned and routine maintenance assignment, including machine breakdowns, should be given an *order number* in accordance with existing work priorities within the production facility. Detailed information related to each maintenance task should be recorded in the **maintenance work progress report**. A typical illustration of such a report is presented in Exhibit 4–26.

Certain maintenance jobs can only be performed while machines are not operating and this should be done outside of regular working hours if possible. Typical examples of such work are inspection and repair of conveyors, overhead

Exhibit 4–24

Equipment Maintenance Planning and Control Procedures

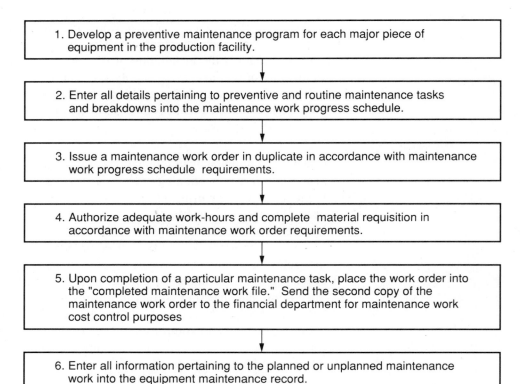

1. Develop a preventive maintenance program for each major piece of equipment in the production facility.

2. Enter all details pertaining to preventive and routine maintenance tasks and breakdowns into the maintenance work progress schedule.

3. Issue a maintenance work order in duplicate in accordance with maintenance work progress schedule requirements.

4. Authorize adequate work-hours and complete material requisition in accordance with maintenance work order requirements.

5. Upon completion of a particular maintenance task, place the work order into the "completed maintenance work file." Send the second copy of the maintenance work order to the financial department for maintenance work cost control purposes

6. Enter all information pertaining to the planned or unplanned maintenance work into the equipment maintenance record.

cranes, and other material handling systems; service and lubrication of machinery and equipment; and tensioning of belts.

It is often advisable to arrange for part of the maintenance team to work during the early hours prior to the start of the morning shift, during lunch time, or after normal working hours when the facility is shut down. The daily planning

Exhibit 4–25

Preventive Maintenance Schedule

Preventive Maintenance Schedule				
Period: September 1989	Machine		Work description	Completion date required
Work allocation	No	Description		
Machine shop	12	NC machine	Monthly	9.15
Welding shop	18	Spot welder	Replace electrodes	9.20
Prepared:		Authorized:		Date:

Exhibit 4–26

Maintenance Work Progress Report

Maintenance Work Progress Report										
Work			Name of maintenance person	Planned Performance			Actual Performance			
				Dates		Time	Dates		Time	
Order No.	Description	Priority 1/2/3		Start	Finish	Hr.	Start	Finish	Hr.	
100	NC machine No. 12 monthly servicing	1	A. Peters	9.15	9.15	4	9.15	9.15	3	
101	Spot welder No. 18 change electrodes	1	B. Thomas	9.20	9.20	1	9.21	9.21	2	

of maintenance work requires, therefore, a considerable amount of effort and cooperation among production personnel.

Accurately specified work assignments prevent conflicting instructions and ensure timely accomplishment of various tasks. It is essential, therefore, to record each job in order to provide a sound basis for equipment maintenance control. Hence, the important rule is that no maintenance work should be done without a written job instruction except in emergency situations. Such written instruction, or **maintenance work order**, should be prepared in advance by the person in charge of the maintenance section and issued to the maintenance personnel prior to the commencement of work. A typical maintenance work order is presented in Exhibit 4–27.

In the event of equipment breakdown, people must be sent by verbal instruction to repair the machine and an appropriate maintenance work order should be issued immediately that specifies the relevant task. The personnel affected by the emergency removal of maintenance workers from jobs they are already on should be notified about the interruption of routine work.

Maintenance work orders usually originate from preplanned regular inspection procedures, equipment maintenance requirements, operating requests for service and repair work, or changes initiated by production management. It is essential that all maintenance work is approved and scheduled by a single authority to avoid conflicting promises and unnecessary production delays. The person in charge of the maintenance section is required to enforce the policy of planned maintenance work and to ensure its execution on a continuous basis.

Written instructions on maintenance work orders should be as brief as possible because more detailed information is normally supplied in the relevant manuals. These manuals provide a comprehensive functional description of machinery and equipment. It is also necessary to prepare a **material requisition** and to specify the materials and spare parts required for the completion of the maintenance work. This requisition could also serve as a receipt for all with-

Exhibit 4–27

Maintenance Work Order

Maintenance Work Order No. 100						
To: A. Peters		From: A. Supervisor		Date required: 9/15/89		
Working instructions: Please complete the monthly service of NC machine No. 12. Replace a spindle with two bearings and inject new lubricant.						
Materials	**Unit**	*Quantity* **Units**	*Unit cost* **$**	*Total cost ($)* **Estimated**	**Actual**	
Spindle	item	1	50	50		
Bearings	item	2	20	40		
Lubricants	gallon	1.5	10	15		
Labor and subcontracting	**Hourly rate**	*Time (hours)* **Estimated**	**Actual**	*Total cost ($)* **Estimated**	**Actual**	
Regular maintenance	$40/hr	2		80		
Total cost				**185**		

drawals of materials from stores. The exact requirements for equipment maintenance service can usually be predetermined, although provision should be made for spares in case a need is identified only after dismantling the machinery. For this reason the maintenance supervisor should be issued with a material requisition book.

The effectiveness of equipment maintenance service depends substantially upon the availability of records of past work. It is essential, therefore, to summarize relevant details of maintenance work in an appropriate **equipment maintenance record**. A typical illustration of such a record is presented in Exhibit 4–28.

Exhibit 4–28

Equipment Maintenance Record

Equipment Maintenance Record						
Machine No. 12		Description: NC machine				
Date	Work order No.	Work description	Cost ($) Material	Labor	Subcontract	Total
9/15/89	100	Monthly service, new spindle, two bearings, and lubricant	105	80	——	185

4.10 Equipment Replacement

The costs of maintenance and repair work may vary depending on the age and quality of machinery and equipment and their degree of utilization in the facility. When these costs are unforeseen and substantial, it is necessary to consider replacement of the equipment if this proves to be more economical. It is essential, therefore, to develop a suitable **equipment replacement program,** to establish a repair limit cost for every major piece of machinery and to monitor the actual expenditure against the budgeted repair limit cost. When the actual repair cost exceeds the budgeted limit, this is the first indication that a particular piece of equipment should be considered for replacement. The value of equipment repair limit cost depends upon the age of machinery and equipment, cost and availability of replacements, possible loss of production output and final resale value. Some of the major objectives of the equipment replacement program are:

- To increase the production capacity of the facility
- To decrease operational running cost per unit of production
- To minimize equipment maintenance and repair costs
- To dispose of broken, worn out, and obsolete equipment
- To improve the quality of manufactured products
- To improve utilization of production personnel
- To simplify manufacturing operations and processes
- To upgrade the efficiency of production planning and control
- To improve the overall productivity of performance in the facility

Whether the equipment is replaced in accordance with a specific replacement program developed by management or as a result of a sudden breakdown, a specific plan of investigation should be prepared. The main objective of such a plan is to adopt standard criteria in the form of a checklist of points on which to examine equipment replacement from the technical suitability and cost-saving point of view. Hence, the two major **equipment replacement factors** are:

- **Technical factors.** These factors, such as accuracy, production output, technical compatibility, quality of production, and safety, relate to the operational suitability of equipment to perform designated tasks in the most effective manner.
- **Cost factors.** These factors, such as equipment operating and maintenance costs, labor and utilities consumption costs, and production output value, relate to the economical viability of equipment.

All progressive manufacturing companies adopt a plan of equipment replacement in accordance with a definite program instead of waiting until the machinery breaks down, deteriorates, or becomes obsolete. The equipment replacement program normally necessitates one of the following steps:

- An annual budget providing a specific amount of money or a fixed percentage of sales revenue in order to allow purchase of new equipment to replace old and inefficient machinery
- Annual replacement of the oldest and most unproductive pieces of machinery by new equipment to ensure higher production capacity, greater operational accuracy, and reduced labor requirements

- Preplanned and continuous study of specific manufacturing processes and evaluation of present production performance with the objective of making equipment replacements where manufacturing costs can be definitely reduced

It is usually profitable to replace equipment during the first 10 to 15 years of its operation depending on the nature of the manufacturing process and production activity. Furthermore, it is advisable to set aside an amount of money equal to the value of annual depreciation of equipment and to use it for new equipment purchases because:

- Depreciation and obsolescence of equipment represent a continuous process and should be compensated for on a continuous basis to avoid increased inefficiency in the production facility.
- Capital investment in modern equipment and tools usually earns a better return in comparison with an investment in other securities.
- Depreciation reserves that are allowed to accumulate instead of being used for their original purpose create the possibility of mismanagement of capital funds.
- It is easier to maintain a steady level of new equipment replacement expenditure programs on an annual basis than to commit the company to an unplanned substantial outlay of capital.

A number of equipment replacement methods and formulas have been developed in the past. The replacement problem usually demands a comparison between the costs of performing specific manufacturing operations with various types of machinery and equipment. This problem is generally important enough to require a detailed investigation into the **equipment replacement study** and should be handled by a senior company executive. The investigation should cover all aspects of the equipment performance and should determine the maximum return on the required capital investment. It is also necessary to consider the cost of tooling, jigs, and fixtures required for specific production purposes, keeping in mind that tools usually have a high rate of deterioration.

The fundamental approach of equipment replacement economics is based on the determination of **equipment annual costs** incurred in production by a particular machine. It is essential to determine the total annual cost related to each machine and to compare it with similar costs of other machines. It is also important to realize that some machines function for different amounts of working hours during one year—some may operate only a half shift, while others work two or three shifts. The study of equipment economics, therefore, should be based on the accurately estimated operating time performance of the machine and not on its full potential capacity. Equipment annual cost can be determined as follows:

$$EAC = FC + LC + OC$$

Key:

EAC = equipment annual cost
FC = finance cost
LC = labor cost
OC = operating cost

Finance cost should consider the direct investment in the present or proposed piece of machinery. For the existing equipment it should be the current net-realizable value, regardless of the original cost or book value, and for the proposed equipment this should be the total cost including transportation, installation, and finance charges. The finance cost should be calculated on the basis of the total percentage of direct investment, allowing for return on the capital investment and depreciation of the equipment. This cost can be determined as follows:

$$FC = (A + B) \times CI$$

Key:

A = annual percentage allowance for return on investment
B = annual percentage allowance for depreciation of equipment
CI = total capital investment

Labor cost should take into account the total cost of direct labor and should correspond to the total projected operating time of a particular machine (e.g., half shift, one shift plus 20 percent overtime, or three shifts). This cost should also include annual vacation and holiday pay as well as total company's contributions toward the direct labor cost, such as pension, medical insurance, social security.

Operating cost should include the total cost of electricity and water consumption, space allotted to the machine, maintenance, and insurance costs.

A particular manufacturer, for example, is considering replacing two milling machines with an NC machine of the same total capacity. The realizable value of each milling machine is $7,000, and the new NC machine is priced at $18,000. The expected rate of return on investment is 20% and annual depreciation of equipment is 15%. The new machine will require only 50% of the labor cost (two operators at $1,000 per month) and 70% of the operating cost ($200 per month) of the existing machines. The equipment replacement study summary is illustrated in the Exhibit 4–29.

It is apparent from this example that the proposed NC machine will show savings that will not only pay back the increased investment in a reasonable period and earn a fair return on investment, but will also provide an additional saving of $11,320 per year ($31,300–$19,980).

The equipment replacement study is easily applicable in cases where a particular machine or set of machines represents part of a continuous manufacturing process that deals with a specific product. This study, however, is also applicable in cases where a particular machine is utilized in various manufacturing processes and is used on many different products. The latter study may require

Exhibit 4–29

Equipment Replacement Study Summary

Description of Cost	Present		Proposed	
		Values in Dollars		
Capital investment	7,000 × 2	= 14,000		18,000
Return on investment	14,000 × 0.2	= 2,800	18,000 × 0.2 =	3,600
Annual depreciation	14,000 × 0.15 =	2,100	18,000 × 0.15 =	2,700
(+) Finance cost	(0.2+0.15)×14,000 =	4,900	(0.2+0.15)×18,000 =	6,300
(+) Labor cost	2 × 1,000 × 12 =	24,000	1 × 1,000 × 12 =	12,000
(+) Operating cost	200 × 12 =	2,400	0.7 × 200 × 12 =	1,680
(=) Total cost		31,300		19,980

more information and could take more time to complete, but its general principles remain the same.

Equipment replacement studies usually provide valuable information related to the decision-making process that takes place during equipment evaluation, selection, and replacement procedures. Any such study will always require skillful managerial judgment in order to make a sound final decision.

4.11 Tool Control

Every manufacturing organization utilizes a substantial quantity of small appliances such as **tools**, **jigs**, and **fixtures** commonly used in the production environment. All tools can be classified into three basic categories:

- **Standard tools.** These tools are interchangeable and can be used on various machines.
- **Special tools.** These tools are not interchangeable, are often very expensive, and are applicable to a specific type of work or product.
- **Perishable tools.** These tools are often termed **consumable tools** because of their short lifespan. Their cost is often substantial as a result of their high consumption.

Tools represent an integral part of the manufacturing process and should be planned and prepared in advance. It is necessary to develop and maintain practical **tool control** to ensure good workmanship and to satisfy the production requirements of the organization. Some of the important requirements of tool control have been outlined by William B. Cornell in *Organization and Management*:

- All tools which have to be made for jobs should be designed by the tool design section.
- Tools needed for each operation should be specified.
- Tools should be standardized.
- A toolroom should be maintained.
- Tools should be inspected and maintained in proper condition.
- Tools should be delivered promptly to the workers when and where required.
- All tools should be fully accounted for and their location known at all times.
- Workmen should be held responsible for all tools used by them.
- Personnel of the tool crib should be carefully selected.
- Records should be kept showing performance and tool cost.
- A perpetual inventory of tools should be provided.

Cornell further specified important advantages arising from the establishment of organized methods for tool control:

- Reduced capital tied up in inventory and less interest charges. Tool stocks are kept consistent with production requirements. New tools are not designed and made when proper tools already exist. Obsolete tools are disposed of.
- Quality of products is maintained. Good tools permit good workmanship.
- Production cost is reduced. Work is turned out in less time with less scrap and spoilage.

- Tool cost is reduced. Proper care prolongs tool life. Worn tools are salvaged. Losses due to waste and pilferage are cut down.
- Production control is aided. Availability of standard stocked tools and procurement of new or special tools is taken care of before work is ready to go into production. Planning can be done with assurance of meeting schedules.
- Tool storage space is conserved and tool crib operating costs are reduced. Centralization, orderly arrangement, proper shelving, adequate indexes and records, capable personnel, all contribute toward such economies.[4]

It is essential to ensure cost effectiveness of tooling in any manufacturing organization and to establish a correct level of expenditure. The amount of capital which should be invested in tooling depends primarily on the particular production requirements and varies substantially among different manufacturing companies. Expenditure for tools is usually required whenever the product must be manufactured in large quantities. Often, however, the capital is tied up in expensive tools, jigs, and dies prepared for products which are in small demand.

Tooling may also provide an important saving in labor costs and so it is essential to invest sufficient capital into the process of developing new tools, jigs, and fixtures in order to simplify and speed up the manufacturing operation. An additional factor to be considered is the estimated life of tools, jigs, and fixtures and the possible discontinuation of a particular product line. Major factors determining the level of capital investment into these supplies can be summarized as follows:

- Economic advantage due to labor cost reduction
- Effective tool cost recovery over a large quantity of products
- Increased accuracy and improved quality of products
- Increased productivity of the manufacturing process

There are a number of important questions to be considered when evaluating the cost of tooling, jigs, and fixtures. Some of these questions are as follows:

- What is the repayment period for a tool used under specific conditions? For example, how long will it take a tool that costs $300 to pay for itself if it saves 10 cents on direct labor cost per unit of product at a specified rate?
- How many products must be manufactured to pay for a jig of a specific estimated cost to show a particular saving in direct labor cost per unit of product? What volume of production will be required to recover the cost of a particular jig valued at $200 to save 5 cents on direct labor cost of each piece?
- What is the estimated cost of a fixture which is required to show a particular estimated unit saving in direct labor cost on a specified number of products? What, for example, should be the "break-even" on a production run of 5,000 units if the fixture can save 10 cents on direct labor cost per unit?
- What profit could be earned by a tool at a specific cost for an estimated saving in direct labor cost per unit and particular rate of production output? What would be the profit generated by a $300 tool if it saves 5 cents in direct labor cost per unit on 800 units?

The decision in regard to the purchase of a particular tool or its manufacture depends upon the cost, quality, and service related to a particular item. Standard and perishable tools can usually be purchased from tool suppliers at reasonable prices, but special tools often present a practical problem. These tools can be manufactured within the company at fair cost if the toolroom facilities are provided. Alternatively, it may become necessary to subcontract the work to outside tooling specialists.

It is advisable to consider the following factors when deciding whether to make or purchase a particular tool, jig or fixture:

- **Tool cost factor.** It is necessary to estimate the cost of making the tooling, taking into account the appropriate cost of materials, labor subcontracting service, and toolroom overheads.
- **Tool quality factor.** It is often more economical to purchase tooling from tool specialists who usually guarantee the quality of their products. If, conversely, the company manufactures its own tooling, breakage usually represents a non-recoverable loss.
- **Tool service factor.** Every tool is designed to provide a service at a specific level of production. Thus, if a particular tool is marginally more expensive than another tool, it is expected to recover the excess cost by means of additional service.

The process of estimating costs of special tools requires completion of a **tool costing sheet.** The prime purpose of cost estimating is to summarize all possible expenses associated with the manufacture of a particular tool, jig, or fixture. A typical tool costing sheet is presented in Exhibit 4–30.

The cost of tooling is usually lower and its quality on an equally acceptable level when tools are manufactured by specialists on the production line basis. It is necessary, therefore, to consider the overall cost of tooling prior to making the final decision in regard to its manufacture or purchase. Sometimes the cost of special tooling may be lower if manufactured in the toolroom, depending on the available facilities and the efficiency of its personnel.

Once tool manufacturing requirements are identified, all tasks must be scheduled for timely execution. Each planned tool manufacturing assignment should be given a job number in accordance with existing work priorities in the toolroom. Detailed information related to each tool manufacturing job should be recorded in the **toolroom work progress report**. A typical illustration of such a report is presented in Exhibit 4–31.

Irrespective of their origin, all tools should be tested on short non-productive runs before their actual use in the production department. The results of such tests must be properly recorded in a **tool trial report** to ensure effective performance of tooling and to avoid unnecessary breakdowns and subsequent loss of production time. A typical illustration of such a report is presented in Exhibit 4–32.

Once the new tool is tested in the manufacturing environment, appropriate comments by the production, toolroom, and drafting office personnel need to be summarized in the tool trial report. Only with their approval can a particular tool be accepted for routine production runs.

It is also necessary to standardize the tooling variety in the production department. This becomes particularly important when the company grows in size and diversifies into various directions. One of the objectives of tool

Exhibit 4–30

Tool Costing Sheet

Tool Costing Sheet				
Tool No. 300		Tool description: Special forming tool		
Section/Shop: Press shop		Part No.: 423-8000		Operation No.: 1,2,3
Material	**Unit description**	**Unit cost**	**Total cost ($)**	
	Quantity/size/weight	**$**	**Estimated**	**Actual**
MS steel	5″ × 7″ × 3″	40/lb	80	
Brass bar	Dia. 1″ ×5″	10/lb	30	
Special cutting knife	1 unit	100/unit	100	
Clamps	10 units	5/unit	50	

Labor and subcontracting	**Hourly Rate**	**Production time (Hours)**		**Total cost ($)**	
		Estimated	**Actual**	**Estimated**	**Actual**
Toolmaker	50	5		250	
Plating	- - -	- - -		60	
Total cost				570	
Prepared: A. Jacks		Authorized: P. King		Date: 9.1.89	

Exhibit 4–31

Toolroom Work Progress Report

Toolroom Work Progress Report											
Toolroom job No.	Tool No.	Work priority 1/2/3	Name of toolmaker	Planned performance			Actual performance			Tool trial report No.	Tool acceptance date
				Dates		Time	Dates		Time		
				Start	Finish	Hr.	Start	Finish	Hr.		
456	300	1	A. Peters	9.11.89	9.13.89	20	9.12.89	9.15.89	24	540	9.20.89

Exhibit 4–32

Tool Trial Report

Tool Trial Report				
Tool trial report No.: 540		Tool No.: 300	Description: Special forming tool	
Section/Shop: Press shop		Machine No.: 12	Setting time: 1 Hr	
Operational details: Use this tool for Part No. 423-800, operations 1, 2, and 3				

Trial			Comments		
No.	Date	Quantity	Production Supervisor	Toolroom Supervisor	Draftsperson-designer
1	9.17	20	Reject operation 3	Adjust the tool	Reject operation 3
	9.18	20	All operations O.K.	Tool is O.K.	Product is O.K.
2					
3					
4					
Tool acceptance date: 9.20.89			Tool acceptance authorized: P. King		

standardization is to minimize the number of suppliers and to reduce the range of special tools. The advantages of a **tool standardization program** are numerous:

- Purchase cost reduction
- Spare parts level reduction
- Storage space reduction
- Administrative work reduction

If a company has more than one facility using the same type of tooling, each facility can keep smaller stocks of replacement parts and thus reduce the overall investment in tooling.

The process of establishing suitable tooling standards should allow sufficient flexibility to accommodate new and more economical types of tools. It is necessary, therefore, to ensure the update of tool performance and maintenance records in order to provide an acceptable standard of tools, jigs, and fixtures. These records will indicate the quality of tooling, the frequency of their servicing, and their degree of suitability for general production purposes.

All records related to operational performance of a particular tool need to be summarized in the **tool performance and maintenance card**. A typical illustration of such a card is presented in Exhibit 4–33.

It is also essential to provide adequate facilities for storage and control of tooling in the production department. Tools are usually stored in a special

Exhibit 4–33

Tool Performance and Maintenance Card

Tool Performance and Maintenance Card						
Tool No. 300			Tool description: Special forming tool			
Section/Shop: Press shop			Part No.: 423-8000		Operation No. 1,2,3	
Tool issue date	Quantity of parts produced	Tool return date	Tool performance and maintenance comments	Material cost ($)	Repair time (Hr.)	Toolroom supervisor signature
10.1.89	1,000	10.1.89	Tool performance is O.K.	- - -	- - -	R. King
10.8.89	4,000	10.9.89	Minor repair	20	0.5	≈

location, commonly termed a **tool crib**, in accordance with the following three methods:

1. **Central tool crib.**   All tools are located in one central storage place from where they are issued on demand. This method is most suitable for small and medium-sized manufacturing companies.
2. **Sub-tool crib.**   All tools are located in one central storage place from where they are distributed to sub-tool cribs which carry the necessary stock of tooling used by a specific production section. Production personnel receive all tools from a particular sub-tool crib, located in a certain production section. This method is most suitable for larger manufacturing companies.
3. **Flexible sub-tool crib.**   This method is similar to the sub-tool crib tooling distribution. However, it represents a movable tool crib which can operate between floors in the form of an elevator and deliver tools to various sections. This method is most suitable for medium-sized and large manufacturing companies accommodated in multistory buildings.

There are a number of factors related to the correct storage procedure of tooling in the manufacturing organization:

*   *Facility size and plant layout.*   Tools can be stored in a central storage place or in a few smaller stores, depending on the size of the facility and the plant layout.
*   *Allocation of space in production department.*   It is important to locate adequate tool storage facilities near those manufacturing sections that use most of the tools.
*   *Nature of product.*   It is important to provide an adequate variety and quantity of tools depending on the nature of manufactured products.

- *Method of operation.* It is essential to ensure a sufficient range and quantity of tools in accordance with requirements of various manufacturing methods.

There are three methods of **tool distribution** commonly used in any manufacturing organization:

1. Tools are distributed to workers in accordance with tool requisitions prepared in advance for particular jobs. These tools are collected from workers and returned to the tool crib upon the completion of work.
2. Tools are distributed to workers and are left in their possession for use on a permanent basis.
3. Tools are collected by workers from the tool crib and subsequently returned by them when the work is completed.

The first method is probably the most practical one since it provides pre-planned and efficient distribution of tools to workers in accordance with current production requirements. In addition, this method ensures that the time wasted by operators and machine idle time is minimized. Finally, this method provides for effective tool maintenance and control, ensuring high overall utilization of tooling in the facility. This method of tool distribution is commonly used by manufacturing companies that operate on a regularly-planned basis and produce for stock or for a progressive set of orders.

The second method is not commonly used for production purposes because it would require a large quantity of tooling to satisfy the needs of all workers if tools were left permanently with the production personnel. This method is, however, useful for various nonmanufacturing work centers in the production department such as assembly, quality control, and maintenance sections. Most tools used by these sections are of a special nature and,therefore, not required by manufacturing sections.

A third method is frequently used by various manufacturing organizations. However, it is recommended that this method be avoided and replaced with an alternative one, depending on the nature of the production activity. This method is undesirable in the normal production environment because it encourages equipment idleness, unnecessary conversations among production personnel, and a waste of time, causing a reduction in the overall productivity level. Nevertheless, this method could be used by certain work centers within the production department involved in irregular manufacturing work such as toolroom or maintenance section.

Regardless of the method used, it is essential to provide good service for tool distribution in the facility. Tools should be kept in a proper storage place and distributed to the production personnel only when required. Certain conditions of good service should be maintained by the toolkeepers on the following basis:

- They should have adequate knowledge of all tools under their control.
- Delivery of tools should be done promptly and accurately in accordance with tool requisitions.
- Tools should always be kept in good working condition.
- All damaged and worn-out tools should be replaced by new or reconditioned ones.
- Tool damage should be assessed and charged to a proper account.
- Tool maintenance should be carried out on a steady basis.

- All unused tools should be collected and returned to the tool crib.
- All records of tool movements should be constantly updated.

There are a few systems of tool distribution commonly used by various manufacturing companies. Some of these systems are:

1. **Single-check system.**   The worker secures a receipt of a tool with a brass disc with his or her number stamped on it. This disc is hung on a hook at the place where the tool is stored, so that when the tool is required, the toolkeeper will know where to locate it in the facility. There is no record, however, of how many tools are in the possession of various workers and for what purpose they are used.

2. **Double-check system.**   This system is similar to the previous one except that an additional brass disc is placed under the name of the worker who is using the tool. The toolkeeper will now be able not only to locate each tool, but also to check the quantity of tools issued to a particular worker.

3. **Triplicate-check system.**   This system requires that the worker complete a tool requisition in triplicate. The form specifies the date of order, worker's clock card number, details of the required tool, and signature upon acceptance of the tool. The first copy is kept by the toolkeeper until the tool is returned, the second one is issued to the worker with the tool and the third one is clipped to the place where the tool is usually kept. When the tool is returned in good condition, the toolkeeper files the first copy away and destroys the other two. Accumulation of requisitions should provide the toolkeeper with accurate information about the usage of various tools. If the tool has not been returned in good condition, certain remarks will be made on the second copy and filed away separately indicating accumulation of damaged tools. This will provide the toolkeeper with information about the source and frequency of tool damage. The second copy can also be used as a tool repair order indicating the nature of the required repair work and directing the allocation of the repair cost.

Modern production management practice suggests that all tools be maintained by toolroom personnel rather than have the workers themselves or even toolkeepers perform this work. The efficiency of tools depends substantially on the condition in which they are kept. Cutting efficiency, for example, depends primarily on the tools' sharpening methods and even slight variation of tool angles will reduce efficiency to a large degree. It is essential, therefore, to ensure that all tools, including the damaged and worn ones, are properly inspected and repaired only by toolmakers or other specialized personnel. An additional reason for sharpening and repairing tools in the toolroom is that it is more economical than to allow the worker to handle this procedure at the expense of his productive time.

4.12 Cost Estimating

When inquiries for jobs, products, services, contracts, or projects are received from prospective customers, it is necessary to prepare accurate cost estimates and to specify delivery or completion dates. The **cost estimating** procedure forms the basis for quotations on pending orders and assists in determining the final selling price of products and services. This procedure entails preparation of a statement summarizing quantities and costs of required materials, production times, bought-out components, and subcontracting services. Furthermore, cost estimating provides a foundation for thorough financial control of operational activities within the organization. Thus, it is important to develop such a procedure for various types of activities and to ensure that all cost factors are properly taken into account. Some of the major factors influencing the cost estimating procedure are:

- Previous cost estimates
- Previous actual cost records
- Current cost of materials
- Current hourly rates
- Current cost of subcontracting services
- Estimated usage of materials, labor, equipment and subcontracting services
- Estimated quantities to be manufactured
- Current level of productivity
- Availability of time for production
- Competitive situation in the marketplace
- Possibility of repeat orders
- Mature judgment and professional expertise

Although the advanced estimation of work represents one of the basic functions within the production department, the success of its implementation also depends upon the accuracy of information supplied by the financial department. Such information, particularly hourly rates, is usually determined in accordance with the specific details of the company's annual budget and should be reviewed from time to time. These rates are expressed in dollars per labor-hour or machine-hour and provide the basis for a standard costing procedure. The effectiveness of cost estimating depends not only upon the estimator but also upon the overall efficiency of the production department and the ability of the production manager to plan, coordinate and control the work in the facility. The basic cost estimating procedure is summarized in Exhibit 4–34.

Cost estimating procedures are constantly used for various operational activities. These procedures are based on two **standard costing methods** discussed in detail in Part 3 (Volume I) and classified as follows:

- **Job order costing.** This method entails costing of raw materials, labor, use of operational capacity, and subcontracting services for each job, product, service, contract, or project on an individual basis.
- **Process costing.** This method entails costing of raw materials, labor, use of operational capacity, and subcontracting services for a particular manufacturing or service process and allocating the overall cost to the total number of product or service units produced.

The job order costing method is commonly used for estimation of costs in a job shop or batch production environment or for custom services, contracts, and long-term projects. The process costing method, on the other hand, is used in a flow production environment and for estimating standard service costs. Irrespective of the costing method used, however, the cost estimating procedure necessitates a thorough understanding of all material, labor, operational capacity, and subcontracting service requirements. These requirements should be identified and summarized in a **costing sheet.** A typical illustration of such a sheet is presented in Exhibit 4–35.

Exhibit 4–34

Cost Estimating Procedure

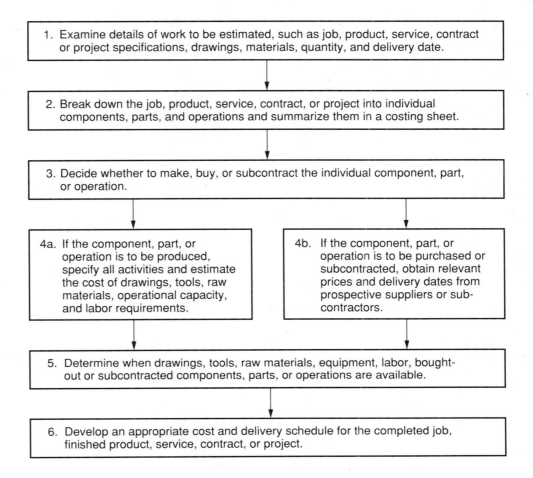

1. Examine details of work to be estimated, such as job, product, service, contract or project specifications, drawings, materials, quantity, and delivery date.

2. Break down the job, product, service, contract, or project into individual components, parts, and operations and summarize them in a costing sheet.

3. Decide whether to make, buy, or subcontract the individual component, part, or operation.

4a. If the component, part, or operation is to be produced, specify all activities and estimate the cost of drawings, tools, raw materials, operational capacity, and labor requirements.

4b. If the component, part, or operation is to be purchased or subcontracted, obtain relevant prices and delivery dates from prospective suppliers or subcontractors.

5. Determine when drawings, tools, raw materials, equipment, labor, bought-out or subcontracted components, parts, or operations are available.

6. Develop an appropriate cost and delivery schedule for the completed job, finished product, service, contract, or project.

Since the product-manufacturing process passes through various work centers, the labor and operational capacity input per work center need to be estimated on a *time basis* and corresponding hourly rates need to be applied.

It is often necessary to decide whether to manufacture a particular component or to purchase it from another supplier. In fact, most **make-or-buy decisions** for operational activities are made during the cost estimating procedure. A company's buyer must obtain appropriate prices of materials and services and pass the information to the cost estimator.

Prior to the commencement of any operational activity it is essential to identify whether operational capacity is available, and if not, to preselect a suitable subcontractor. The cost of all subcontracting services should be identified in advance and specified in the final estimate sheet.

Cost estimating procedure also entails determination of a product or service delivery date. This, in turn, is a part of the production scheduling process which is discussed later in this part. Hence, the cost estimator should determine the total working time and identify the existing availability of operational capacity and labor resources. Each operation should be fitted into the existing production schedule in accordance with available operational capacity, that is, total capacity less the existing workload in the production department. If the existing workload does not permit timely completion of a particular assignment, the cost estimator should consider whether to use overtime operational capacity or to quote a late delivery to a customer.

Exhibit 4–35

Costing Sheet

Costing Sheet				
Job/Part/Product No. 423-8000	Description: Special box for customer A			
Quantity: 1,000	Date required: 10.10.89		Reference No.:	
Other details: Refer to job No. 1828				

Materials	Unit description	Unit cost	Total cost ($)	
	Quantity/size/weight	$	Estimated	Actual
Mild steel	2′ × 3′ × 0.02′ × 2	80.00	160.00	
Stainless steel pins	Dia 0.3″ × 2,000	0.05	100.00	
Bolts	0.3″ × 1,000	0.10	100.00	

Labor per work center and subcontracting	Hourly rate	Production time (Hr.)		Total cost ($)	
		Estimated	Actual	Estimated	Actual
Machine shop	20.00	25		500.00	
Welding shop	15.00	20		300.00	
Paint shop	30.00	5		150.00	

Total cost	1,310.00	
Profit markup: 40%	524.00	
Commission and discount allowances: 5%	65.00	
Total selling price per 1,000 items	1,899.50	
Total selling price per item	1.90	
Prepared: A. Jackson	Authorized: B. Hall	Date: 9.10.89

4.13 Production Planning

Production planning represents an integral part of an efficient manufacturing process. Production planning is based on the systematic predetermination of the methods and procedures required for completion of products in the most suitable manner. The main objective of effective planning is to ensure the most economical utilization of operational capacity, human energy, and material resources available in the facility. Production planning is often a complex task and has to remain flexible enough to accommodate constantly changing requirements while manufacturing products for stock or customers' orders.

The basic principles of production planning, outlined in Exhibit 4–36, are similar for most manufacturing companies. The two most common principles are:

• The production plan should include all products or groups of products processed by common manufacturing facilities.

Exhibit 4–36

Production Planning Sequence in a Manufacturing Organization

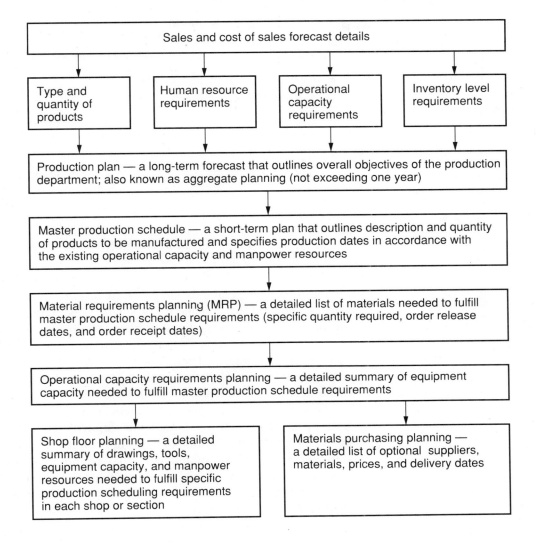

- The production plan should be expressed in the simple terms meaningful to the production personnel.[5]

Production planning in a job shop or batch production environment is usually more complex in comparison with flow production since there is a much broader range of products and manufacturing operations. Regardless of the manufacturing method, however, it is essential to ensure that the production output is carefully matched with a company's sales and financial budgets for a particular fiscal period.

The planning process usually starts with an annual manufacturing forecast which considers overall operational requirements. This type of planning, also known as **aggregate planning,** is designed to minimize the cost of meeting production demands by regulating three basic variables:

- The production output requirements
- The production manpower requirements
- The inventory level requirements

Exhibit 4–37

Aggregate Production Plan (Manufacturing Forecast)

Aggregate Production Plan			
Year: 1990	**Number of units — Product line A**		
Month	**Sale**	**Production**	**Inventory**
Year-end balance	— —	— —	50,000
January	25,000	15,000	40,000
February	20,000	10,000	30,000
March	15,000	15,000	30,000
April	25,000	20,000	25,000
May	5,000	10,000	30,000
June	30,000	15,000	15,000

A typical example of an aggregate production plan for a six-month period is illustrated in Exhibit 4–37.

If the production demand remains steady during the fiscal period, production planning becomes relatively simple. In reality, however, a company often experiences a nonuniform demand for products. This, in turn, puts additional pressure on the production manager and further complicates the planning process. It is necessary, therefore, to select effective strategies in order to meet a nonuniform manufacturing demand. These strategies, summarized in Exhibit 4–38, may be implemented individually or applied in any combination depending upon the manufacturing operations.

One of the prime approaches frequently used in aggregate planning is a **bottom-up approach**, or **rough cut capacity requirements planning**. This approach prescribes formulation of operational plans for each product and subsequent summation of all individual requirements into an aggregate plan. Operational capacity requirements planning involves **material requirements planning (MRP)** and estimation of equipment capacity requirements for a specified manufacturing period.

Throughout production planning it is necessary to obtain certain information and consider the following factors:

- *Production materials*—determining type, quantity, quality and availability of materials
- *Production facilities*—determining operational capacity, tooling, and availability of machinery and equipment
- *Production methods*—determining the most efficient procedure for each operation on each part of the product, specifying the auxiliary equipment, and grouping product parts into final assembly
- *Production operations*—determining the sequence in which operations must be carried out on each part of the product
- *Production standards*—determining the level of quality for each part in accordance with required specifications
- *Production time*—determining the time allowance for each operation in accordance with specified production methods
- *Production "due dates"*—determining dates for commencement and completion of each operation taking into account all factors mentioned above

Exhibit 4–38

Production Planning Strategies for Meeting Nonuniform Demands

Methods	Costs	Remarks
Strategy: Absorb demand fluctuations by varying inventory level, backordering, or shifting demand.		
Produce in earlier period and hold until product is demanded.	Cost of holding inventory.	Service operations cannot hold service inventory. They must staff for peak levels or shift demand.
Offer to deliver the product or service later when capacity is available.	Causes a delay in the receipt of revenue at the minimum. May result in lost customers.	Manufacturing companies with perishable products often are restrained in the use of this method.
Special marketing efforts to shift the demand to slack periods.	Costs of advertising, discounts, or promotional programs.	This is another example of the interrelationship between functions within a business.
Strategy: Change only the production rate in accordance with the nonuniform demand pattern.		
Work additional hours without changing the work force size.	Requires overtime premium pay.	Reduces the time available for maintenance work without interrupting production.
Staff for high production levels so that overtime is not required.	Excess personnel wages during periods of slack demand.	Sometimes work force can be utilized for deferred maintenance during periods of low demand.
Subcontract work to other firms.	The company must still pay its own overhead plus the overhead and profit for the subcontractors.	Utilizes the capacity of other firms but provides less control of schedules and quality levels.
Revise make-or-buy decisions to purchase items when capacity is fully loaded.	The company must have skills, tooling, and equipment that will be unutilized in slack periods.	All of these methods require capital investments sufficient for the peak production rate, which will be underutilized in slack periods.
Strategy: Change the size of the work force to vary the production level in accordance with demand.		
Hire additional personnel as demand increases.	Employment costs for advertising, travel, interviewing, training, etc. Shift premium costs if an additional shift is added.	Skilled workers might not be available when needed since they are more likely to be employed elsewhere.
Lay off personnel as demand subsides.	Cost of severance pay and increases in unemployment insurance costs. Loss of efficiency because of decreased morale and higher-seniority workers being moved into jobs for which they are inexperienced as they move into ("bump") jobs of workers with less seniority.	The company must have adequate capital investment in equipment for the peak work force level.

SOURCE: James B. Dilworth, *Production and Operations Management*, 2nd ed. (New York: Random House, 1983), p. 111. Reprinted with permission.

Two major functions of production planning are **scheduling** of manufacturing processes into acceptable timetables and **loading** various machines or operators in accordance with scheduled programs. A **master production schedule**, illustrated in Exhibit 4–39, is usually prepared on a weekly, biweekly, or monthly basis, depending on the nature of manufacturing activities. The scheduling of work facilitates a short-term production plan for various manufactured products, considering the production method, required quantities of materials, and labor force.

The complexity of the detailed scheduling task, also known as **shop floor control**, depends upon the type of production method employed by a company. The scheduling process starts by breaking the total assignment into a number of operations and selecting the most economical ways to accomplish these operations. In a manufacturing company, for example, this means identi-

Exhibit 4–39

Master Production Schedule

Master Production Schedule					
Product	**Production department—week no. 12**				**Total Quantity**
	1	2	3	4	
A	1,000	3,000	2,000	3,000	9,000
B	3,000	2,000	1,000	2,000	8,000
C	2,000	4,000	2,000	1,000	9,000
D	3,000	1,000	3,000	1,000	8,000
Std. hour loaded	2,500	2,200	2,500	2,300	— —
Std. hour available	2,200	2,200	2,200	2,200	— —

fying every component specified in the parts list or bill of materials; checking availability of appropriate drawings, tools, materials, labor, and operational capacity; and scheduling the requirements. Furthermore, it is necessary to place purchase orders for all buy-outs and finalize the selection of suitable subcontractors.

The scheduling of work in a job shop or a batch production environment entails summarizing individual manufacturing requirements into a **job card.** An individual job number must be allocated to every assignment handled in the job shop and a job card prepared accordingly. Products manufactured in a batch production environment, on the other hand, can be identified by an appropriate batch number. Job cards for batch production are usually issued

Exhibit 4–40

Illustration of a Job Card

Job Card							
Work center: Machine shop					Job No.: 118		
Job description: Part 423–800, Op. 1 and 2					Quantity: 1,000		
Drawing No.: 12487				Completion date required: 10.10.89			
Material: Mild steel					Size or weight: 100lb.		
Op. No.	**Machine No.**	**Tool No.**	**Description of operation**	**Norm**	**Time (hours)**		
				Op./hr.	Est.	Act..	Var.
1	8	121	Cut the blank	50	20	19	+1
2	12	180	Drill and tap	40	25	26	−1
3							
4							
5							
6							
7							
Prepared: A. Stevens		Authorized: B. Press			Date: 10.1.89		

for every component or operation depending upon the specific manufacturing requirements. A typical job card is illustrated in Exhibit 4–40.

The scheduling of work in a flow production environment requires a particularly high degree of accuracy since all operations are built into the manufacturing process. It is very important, therefore, to ensure that appropriate drawings, tools, and materials become available in accordance with master production schedule requirements.

The majority of small and medium-sized manufacturing companies usually operate as job shops or utilize a batch production method. The sequence of production scheduling and control for both methods is illustrated in Exhibit 4–41.

Exhibit 4–41

Production Scheduling and Control Sequence

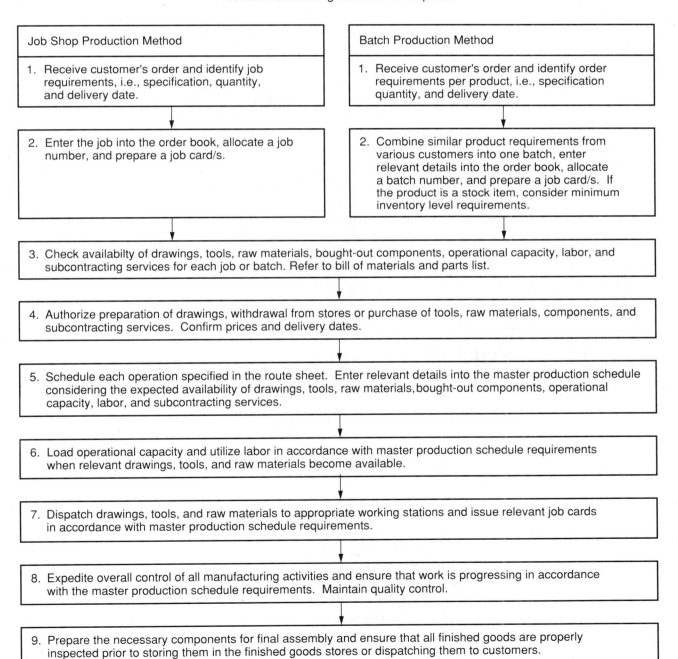

Job Shop Production Method	Batch Production Method
1. Receive customer's order and identify job requirements, i.e., specification, quantity, and delivery date.	1. Receive customer's order and identify order requirements per product, i.e., specification quantity, and delivery date.
2. Enter the job into the order book, allocate a job number, and prepare a job card/s.	2. Combine similar product requirements from various customers into one batch, enter relevant details into the order book, allocate a batch number, and prepare a job card/s. If the product is a stock item, consider minimum inventory level requirements.

3. Check availabilty of drawings, tools, raw materials, bought-out components, operational capacity, labor, and subcontracting services for each job or batch. Refer to bill of materials and parts list.

4. Authorize preparation of drawings, withdrawal from stores or purchase of tools, raw materials, components, and subcontracting services. Confirm prices and delivery dates.

5. Schedule each operation specified in the route sheet. Enter relevant details into the master production schedule considering the expected availability of drawings, tools, raw materials, bought-out components, operational capacity, labor, and subcontracting services.

6. Load operational capacity and utilize labor in accordance with master production schedule requirements when relevant drawings, tools, and raw materials become available.

7. Dispatch drawings, tools, and raw materials to appropriate working stations and issue relevant job cards in accordance with master production schedule requirements.

8. Expedite overall control of all manufacturing activities and ensure that work is progressing in accordance with the master production schedule requirements. Maintain quality control.

9. Prepare the necessary components for final assembly and ensure that all finished goods are properly inspected prior to storing them in the finished goods stores or dispatching them to customers.

Exhibit 4–42

Gantt Chart Application

Weekly Production Schedule						
Work Center	Production Department — Week No. 12					
	Monday	Tuesday	Wednesday	Thursday	Friday	Saturday
1	Job A	Job A	Job A	Job B	Job B	Job C
2	Job D	Job D	Job E	Job F	Job F	Job F
3	Job G	Job G	Job G	Job G	Job H	Job H

Among the most important tools for production scheduling is graphical display of work allocation in various work centers. Such a display, known as the **Gantt Chart**, provides a very effective indication of workload status within the production department. A typical example of Gantt Chart is illustrated in Exhibit 4–42.

Each job or batch number must be entered into the Gantt Chart prior to the commencement of operational activities. This chart can subsequently be used to show the duration and sequence of specific jobs that are scheduled for each individual work center.

Finally, when the production master schedule is completed, the loading of work may begin. The prime purpose of this procedure is to allocate the existing workload to various machines and to ensure maximum utilization of available operational capacity and manpower resources. Production loading is normally carried out on a daily or weekly basis depending upon the specific production requirements. The loading of each machine depends upon the availability of drawings, tools, operators, and materials for every job. If materials are available early, they must be held in an appropriate material control area until the job is released to the work center. Additional details pertaining to material requirements planning (MRP) are discussed next.

4.14 Material Requirements Planning

Material requirements planning (MRP) is a system which aims to calculate the quantity and determine the timing of materials, parts, and components required to complete a finished product. The MRP is considered one of the most important production and inventory management methods used by many manufacturing organizations. The three principal functions of the MRP system have been summarized by Joseph Orlicky:

1. **Inventory control**
   - Order the right part.
   - Order the right quantity.
   - Order at the right time.
2. **Priority planning**
   - Order with the right due date.
   - Keep the due date valid.
3. **Capacity requirements planning**
   - Plan for a complete load.
   - Plan an accurate (valid) load.
   - Plan for an adequate time span to view future loads.[6]

Some small and medium-sized manufacturing companies use a computerized version of an MRP system or plan to install one in the near future. This type of system generally handles a large variety of products, parts, components, and raw materials. In addition, a computerized MRP system may offer the following advantages:

- Reduction of the average level of inventory
- Improved availability of raw materials, components and parts
- Improved utilization of operational capacity and manpower resources
- Reduction in idle time in the facility
- Reduction in machine setup and tear-down costs
- Improved flexibility of master production schedule
- Improved production flow
- Reduction in overall manufacturing costs
- More reliable delivery dates to customers

The MRP system can also inform the production manager in advance if required delivery dates are achievable. Furthermore, it changes due dates for orders and facilitates capacity requirements planning. Many companies that have used the MRP system have reported a substantial reduction in inventory investment costs—up to 40%—and an overall improvement in productivity.

In order to use the MRP system it is necessary to collate information from three sources:

- **The master production schedule (MPS).** This schedule is prepared on the basis of actual customers' orders and predicted demand. The MPS indicates the quantity and date of each production order.
- **The bill of materials file (BOM).** This file contains details of all raw materials, parts, components, subassemblies, and assemblies required to complete a product.
- **The inventory status file.** This file contains detailed information about the quantity of each item available on hand, on order, and committed for use in the manufacturing process.

The MRP system is designed to run on a regular basis, say once a week, and must be supported by accurate and updated information drawn from all the aforementioned sources. This system is schematically presented in Exhibit 4–43.

The master production schedule, or **master schedule,** is the prime input element for the MRP system. This schedule is generally developed on a regular basis and contains all confirmed customer orders and additional inventory requirements. The customer orders include the quantities and delivery dates of required products while additional inventories are determined in accordance with forecast for product demands. The types and quantities of products may vary from one week to another depending upon immediate customer needs and short-term forecast demands. Master production schedules, therefore, should be examined for availability of materials, operational capacity, and labor, and then revised and developed again. Consider, for example, a master production schedule for ABC Manufacturing Company which makes filing cabinets and office furniture. A portion of such a schedule is presented in Exhibit 4–44.

The bill of materials file contains detailed information about the quantity of materials and components which must be pre-purchased or manufactured in order to complete a specified number of finished products. This file includes

Exhibit 4–43

Material Requirements Planning System

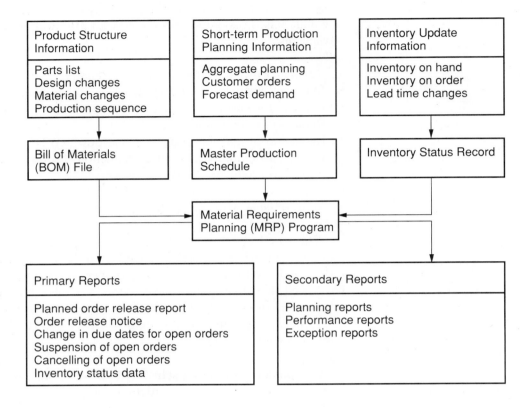

a detailed breakdown, or "explosion" of all components for every product manufactured by the company and provides the second input for the MRP system. Each bill of materials contains a comprehensive parts list which summarizes the exact quantities of all components, subassemblies, and assemblies required to complete a particular product. In addition, such a bill provides information pertaining to the manufacturing methods of each component as summarized in the appropriate route sheet. All product design modifications and changes in material and production sequence are also included in this file. Since the final assembly might consist of several subassemblies, the end-product may be presented as a multi-level component structure, or a **product structure tree**. The bill of

Exhibit 4–44

Portion of the Master Production Schedule for ABC Manufacturing Company

Item	Week number										
	1	2	3	4	5	6	7	8	9	10	11
001 3-drawer file						100			100		100
005 4-drawer file			60			60	120		60		
007 desk					150			150		90	

SOURCE: This example and the following illustrations are adapted from James B. Dilworth, *Production and Operations Management,* 2nd ed. (New York: Random House, 1983), pp.242—251. Reprinted with permission.

materials and product structure tree for the filing cabinet produced by ABC Manufacturing Company are presented in Exhibit 4–45.

The product structure tree for the filing cabinet contains four levels of products, components, and materials. Each "lower" level represents the "component" level for the one above it. Level 3, for example, contains materials which are needed for manufacturing components presented in Level 2. Components in

Exhibit 4–45

Bill of Materials and Product Structure Tree

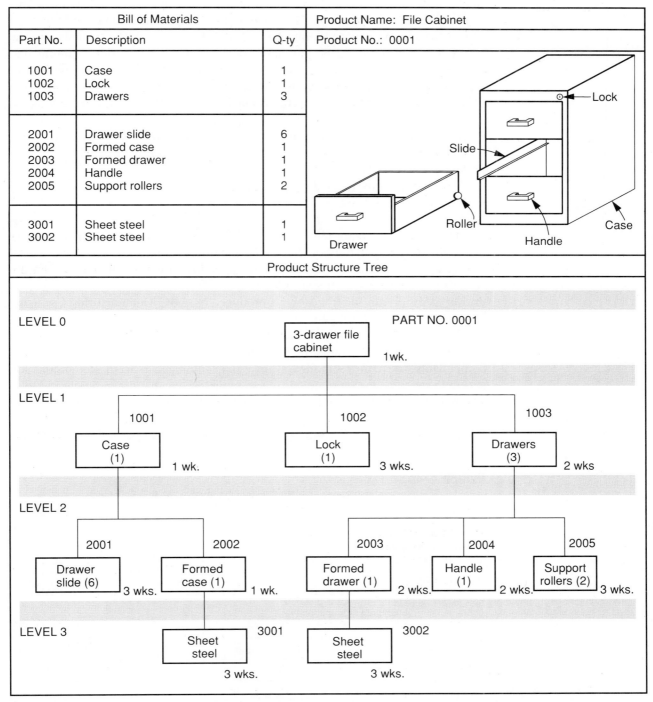

Level 2, in turn, are required for completing "parent" subassemblies in Level 1. Finally "parent" subassemblies and components in Level 1 are used in the assembly of the finished product in Level 0.

Each item specified in the product structure tree is identified by its part number, quantity per one assembly, and lead time. **Lead time** is the estimated number of weeks which has to be allowed for obtaining specific materials and parts, manufacturing and subassembling components, and assembling the final product.

The third major input for the MRP system is provided by the inventory status file. This file contains a detailed and updated record regarding the status of every inventory item, i.e., raw materials, components, subassemblies, and assemblies. Some items required for a particular job could be available in the stores, but others should be purchased to meet specific material requirements. Inventory items are usually grouped into categories and coded by an individual identification number for easy reference. The details regarding each item are summarized in an **inventory status record** and include such information as:

- Item number or code, description, name, and lead time
- Gross requirements of inventory
- Scheduled receipt of inventory (open orders)
- Expected quantity of inventory on hand
- Planned order releases

The inventory status record may contain additional information pertaining to subsidiary data such as order details, pending action, or order changes. All information pertaining to inventory status is updated on a regular basis to ensure effective material requirements planning. A typical inventory record of the drawer assembly for the file cabinets produced by ABC Manufacturing Company is presented in Exhibit 4–46.

The MRP system uses the master production schedule, the bill of materials file, and the inventory status file to determine the net requirements for materials, components, and subassemblies at any given moment. The master production schedule specifies the type, quantity, and completion date of a particular product. The bill of materials file provides information about the type, quantity, and lead time of all materials and components required for any finished product. Finally, the inventory status file summarizes the quantities on hand and scheduled receipts

Exhibit 4–46

Inventory Record for the Drawer Assembly for File Cabinets

Item: 1003; LT: 2 weeks 3-drawer assembly file cabinet	Week										
	1	2	3	4	5	6	7	8	9	10	11
Gross requirements						300			300		300
Scheduled receipts		400									
On hand 20	20	420	420	420	420	120	120	120	−180	−180	−480
Net requirements									180		300
Planned order releases							180		300		

SOURCE: James B. Dilworth. Reprinted with permission.

per component (i.e., previously released orders). Once all the aforementioned information is processed by the MRP program, the following two options become available:

1. The inventory on hand plus previously released orders is sufficient to meet scheduled manufacturing requirements. Hence, there is no need to release additional purchase or production orders.
2. The inventory on hand plus previously released orders is not sufficient to meet scheduled manufacturing requirements. In this instance, additional purchase or manufacturing orders should be released in accordance with the net requirements and lead time for a particular component.

Consider, for example, the inventory status record for the drawer assembly presented in Exhibit 4–46. According to this example, the net requirement for the item in Period 9 can be determined as follows:

(+)Gross requirements	+300
(−)Scheduled receipts	− 0
(−)On hand	−120
(=)Net requirements	+180

Since the lead time for the drawer assembly is two weeks, the net requirement must be scheduled two weeks ahead. Thus, the planned order release of 180 is entered in Period 7 to meet the above manufacturing requirements.

All information must be fed into the MRP system continuously to ensure effective production performance. The MRP system, in turn, will process such information and determine net requirements and order release dates for every material and component required for current manufacturing needs. The action of the MRP system cuts across all levels of the product structure tree and converts gross requirements of the master production schedule into net requirements for individual components. The conversion of such requirements is illustrated in Exhibit 4–47.

Once all net requirements of individual components are identified, a **time-scaled assembly chart** needs to be prepared. The prime purpose of this chart is to illustrate when orders for various materials and components should be released to ensure timely assembly of the finished product. A typical time-scaled assembly chart for the three-drawer file cabinet is presented in Exhibit 4–48.

As a result of extensive computations, the MRP system produces a number of important documents. These documents are generally classified as **primary reports** and **secondary reports.** The primary reports, for example, include the following:

1. *Planned orders* to be released at a future time
2. *Order release notices* to execute the planned orders
3. *Changes in due dates* of open orders due to rescheduling
4. *Cancellations or suspensions* of open orders due to cancellation or suspension of orders on the master production schedule
5. *Inventory status data*

Additional reports, which are optional under the MRP system, fall into the following main categories:

1. *Planning reports* to be used, for example, in forecasting inventory and speci-fying requirements over some future time horizon

Exhibit 4–47

Conversion of Master Production Schedule Requirements into the Net Requirements of Individual Components

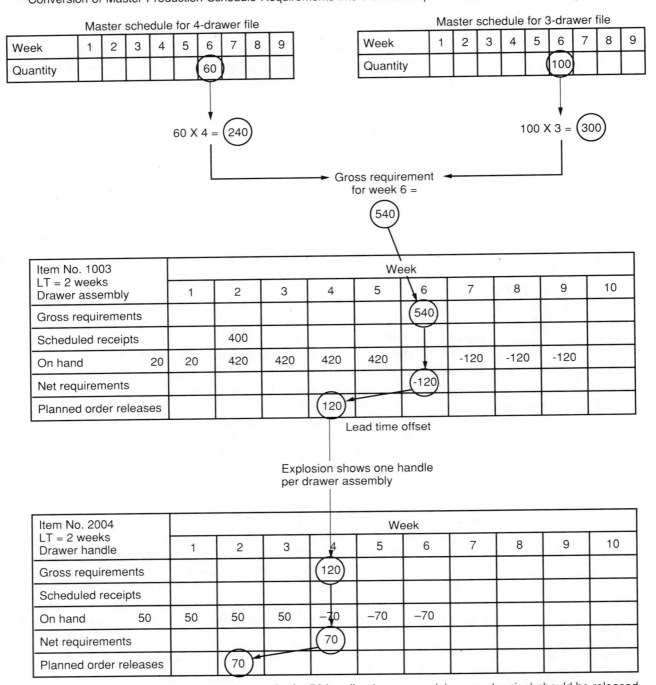

Master schedule for 4-drawer file

Week	1	2	3	4	5	6	7	8	9
Quantity						60			

Master schedule for 3-drawer file

Week	1	2	3	4	5	6	7	8	9
Quantity						100			

60 X 4 = 240

100 X 3 = 300

Gross requirement
for week 6 =

540

Item No. 1003 LT = 2 weeks Drawer assembly	Week									
	1	2	3	4	5	6	7	8	9	10
Gross requirements						540				
Scheduled receipts		400								
On hand 20	20	420	420	420	420		-120	-120	-120	
Net requirements						-120				
Planned order releases				120						

Lead time offset

Explosion shows one handle
per drawer assembly

Item No. 2004 LT = 2 weeks Drawer handle	Week									
	1	2	3	4	5	6	7	8	9	10
Gross requirements				120						
Scheduled receipts										
On hand 50	50	50	50	-70	-70	-70				
Net requirements				70						
Planned order releases		70								

If master schedule remains unchanged, an order for 70 handles (or some minimum order size) should be released next week.

SOURCE: James B. Dilworth. Reprinted with permission.

2. *Performance reports* for purposes of pointing out inactive items and determining the agreement between actual and programmed item lead times and between actual and programmed quantity usages and costs

3. *Exceptions reports* that point out serious discrepancies, such as errors, out-of-range situations, late or overdue orders, excessive scrap, or nonexistent parts.[7]

Exhibit 4–48

Time-scaled Assembly Chart

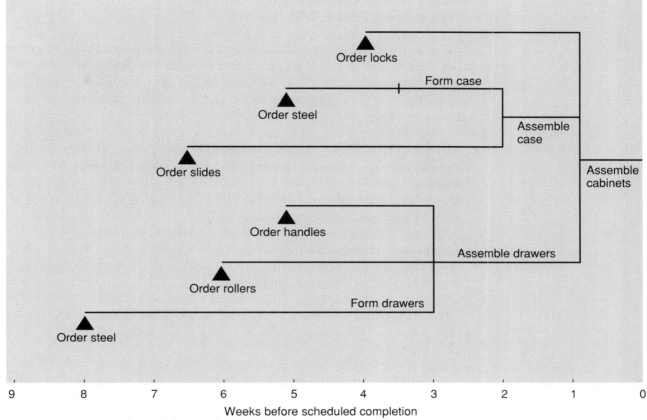

SOURCE: James B. Dilworth. Reprinted with permission.

The MRP system is widely used in various manufacturing industries and has often proved successful. This system has been modified recently to incorporate additional functional parameters. Such a system is known as *manufacturing resource planning (MRP II)*. The main purpose of the MRP II is to plan and monitor various resources of a manufacturing company including production, purchasing, accounting, and marketing. This system has since been modified further to incorporate other functional activities on a company wide basis. It is known as the *Communications Oriented Production Information and Control System (COPICS)*. This system is designed to facilitate efficient planning and control within a manufacturing company by providing extensive database through a network of computer terminals.

4.15 Production Control

Production control is one of the most critical functions of the production manager. The main purposes of production control are to authorize operational activities, to ensure effective implementation of production planning efforts, and to control production costs within the facility. The effectiveness of production control depends upon several factors:

- Detailed preliminary planning of each job
- Thorough preparation of drawings, tools, and materials for each job

- Timely availability of operational capacity and human resources
- Built-in flexibility in the master schedule requirements
- Continuous coordination of shop-floor activities
- Clear communication in the production department
- High quality of operational performance

The two basic functions of production control are **dispatching** and **expediting** work in accordance with preplanned manufacturing activities. The main purpose of work dispatching is to authorize and initiate coordinated manufacturing activities by means of releasing orders and instructions. It should also ensure that:

- Materials are available and are transferred to the relevant working stations.
- Production aids, such as tools or jigs, are available and issued to relevant working stations.
- Drawings, specifications, bills of materials, and parts lists are prepared and issued to relevant working stations.
- Job cards or reports are prepared for all manufacturing operations.
- Quality control inspection reports are prepared.
- All production aids and drawings are returned to their correct locations upon completion of the manufacturing process.

The main purpose of work expediting, or **progress chasing**, is to provide overall control of all manufacturing activities once production has been set in motion and to ensure that:

- Any details which have been overlooked or which do not proceed according to plan are rectified.
- Job cards or reports are completed with all the necessary data related to performance and cost control.
- The progress of work between various stations and sections is in accordance with the master production schedule.
- Quality control is maintained on a continuous level.

The production control system depends upon the type of manufacturing method employed by the company. This system is classified as **job control** for a job shop, **batch control** for batch production, and **flow control** for a flow production environment.

The major characteristics of the job shop, or intermittent manufacturing operation, include diversity of products and operations, small volumes, and short production runs. Manufacturing orders arrive from different sources in a relatively unpredictable manner and often at short notice. Many of these orders require the manufacturing of new products and the preparation of additional drawings and tools. Furthermore, the job shop operation is accompanied by a diversity of raw materials and complicated inventory control requirements. Some of the features of job control are:

- Each order must be planned and controlled on an individual basis.
- A new parts list and route sheet must be prepared for every non-repetitive order.
- Special raw materials must be purchased for every new order.
- Operational capacity and labor resources can be planned only on a short-notice basis.

Control of manufacturing activities in a batch production environment, or batch control, is quite similar to the job control procedure. This has been illustrated previously in Exhibit 4–41. Manufacturing orders arrive from various customers and are grouped into batches of similar products. Since many manufacturing orders are received on a repetitive basis, various components and products are manufactured and kept in stock. Thus, the economical level of work-in-process and finished goods inventory should be established and manufacturing activities planned and controlled accordingly. Batch production usually entails manufacture of tens, hundreds, and thousands of the same item for delivery to customers over an extended period of time. Hence, it becomes easier to schedule and control manufacturing operations during a longer production cycle. The number of drawings and tools and the diversity of raw materials are also reduced in the batch production environment. Some of the features of batch control are:

- Most orders must be incorporated into batches of similar products.
- Each batch must be planned and controlled on an individual basis.
- A new parts list and route sheet must be prepared for every non-repetitive batch.
- Raw materials must be purchased in accordance with economic inventory level requirements.
- Operational capacity and human resources can be planned one or more weeks in advance.

Manufacturing control in a flow production environment is very different in comparison with job shop or batch production. The prime characteristic of flow control is the continuity of the manufacturing process. This process is best described by a conveyor line, where a small range of standard products is manufactured in large quantities. High volume production ensures additional economies in the manufacturing process provided production facilities are adapted to the manufactured item.

Similar items are produced on a repetitive basis for stock, mainly, not for specific customer orders. All work stations are arranged to facilitate uniform and continuous production flow. Optimally, the production line should be organized to allow the most effective use of the operational capacity and manpower resources on a regular basis. When a production line is being used, the detailed routing of operations is incorporated in the manufacturing process. The maximum production output available from each work station depends upon its capacity. Each station must be manned by an appropriate number of employees to facilitate smooth production flow. Some of the features of flow control are:

- All materials flow through work stations at a constant rate.
- The constant flow of materials demands that operational capacity and human resources can handle the given production volume.
- Production scheduling and control of individual operations must be synchronized with the overall production planning requirements.
- The repetitive nature of manufacturing operations simplifies the requirements for daily instructions and production reporting procedure.
- The availability of all materials, operational capacity, and human resources must be coordinated well in advance to ensure a smooth production flow.

Effective production control necessitates that all stages of any manufacturing operation are properly balanced well in advance. It is advisable, therefore, to balance the workload at each station despite some time variation or idle time which may occur. Line balancing entails selecting the most suitable combination of operations to be carried out at each work station in accordance with overall production requirements. It involves minimizing the number of operations, work stations, operational capacity, materials, and human resources required to attain a predetermined production level.

Exhibit 4–49
Summary of Production Control and Related Activities that Must Be Coordinated in a Manufacturing Process

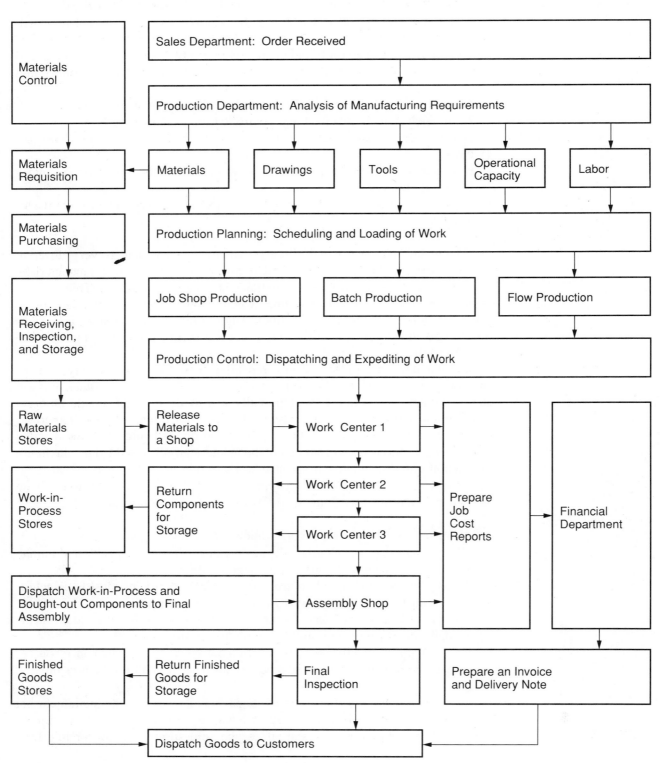

Production control requires continuous coordination of activities in various departments within an organization. This is illustrated in Exhibit 4–49.

Another essential function of production management is correlation of efforts with the financial department to facilitate thorough control of manufacturing costs and to ensure effective recovery of the company's expenditure. This task is usually carried out by a suitable **production cost control system**. The main objective of such a system is to provide correct allocation of material, equipment, labor, and subcontracting service costs to various manufacturing assignments and to secure the desired level of company profitability.

The control of production costs is frequently handled by a cost control clerk and is based on two costing methods, **job order costing** and **process costing**. Both methods were discussed earlier as part of cost estimating procedures within the production department. Thus, in order to determine the actual cost of a particular job, be it a product or a service, it is necessary to record all individual costs in the cost sheet presented in Exhibit 4–35.

Major parameters of the production cost control include the following:

- Raw materials and bought-out components used on a particular assignment—to calculate total material cost contribution
- Production time spent on a particular assignment—this time is converted into an applicable hourly rate in order to calculate total labor and operational capacity cost contribution
- Subcontracting services utilized on a particular assignment—to calculate total subcontracting services cost contribution

Recording material costs is usually done using material requisitions prepared in advance for various jobs. The recording of production time, on the other hand, is carried out by means of daily or weekly time sheets summarizing the total number of hours spent on a particular job, or alternatively, by means of job cards prepared separately for various assignments. The recording of subcontracting service costs is normally accomplished in a manner similar to the recording of material costs. Subsequently, all costs incurred during a particular manufacturing process are compared with the corresponding estimates, and all variances are identified and investigated.

4.16 Planning and Control of Services and Projects

Planning and control of nonmanufacturing activities may represent a complex task depending upon the nature of such activities. **Planning and control of services,** for example, entails steps similar to those undertaken in the manufacturing environment. Such steps have been discussed earlier in the context of job shop production, batch production, and flow production.

All services have been previously classified as **custom (specialized) services**, or **standard services**. Some examples of custom services have been illustrated in Exhibit 4–3. These services are provided either by tradespeople (plumbers, electricians, or hairdressers) or professional people (doctors, accountants, or lawyers). Each of theses services is, in essence, provided to an individual customer on a special order basis similar to the job shop production method. The basic difference, however, is that the service process does not require that inventory be kept except for consumable items like spare parts kept by plumbers or medicine kept by doctors. The basic comparison between the custom service and a job shop is illustrated in Exhibit 4–50.

Exhibit 4–50

Comparison between Custom Service and Job Shop Production Method

Description	Custom Service (Job Shop Production)
Process	Service (manufacturing) to customers orders, only
Type of Order	Mostly unique and nonrepetitive
Service (Product) Range	No standard range of services (products)
Service (Product) Unit Cost	High
Volume of Operations	Very low, often one-off item
Method of Operations	Very diversified, sometimes repetitive
Equipment Application	Very general application to various operations
Operational Capacity Planning	Can be scheduled at short notice only
Personnel Skill Requirements	Very high level for general and specialized application

Standard service, on the other hand, can be compared with a flow production environment. This service has also been illustrated in Exhibit 4–3. Some typical examples of standard service are child day-care, education, or insurance. Each of these services is provided on a "flow production" basis, not to a particular customer order. Standard service entails rendering a regular range of services to customers at a predetermined fee. This service may be offered to a large number of customers simultaneously. The standard service, like the custom one, does not require that inventory be kept except for consumable items such as food stuffs kept by a fast food outlet or chemicals kept by an electroplating company. The basic comparison between the standard service and flow production is illustrated in Exhibit 4–51.

Operational planning and control represent an integral part of an efficient service process. Operational planning necessitates a continuous formulation of methods and procedures required for the completion of services in the most suitable manner. The prime purpose of effective planning is to ensure the most economical utilization of human skills, energy, and equipment available in the organization. There are three basic types of operational planning:

1. Planning that relates to volume of service and synchronization of service operations with sales requirements

Exhibit 4–51

Comparison between Standard Service and Flow Production Method

Description	Standard Service (Flow Production)
Process	Service (manufacturing) to customers on a continuous basis
Type of Order	All standard and repetitive
Service (Product) Range	Limited range of standard services (products)
Service (Product) Unit Cost	Low
Volume of Operations	High
Method of Operations	Standard
Equipment Application	Very specialized application to a narrow range of operations
Operational Capacity Planning	Must be planned and scheduled well in advance
Personnel Skill Requirements	Average level for a highly standardized application

2. Planning that relates to the particular service method
3. Planning that relates to detailed timing necessary for attaining the desired results

The first type of operational planning depends upon seasonal fluctuations in service demands, such as preparation of tax returns or renewal of an insurance policy. This method specifies the required level of service efforts in accordance with such demands. The second type of operational planning depends upon the nature of the service method, namely custom service or standard service. Finally, the third type of operational planning conforms to particular timing such as promised completion dates or specific time limitations imposed on the service process.

The fundamental principles of operational planning are similar for most service companies:

- The operational plan should include all services or groups of services handled by the organization.
- The operational plan should be expressed in clear terms meaningful to company employees.

Operational planning of custom services is generally more complex than planning of standard services since there is a much broader range of services offered to customers. Irrespective of service method, however, it is necessary to ascertain that the service activity is constantly coordinated with a company's revenue and expenditure budgets for a particular fiscal period.

Operational planning sequence of service operations is illustrated in Exhibit 4–52. The planning process normally starts with an annual service forecast which

Exhibit 4–52

Operations Planning Sequence in a Service Organization

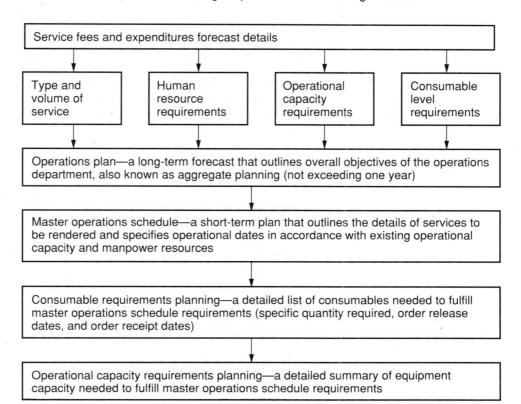

considers overall operational requirements. This type of planning has been discussed earlier in the context of manufacturing activities and is termed **aggregate planning**. The basic variables of aggregate planning for service operations are:

- Operational output requirements
- Operational human resource requirements
- Consumable level requirements (optional)

If the demand for services remains steady during the fiscal period, operational planning and control become relatively simple. Most service companies, however, experience a non-uniform demand for services. This necessitates that managers develop suitable strategies for dealing with such conditions. Some of these strategies have been illustrated earlier in Exhibit 4–38. Service operations may benefit from the aforementioned strategies considering that inventory requirements are excluded. Additional strategies frequently utilized by the service companies are summarized in Exhibit 4–53.

Planning and control of projects represent a different type of problem in comparison with manufacturing and service activities. A **project** is a long-term task to develop and produce a special, often one-off, product. Several examples of special projects have been illustrated in Exhibit 4–3. These projects may be undertaken by one person—a writer, a scientist, or a group of people such as publishers, or research laboratory group. Other projects may involve a long-term contract to construct a bridge or to build a house. These projects are carried out by **contractors** and entail utilization of special materials, equipment, and human resource capacity. Hence, projects are in essence a "long-term job shop" where some tasks may last for several months or years.

Among the methods most frequently used in planning and controlling long-term projects are *Program Evaluation and Review Technique (PERT)* and *Critical Path Method (CPM)*. The CPM has been discussed earlier in the context of product design and illustrated in Exhibit 4–10. Both methods are based on the use of a graphical representation of tasks to be performed, or **network scheduling.** Some of the advantages of network scheduling have been outlined by James Dilworth:

1. They lead to planning a project to the selected level of detail so that all parts of the project and their intended order of accomplishment are known.
2. They provide a fairly accurate estimate of the length of time it will take to complete the project and the activities that must be kept on time to meet the schedule.
3. They provide a graphic picture and standardized vocabulary to aid in understanding work assignments and communicating among people involved in the project.
4. They provide a means of tracking progress on a project (that is, show where work is with respect to the plan).
5. They identify and focus attention on potentially troublesome activities to facilitate management by exception.
6. They provide a means of estimating the time and cost impact of changes to the project plan at any stage.

The network scheduling of special projects and contracts entails detailed planning of all relevant activities. This process involves three basic steps and, according to Dilworth, can be summarized as follows:

1. *Plan the project.*
   1.1 Analyze the project by determining all of the individual activities (sometimes called tasks, jobs, or operations) that must be performed to complete it.

Exhibit 4–53

Operational Planning and Control Strategies for Meeting Nonuniform Demands

Methods	Costs	Remarks
Strategy: Absorb demand fluctuation by shifting manpower capacity		
Moving employees from one position to another where the demand is higher	No additional cost is involved except perhaps the cost of additional training of employees	The motivation level of some employees may decrease as a result of a frequent shifting to different positions
Strategy: Use part-time employees		
Hire part-time employees when the demand increases	Additional cost of searching for and compensating part-time employees	Part-time employees may not perform effectively enough if they do not get sufficient training
Strategy: Use existing employees for overtime		
Work overtime to accommodate peak demands	Additional cost of overtime	Additional compensation may enhance motivation of employees
Strategy: Reschedule the vacation period of employees		
Rescheduling the vacation period to accommodate peak demands	No additional cost except perhaps an "appreciation" bonus	Occasionally employees may get dissatisfied for not having vacations when they want them
Strategy: Use variable work shifts		
Assign employees to various work shifts to meet specific operational requirements	No additional costs except perhaps increased pay rate for night shifts	Sometimes employees may get discouraged through not working during steady hours
Strategy: Stabilize demand pattern for services		
Offer special price reductions or discounts during a period of low demand	Cost of discounts only	Stabilizing demand pattern may create a more uniform operational procedure
Strategy: Use an appointment procedure		
Develop and maintain an appointment schedule for specialized services	No additional cost	Stabilizing the equipment and human resource capacity utilization
Strategy: Use a priority procedure		
Develop and maintain a priority procedure to accommodate the operational demands	No additional cost	Stabilizing the equipment and human resource capacity utilization
Strategy: Use a delayed delivery procedure		
Develop and maintain a delayed delivery schedule to meet operational requirements	No additional cost	Stabilizing the equipment and human resource capacity utilization
Strategy: Maintain a fixed operational schedule		
Develop and maintain a fixed operational schedule for standard services	Cost per unit service is reduced to a minimum	This is one of the most popular methods of rendering a standard service

1.2 Show the planned sequence of these activities on a network (a graph using arrows and circles to represent the relationships among projects activities).

2. *Schedule the project.*
   2.1 Estimate how long it will take to perform each activity.
   2.2 Perform computations to locate the critical path (the longest time chain of sequential activities that determines the duration of the project). This step also provides other information that is useful in scheduling.
   2.3 Use this information to develop a more economical and efficient schedule if one is indicated.

3. *Monitor the project.*
   3.1 Use the plan and schedule to control and monitor progress.
   3.2 Revise and update the schedule throughout execution of the project so that the schedule represents the current plans and current status of progress.[9]

Effective use of both methods has recently been popularized by several computer programs. These programs are particularly useful for large projects where a substantial amount of information must be scheduled, controlled, and revised during a long period of time.

4.17 Quality Control

The effectiveness of the manufacturing organization is measured not only by the ability of production management to plan and control manufacturing activities, but also by its ability to supply high-quality products and services to customers. An important function of the production manager, therefore, is to develop and maintain effective quality control within the organization. The ultimate purpose of an effective quality control procedure is to establish a suitable **quality assurance program**, which has been outlined by James Dilworth as follows:

1. *Reliability engineering*, to ensure that the design will have an adequate expected useful life.
2. *Value engineering*, to ensure that the product will perform the necessary function at the minimum cost.
3. *Evaluation of usability*, to see that the product will be convenient and safe in the hands of the user.
4. *Process control*, to ensure that the materials, processes, and other inputs to the transformation process are adequate for the intended product.
5. *Product screening and appraisal*, to see that the output that is sold to customers is of sufficient quality.
6. *Service assurance*, to see that the customer is adequately trained to use and maintain the product and that service parts and manuals are made available.
7. Quality feedback to provide *corrective action* when field use indicates inadequate quality.[10]

The aforementioned elements of the quality assurance program aim to ensure three following aspects:

- Quality of design
- Quality of conformance
- Quality of performance

Quality of design for products and services must meet minimal standards for usage in the marketplace. An essential element of quality is built into products and services at the design stage. It is important that designers consider the relationship between cost and quality and the precision required by the customers. It is also evident that the quality of products and services is closely interwoven with the degree of manufacturing costs and the level of the selling price. Futhermore, quality of design is of paramount importance because of the necessity of carrying product or service liability by various companies. Product and service safety requirements are regulated by several federal laws, one of these being the Consumer Product Safety Act of 1972. The prime objective of these laws is to define and maintain appropriate standards for products and services in the marketplace.

Quality of conformance for products and services to the original standards of their design is determined by inspection procedures within the production department. These procedures require the use of expensive equipment and skilled personnel during various stages of the manufacturing or operational processes. Such procedures include *partial sampling* of products, for example, or application of *statistical quality control* methods in assessing the standard of selected products. A partial sampling of products is frequently used when the possibility of products being defective is relatively low. In other instances, certain allowances for defective goods may be imposed by a customer, which calls for statistical quality control. Another type of product inspection is an *acceptance sampling* procedure. This procedure is usually applied to a specific batch of products, a lot, and it aims to accept or reject such a lot by inspecting a limited number of product samples. Finally, *process control* procedure is used to examine the standard of operations and processes employed by a manufacturing or service organization.

Quality of performance suggests that the standards of products and services must comply with the original requirements specified by customers. Quality of performance does not remain static—it usually varies throughout the product's or service's life cycle. This depends upon the degree of reliability built into the product or service at the design stage. **Reliability** is the ability of a product or service to perform a specified function without failure under particular working conditions during a defined period of time. Obviously, no product can function forever, but the degree of reliability is a decisive factor in the overall functional performance. Despite current trends to reduce manufacturing costs, the product's reliability represents an exceedingly important variable. It is necessary, therefore, to ensure an acceptable level of product and service reliability by means of sound design practice, high quality of raw materials, professional workmanship, and proven manufacturing methods.

Quality control entails evaluation and progressive refinement of manufacturing processes, identification of defects, and correction of problems before the quality of products and services deteriorates. In order to ensure high quality products and services, it is essential to maintain a similar standard of equipment, materials, and production personnel in the organization. This can be accomplished by constant **quality control inspections** in three stages:

1. Prior to the beginning of the manufacturing or service process
2. During the manufacturing or service process
3. At the end of the manufacturing or service process

The first stage of quality control entails adherence to all requirements specified by the engineering department. This includes checking that all drawings contain the latest product modifications and that all equipment, tools, and instruments are in good working order. In addition, all raw materials, bought-out components and subcontracting services must be carefully inspected upon their delivery. Inspection of raw materials and bought-out components may be carried out using partial sampling, statistical quality control, or acceptance sampling methods. All unsatisfactory raw materials, goods, and services purchased from other companies should be returned without delay and new suppliers must be found.

The second stage of quality control necessitates a regular examination of production personnel performance and evaluation of standard manufacturing and service methods. Furthermore, it entails inspection of work-in-process and observation of services rendered to customers.

The nature of quality control inspection depends upon the level of accuracy and precision, measured characteristics, and skills of inspection personnel. These inspections are usually conducted on a continuous basis and are accomplished by means of visual examination or utilization of gauging tools and measuring instruments.

The last stage of quality control entails final inspection of products manufactured or examination of services rendered to customers. The inspection methods utilized at this stage are similar to those applied at earlier stages.

An effective production quality control system provides a number of advantages and contributes to improved production performance and results. Some important benefits of this system are:

- Reduction of the cost of damaged goods and scrap
- Reduction of the cost of production rework
- Reduction of the cost of quality control inspection
- Improved standard of products and services
- Improved satisfaction of customers

Another important element to be considered by the production manager relates to the actual cost of the quality assurance program. An excessive investment of material and labor in such a program may cause a dramatic increase in the total manufacturing cost of a specific product. It is necessary, therefore, to establish an optimal level of quality control, thereby reducing the potential cost of product failure and minimizing manufacturing costs. The relationship between the cost of product quality control, the cost of possible failure, and the manufacturing cost is illustrated in Exhibit 4–54.

A useful quality control technique has been introduced by the Japanese and recently became popular in the United States. This technique is known as **quality circles (QC)**, and its prime objective is to improve the quality of products and processes within a company. A quality circle is a group of volunteer employees from the same work center who meet on a scheduled basis to discuss job-related issues and problems. Such a group is usually led by a supervisor or by an experienced production worker and includes no more than 10 to 12 employees. Quality circle meetings are usually held once a week outside regular working hours. Employees are normally compensated for their time by the company. During such meetings, members use various brain-storming techniques, define and discuss particular problems, and evaluate possible solutions. This is followed by summarized proposals which are subsequently presented to the company management. For quality control to succeed, it is essential that management provides full support for such an activity. If successful, quality circles may contribute toward further growth of productivity, improved morale, and better labor–management relations within the organization.

Exhibit 4–54

Relationship of the Cost of Quality Control, the Cost of Failure, and the Total Cost of a Product

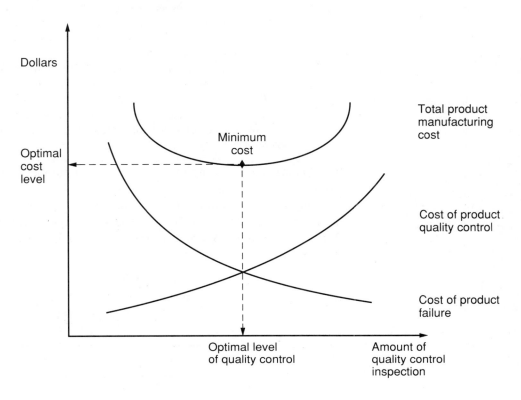

4.18 Materials Purchasing

A broad range of material-related activities is constantly conducted within a company. All such activities fall into the scope of **materials management (MM)**, which is defined as the "coordinated function responsible to plan for, acquire, store, move, and control materials and final products to optimize usage of facilities, personnel, capital funds, and to provide customer service in line with corporate goals"[11]. Materials management is becoming increasingly important in manufacturing as well as nonmanufacturing organizations. The various activities included in this function are materials purchasing and receiving, inventory control, and dispatch of finished products.

Materials purchasing is the responsibility "to buy materials of the right quality, in the right quantity, at the right time, at the right price from the right source with delivery at the right place."[12] Materials purchasing involves a number of activities which have been outlined by James Dilworth:

1. To locate, evaluate and develop sources of the materials, supplies and services that the company needs.
2. To ensure good working relations with these sources in such matters as quality, delivery, payments, and exchanges or returns.
3. To seek out new materials and products and new sources of better products and materials so that they can be evaluated for possible use by the company.
4. To purchase wisely the items that the company needs at the best price consistent with quality requirements and to handle the necessary negotiations to carry out

this activity. The best value does not always represent the lowest initial cost, so products should also be evaluated for their expected lifetime, serviceability, and maintenance cost.

5. To initiate if necessary and to cooperate in cost-reduction programs, value analyses, make-or-buy studies, market analyses, and long-range planning. Purchasing should keep abreast of trends and projections in prices and availability of the inputs that a company must have.

6. To work to maintain an effective communication linkage between departments within the company and between the company and its suppliers or potential suppliers.

7. To keep top management aware of costs involved in the company's procurement and any market changes that could affect the company's profits or growth potential.[13]

Materials purchasing procedure entails a number of steps which are summarized in Exhibit 4–55.

Substantial quantities of raw materials, bought-out components, consumables, tools, and subcontracting services are constantly required by companies. It is essential, therefore, to recognize the need for particular material and services and specify these accordingly.

Exhibit 4–55
Materials Purchasing Procedure

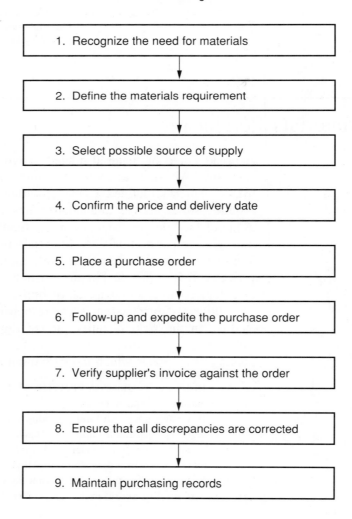

1. Recognize the need for materials

2. Define the materials requirement

3. Select possible source of supply

4. Confirm the price and delivery date

5. Place a purchase order

6. Follow-up and expedite the purchase order

7. Verify supplier's invoice against the order

8. Ensure that all discrepancies are corrected

9. Maintain purchasing records

The purchasing procedure has been described in Exhibit 3–29 in Part 3 (Volume I). This procedure should be initiated by means of a **purchase requisition** illustrated in Exhibit 3–30 that outlines a detailed description, quantity, and delivery date of required materials or services. Each purchase requisition is completed in duplicate by a requisition originator in accordance with specific operational requirements. The first copy of the requisition is sent to the head of the department for approval to ensure effective control over purchasing activities. The second copy is kept by the purchasing requisition originator. Upon its approval the requisition is forwarded to the company's buyer and is used as a detailed purchasing instruction.

In order to ensure effective performance of the purchasing function, it is important to identify and select a range of the most suitable suppliers of materials and services. The evaluation of these suppliers includes the following factors:

- Quality of materials and services
- Timing of deliveries
- Comparative cost of materials and services
- Effectiveness and reliability of the supplier's service

It is the responsibility of the company's buyer to develop and maintain an effective purchase control system and to prepare a separate **materials purchase control card** for every frequently-purchased item. The prime purpose of such a card is to provide an updated record of inventory requirements and a purchasing history of a specific item. A typical materials purchase control card is presented in Exhibit 4–56.

After selecting possible sources of materials or services supply, the buyer must confirm the prices and delivery dates in order to meet operational requirements. When the final selection is made, a **purchase order,** as illus-

Exhibit 4–56

Materials Purchase Control Card

Materials Purchase Control Card											
Product description			**Required inventory level**								
5″ × 2″ stainless steel plate			Maximum: 1,000		Reorder: 400		Minimum: 100				
Name of supplier			**Phone No.**	**Contact name**		**Terms**		**Comments**			
1. ABC supplies, Inc.			123-4567	Alice		2/30					
2. KLM Supplies, Inc.			234-5678	Linda		2/60					
3. XYZ Supplies, Inc.			345-6789	Peter		C.O.D.					
Date	Purchase order No.	Supplier	Quantity ordered	Price ($) Unit	Price ($) Total	Date	Purchase order No.	Supplier	Quantity ordered	Price ($) Unit	Price ($) Total
8.1.89	123	ABC	800	0.5	400						
9.1.89	234	KLM	1,000	0.6	600						

trated in Exhibit 3–31,should be prepared and sent to the most suitable supplier. Purchase orders are usually made out in triplicate: the original is sent to the supplier, the second copy and a copy of the requisition are sent to the store-keeper, and the last copy remains in the file in the buyer's office. Relevant details pertaining to each purchase order must be confirmed by the supplier and clearly marked by the buyer on the remaining copy of the purchase order. Some companies send an additional copy of the purchase order, an **acknowledgment copy,** to the supplier. On this copy the supplier confirms the acceptance of the purchase order, specifies the promised delivery date, and returns the completed copy to the buyer.

The buyer enters each purchase order into the "order follow-up" file until actual delivery takes place. The follow-up of each order is essential to ensure that all promised delivery dates are met by suppliers. When materials or services are finally delivered they should be received in the company's stores. The storekeeper has been already notified about pending delivery by means of copies of the requisition and the purchase order issued to him earlier. These documents are kept by the storekeeper in the "pending delivery" file until the actual arrival of materials or services.

Upon their delivery, all materials or services must be properly inspected and the supplier's delivery note and invoice verified against the original purchase order. A typical delivery note and invoice are illustrated in Exhibit 3–32 and Exhibit 3–33, respectively. It is essential to ensure that there are no discrepancies in the documentation and that the delivery is found in good order. If any materials are rejected by the storekeeper, they must be returned to the supplier and replaced as soon as possible. Both copies of the delivery note must be signed by the storekeeper to confirm complete or partial acceptance of the delivery. A signed delivery note, an invoice (if supplied), copies of the purchase requisition, and the purchase order should be sent to the financial department for further processing and payment of accounts. Sometimes suppliers send the invoice directly to the financial department after the delivery takes place. Finally, a record should be entered into the **material received report** giving the details of the delivery. This record provides entry information for inventory control purposes and has been illustrated in Exhibit 3–34 in Part 3 (Volume 1).

Depending on the company's size and subsequent requirements for materials and services, the purchasing procedure can be carried out manually or through a computer. Manual procedure is frequently used by smaller organizations where the volume of paperwork is relatively small. When the company grows, however, and places more and more orders with various suppliers, the volume of the paperwork may increase dramatically. This often necessitates automation of the purchasing procedure and reduction of the number of forms. At this stage a **traveling requisition** for all frequently purchased items should be introduced. The traveling requisition lists in permanent blocks all descriptive information about the item requested, the approved suppliers, their phone numbers, and past pricing information. A typical traveling requisition is illustrated in Exhibit 4–57.

The traveling requisition is kept in the work center where a particular item is being used, and lists the current stock of the item, the desired quantity, and the date. This form is then sent to the company's buyer and serves as an instruction for a purchase order. Thereafter the traveling requisition is returned to the requisitioning work center and is kept there for future use. This procedure saves time and helps reduce the volume of paperwork in companies that use a manual system.[14] If the company continues to grow, management may decide to computerize the purchasing procedure and incorporate it with other functional activities.

Exhibit 4–57

Traveling Requisition

Traveling Requisition											
Product description			**Required inventory level**								
10″ × 2″ mild steel plate			Maximum: 2,000		Reorder: 600			Minimum: 400			
Name of supplier			**Phone No.**		**Contact name**		**Unit price**		**Terms**		
1. ABC Supplies, Inc.			123-4567		Alice		$0.5		2/30		
2. KLM Supplies, Inc.			234-5678		Linda		$0.6		2/60		
3. XYZ Supplies, Inc.			345-6789		Peter		$0.45		C.O.D.		

Date	Quantity			Purchase order No.	Supplier	Date	Quantity			Purchase order No.	Supplier
	In stock	On order	Required				In stock	On order	Required		
8.1.89	600	1,000	2,000	123	ABC						
9.1.89	400	—	1,000	234	KLM						

4.19 Materials Control, Storage, and Dispatch

Materials control, or **inventory control,** is one of the critical elements of production and operations management. It is particularly important since many companies are compelled to keep a broad range of costly inventories in order to meet their operational requirements. The classification of inventories, as discussed in Part 3 (Volume I), can be summarized as follows:

- Service companies—spare parts and consumables inventory
- Merchandising companies—merchandise inventory
- Manufacturing companies—raw materials, work-in-process, and finished goods inventory

Inventory is important for several reasons. It enables a company to meet fluctuating customer requirements, to stabilize the utilization of operational capacity and human resources, and to minimize the effect of material shortages. However, inventory is often associated with substantial costs:

- *Cost of goods ordered.* This includes the actual investment in goods purchased by the company.
- *Setup cost.* This includes the overall administrative overhead, which relates to the purchasing function within the company.
- *Goods holding cost.* This includes the interest payable on investment that has been used to purchase the goods.
- *Storage cost.* This includes the overall costs of keeping and handling goods in the stores.

• *Stock shortage cost.* This includes all losses which may occur as a result of inventory shortage, like loss of sale, idle machine, and labor time.

It is essential, therefore, to determine when a certain type of inventory should be purchased and in what quantity. Various types of **material ordering systems** deal with these important questions. Some systems are based on a *dependent demand for inventory,* such as MRP, while others are based on an *independent demand for inventory.* The basic difference between the two systems is illustrated in Exhibit 4–58.

Material ordering based on a dependent demand for inventory has been discussed earlier in the context of the MRP system. The second type of material ordering is based on an independent demand for inventory and includes two systems:

• Reorder point system
• Periodic review system

A **reorder point system** entails a predetermination of the minimum inventory level for every item kept in stock. Whenever the inventory on hand reaches the minimum level, or **reorder point,** a purchase order must be placed for a pre-specified quantity of goods. The reorder point is established so that the inventory on hand will be sufficient to meet the production demand during the **lead time,** the time between placement of a purchase order and receipt of materials. The reorder point system is clarified in Exhibit 4–59.

The lead time for different materials varies, depending upon the particular suppliers. It is necessary, therefore, to establish the lead time for every inventory item well in advance in order to determine the minimum inventory level. The prespecified quantity of inventory to be purchased at the reorder point is generally based on the **economic order quantity (EOQ) model**. The basic assumptions underlying the EOQ model are:

• Constant demand for products
• The lead time is known well in advance
• Every order arrives in one complete delivery without partial order deliveries or back-orders
• The cost of placing and receiving an order remains constant irrespective of the order size

Exhibit 4–58

The Two Basic Material Ordering Systems

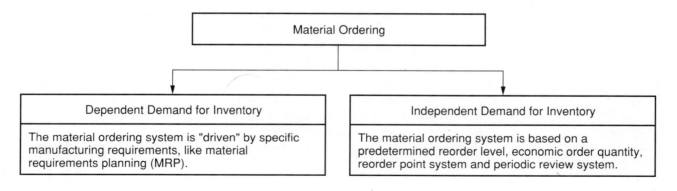

Exhibit 4–59

Reorder Point System

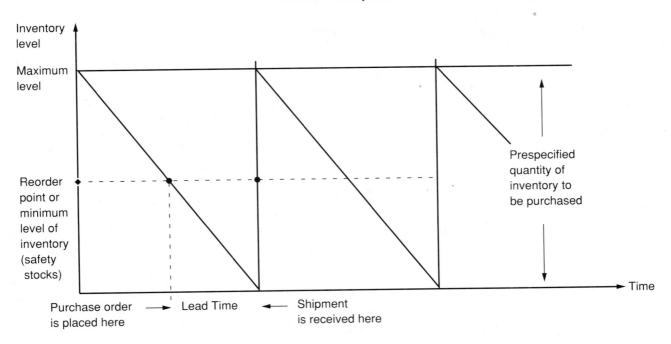

- The cost per item remains constant irrespective of the order size
- The cost of holding an inventory item remains constant irrespective of the number of items held in stock

The EOQ model does not provide a perfect answer since the aforementioned assumptions are seldom realized in the actual business environment. Under suitable conditions, however, this model may provide a starting point for determining the economic order quantity. The EOQ formula is recorded as follows:

$$\text{EOQ (in units)} = \sqrt{\frac{2 \times N \times S}{H}}$$

Key:

N = number of units used during one year.

S = average order related cost (this includes the cost of preparing the order, driver, transportation, and other relevant administrative expenses).

H = the cost of holding a unit of inventory during one year.

An application of the EOQ formula is illustrated in the following example. A company is using 10,000 units of Product A during one year. The average order-related cost is $15. The cost of holding a product unit during one year is $5, since an item costs $50 and the annual interest rate is 10%. Thus, the economic order quantity can be computed as follows:

$$\text{EOQ} = \sqrt{\frac{2 \times 10,000\text{units} \times 15}{5}} =$$

$$\sqrt{60,000} = 244.9 \approx 245 \text{ units}$$

A **periodic review system,** as its name implies, entails reviewing the inventory level at equal intervals and maintaining it at a predetermined level by ordering additional quantities of materials. A "maximum" level of inventory needs to be established for each stock item to secure correct reordering of required materials. The quantity of materials that need to be reordered can be determined as follows:

Reorder quantity $= A - B - C + D$

Key:

A = Maximum level of inventory
B = Inventory "on-hand" i.e., available in stock
C = Inventory "on-order" i.e., materials ordered but not yet received
D = Expected demand of inventory during the lead period

Depending upon the company's size, nature of operations, and range of materials and products, the **inventory control system** can be maintained on a manual basis or in computerized form. The two basic inventory control systems that can be used by the company have been described earlier in Part 3 (Volume I) and include:

- **Periodic inventory system.** This system is based on counting inventory on a periodic basis, possibly once every six or twelve months. Under this system no detailed record of inventory status is kept during the year.
- **Perpetual inventory system.** This system entails recording every transaction pertaining to the movement of inventory on a continuous basis. Under this system every purchase, entry, withdrawal, and sale of inventory is recorded in a **perpetual inventory record card**. A typical illustration of such a card was presented in Exhibit 3–45.

A perpetual inventory control system is commonly used by small and medium-sized companies. Under this system the following information becomes available for each inventory item:

- Inventory description and number
- Required level of inventory—reorder level and minimum level
- Storage location
- Inventory movement in the stores—date; quantity received, sold, and balance; unit and total costs

In practice, companies keep fluctuating quantities of different types of inventories in their stores. These inventories usually fall into three major categories in accordance with an **ABC classification** that can be summarized as follows:

- *Category A—high value items.* Approximately 20 percent of all items account for about 70 percent of the total annual inventory value.
- *Category B—medium value items.* Approximately 30 percent of all items account for about 20 percent of the total annual inventory value.
- *Category C—low value items.* Approximately 50 percent of all items account for about 10 percent of the total annual inventory value.

It is advisable to recognize the use of each inventory item and categorize it according to the ABC classification. Furthermore, it is useful to examine the movement of each inventory item in order to identify the current demand for products and future trends. This will necessitate a regular maintenance and control of all inventory records. One of the popular methods for achieving accurate inventory records is **cycle counting**. This method entails periodic counts and verification of inventory records for various items used by the production department. Using the cycle counting procedure, management has constant access to updated inventory records.

When the delivery of inventories takes place, all items must be inspected and placed within the company's stores to ensure their safekeeping. Hence, **materials storage** also represents an integral part of the material management and control system. The types of stores maintained by the company usually depend upon the manufacturing or operational requirements and may be classified as:

- Raw materials stores
- Components or work-in-process stores
- Finished goods stores
- Consumables stores

Stores layout and location depends upon the individual needs and the size of the organization. The variation of requirements results from differences in facilities; specific arrangement of manufacturing, finishing, and assembly processes; and the nature of the production operation. Type, size, and quantity of materials also play an important role in the layout of stores. However, some of the common principles applied to the process of locating stores are as follows:

- Stores should be developed to provide maximum space at a minimum cost
- Stores should be located to meet the requirements of the manufacturing processes
- Stores should provide for maximum flexibility to accommodate changing conditions
- Stores should facilitate effective material handling procedures

Stores are usually located on a centralized or decentralized basis, and each type of location has certain advantages and disadvantages. The advantages of the centralized storing facilities arise largely from:

- Improved supervision in the stores
- Improved control over inventories
- Improved stores service efficiency
- Improved accuracy of the inventory counting procedure
- Reduced space requirement
- Reduced personnel requirement

The storage and control of inventory plays an important role within the organization. This function is carried out by one or several storekeepers depending upon the size and specific requirements of the company. The usual duties of a storekeeper cover a wide range of activities:

- To receive and record all deliveries
- To unpack goods and check the quantities and the quality against the relevant purchase order
- To return defective goods and to prepare supporting documentation
- To inform the buyer and the purchase originator of the receipt of goods

- To arrange proper storage of raw materials, components, work-in-process, finished goods, consumables, and tools
- To issue goods against authorized material, stores, or tool requisition
- To maintain updated inventory control records
- To arrange the dispatch of finished goods to customers
- To count inventory of all materials placed in the stores

Another important task of production management is to ensure timely delivery of products to customers. In order to facilitate economical and prompt delivery, it is necessary to develop and maintain an effective **materials dispatch** procedure. This function is usually carried out by the dispatch supervisor, but if the company's size does not justify a separate position, it may be performed by the store's supervisor.

The dispatch of finished products to various customers necessitates effective coordination of all activities related to materials management procedures. Some of the important requirements of the materials dispatch are:

- Availability of all materials and components required for the manufacture and assembly of finished products
- Timely assembly of finished products in accordance with a predetermined production schedule
- Availability of packaging materials
- Availability of sufficient storage facilities
- Availability of transport facilities

It is necessary to plan all deliveries in advance in order to reduce the delivery costs and to increase the efficiency of transport facilities. The nature of the **transport control system** usually depends upon the number of commercial vehicles utilized by the company. Some of the essential requirements of effective transport control facilities are:

Exhibit 4–60

Daily Shipping Schedule

Daily Shipping Schedule							
Date: 10.1.89		Name of driver: A. Kemp		Truck reg. No. 567-890			
Delivery note No.	Customer		Distance (miles)		Time		Signature of customer
	No.	Name	Start	Traveled	In	Out	
123	50	Customer A	10,000	20	8:00	8:20	
156	75	Customer B	10,000	15	9:00	9:20	

- Daily delivery routing schedule
- Restricted loading of vehicles
- Skilled drivers
- Constant control of the drivers' performance
- Regular servicing and maintenance of vehicles
- Monthly vehicle performance control
- Monthly vehicle maintenance and repair cost control

An integral element of the materials dispatch procedure is preparation of a **daily shipping schedule**. The prime purpose of this schedule is to summarize details of daily deliveries and to maintain control in the dispatch section. A typical daily shipping schedule is presented in Exhibit 4–60.

4.20 Just-in-Time Manufacturing Philosophy

All information contained in this part is based on the usual and widely-accepted production and operation practices used by Western manufacturers. Since the beginning of 1980, however, a strong Japanese influence became evident in the Western World in the form of a **Just-in-Time (JIT) manufacturing philosophy.** In fact, this philosophy turned many Japanese companies into real success stories during recent years.

One expert, Edward J. Hay, describes the Just-in-Time as a philosophy of eliminating waste in the total manufacturing process from purchasing through distribution.[15] Elimination of waste includes three fundamental and equally important elements:

- Balance and synchronization of all activities in the manufacturing process
- Total quality of operations and products based on the principle "doing it right the first time"
- Constructive cooperation between all employees within the organization

The Just-in-Time methodology was introduced by Toyota after World War II. In the late 1970s the JIT became more and more popular among Japanese manufacturers. It is still not totally adopted in that part of the world, however. Around 1980, several American experts began a detailed study of various Japanese management methods, including the JIT methodology. The prime objective of that study has been to identify the secret weapon that made Japanese manufacturers so successful and competitive in the world markets. The study revealed that Japanese companies use an approach which includes several important elements. Some of these elements, described earlier in Part 1 (Volume I), relate to the issue of human relations and propagate the concepts of "respect, trust, loyalty and positive attitude toward people" (Theory Z).[16] It is apparent that such elements represent a fundamental ingredient of the Japanese culture. Additional elements that have been identified as most suitable for Western culture include:

1. *The JIT philosophy.* This philosophy of economy and total elimination of waste represents the foundation, or the umbrella, of the JIT methodology.
2. *Quality of people, operations, and products.* The concept of total quality is a major and integral element of the JIT methodology.
3. *The JIT manufacturing methods.* These methods include uniform produc-

tion load, overlapping operations, reduced setup time, pull system, and JIT purchasing.

4. *Employee participation and teamwork.*   This concept is based on complete cooperation between employees and commitment to the organization.

The Just-in-Time methodology can be visualized as a pyramid, as illustrated in Exhibit 4–61. At the top of the JIT pyramid is the JIT philosophy. The philosophy applies to the quality of people, operations, products, and manufacturing methods. The underlying foundation of the JIT pyramid is unconditional commitment by management to the implementation of JIT methodology within the organization and continuous cooperation between employees.

One of the most important objectives of the JIT philosophy is to minimize or eliminate waste throughout all stages of the manufacturing process. Toyota defines waste as "anything other than the minimum amount of equipment, materials, parts, and working time absolutely essential to production." Everything in excess of such a minimum is considered by the JIT philosophy as additional and unnecessary expense. According to the JIT philosophy, it is essential to achieve a situation in which the manufacturing process will utilize minimal resources. For example:

- Minimum suppliers
- Minimum personnel, equipment, and space
- Minimum inventory
- Minimum setup and operational times
- Minimum scrap and rework

Perhaps, one of the most important tasks prior to the implementation of the JIT methodology is the conducting of a **value-added analysis**. This analysis will help to establish what the Just-in-Time methodology can do for a company. The prime purpose of this analysis is to identify the areas of inefficiency related to the existing manufacturing procedure.

Value-added analysis is usually carried out by selecting a set of existing manufacturing operations and recording in detail every single activity that takes place. When the description of all activities is completed, it is necessary to establish which ones actually add value to the product. All those activities which

Exhibit 4–61

The Just-in-Time Pyramid

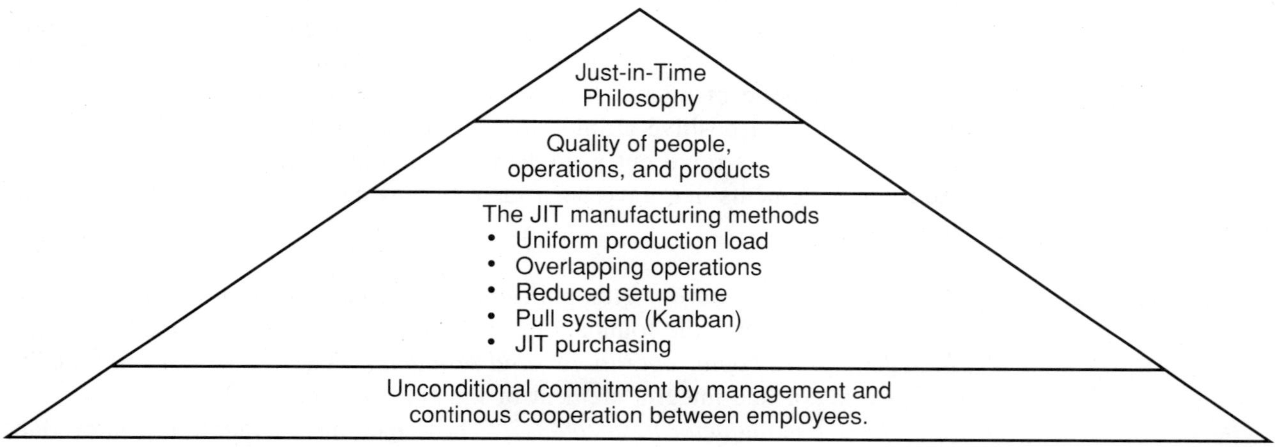

Exhibit 4–62

Value-Added Analysis

Value-Added Analysis

Activity No.	Operation No.	Description	Adds value
1	1	Cut material into blanks	yes
2		Check size	no
3		Move to the next station	no
4		Wait for next operation	no
5	2	Bend blanks into shape	yes
6		Inspect	no
7		Move to the next station	no
8		Wait for tools	no
9		Set the machine	no
10	3	Drill and tap	yes
11		Inspect	no
12		Move to the assembly	no
13		Wait for other components	no
14	4	Assembly of all components	yes
15		Inspect	no

do not add value should be carefully examined, reduced, and eliminated if possible. A typical value-added analysis is illustrated in Exhibit 4–62.

Reduction of nonproductive activities associated with manufacturing operations helps to improve the overall productivity and adds real value to the final product. This process ultimately results in elimination of waste and represents an integral part of the Just-in-Time methodology. Proper implementation of this methodology may produce a number of positive results and benefits, some of which are outlined in Exhibit 4–63.

Exhibit 4–63

Expected Results and Benefits
of the JIT Methodology

Description of benefit	Range of improvement (%)
Lead-time reduction	83–92
Productivity increase	
Direct labor	5–50
Indirect salary	21–60
Cost of quality reduction	26–63
Purchased material price reduction	6–45
Inventory reduction	
Purchased material	35–73
Work-in-process	70–89
Finished goods	0–90
Setup reduction	75–94
Space reduction	39–80

SOURCE: Edward J. Hay, Rath, & Strong, *The Just-In-Time Breakthrough* (New York: John Wiley & Sons, Inc., 1988), p. 23. Reprinted with permission.

The Just-in-Time manufacturing methodology is based on principles largely associated with assembly line processes. In fact, the JIT philosophy suggests that assembly line principles should be applied to all manufacturing and related operations. This includes purchasing raw materials, production and assembly operation, quality control, storage, distribution of finished products, and even administrative flow of work in the office.

One of the basic tasks of the Just-in-Time methodology is to ensure a balanced and synchronized production flow. The planning of such a flow should start with the last operation in accordance with specific customer requirements. For example, if a customer needs 100 units of Product A per day, the planning process should consider all operations in reverse order and determine an appropriate **cycle time**. In accordance with JIT methodology, the cycle time measures the rate of requirement for products as dictated by a customer and not by the manufacturing ability of the production facility. The process of synchronization and balancing of a production flow entails a number of steps that are presented in Exhibit 4–64.

The Just-in-Time philosophy suggests that all production operations should be geared to accommodate specific customer needs at short notice. Products should be manufactured to meet the demand rather than being produced for stock irrespective of the available operational capacity and human resources. Furthermore, the JIT methodology prescribes a **level-loading** and scheduling of all operations at a frequency dictated by customer requirements. As a result of the level-loading of manufacturing operations, the company may expect to benefit through smooth production flow, increased flexibility of operations, reduced inventory requirements, shorter lead times, and overall quality improvements.

One of the key issues in the level-loading of manufacturing operations is **reduction of setup times**. The process of setup time reduction, similar to the process of waste elimination, requires an in-depth examination of all activities associated with setting a particular machine. These include preparing a machine for a manufacturing operation, handling a workpiece, setting tools, and clamping

Exhibit 4–64

Synchronization of the JIT Production Plan

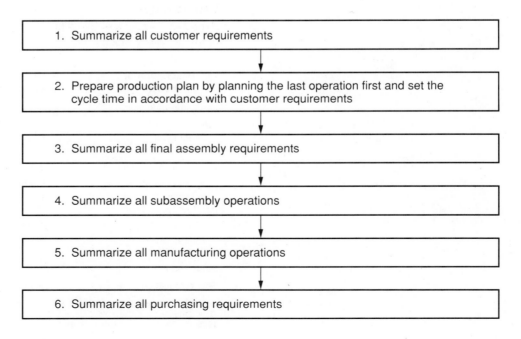

a workpiece in the machine. The Just-in-Time methodology includes a number of steps which lead to an effective reduction of time during the machine setup procedure. The JIT philosophy also suggests that such time savings should be applied to the level-loading of manufacturing operations, thus gearing production facilities toward immediate customer needs.

Another important element involved in the level-loading of manufacturing operations is the **flexibility** of production facilities. Traditionally, machinery and equipment are laid out in accordance with their functional designation within the production department. This type of plant layout has been discussed earlier and described as process layout. Many small and medium-sized companies that operate as job shops and manufacture products in batches utilize process layout principles. Here a batch of products undergoes the first operation in one section and thereafter is moved to another section for the second operation and so on. This procedure entails a continuous scheduling of all production activities and usually does not provide much operational flexibility.

The Just-in-Time philosophy, on the other hand, prescribes that machinery and equipment should be laid out by product rather than by function. This type of plant layout is similar to the product layout which has been also discussed earlier. The Just-in-Time methodology entails an arrangement of equipment in which "**machine cells**" or "**work cells**" are created. The prime purpose of these cells is to provide a universal and highly flexible manufacturing facility where the product can undergo a number of different operations on a "mini-assembly line" basis. This arrangement of machinery offers several advantages similar to those associated with the ordinary assembly line.

One of the major differences between an ordinary manufacturing approach and the Just-in-Time philosophy is the actual method of linking various operations. Traditionally, each step of a particular manufacturing process is identified during the process design stage and recorded in an appropriate route sheet. Thereafter the information contained in the route sheet is used as a prime source for scheduling and controlling of manufacturing activities. Ordinary manufacturing approach is frequently termed a "push system" since all operations are pushed through the production department in accordance with master production schedule requirements.

The Just-in-Time methodology, conversely, prescribes that all manufacturing operations should be linked into a uniform production process on a **pull system** basis. The pull system can be described by a chain of procedures which usually take place in an ordinary supermarket. These procedures are initiated by customers who come to the supermarket, purchase certain goods by withdrawing them from shelves, and finally pay the money to the cashier. At a regular interval, the supermarket employee is instructed to check which products have been withdrawn from the shelves. All product withdrawals are recorded in a summary sheet which, in turn, serves as an authorization to replace such products with new ones.

The Japanese carefully studied the "supermarket" procedure and introduced it into the manufacturing environment. This procedure contains two prime types of signals called **Kanbans**, which are used to "pull" all manufacturing operations. The supermarket procedure provides the basis for scheduling and controlling manufacturing activities and is described by an example in Exhibit 4–65.

The first signal that initiates the production activities in the example is issued by the assembly section. Various products must be assembled in this section on a daily basis in order to meet customer demands. Hence, the assembly section may be viewed as an "internal customer" withdrawing the required components and subassemblies from various work centers within the production department, or

Exhibit 4–65

Production Scheduling and Control by Kanban

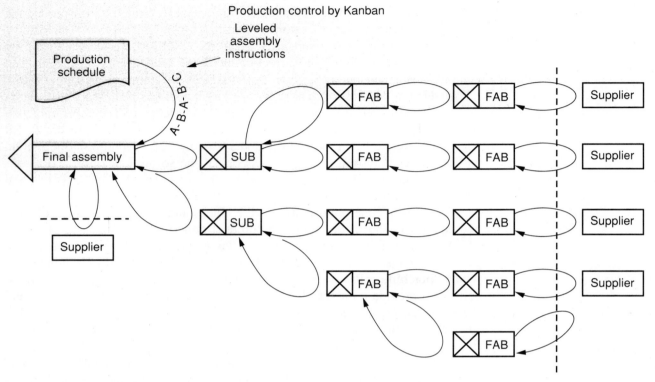

SOURCE: Edward J. Hay, *The Just-In-Time Breakthrough* (New York: John Wiley and Sons, 1988), p. 108. Reprinted with permission.

"supermarket." All components are placed in special containers ready for immediate consumption in accordance with specific production requirements.

A special **Kanban card** that specifies the description and quantity of a particular component is placed in each container. After withdrawal of components from the production department, the Kanban card should be removed from the container and returned to the work center where the components' manufacturing operations can take place. This card serves as the second signal, or authorization, issued to the specific work center to produce another container-full of components in a given period of time.

As a result of the "chain reaction," the entire manufacturing process can run on a series of pull signals or Kanbans as illustrated in Exhibit 4–65. These signals become the "money" which are used throughout the manufacturing process from the final assembly through subassembly, fabrication, and purchasing activities.

Purchasing raw materials and components plays a critical role in the balancing and synchronization of the Just-in-Time manufacturing process. The prime objective of **Just-in-Time purchasing** is to develop firm relations with suppliers and to ensure that minimal quantities of materials are delivered *just in time* for production. The prime characteristics of JIT purchasing have been outlined by Richard Schonberger as follows:

Suppliers:
• Few suppliers
• Nearby suppliers
• Repeat business with same suppliers

- Active use of analysis to enable desirable suppliers to become/stay price competitive
- Clusters of remote suppliers
- Competitive bidding mostly limited to new part numbers
- Buyer plant resists vertical integration and subsequent wipeout of supplier business
- Suppliers are encouraged to extend JIT buying to their suppliers.

Quantities:
- Steady output rate (a desirable prerequisite)
- Frequent deliveries in small lot quantities
- Long-term contract agreements
- Minimal release paperwork
- Delivery quantities variable from release to release but fixed for whole contract term
- Little or no permissible overage or underage of receipts
- Suppliers encouraged to package in exact quantities
- Suppliers encouraged to reduce their production lot sizes (or store unreleased material).

Quality:
- Minimal product specifications imposed on supplier
- Help suppliers to meet quality requirements
- Close relationships between buyers' and suppliers' quality assurance people
- Suppliers encouraged to use process control charts instead of lot sampling inspection.

Shipping:
- Scheduling of inbound freight
- Gain control by use of company-owned or contract shipping, contract warehousing, and trailers for freight consolidation/storage where possible instead of using common carriers.[17]

The JIT purchasing procedure presents several benefits to the purchasing organization and suggests that suppliers should be viewed as outside partners who can contribute to the long-run welfare of the buying firm rather than as outside adversaries. The effectiveness of the JIT purchasing strongly depends upon the quality of the materials being supplied. In fact, the Just-in-Time philosophy states that quality at the source is of a paramount importance in a successful waste elimination program. Hence, it is essential to ensure that the quality of all materials supplied to the company is always maintained on an acceptable level. Ideally, every supplier should guarantee the quality of his products, thus minimizing the inspection requirements of incoming goods.

In order to maintain high quality of operations and products in the JIT manufacturing environment, specific quality requirements need to defined. All manufacturing processes should be controlled on a continuous basis to provide immediate feedback to management. The Just-in-Time philosophy also suggests operating the production equipment at lower speeds so that the process can be stopped when problems occur.

Planned maintenance of machinery and equipment also plays an important role in JIT manufacturing environment. This entails correct selection of suitable equipment and continuous operator involvement in total productive maintenance efforts. All maintenance procedures including preventive maintenance and equipment breakdowns should be recorded on a regular basis.

The crucial factor in the successful implementation of the Just-in-Time methodology is probably the total commitment by the company's management

Exhibit 4–66

Effects of the Just-in-Time Philosophy

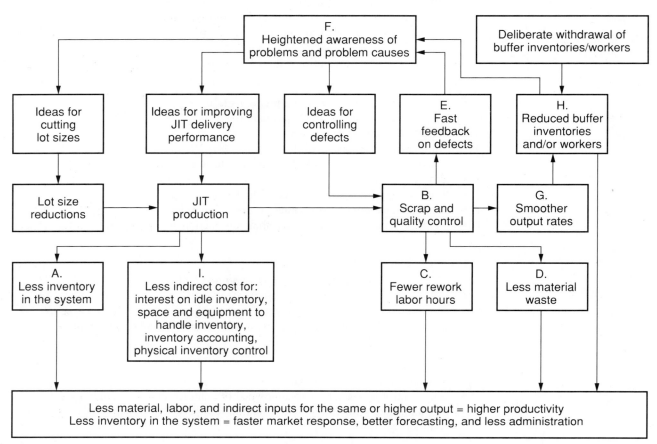

SOURCE: Adapted with permission of The Free Press, a division of Macmillan, Inc. from *Japanese Manufacturing Techniques: Nine Hidden Lessons in Simplicity* by Richard J. Schonberger. Copyright ©1982 by Richard J. Schonberger.

toward the JIT philosophy. Although this philosophy proved to be effective for large manufacturing corporations, small and medium-sized organizations may also benefit from the JIT methodology. Several effects that can be expected as a result of the Just-in-Time methodology have been summarized by Richard Schonberger and presented in Exhibit 4–66. Finally, when various elements related to JIT manufacturing activities are implemented, it is imperative to stimulate a spirit of cooperation and teamwork among employees.

4.21 Working Instructions and Forms

All information related to production and operations management principles has been presented in Sections 4.01–4.20. It is essential to understand this information and to proceed with the compilation of forms provided at the end of Part 4. Working instructions for completing these forms follow immediately. The instructions require that management rates its knowledge of production and operations management principles and evaluates company performance in the area of production and operations management. Aggregate scores will help to identify possible problems and to assign priorities for implementing the most effective solutions. The sequence of activities pertinent to completion of working forms is presented in Exhibit 4–67.

Exhibit 4–67

Summary of Forms for Part 4

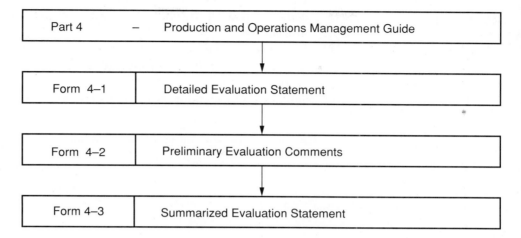

| Part 4 | – | Production and Operations Management Guide |

| Form 4–1 | Detailed Evaluation Statement |

| Form 4–2 | Preliminary Evaluation Comments |

| Form 4–3 | Summarized Evaluation Statement |

4–1 Detailed Evaluation Statement

22. Study the description of all checkpoints related to *production and operations management principles* as outlined in Part 4.

23. Evaluate your personal knowledge in the area of production and operations management and score your *personal knowledge level* of each checkpoint. Scores should be based on the scale shown below:

0 – 20(%)	Very poor level of knowledge
21 – 40(%)	Poor level of knowledge
41 – 60(%)	Fair level of knowledge
61 – 80(%)	Good level of knowledge
81 – 100(%)	Very good level of knowledge

24. Evaluate your company's performance in the area of production and operations management and score your *company's performance level* on each checkpoint. Scores should be based on the scale shown below:

0 – 20(%)	Very poor level of performance (the checkpoint has never been implemented)
21 – 40(%)	Poor level of performance (the checkpoint is implemented sometimes)
41 – 60(%)	Fair level of performance (the checkpoint is implemented, but not managed well)
61 – 80(%)	Good level of performance (the checkpoint is implemented and managed well)
81 – 100(%)	Very good level of performance (the checkpoint is constantly implemented and managed very well)

25. Determine the *average evaluation level* pertaining to your personal knowledge and the company's performance within each area of production and operations management as follows:

$$\text{Average Evaluation Level } (\%) = \frac{\text{Total Score}}{\text{Number of Applicable Checkpoints}}$$

Form 4–2 Preliminary Evaluation Comments

26. State your personal opinion related to production and operations management principles currently employed by your company and summarize *preliminary evaluation comments*.

Form 4–3 Summarized Evaluation Statement

27. Issue Form 4–1 and Form 4–2 to key executives within your company who are actively involved in the *production and operations management activities* and ensure that both forms are completed in accordance with instructions.

28. Designate a *final evaluation level*[a] for each checkpoint as a result of a meeting between the company executives.

See continuation of working instructions on page 200 (Part 5)

---

[a]The final evaluation level may not represent an average value of the individual results and should be determined by mutual consent.

NAME OF COMPANY:		FORM 4 – 1	
		PAGE 1 OF 1	

PRODUCTION AND OPERATIONS MANAGEMENT ANALYSIS
DETAILED EVALUATION STATEMENT

No.	DESCRIPTION	PERSONAL KNOWLEDGE LEVEL (%)	COMPANY'S PERFORMANCE LEVEL (%)				
			VERY POOR	POOR	FAIR	GOOD	VERY GOOD
		0 - 100	0 - 20	21 - 40	41 - 60	61 - 80	81 - 100
4.01	The Production and Operations Management Process						
4.02	Classification of Operational Activities						
4.03	Facility Design, Location, and Organization						
4.04	Product Selection, Design, and Standardization						
4.05	Process Design						
4.06	The Drafting Office						
4.07	Equipment Evaluation and Selection						
4.08	Plant Layout						
4.09	Equipment Maintenance						
4.10	Equipment Replacement						
4.11	Tool Control						
4.12	Cost Estimating						
4.13	Production Planning						
4.14	Materials Requirements Planning						
4.15	Production Control						
4.16	Planning and Control of Services and Projects						
4.17	Quality Control						
4.18	Materials Purchasing						
4.19	Materials Control, Storage, and Dispatch						
4.20	Just-in-Time Manufacturing Philosophy						
→	AVERAGE EVALUATION LEVEL						

NAME:	POSITION:	DATE:

PRODUCTION AND OPERATIONS MANAGEMENT ANALYSIS
PRELIMINARY EVALUATION COMMENTS

No.	DESCRIPTION	PRELIMINARY EVALUATION COMMENTS
4.01	The Production and Operations Management Process	
4.02	Classification of Operational Activities	
4.03	Facility Design, Location, and Organization	
4.04	Product Selection, Design, and Standardization	
4.05	Process Design	
4.06	The Drafting Office	
4.07	Equipment Evaluation and Selection	
4.08	Plant Layout	
4.09	Equipment Maintenance	
4.10	Equipment Replacement	
4.11	Tool Control	
4.12	Cost Estimating	
4.13	Production Planning	
4.14	Materials Requirements Planning	
4.15	Production Control	
4.16	Planning and Control of Services and Projects	
4.17	Quality Control	
4.18	Materials Purchasing	
4.19	Materials Control, Storage, and Dispatch	
4.20	Just-in-Time Manufacturing Philosophy	

NAME:	POSITION:	DATE:

PRODUCTION AND OPERATIONS MANAGEMENT ANALYSIS
SUMMARIZED EVALUATION STATEMENT

No.	DESCRIPTION	COMPANY'S PERFORMANCE LEVEL (%)				
		ASSESSED BY PRESIDENT	ASSESSED BY OPERATIONS EXECUTIVE	ASSESSED BY	ASSESSED BY	FINAL EVALUATION LEVEL
4.01	The Production and Operations Management Process					
4.02	Classification of Operational Activities					
4.03	Facility Design, Location, and Organization					
4.04	Product Selection, Design, and Standardization					
4.05	Process Design					
4.06	The Drafting Office					
4.07	Equipment Evaluation and Selection					
4.08	Plant Layout					
4.09	Equipment Maintenance					
4.10	Equipment Replacement					
4.11	Tool Control					
4.12	Cost Estimating					
4.13	Production Planning					
4.14	Materials Requirements Planning					
4.15	Production Control					
4.16	Planning and Control of Services and Projects					
4.17	Quality Control					
4.18	Materials Purchasing					
4.19	Materials Control, Storage, and Dispatch					
4.20	Just-in-Time Manufacturing Philosophy					
→	AVERAGE EVALUATION LEVEL					

NAME :	POSITION :	DATE :

4.22 References

1. L.C. Hoch, "Guidelines for Selecting a New Plant Site," *Modern Manufacturing*, May 1969, pp. 131–140.
2. L.P. Alford and John R. Bangs. *Production Handbook* (New York: The Ronald Press Company, 1952), p. 4.
3. Belverd E. Needles Jr., Henry R. Anderson, and James C. Caldwell, *Financial and Managerial Accounting* (Boston, MA: Houghton Mifflin Company, 1988), pp. 535–536.
4. Cornell, *Organization and Management*.
5. James H. Greene and George W. Plossl, "Short-Range Planning," *Production and Inventory Control Handbook*, Chapter 9 (New York: McGraw-Hill, 1970), p. 4.
6. Joseph A. Orlicky, *Material Requirements Planning: The New Way of Life in Production and Inventory Management* (New York: McGraw-Hill, 1974), pp. 181–183.
7. Richard B. Chase and Nicholas J. Aquilano, *Production and Operations Management* (Homewood, IL: Richard D. Irwin, 1985), p. 542.
8. James B. Dilworth, *Production and Operations Management*, 2nd ed. (New York: Random House, 1983), p. 335. Reprinted with permission.
9. Ibid., pp. 335–336.
10. Ibid., pp. 384–385.
11. Robert B. Ballot, *Materials Management: A Results Approach* (New York: American Management Association, 1971), p. 6.
12. Gary J. Zenz, *Purchasing and the Management of Materials* (New York: John Wiley & Sons, 1987), p. 6.
13. Dilworth, p. 181.
14. Zenz, pp. 111–112.
15. Edward J. Hay, Rath, & Strong, *The Just-in-Time Breakthrough* (New York: John Wiley & Sons, 1988), pp. 1–20.
16. William G. Ouchi, *Theory Z* (New York: Addison-Wesley, 1981). p. 7.
17. Richard J. Schonberger and James P. Gilbert, "Just-In-Time Purchasing: A Challenge for U.S. Industry," *California Management Review*, Fall 1983, p. 58.

Part 5

Marketing and Sales Management Guide

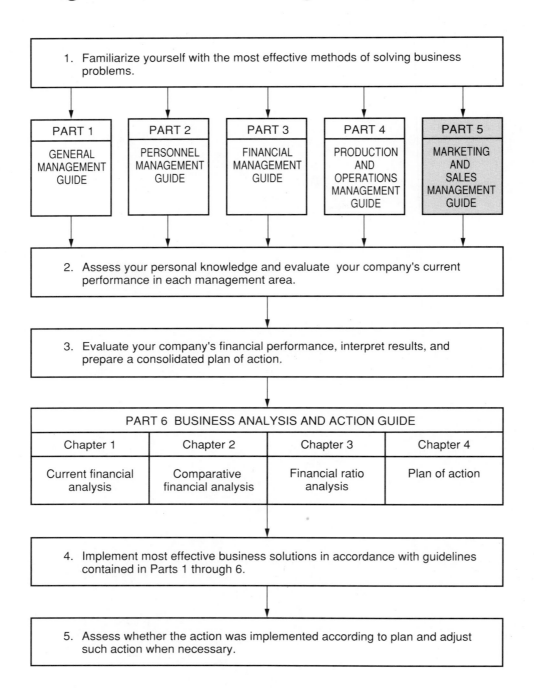

1. Familiarize yourself with the most effective methods of solving business problems.

PART 1	PART 2	PART 3	PART 4	PART 5
GENERAL MANAGEMENT GUIDE	PERSONNEL MANAGEMENT GUIDE	FINANCIAL MANAGEMENT GUIDE	PRODUCTION AND OPERATIONS MANAGEMENT GUIDE	MARKETING AND SALES MANAGEMENT GUIDE

2. Assess your personal knowledge and evaluate your company's current performance in each management area.

3. Evaluate your company's financial performance, interpret results, and prepare a consolidated plan of action.

PART 6 BUSINESS ANALYSIS AND ACTION GUIDE			
Chapter 1	Chapter 2	Chapter 3	Chapter 4
Current financial analysis	Comparative financial analysis	Financial ratio analysis	Plan of action

4. Implement most effective business solutions in accordance with guidelines contained in Parts 1 through 6.

5. Assess whether the action was implemented according to plan and adjust such action when necessary.

- *The 20 elements of practical marketing and sales management*
- *Working instructions and forms for evaluating your company's marketing and sales management*
- *Guidelines for implementing effective marketing and sales strategies and much more*

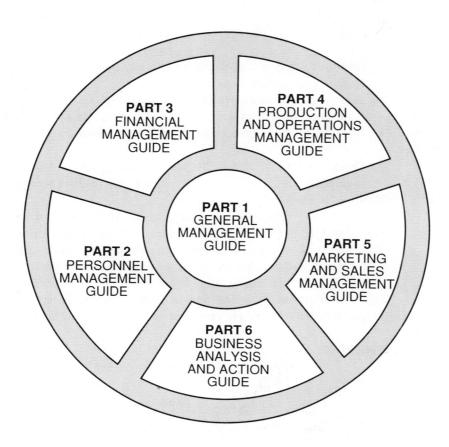

Contents

5.00 Introduction

The prime purpose of the **marketing and sales management guide** is to identify business problems and implement the most effective solutions in the area of marketing and sales management. This guide highlights a variety of issues, such as:

- How to identify market requirements and to develop sound marketing strategies
- How to formulate and to implement a marketing plan
- How to prepare sales budgets
- How to develop an effective sales organization
- How to recruit, train, compensate, and motivate the salesforce
- How to evaluate and to control sales performance

These and other related issues are addressed in the marketing and sales management guide. All issues are described in **20 checkpoints** presented in **Sections 5.01–5.20.**

To develop the most suitable solutions in the area of marketing and sales management, it is necessary to understand the issues discussed in this part. Thorough self-assessment by company executives and evaluation of company performance in the aforementioned area will indicate the effectiveness of current marketing and sales management principles. This, in turn, will help to formulate a sound plan of action and to implement the most effective solutions in accordance with the **work program** presented in Exhibit 5–1.

Exhibit 5–1

Work Program for Part 5

Work Program

Planned Action	Objective
1. Study of marketing and sales management principles	To attain an adequate level of knowledge in the area of marketing and sales management
2. Self-evaluation of knowledge by members of the management team in the area of marketing and sales management	To identify individual strengths and weaknesses of members of the management team in the area of marketing and sales management
3. Evaluation of company performance in the area of marketing and sales management	To identify the level of company performance in the area of marketing and sales management and to establish the average evaluation level
4. Formulation of a plan of action in the area of marketing and sales management	To summarize the range of activities that must be undertaken in the area of marketing and sales management
5. Implementation of the most effective business solutions in the area of marketing and sales management	To develop a set of the most suitable solutions in accordance with guidelines presented in this part
6. Evaluation and control of actions in the area of marketing and sales management	To assess whether the action was implemented according to plan and to adjust such action when necessary

Note: Please familiarize yourself with relevant working instructions prior to completing forms at the end of this part. Additional information on these forms is available from Business Management Club, Inc. upon request.

5.01 The Marketing Management Process

In 1985 the American Marketing Association defined marketing as "the process of planning and executing the conception, pricing, promotion, and distribution of ideas, goods, and services to create exchanges that satisfy individual and organizational objectives."[1] In other words, marketing management entails analysis, planning, implementation, and control of activities designed to develop and maintain a beneficial exchange of ideas, products, and services in the marketplace to meet personal and corporate goals.

Many business practitioners confuse marketing management with sales management. Although these functions are strongly interrelated, they do differ in purpose and description. Harvard professor Theodore Levitt defines the difference between the two functions as follows:

> Selling focuses on the need of the seller; marketing on the needs of the buyer. Selling is preoccupied with the seller's need to convert his product into cash; marketing with the idea of satisfying the needs of the customer by means of the product and the whole cluster of things associated with the creating, delivering and finally consuming it.[2]

Another well known management expert, Peter F. Drucker, suggests that:

> Selling and marketing are antithetical rather than synonymous or even complementary. There will always, one can assume, be a need for some selling, but the aim of marketing is to make selling superfluous. The aim of marketing is to know and understand the customer so well the product or service fits him and sells itself.[3]

The most important task of a marketing manager is to initiate the **marketing management process** and develop a marketing department within the organization. The planning and control of the marketing management process entail a number of steps that are outlined in Exhibit 5–2.

The marketing management process begins with the gathering and collating of marketing information. It is essential, therefore, to develop a strong market intelligence team and to utilize appropriate sources of information. These sources may include publications, statistical data, reports from sales personnel, and market research bureaus.

Examination of strategic marketing variables entails evaluation of internal factors (company size, strengths, weaknesses, organizational and management structure, corporate objectives, and products or services) and external factors (current market demand, influence of competition, legal requirements, and technological developments). Comprehensive examination of relevant strategic marketing factors enables the marketing manager to evaluate the company's existing position in the marketplace. This in turn provides a sound foundation for formulating the company's marketing objectives for the forthcoming fiscal period.

After formulating marketing objectives, it is necessary to identify suitable market segments where the company may have an opportunity to offer its products or services. Market opportunity represents a suitable field of marketing action where a company may have a potential trading advantage. Each feasible opportunity should be viewed more closely to establish a suitable method of entering into a specific market.

There are many different market segments where a company may identify sound business opportunities. These segments, known as target markets, must be classified according to their industrial activity and grouped into separate target market areas. The sales potential of each area should be evaluated and the

Exhibit 5–2

The Marketing Management Process

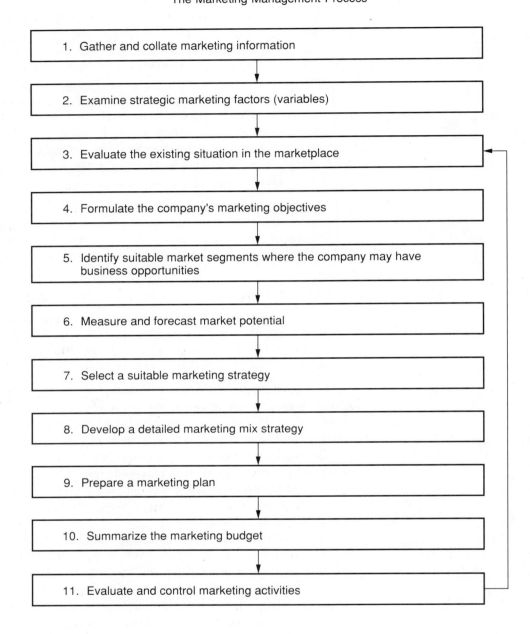

1. Gather and collate marketing information

2. Examine strategic marketing factors (variables)

3. Evaluate the existing situation in the marketplace

4. Formulate the company's marketing objectives

5. Identify suitable market segments where the company may have business opportunities

6. Measure and forecast market potential

7. Select a suitable marketing strategy

8. Develop a detailed marketing mix strategy

9. Prepare a marketing plan

10. Summarize the marketing budget

11. Evaluate and control marketing activities

most suitable market opportunities selected in accordance with the company's capabilities to gain and maintain a market position.

Once the marketing manager has evaluated the company's existing position, formulated appropriate objectives, and identified and measured target markets, it is necessary to select a suitable marketing strategy. There are five basic strategies that can be chosen at this stage: new venture strategy, growth strategy, market development strategy, market retention strategy, or balancing strategy.

The next stage of the marketing management process involves development of a detailed marketing mix strategy. Marketing mix will be defined later as a combination of four important elements: product, price, promotion, and place (distribution). Thus, it is necessary to develop a comprehensive product or service strategy, pricing strategy, promotional strategy, and distribution strategy.

Preparation of the marketing plan represents the culmination of the marketing management process. This plan must be prepared for at least one fiscal year and should include:

- Summarized analysis of the existing situation in the marketplace
- Outline of the company's marketing objectives
- List of suitable market segments
- Summarized forecast of market potential
- Outline of the overall marketing strategy
- Summary of the marketing mix strategy
- Summary of marketing and sales action program
- Summary of marketing and sales budgets

Finally, when the marketing plan is prepared and all relevant budgets have been approved, it becomes essential to implement the plan and ensure effective control over all related functions. This in turn requires the creation of a marketing department to handle evaluation, planning, implementation, and control of all marketing and sales activities.

5.02 Buying Behavior

Successful implementation of the marketing management process requires a thorough understanding of **buying behavior** in various markets. These markets differ in their nature and size and include the following:

- **The consumer market.** This market consists of all individuals and households that purchase products and services for personal use.
- **The producer market.** This market consists of all individuals and organizations that purchase products and services for their own manufacturing needs and supply the produced goods and services to others at a profit.
- **The reseller market.** This market consists of all individuals and organizations that purchase products with the sole purpose of reselling them to others at a profit.
- **The government market.** This market consists of local, state, and federal governmental organizations that purchase products and services to fulfill their functional objectives.

In order to understand buying behavior in these markets, it is necessary to provide answers to certain questions:

- *Who buys?* What kind of people initiate the purchasing procedure and who places the actual purchase order?
- *What do they buy?* What kind of products or services are purchased?
- *How much do they buy?* In what quantities and how frequently are products or services purchased?
- *How do they buy?* What procurement methods are used during the purchasing procedure?
- *Why do they buy?* What are the reasons for purchasing specific products or services?

The consumer market, with a population of about 250 million in 1989, has the largest number of buyers in the United States. The average household size is approximately 2.7 persons per family and the median age of the population is about 32 years. Additional statistical information pertinent to consumer markets may be found in sources such as the U.S. Government Printing Office or the U.S. Bureau of Census.

The study of consumer behavior entails examination of several issues which have been summarized by Paul S. Busch and Michael J. Houston:

1. Consumer behavior deals primarily with the behavior of individuals in the marketplace—the manner in which they purchase and use products and services.
2. Consumer behavior is multidisciplinary. Its understanding is enhanced by contributions from such areas as psychology, social psychology, sociology, cultural anthropology, and economics.
3. Consumer behavior is concerned with factors that influence product purchase decisions and product usage.
4. Consumer behavior is concerned with the process by which consumers arrive at buying decisions and how that process differs across individuals and products.
5. Finally, consumer behavior includes postpurchase phenomena: satisfaction with the outcome of a purchase and usage behavior surrounding a product, for example.[4]

The framework for consumer behavior, outlined in Exhibit 5–3, is influenced by three important factors that must be understood by the marketing and sales executives. These are:

*   *Marketing strategy factors*—product, price, promotion, and distribution
*   *Personal factors*—values, needs, attitudes, beliefs, and personality of individual consumer
*   *Social factors*—social and economic environment, family, friends, and lifestyle

The integral part of ordinary buying behavior is the **consumer decision process.** This process has a number of steps that enable the consumer to satisfy a particular need:

Exhibit 5–3

Framework for Evaluating Consumer Behavior

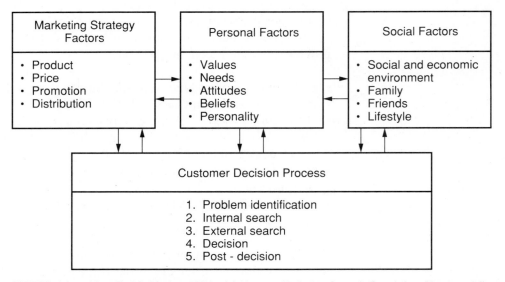

SOURCE: Adapted from Paul S. Busch and Michael J. Houston, *Marketing: Strategic Foundations* (Homewood, IL: Richard D. Irwin, 1985), p. 231. Reprinted with permission.

1. *Problem identification.* The consumer identifies a specific problem and recognizes the need to solve it.
2. *Internal search.* The consumer evaluates existing knowledge and past experience in solving a similar problem.
3. *External search.* The consumer examines new information in the market–place that may lead to solution of the existing problem.
4. *Decision.* The consumer decides on the most suitable method of solving the existing problem.
5. *Post–decision.* The consumer evaluates the decision and subsequent action and utilizes the acquired experience in making similar decisions in the future.

The **organizational market** represents another important consideration for the marketing manager. Although this market is much smaller than the consumer market in terms of the number of buyers, it generates the largest aggregate dollar volume of purchases. This market includes all industrial and commercial organizations such as manufacturers, service companies, wholesalers, retailers, contractors, farmers, and government organizations.

The organizational market is best characterized by the size of various companies in the marketplace. This is illustrated in Exhibit 5–4.

The organizational market generates a continuous need for three types of products and services:

- **Consumer goods.** These include all products that are ultimately purchased and used by individual consumers.
- **Industrial goods.** These include raw materials, components, capital equipment, accessory equipment, and consumables purchased by organizations.
- **Organizational services.** These include all services rendered by individuals or organizations for other organizations.

A broad range of products and services is purchased by various organizations in accordance with specific buying practices discussed earlier in Part 4. These practices are guided by organizational buying behavior and are influenced by factors such as:

Exhibit 5–4

Size Distribution of Organizational Market

Type of Organization	Number of Employees	Percent of Total Companies	Percent of Total Employees
Manufacturers	1 – 9	45	2
	10 – 49	34	10
	50 – 249	16	24
	250 – 999	4	27
	1000 – over	1	36
Wholesalers	1 – 4	43	7
	5 – 9	24	12
	10 – 49	29	44
	50 – over	4	37
Retailers	1 – 4	48	7
	5 – 9	24	12
	10 – 49	24	44
	50 – over	4	37

SOURCE: Adapted from *County Business Patterns,* 1981.

Exhibit 5–5

Framework for Evaluating Organizational Buying Behavior

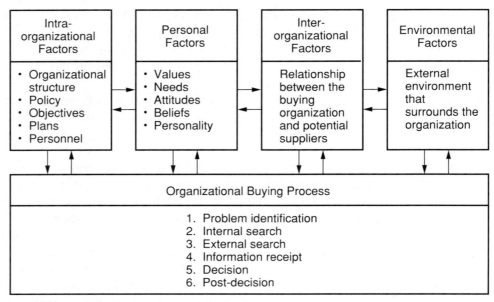

SOURCE: Adapted from James H. Meyers and Richard R. Mead, *The Management of Marketing Research* (Scranton, PA: International Textbook Company, 1969), pp. 27-46. Reprinted in Busch and Houston, p. 781. Reprinted with permission.

- *Intra-organizational factors*—organizational structure, policy, objectives, plans, and personnel involved in the decision-making process
- *Personal factors*—values, needs, attitudes, beliefs, and personality of each participant in the buying process
- *Inter-organizational factors*—relationship between the buying organization and potential suppliers
- *Environmental factors*—external environment surrounding the organization

The actual decision-making process used by organizational buyers is similar to the consumer decision process described earlier. It includes the following:

1. Problem identification
2. Internal search
3. External search
4. Information receipt
5. Decision
6. Post-decision

The overall framework of organizational buying behavior is outlined in Exhibit 5–5.

5.03   Marketing Information and Research

One critical task in the marketing management process is identification and selection of suitable sources of **marketing information.** This is particularly important because marketing managers often experience uncertainty regarding trends and their implications in the environment and in the marketplace. Updated marketing information therefore plays a vital role in effective planning, problem solving, and control of marketing activities. Some questions about these activities have been summarized by James H. Myers and Richard R. Mead as follows:

1. *Planning*
   - What are the basic trends in the domestic economy? How, specifically, will these affect the market for our products?
   - What changes can we expect in customer purchasing patterns? Will these be based on changes in real income, on changing tastes and values, or on changes in patterns of distribution?
   - What will our needs be over the next three years for sales representatives? branch offices? distribution centers (warehouses)?
   - What new markets are likely to open up? What types of products or services will be needed to serve them? Are there promising markets we are not now serving?
   - Who are our competitors? What is their direction? How will they affect our plans?

2. *Problem solving*
   2.1 Product
       - Which of several alternative new-product designs is most likely to be successful? What specific features should the final product have?
       - What action should we take to counter a new-product offering by competitors?
   2.2 Price
       - How should we price new products? Should we use a penetration (low) price or a skimming (high) price?
       - What is the shape of our demand curve?
   2.3 Distribution
       - What types of intermediate deals should be used at the agent, whole-sale, or retail levels? How intensive should this coverage be?
       - How many manufacturing and warehousing facilities should the firm operate? In what locations?
   2.4 Promotion
       - What should the total promotion budget be? How should it be allocated among products, among geographic areas, and among the various forms of promotion (advertising, personal selling, and so on)?
       - To what extent should we use such sales stimulants as coupons, premiums, deals, and contests to increase customer traffic in retail stores?

3. *Control*
   - What are current sales and market shares for each of our product lines? for each geographic area? for each major customer type?
   - What is our corporate image among present customers? among our potential customers? among our distributors?[5]

Several sources of information are usually available to marketing managers, including marketing intelligence, sales personnel employed by a company, market research firms, suppliers, and business associates. It is essential to collect marketing information on a continuous basis and to utilize all available sources in order to develop an effective marketing information system.

Marketing information system (MIS) has been defined as a set of procedures and methods for the consistent planned collection, analysis, and presentation of information for use in making marketing decisions.[6] A more elaborate definition describes MIS as a structured interacting complex of persons, machines, and procedures designed to generate an orderly flow of pertinent information collected from both intra-and extra-firm sources for use as the basis for decision-making in specified responsibility areas of marketing management.[7] As the definition implies, the prime purpose of the MIS is to collate relevant information from various sources to ensure most effective performance of the marketing department. Four major functions performed in the operation of the MIS have been outlined by Paul S. Busch and Michael J. Houston:

1. *Organize.* With the variety of types and sources of information available to marketing managers, a crucial function of the MIS is to categorize the information as it is collected.
2. *Store.* Not all information is used at the same time or by the same people. Consequently, it is necessary to store the information so it is available to those who need it when they need it.
3. *Analyze.* Some information is not useful until it is analyzed and transformed into a new form. For example, information may enter the system for use in demand assessment. It is not used in its raw form but rather as input to a forecasting model that generates a short-run or long-run forecast of demand.
4. *Transmit.* Raw or transformed information must be transmitted to decision-makers in order for it to be used. The MIS must allow for a smooth flow of information to its users on demand.[8]

In order to develop an effective MIS, marketing managers must gather relevant information from sources such as:

- *Marketing intelligence.* This includes salesperson reports; trade journals; reports from customers, suppliers, and business associates; reports about competitors; press clippings; trade show data; and information about tax and law.
- *Internal accounting.* This includes several monthly reports: accounts receivable; accounts payable; inventory status reports; product and service cost reports; sales and profitability reports per product, service, customer, sales area, and sales person; monthly budget and variance reports.
- *Marketing research.* This includes special marketing surveys and census data; local Chamber of Commerce, Small Business Administration, and Direct Marketing Association research data; specialized marketing forecast; and stock market data.

A well-maintained MIS enables a marketing manager to provide the most updated information to the executive management team. This information plays a critical role in the pending success or failure of the company's efforts in the marketplace. Depending on the specific requirements and size of the organization, the MIS may be maintained on a manual basis or in computerized form. The MIS is generally utilized in a broad variety of applications, some of which are outlined in Exhibit 5–6.

Although the role of MIS has increased substantially during recent years, the need for traditional marketing research has not diminished. A new definition of **marketing research** was adopted by the American Marketing Association in 1987:

Marketing research is the function which links the consumer, customer, and public to the marketer through information—information used to identify and define marketing opportunities and problems; generate, refine, and evaluate marketing actions; monitor marketing performance; and improve understanding of marketing as a process.

Marketing research specifies the information required to address these issues; designs the method for collecting information; manages and implements the data collection process; analyzes the results; and communicates the findings and their implications.[9] The marketing research process occurs in several stages which are outlined in Exhibit 5–7.

Exhibit 5–6

Marketing Information System (MIS)

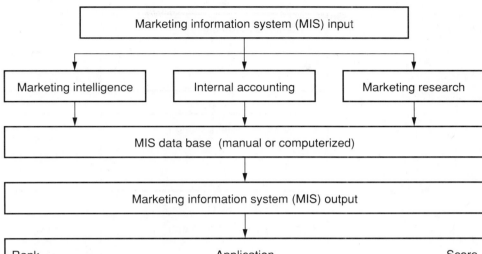

Rank	Application	Score
1.	Sales analysis: company sales	4.72
2.	Sales forecasting	4.36
3.	Sales analysis: company versus competitor sales	4.27
4.	Develop sales budgets	4.25
5.	Develop sales performance ratios by sales representative	4.09
6.	Determine developmental potentials by territory	4.09
7.	Sales analysis: company versus industry sales	4.00
8.	Produce sales quotas	3.73
9.	Maintain customer profiles	3.72
10.	Develop sales quotas	3.72
11.	Manage sales inquiries and leads	3.69
12.	Maintain internal company information (products, pricing, technical, etc.)	3.61
13.	Develop competitive performance parameters	3.58
14.	Maintain information on sales personnel	3.53
15.	Measure return on time invested	3.46
16.	Generate customized graphics for sales presentations	3.46
17.	Determine alignment of sales representatives	3.45
18.	Develop market penetration ratios	3.45
19.	Maintain competitive information data base	3.36
20.	Generate customized presentation reports for sales calls	3.23
21.	Monitor sales call costs	3.07
22.	Maintain customer mailing lists	3.00
23.	Maintain file of stock letters for personalized business correspondence	2.69
24.	Maintain data base of all key sales-related facilities (hotels/motels, restaurants, conference centers, etc.)	2.69
25.	Generate prefiled order forms for sales representatives	2.53
26.	Maintain log of sales representatives' call routes	2.27

Scale 1 to 5: 1 = no interest; 5 = high interest.

SOURCE: Partially adapted from Norman Wiener, "PCs and Marketers Forge a Productive Alliance," *Sales & Marketing Management* (February 6, 1984), p. 38. Reprinted with permission.

Exhibit 5–7

The Marketing Research Process

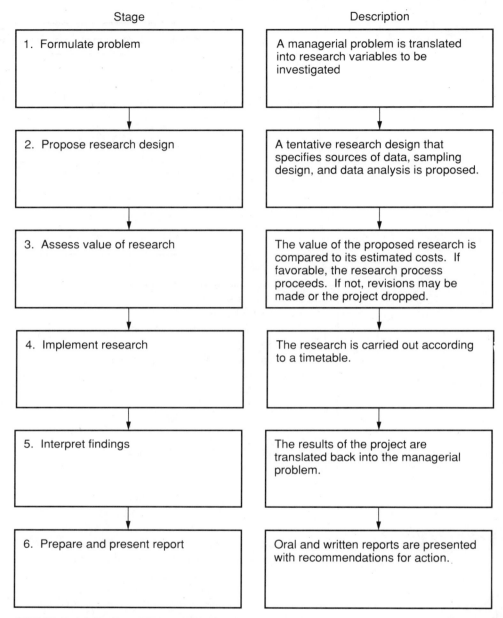

Stage	Description
1. Formulate problem	A managerial problem is translated into research variables to be investigated
2. Propose research design	A tentative research design that specifies sources of data, sampling design, and data analysis is proposed.
3. Assess value of research	The value of the proposed research is compared to its estimated costs. If favorable, the research process proceeds. If not, revisions may be made or the project dropped.
4. Implement research	The research is carried out according to a timetable.
5. Interpret findings	The results of the project are translated back into the managerial problem.
6. Prepare and present report	Oral and written reports are presented with recommendations for action.

SOURCE: Paul S. Busch and Michael J. Houston, *Marketing: Strategic Foundations* (Homewood, IL: Richard D. Irwin, 1985), p. 788. Reprinted with permission.

Proper research and evaluation of various markets usually provides the company with the basic information required for the development of new marketing strategies, policies, and plans. A great variety of public and private sources of statistical information is available to marketing managers. Some of these sources are summarized in Exhibit 5–8.

In addition, several research agencies compile specialized data and provide standardized marketing information services on a continuous basis. Two major organizations that provide these services are:

- *Dun & Bradstreet "Market Identifiers" (DMI).* DMI is a roster of over 4.3 million establishments that contains descriptive information for each company on the roster; information including location, SIC codes, line of business, sales

Exhibit 5–8

Public and Private Sources of Statistical Data

Sources of Statistical Data

Public Sources	Private Sources
Current Population Reports	Almanac of Business and Industrial Financial
Census of Housing	Ratios
Census of Retail Trade	Commodity Yearbook
Census of Service Industries	Consumer Market and Magazine Report
Census of Wholesale Trade	Editor and Publisher Market Guide
Census of Manufacturers	Fortune Directory
Census of Mineral Industries	A Guide to Consumer Markets
Census of Transportation	Handbook of Basic Economic Statistics
Census of Agriculture	Million Dollar Directory
Census of Government	Moody's Manuals
Business Cycle: Handbook of Indicators	Predicasts
Survey of Current Business	Sales & Marketing Management Survey of Buying
County and City Data Book	Power
Economic Indicators	World Almanac and Book of Facts
Federal Reserve Bulletin	
Monthly Labor Review	
State and Metropolitan Area Data Book	
Statistical Abstract of the United States	
Statistics of Income	
U.S. Industrial Outlook	

SOURCE: Paul S. Busch and Michael J. Houston, *Marketing: Strategic Foundations* (Homewood, IL: Richard D. Irwin, 1985), p. 793. Reprinted with permission.

volume, and number of employees. DMI is a useful source for industrial goods manufacturers in planning their marketing operations.

- *Nielsen Retail Index.* Every two months, from national samples of 1,600 super-markets, 750 drugstores, and 150 mass merchandisers, the A. C. Nielsen Company tracks data on individual brands of consumer goods. Information gathered includes inventory change, sales to consumers, price, and the amount of advertising and sales promotion for the brand during the two month period. This information is broken down by geographic area, store type, and store size. The Nielsen Retail Index is useful to consumer goods manufacturers and wholesalers.[10]

Regular gathering of marketing information helps management develop effective marketing strategies, policies, and plans. These are discussed later in this part.

5.04 Market Segmentation

Marketing information systems and marketing research normally reveal the extent of the trading potential and specific size of various markets. Each market is filled with many individuals and organizations representing different needs, and buying habits. It is essential to identify various markets, to break them into logical **market segments,** and to plan each segment individually. This process is known as **market segmentation,** and it represents one of the important functions of the marketing manager.[11] Market segmentation entails the grouping of various customers on the basis of similarity of their requirements and characteristics. The main objective of market segmentation is to determine a set of **target markets** that can be effectively reached and served by the company, utilizing a suitable marketing mix.

Marketing mix represents one of the key concepts in modern theory on marketing management. It is known as the **"four P"** concept and includes the following marketing variables:

1. **P—Product**—features, size, quality, brand name, packaging, service, and warranties
2. **P—Price**—selling price, discounts, and credit terms
3. **P—Promotion**—advertising, selling, and publicity
4. **P—Place**—distribution channels, area coverage, geographic location, and transportation

Correct balancing of resources allocated to each element of the marketing mix plays an important role in the market segmentation process. Markets consist of customers who may differ in product and service requirements, buying practices, size, resources, and geographic location. Market segmentation depends on the type of market, namely, consumer, producer, reseller, or government. Industrial market segmentation normally takes into account the following factors:

- Type of business
- Size of organization
- Geographic location
- Product or service application
- Product or service usage rate

The federal government has developed a **standard industrial classification (SIC) system** in which all business organizations are categorized in accordance with their economic activities. In general, all organizations are categorized into the following major divisions:

- Manufacturers
- Service organizations
- Wholesalers
- Retailers
- Nonprofit groups
- Government groups, agencies, and institutions

In addition, all business organizations are classified into major subgroups, industry subgroups, detailed industry, product or service range, and specific product or service description. A typical example of a **SIC structure** is illustrated in Exhibit 5–9.

Another important element in market segmentation is classification of business organizations according to size. The prime indicators of company size are the number of employees in the organization, the monthly or annual level of sales, and the number of subsidiary companies within the organization.

Many banks and financial institutions, for example, categorize business organizations according to their size and financial capabilities. Subsequently, larger organizations are sometimes offered additional incentives like lower interest rates or more favorable credit conditions. Business organizations themselves also frequently categorize customers by company size and future business potential. Many organizations develop a special pricing procedure for preferred customers and maintain a discount structure based on the average volume of business placed by a particular customer.

It is often convenient to classify business organizations by their geographic location. Depending upon the specific marketing requirements, such a classification may take place on the following basis:

- Classification by state
- Classification by county

Exhibit 5–9

Structure of the Standard Industrial Classification System

Classification	SIC Number	Description
Division	D	Manufacturing
Major group	34	Manufacturers of fabricated metal products
Industry subgroup	344	Manufacturers of fabricated structural metal products
Detailed industry	3441	Manufacturers of fabricated structural steel
Manufactured products	34411	Manufacturers of fabricated metal for buildings
Manufactured products	3441121	Manufacturers of fabricated structural metal for buildings– iron and steel (for sale to companies): industrial

SOURCE: Adapted from Office of Management and Budget, 1972, *Standard Industrial Classification Manual* (Washington DC: U.S. Government Printing Office, 1972); U.S. Bureau of the Census, 1977, *Census of Manufacturers: Fabricated Structural Metal Products* (Washington DC: U.S. Government Printing Office, 1980).

- Classification by city
- Classification by ZIP code
- Classification by industrial or rural area

Market segmentation based on a geographic location is particularly useful when the sales potential of a specific target market area is evaluated. This method of segmentation provides basic information for allocating different market areas and sales quotas to sales personnel.

Sometimes it may be useful to classify business organizations and consumers on the basis of product or service application and usage rate. This type of classification is particularly important because other classification methods do not always provide accurate data.

Apart from identifying the type and size of a business organization and evaluating the sales potential of a particular geographic location, it is often necessary to develop a **composite profile** of each market segment. This requires a sound understanding of buying behavior in a specific market segment and an examination of what is purchased, when, and in what quantities.

Small and medium-sized companies, just like the larger organizations, have to constantly fight for additional business in the marketplace, so it is essential that the marketing manager pay serious attention to the market segmentation process. This process provides meaningful information for the formulation of the company's marketing strategy and the development of an overall marketing plan.

An ordinary market segmentation process entails a number of steps which should be undertaken by the marketing manager. These steps are:

1. *Identification of market segments.* Various segments should be identified in accordance with the SIC system by type and size of business, geographic location, application, and usage rate of products and services.
2. *Collation of marketing information.* This includes data extracted from the MIS and results obtained from appropriate marketing research.
3. *Development of composite profiles.* This entails profiling each market segment in terms of who buys, what they buy, how much they buy, how they buy, and why they buy.

4. *Estimation of market potential.*   This entails evaluation of possible business volume that may be generated by each market segment that is identified and examined in the above process.

5. *Analysis of marketing opportunity.*   This entails examination of competitive situations in the marketplace and development of a suitable marketing program for each market segment in terms of an estimated profit potential.

6. *Selection of a preliminary marketing strategy.*   This represents the beginning of an important process in which various marketing strategies are evaluated in terms of current positioning of the company in the marketplace, existing and potential market requirements, and prevailing competition.

The market segmentation process represents the beginning of an active marketing planning effort. This process is followed by a comprehensive measurement of selected market segments, forecasting of business potential, formulation of a suitable marketing strategy, and development of an effective marketing plan. A typical market segmentation process is summarized in Exhibit 5–10.

The market segmentation process provides the company with a number of important advantages:

- Management is in a better position to identify suitable market opportunities.
- Management can make improved adjustments of their products and services in accordance with particular market requirements.
- Management can develop the most suitable marketing mix of product, price, promotion and place.
- Management can develop sound marketing programs and budgets based on well-identified factors of specific market segments.

After completing the market segmentation process, management should proceed with measurement and forecasting of selected market segments. These activities are discussed next.

Exhibit 5–10

The Market Segmentation Process

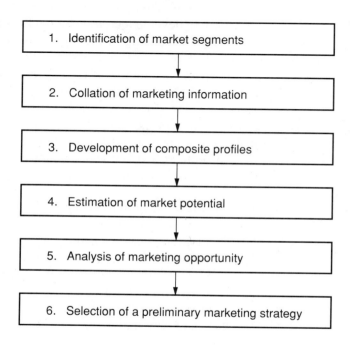

5.05 Market Measurement and Forecasting

Once market segmentation has been accomplished it is necessary to provide a quantitative estimate for each selected market segment. This process, known as **market measurement,** entails evaluation of specific demand for a particular product or service, territory, and type of customer. **Market demand** for a particular product or service is represented by the total volume that could be purchased by a specified group of customers in a particular geographical area during a predetermined period of time. Proper measurement of the market demand is useful in the process of forecasting and sales budget preparation.

Forecasting is predicting the future by analyzing the past. For estimation of future demand, the marketing manager frequently uses the sales information from previous years, sales force estimates, and statistical information from governmental and other sources. This does not necessarily mean that what happened in the past will also happen in the future, but that analysis of the past begins the process. Why is it important? Through forecasting, the marketing manager is able to determine markets for products, plan corporate strategy, develop sales quotas, determine the need for and number of salespeople, decide on distribution channels, price products, or services, analyze products and product potential in different markets, decide on product features, determine profit and sales potential for different products, help determine advertising budgets; determine the potential benefits of sales promotion programs, and decide on the use of various elements of the marketing mix. In fact, not only does forecasting have a central role in marketing, but it is also important for the planning of production, finance, and other operational activities.[12]

Some of the key concepts related to the market measurement and forecasting process have been summarized by Paul S. Busch and Michael J. Houston as follows:

- **Demand assessment** refers to the process by which a firm arrives at a quantified estimate of the level of demand for a generic product or brand that exists or will exist during a given time period.
- **Market potential** is the maximum sales of a generic product, product-form, or service for an entire industry in a market during a given time period, presuming a given environment and a maximum marketing effort by all marketers.
- **Market forecast** is an estimate of the expected sales of a product or service that will be realized by the industry in the market (or portion thereof) during a specified time period.
- **Sales potential** refers to the maximum sales available to a company under maximum marketing effort by the company for a given time period.
- **Sales forecast** is an estimate of a company's actual sales that will be realized in a market during a given time period under a planned marketing program and expected environmental conditions.
- **Market share** is the ratio of actual company sales to actual industry sales.[13]

All of these marketing concepts can be visualized as a number of squares with a gradually-reduced surface area. The graphic presentation of these concepts in illustrated in Exhibit 5–11.

Market measurement and forecasting may be carried out for a short-term period (up to one year) or for a long-term period (between one and three years or more), depending upon the specific company requirements. Short-

Exhibit 5–11

Key Concepts in Market Measurement and Forecasting

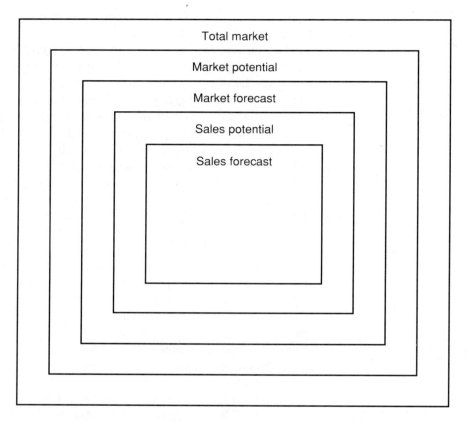

term market measurement and forecasting, for example, involves the following five steps:

1. Establish the boundaries of the total market for the current fiscal year.
2. Estimate a short-term market potential for the current fiscal year—assess the total market demand.
3. Develop a short-term market forecast for the current fiscal year—estimate the potential value of sales for the total market.
4. Estimate a short-term sales potential for the current fiscal year—assess the maximum sales available to a company under maximum marketing effort conditions.
5. Develop a short-term sales forecast for the current fiscal year—estimate the company's actual sales that are expected to be realized under the planned marketing program and anticipated environmental conditions.

A long-term market measurement and forecasting is carried out in a similar manner in which the "current fiscal year" is replaced by an appropriate long-term period. This procedure is particularly important to larger organizations with an established share in the marketplace and to organizations that plan to enter into new markets.

Several methods of assessing current market demands are frequently used by the marketing managers. These methods are:

*   Chain-ratio method
*   Market-buildup method
*   Buying-power-index method

The **chain-ratio method** entails assessment of the current demand based on user characteristics and consumption rates. This method starts with an estimate of overall market demands and establishes the demand for a specific product or service through usage rates. *User characteristics* relate to a particular market or market segment and include relevant *demographic* (age, sex, marital status, family size, etc.), *socioeconomic* (income, education, occupation), and geographic (city, county, state, etc.) variables. *Product consumption* or *usage rate* provides the basic information about the quantity and frequency of products or services being purchased. The chain-ratio method also considers the expected life period of a particular product or service.

The chain-ratio method is particularly useful in a consumer environment. A golf club manufacturer, for example, caters to people between 30 and 70 years of age with annual income in excess of $60,000. These people reside in state X and represent 25 percent of the total population of 10 million. It may be assumed from past experience that 8 percent of these people play or are interested in golf. This, in turn, leads to the establishment of boundaries of the total market for golf clubs in state X. In order to determine the annual consumption rate per unit of product in this example, it should be recognized that 15 percent of the total market consists of first-time buyers and an additional 10 percent purchases the product for replacement purposes. Thus, the annual consumption rate includes both new and replacement demand.

Taking this data into consideration, it becomes possible to assess the current market demand and evaluate sales potential for the current fiscal year, assuming that the company's market share is 30 percent.

1. *Boundary of the total market:*
   Total population   100% = 10,000,000

2. *Market potential for golf clubs:*
   People between 30 to 70 years of age with annual income in excess of $60,000   × 25% = 2,500,000
   People who play or are interested in golf   × 8% = 200,000

3. *Market forecast:*
   People who are first-time buyers   × 15% = 30,000
   People who buy for replacement   10% = 20,000
   Total number of buyers   50,000
   Potential value of sales at $100 per set   × $100 = $5,000,000

4. *Sales potential for the company:*
   Estimated company share in the market   × 30% = $1,500,000

The **market-buildup method** requires assessment of the current demand for several identifiable market segments. Thereafter, all individual estimates are added together to obtain the value of the total market demand. A particular requirement of this method is that sales potential of each market segment be estimated by means of a common market denominator. A *common market denominator* is a descriptive factor which may be applicable across all market segments in the task of assessing the total market demand for a particular product or service.

The market-buildup method is suitable for estimating potential in industrial and consumer market environments. One of the prime sources of market segmentation frequently used by the industrial marketer is the standard industrial classification (SIC) system discussed earlier. The common market denominators that are applied throughout this estimating procedure generally represent a certain measure of size or activity pertinent to all market segments, like the number of employees, unit sales over 1,000 employees, or revenue per 1,000 employees.

The market buildup method entails a number of steps which are outlined below. These steps are as follows:

1. Break down total market into individual market segments; using for example, the SIC system.
2. Determine unit sales per common market denominator for each segment; for example, determine unit sales per 1,000 employees.
3. Determine total value of variables used as common market denominator for each segment like the total number of employees in each segment;
4. Combine steps two and three into an estimate of market potential for each segment.
5. Add estimates of market potential for each segment and determine total market potential.
6. Consider product unit price and develop a market forecast like the estimated value of sales for the total market.
7. Consider the company's specific market share and estimate the sales potential.

A particular company, for example, specializes in the manufacture of safety gloves for building and construction industries and special trade contractors. Using SIC codes, the company's marketing manager identifies the appropriate market and breaks it into the following segments:

SIC code 15—Building construction
SIC code 16—Construction other than building
SIC code 17—Special trade contractors

The common market denominator used in this instance reflects the demand for safety gloves per 1,000 employees in each market segment. Historical data on safety gloves purchased by each market segment may provide a good starting point for the estimating procedure. Suitable information may be obtained from a local branch of the Chamber of Commerce or from private organizations specializing in commercial marketing information such as Economic Information Services, Inc. The particular information pertinent to the annual consumption of safety gloves per 1,000 employees is as follows:

SIC code	Unit sales per 1,000 employees
15	2,000
16	2,800
17	1,200

The next stage is the determination of the total number of employees per market segment in a specific geographic location (county, state, country). This information may be obtained from the local Chamber of Commerce or from special publications such as the Census of Manufacturers or County Business Patterns. The specific information pertinent to the number of employees in a defined geographic area is assumed to be:

SIC code	Number of employees (000)
15	500
16	300
17	200

The combined information of the average number of units sold per 1,000 employees and the total number of employees in a defined geographic area provides the basis for estimating the market potential of each segment:

SIC code	Unit sales per 1,000 employees	×	Number of employees (000)	=	Market potential (units)
15	2,000	×	500	=	1,000,000
16	2,800	×	300	=	840,000
17	1,200	×	200	=	240,000
Total market potential for the above industries				=	2,080,000

Considering that the average product unit price is $3, the total market forecast for three market segments in the defined geographic area is as follows:

$$\$3 \times 2,080,000 \text{ units} = \$6,240,000$$

If the company has a 20 percent share in the aforementioned market, the sales potential can be determined as follows:

$$0.20 \times \$6,240,000 = \$1,248,000$$

The **buying-power-index (BPI) method** is based on information provided by *Sales & Marketing Management,* a marketing trade publication. In its "Annual Survey of Buying Power," this publication provides a buying power index for specific geographic areas. The BPI method enables the marketing manager to determine the relative buying power of different metropolitan areas, counties, states, and other regions through the following calculations:

$$BPI = 0.5Y + 0.2P + 0.3R$$

Key:

   BPI = Proportion of aggregate national buying power contained in the area
   Y = Proportion of aggregate national disposable personal income contained in the area
   P = Proportion of national population contained in the area
   R = Proportion of aggregate national retail sales occurring in the area

The BPI for the State of Texas, for example, can be calculated as follows:

   $Y = 6.69; \quad P = 6.56; \quad R = 7.52$
   $BPI = 0.5 \times 6.69 + 0.2 \times 6.56 + 0.3 \times 7.52 = 6.91$

As Paul S. Busch and Michael J. Houston suggest, the BPI provides a useful basis for estimating the geographic market potential for an entire industry because its three factors—income, population, and retail activity—are tied to the level of demand for many consumer products.

Sales & Marketing Management also includes a "Survey of Industrial Purchasing Power" that aids industrial marketers in allocating the available market potential. The "Survey of Industrial Purchasing Power" analyzes markets by both geographic area and SIC code. Several factors relating to demand for industrial goods are presented for a specific geographic area or SIC category. They include:

1. Total number of manufacturing companies with 20 or more employees
2. Total number of companies contained in factor 1 with 100 or more employees
3. Dollar value of goods produced in the market
4. The percentage of the dollar value of all goods produced in the United States that factor 3 represents
5. The percentage of the market's manufacturing output produced by companies contained in factor 2
6. Average value of goods produced per company

Factors 1, 3, and 4 provide indexes of industrial activity in a market and reflect market potential. Factors 2, 5, and 6 indicate how concentrated this activity is. They have implications for marketing strategy. For example, a higher percentage of activity concentrated in large companies would suggest the need for a smaller sales force.[14]

5.06 Marketing Strategy

One major responsibility of the marketing manager is the development of an effective marketing strategy. A **marketing strategy** is a general statement outlining the way an organization plans to achieve its overall marketing objectives. The marketing strategy provides a general explanation of how a company intends to implement its marketing plan in a specific competitive environment. The marketing strategy development process entails five steps that are outlined in Exhibit 5–12.

The marketing strategy development process begins with a comprehensive analysis of the existing situation in the marketplace. This requires examination of several **strategic marketing factors:**

1. *Company specialization and resources*
   - What types of products or services are offered to customers at present?
   - Should certain products or services be phased out and new ones added?
   - Does the company have sufficient personnel, financial resources, equipment, and experience to meet the demand for products or services?
2. *Market demand*
   - How strong is the demand for specific products or services in the marketplace?
   - What is the trend of the market demand?
   - What are the requirements for new products or services?
   - How is the demand for products and services generated by different market segments?
3. *Customers*
   - How do different customers make their buying decisions?
   - How satisfied are different customers with the company's ability to meet their needs?
   - Which elements of the marketing mix are particularly influential in the company-customer relations?
4. *Competition*
   - Who are the major competitors?

Exhibit 5–12

Marketing Strategy Development Process (Steps 1–5)

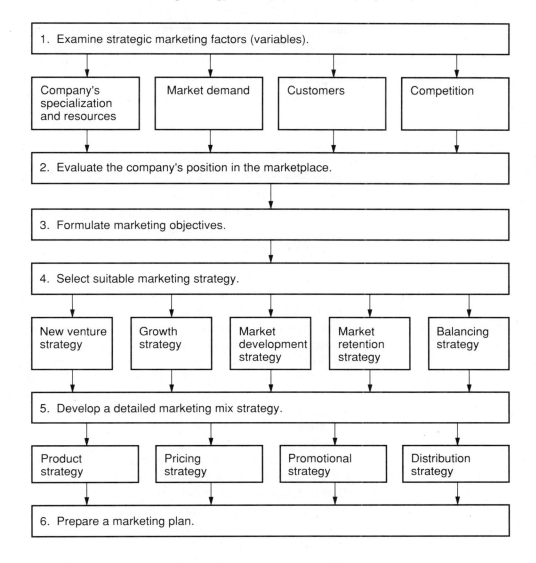

- What is the strategy of major competitors regarding the elements of the marketing mix?
- What is the influence of major competitors on the company's performance in various market segments?
- What is the company's growth potential in the existing competitive market environment?

Situation analysis starts with a detailed examination of the company's offerings in the marketplace. The marketing manager must obtain a clear picture about the market environment in which the company operates at present. The whole range of products or services offered by the company needs to be examined in terms of profitability and competitiveness in the marketplace. Those products or services that prove to be unprofitable, ineffective, or unpopular with customers should be examined with an option of being phased out. New products or services, on the other hand, should be considered in order to meet the changing market requirements.

Company's ability to satisfy existing and future market requirements should be carefully examined at this stage. This entails brief evaluation of marketing factors like the company's organizational structure, experience of management, quality of employees, financial resources, equipment, and overall functional efficiency. In addition, all company offerings should be evaluated in light of the existing laws and regulations imposed by federal and local governments and other relevant organizations.

The actual demand for products and services in the marketplace represents the second strategic marketing factor that needs to be considered. It is essential that the marketing manager obtain relevant information pertinent to the specific demand generated by various market segments. The prime sources of this information are MIS and market research. All market segments which may generate meaningful demand for the company's products or services should be identified and examined by a market segmentation process. In addition, a detailed market measurement and forecasting procedure should be completed. This procedure will provide the marketing manager with in-depth knowledge about specific requirements for products or services, trends, and opportunities in the marketplace.

The third strategic marketing factor to be examined by the marketing manager relates to customers. The manager should understand the real needs of current and prospective customers, the nature of their activities, and how they make their buying decisions. It is also important to obtain feedback from sales personnel about customer satisfaction with the company's products or services. All problems related to product or service performance and poor quality should be identified at this stage. All elements of the marketing mix—product, price, promotion, and distribution—should be carefully examined in light of an effective market penetration. Any inefficiencies in this regard should be evaluated and minimized or eliminated, if possible.

Competition represents the fourth important strategic marketing factor. All competitors must be identified and their respective size and activities carefully examined by the marketing manager. The prime issue for consideration is the strategy adopted by each competing organization in product or service development, price, promotion, and distribution in the marketplace. It is also essential to understand and evaluate the influence of competing organizations on the company's performance in various market segments. Since it is often difficult to obtain meaningful information about competition, it is important to develop a competitive intelligence system which should become an integral part of the MIS. This kind of system could provide important information during the marketing strategy development process and could enhance the company's chance for successful performance.

Examination of strategic marketing factors enables the marketing manager to assess the company's position in the marketplace and to establish preliminary objectives. Philip Kotler, for example, suggests that any organization may be identified as a market leader, challenger, follower, or nicher.

A **market leader** usually has three basic objectives: expansion of the total market, protection of its market share and steady increase of this share. The main objective of the **market challenger** is to attack the market leader and to expand aggressively in the marketplace taking the place of other competing firms in the industry. Some of the common strategies used by the challenger firm are price cutting, price discounts, longer credit facilities, improved quality and service, and an intensive advertising campaign. All other firms follow the market and are classified as **market followers** and **market nichers**, depending on their size. The market followers are the larger firms, and their basic philosophy is to "not rock the boat," usually because of fear that they may lose more than they can gain in the process. The main objectives of market followers are to ensure their active participation in the growth of the market and to maintain their market share. The market nichers, on the other hand, are smaller firms that choose to operate in a particular part of the market without attracting attention from the larger firms. The main objective of the market nichers is to specialize in a narrow market, to service a particular type of customer, and to offer a special range of products and services within a limited geographic area.[15]

Proper evaluation of the company's position in the marketplace makes it possible to establish accurate objectives for a specified period of time. These objectives are usually defined for one fiscal year, providing initial budget parameters for the company's planned performance. Typical marketing objectives may be summarized as follows:

- To increase sales of product line A by 20 percent
- To develop five market segments for a new product line B
- To maintain a 25 percent market share for product line C

Depending upon the company's position in the marketplace and its specific objectives, the marketing manager must select a suitable strategy. Five basic **marketing strategies** may be selected by the company at this stage:

- **A new venture strategy.** This strategy represents a totally new undertaking by the organization. This may entail, for example, developing a new manufacturing facility or launching a new product line.
- **A growth strategy.** This strategy directs the organization toward continuous expansion of business activities in the marketplace, modification of existing products and services, and development of new ones.
- **A market development strategy.** This strategy prescribes a continuous improvement of the existing lines of products or services offered by the organization in conjunction with the development of additional markets.
- **A market retention strategy.** This strategy guides the organization in maintaining its existing position in the marketplace. A certain product or service line may be modified and business activity may be increased. However, the company is expected to offer the same products or services in the existing market.
- **A balancing strategy.** This strategy directs the organization in balancing the level of its business activities in order to achieve the desired profit and market share objectives. In this instance, the company is not expected to develop new products or services, nor is it required to expand into new markets.

Selection of an appropriate marketing strategy provides overall direction for the company's business activities during the forthcoming fiscal year. Specific details pertinent to the selected strategy need to be examined and summarized in conjunction with all elements of the marketing mix. These include the following:

- Product strategy
- Pricing strategy

- Promotional strategy
- Distribution strategy

The specific marketing strategies related to each element of the marketing mix are discussed next. Upon the development of detailed marketing strategies, the marketing manager is expected to proceed with the formulation of a suitable marketing plan.

5.07 Product Strategy

The prime purpose of any business organization is to supply products and services in the marketplace at a profit. A **product** can be defined as "anything capable of satisfying a consumer want or need. A product can take a variety of forms, including a physical object, a service, a place, an organization, an idea, or a personality." The American Marketing Association suggests that all products can be classified as:

- **Consumer goods.** These include all products used by the ultimate consumer or household in such forms that they can be used without further processing.
- **Industrial goods.** These include all products that are to be sold primarily for use in producing other goods or rendering services, as contrasted with goods destined to be sold primarily to the ultimate consumer.[16]

The meaning of a concept "product" is widely used in various aspects of business management. In production, for example, the term "product" describes the outcome of people's work in a specific manufacturing process.

It is generally accepted that every product is created, manufactured, and supplied in order to meet particular customer needs. Naturally, such needs vary at times and this subsequently creates the necessity for a wide range of products required in the open market. These products differ in design, quality, price, size, color, shape, life span, and other descriptive characteristics, but their main and common purpose is to perform effectively and to ensure the satisfaction of the users. The process of product creation and development is usually accompanied by the following factors:

- *Profit.* This is probably the most essential factor motivating the shareholders and management to invest their capital and skills in order to initiate the process of creating various products.
- *Employment.* It is an important factor to provide the necessary work opportunities and fair income to employees during the process of creating various products.
- *Satisfaction.* This is a vital factor stimulating shareholders and employees to ensure momentum throughout the process of creating various products.
- *Growth.* This is an essential outcome of the positive development of a company involved in the process of continuous creation of various products.

A successful **product development cycle** can be maintained for a substantial period of time regardless of the type or size of a product providing that it satisfies a need of the users in the marketplace. As a result of limited product life, it is necessary to ensure constant development of new products to provide continuity of the company's performance. **New product development** represents, therefore, an important function of marketing management. This process consists of six stages which are summarized in Exhibit 5–13.

Exhibit 5–13

New Product Development Process

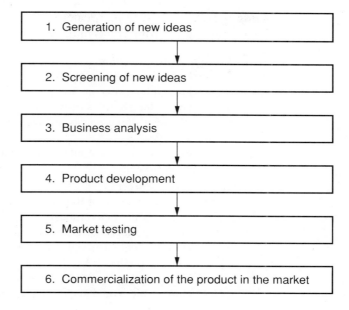

1. Generation of new ideas

2. Screening of new ideas

3. Business analysis

4. Product development

5. Market testing

6. Commercialization of the product in the market

The main objective of each stage of new product development is to establish the overall viability of the product without incurring unnecessary expenditures. Each stage should be properly conducted to ensure a successful launch of the product into the market in accordance with the overall objectives of the organization.

The product development process starts with the acquisition of new ideas. These ideas may come from a number of different sources such as:

- *Customers.* According to the marketing concept, the customer plays a central role in generation of new ideas. This is particularly important because only satisfied customers create a continuous demand in the marketplace.
- *Salespeople.* Probably one of the best sources for new ideas are salespeople because they are constantly dealing with different customers. Salespeople usually have firsthand experience through their contacts with buyers and may provide valuable information.
- *Competition.* Many new ideas come from competing organizations. It is useful, therefore, to study new product developments in the marketplace and to be prepared to follow a good example. Every new product launched by a competitor should, be carefully examined from the company's profitability point of view.
- *Executive management.* New ideas are frequently generated by senior management personnel who are expected to have a better understanding of overall requirements in the marketplace. Since senior managers have an improved knowledge about the company's capabilities, their suggestions may be highly valuable.
- *Research and development department.* One of the prime objectives of this department is to generate new ideas and to develop new products on the company's behalf. Employees who are engaged in research and development usually have a solid technical background and are familiar with all the latest developments in the marketplace.

The second stage involves screening of various ideas and evaluation of new product opportunities. Typical screening questions that should be answered at this stage relate to the company's operations, market potential, concept marketability, engineering, production, financial and legal issues. These questions have been summarized by Tom W. White, as follows:

1. *Company Operations*
   - How compatible is the concept with the current product lines?
   - Does it represent an environmental hazard or threat to our production facility and to the facilities of our neighbors?
   - Would it unreasonably interrupt manufacturing, engineering, or marketing activities?
   - Could we meet the after-sale service requirements that would be demanded by customers?

2. *Potential Market*
   - What is the size of the market?
   - Where is the market located?
   - What would be our potential market share?
   - How diversified is the need for the product? Is it a one-industry or multi-industry product?
   - How fast do we anticipate the market for the concept to grow?
   - How stable would such a market be in a recession?

3. *Concept Marketability*
   - Who would be our competitors?
   - How good is their product?
   - How well capitalized are potential competitors?
   - How important is their product to the survival of their business?
   - How is our product differentiated from the competition's? Will the differentiation provide a market advantage?
   - Could we meet or beat the competition's price?
   - Is the product normally sold through our current distribution channels, or would we have to make special arrangements?
   - Do we have qualified sales personnel?
   - Do we have a suitable means by which to promote the product?
   - What would we anticipate to be the life expectancy of the product? Is it going to move through the various life-cycle stages in 6 months, 6 years, or 60 years?
   - Will the product be offensive to the environment in which it will be used?

4. *Engineering and Production*
   - What is the technical feasibility of the product?
   - Do we have the technical capability to design it?
   - Can it be manufactured at a marketable cost?
   - Will the necessary production materials be readily available?
   - Do we have the production capabilities to build it?
   - Do we have adequate storage facilities for the raw materials and completed product?
   - Do we have adequate testing devices for proper quality control of the product?

5. *Financial*
   - What is our required return on investment (ROI)?
   - What is our anticipated ROI for this product?
   - Do we have the available capital?
   - What would be the payback period?
   - What is our break-even point?

6. *Legal*
   - Is the product patentable?

- Can we meet legal restrictions regarding labeling, advertising, shipment, and the like?
- How significant are product warranty problems likely to be?
- Is the product vulnerable to existing or pending legislation?[17]

The next stage, business analysis, is summarized by the financial and legal questions outlined above. One of the elements of the business analysis relates to the evaluation of **return on investment (ROI)** as discussed earlier in Part 3 (Volume I). The average rate of return on investment for a new product may be calculated as follows:

$$\text{Average rate of return on investment} = \frac{\text{Average annual net income}}{\text{Total investment cost}}$$

In order to determine an accurate value of ROI, it is necessary to consider the average life period of the new product. This is particularly important since the **product life cycle** consists of several stages, causing a substantial fluctuation of ROI value. The four distinct stages in the product life cycle are illustrated in Exhibit 5–14. These stages can be summarized as follows:

- *Stage 1—Introduction.* This stage is characterized by heavy expenditures, slow growth, and low profits.
- *Stage 2—Growth.* This stage is characterized by a rapid increase in sales and profits.
- *Stage 3—Maturity.* This stage is characterized by a stabilized and sometimes declining level of sales and profits.
- *Stage 4—Decline.* This stage is characterized by a rapid decrease in sales and profits.

Another important element which is usually evaluated during the business analysis stage is the payback period. The **payback period** is defined as the number of years required to recover the initial cash invested in new product development. This period can be calculated as follows:

Exhibit 5–14

The Product Life Cycle

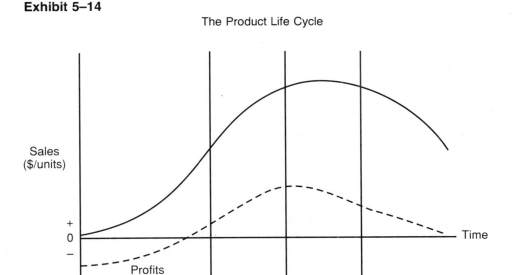

SOURCE: Reprinted by permission of the publisher from "Product Life Cycle: A Literature Review," by David R. Rink and John E. Swan, *Journal of Business Research*, 1979, p. 222. Copyright 1979 by Elsevier Science Publishing Co., Inc.

$$\text{Payback period (in years)} = \frac{\text{Total investment into the project}}{\text{Annual net cash inflow}}$$

The payback period should be determined in conjunction with the expected product life cycle period. Thus, for example, if the total investment into the project is $150,000, it can be recovered in three years if the additional annual net cash inflow generated by the project is as follows:

Year 1	$ 10,000
Year 2	$ 50,000
Year 3	$ 90,000
Total	$150,000

The next step, product development, represents a combined effort of the marketing and engineering departments. This process, consisting of several stages that were discussed in Part 4, can be summarized as follows:

1. Product conception
2. Feasibility study
3. Preliminary design
4. Prototype construction
5. Prototype test
6. Final design
7. Pre-production test

The last element of product development, the pre-production test, leads to the beginning of the market testing procedure. The primary purpose of this procedure is to introduce the new product in limited geographic areas to establish whether the product should be introduced to a larger market. The market testing of the new product will accomplish several major objectives. First, management will gain detailed information and experience with the product before entering into larger markets and committing additional funds. All potential problems that relate to the new product are expected to be identified at this stage. Second, market testing helps to measure the customers' response to the new product and to identify possible inefficiencies in product application. Third, market testing is instrumental in assessing the competitors' influence on the potential success or failure of the new product. Finally, market testing assists the company's management in preparing accurate sales projections for the new products.

The last stage, commercialization of the product in the marketplace, requires maximum coordination of the company's functional abilities. Particular cooperation should be demonstrated by marketing, manufacturing, and distribution departments. Commercialization of new products usually requires a substantial investment in advertising and promotion, distribution of free samples, and other incentives. The performance of new distribution channels should be monitored on a continuous basis, and all inefficiencies identified and eliminated.

Development of new products may sometimes prove to be an expensive and lengthy exercise for a organization. In fact, many organizations do not develop their own products but instead acquire designs of new products from other sources. This process is known as **licensing,** and it offers the company several advantages:

- It saves time and money at the design stage.
- It allows the company to introduce a proven product into the marketplace.

- It reduces the financial risk to a minimum.
- It provides an opportunity to serve customers in a competitive market environment.

Another method of acquiring the right to offer newly developed products is known as **franchising**. By this method the original designer, or *franchisier*, allows other organizations, *franchisors*, to sell newly-developed products in various geographic locations under a *franchise agreement*.

Most firms develop a number of products to meet the requirements of their customers. One of the functions of the marketing manager is to establish a suitable product mix and to monitor the profitability of product lines. The more profitable product lines should receive stronger support and further development, and the less profitable lines should be phased out and replaced by new products.

5.08 Pricing Strategy

Price can be defined as the value assigned to the utility one receives from products or services. Usually, the price is the amount of money that is given up to acquire a specific quantity of goods or services.[18]

The concept of price is an integral part of the **product-for-money exchange process** and is an inherent part of marketing management. All parties involved in the exchange process are expected to establish a suitable price for products or services in order to satisfy both buyer and seller. The buyer must feel that the price paid for products or services is a fair one. The seller, on the other hand, must believe that the price received from the buyer is sufficient to cover the initial expense and produce profit commensurate with the risk involved.

Price is an important tool for allocating products or services in the marketplace. Only if buyers feel that they are getting a good deal will the product or service be purchased. The "right price" concept can therefore be an effective marketing tool that determines who purchases what. Moreover, price determines what will be produced by the sellers and regulates the quantity of products or services purchased by the buyers.

Price is one of the four-P elements of the marketing mix: product, price, promotion, place (distribution). Hence, **price setting,** or **pricing,** represents one of the critical tasks in the marketing management process. Some studies indicate that pricing is considered the most important marketing variable.

Management uses several methods to price products or services. Some of these methods have been discussed in detail in Part 3 (Volume I). Although manufacturers do consider basic costs, potential demand, and competitive prices charged for similar products or services, the ultimate pricing procedure must combine seasoned executive judgement and an analytical approach.

The price-setting procedure in a small or medium-sized organization requires coordination of efforts of marketing, production, and financial personnel. Pricing of products or services must be carried out in accordance with the overall financial and marketing objectives of the company. Pricing may present a problem in certain types of situations such as:

- The price must be set for the first time. This happens when a new product is being developed and introduced into the market.

- The price must be changed in accordance with trading circumstances. This may be a result of increased costs, inflation, or a change in the product demand, or it may be initiated by the competition.
- The price must be set for several products. This is frequently required when the company is producing various product lines that have interrelated manufacturing and distribution costs.

The main objective of the pricing strategy is to determine a suitable price and price fluctuation through time in order to support the product in the marketplace and to meet the sales and profit objectives of the organization. Most firms establish their **pricing strategy** in accordance with one of the following factors:

- **Cost.** The price is determined on the basis of the total manufacturing or service cost plus a profit markup.
- **Demand.** The price is established in accordance with a particular need for the product in the marketplace.
- **Competition.** The price is established in accordance with the going market rate.

Cost represents one of the basic parameters used throughout the ordinary pricing procedure. All costs have been classified in Part 3 as either **direct costs** and **indirect costs** (refer to Exhibit 3–59). The actual pricing of products or services is normally carried out by financial personnel using information provided by the production and marketing departments.

From the strategic marketing point of view, the pricing strategy is particularly important when new products are introduced into the marketplace. Three basic types of pricing strategies may be adopted at this stage by the marketing manager.[19] These strategies are:

1. Penetration pricing
2. Meet-the-competition pricing
3. Price-skimming

Penetration pricing strategy is the strategy of entering into the market with new products at the lowest possible prices. This will allow the company to capture a significant portion of the existing market and to attract valuable customers. Since the low price means lower profit margins for the company, it may discourage competitors from entering the market. Low pricing of products can be used as a prime advantage, provided, of course, that the quality is maintained on an acceptable level. Once the company is successful in establishing itself in the marketplace, the price should be adjusted and raised accordingly. The price increase, however, should not exceed the price level imposed by competitors. At a later stage, if circumstances allow, the price could be increased more in order to maximize the company's level of profitability. Many organizations, small and large, use the penetration pricing strategy as an effective tool in developing a strong business momentum and opening additional markets for their products.

Meet-the-competition strategy directs that new products enter the marketplace at the existing price level established by competitors. In order to ensure successful implementation of this strategy, it is necessary to offer additional advantages to potential customers. Such advantages, for example, could be a simplified functional application, improved quality, or reduced weight of a particular product. All additional benefits should be clearly explained to potential customers and used to stimulate new business in the competitive environment. Once the company is successful in implementing the meet-the-competition strategy, the price of products could be adjusted in order to maximize the level of profitability. The price adjustment, however, should be carried out with particular care to ensure that the company's market share is maintained.

Price-skimming strategy prescribes the use of a high price for new products in a developing market environment. This strategy is frequently used by manufacturers who are the first to introduce a brand new product into the market. The prime purpose of the price-skimming strategy is to maximize the profits from the very beginning while there is no competition in the marketplace. If the new product proves to be a success, the company should expect competition in the future. In the meantime, however, the company should attempt to sell as many products as possible and accumulate additional funds. These funds should be used for advertising and promotion to strengthen the company's position in the marketplace. When the product's novelty is gone and other organizations enter the market, it will be necessary to lower the price and to ensure that the company's market share is maintained. Price-skimming is considered a safe strategy since the company is constantly reducing the price of a particular product and accommodating the ever-changing needs of customers.

Another aspect of pricing strategy relates to discounts which are frequently offered to selected customers. A **discount** is a reduction in a defined selling price. Different types of discounts can be offered to customers. They can focus, for example, on:

- Customers who buy large quantities of products
- Customers who buy on a regular basis
- Customers who settle their accounts within a predetermined period of time
- Customers who pay cash
- Customers who bring other customers

In order to accommodate different situations in a competitive business environment, it is essential to develop a suitable **discount structure**. Several types of discounts should be considered by the marketing manager. These types are:

- Trade discounts
- Quantity discounts
- Cash discounts
- Promotional discounts

A **trade discount** is a reduction in a nominal list price which is offered to regular customers. A **list price** or **suggested retail price** is the final price attached to a particular product or service. Regular customers usually expect a trade discount, which is determined by the supplier. Manufacturers, for instance, may publish a standard list price that includes several trade discounts. These discounts are normally granted to wholesalers and retailers, depending upon the function they perform. Manufacturers often use a **chain discount**, or a series of trade discounts offered to customers. For example, if the product's list price is $50 per unit and the chain discount is "40/20," this means that:

The wholesaler's price to a retailer is
$100 − 0.40 × $100 = $60 per unit

The manufacturer's price to a wholesaler is
$60 - 0.20 \times $60 = 48 per unit

A **quantity discount** is a reduction of the purchase price based on the quantity of purchased products, measured either in units or dollars. Quantity discount is applied on a noncumulative or cumulative basis. A **noncumulative quantity discount** can be applied only to individual purchases. For example, a supplier may offer a 1 percent discount on the purchase of 10,000 units and a 2 percent discount on the purchase of 20,000 units. Noncumulative quantity discounts usually stimulate customers to place larger orders on a less frequent basis. This in turn helps reduce the supplier's administration, production, and distribution costs.

A **cumulative quantity discount**, conversely, can be applied to the total volume of business placed by a particular customer during a specific period of time, usually one year. A typical structure of this discount is illustrated in Exhibit 5–15.

Cumulative quantity discount does not encourage customers to place larger orders, so it causes higher administrative, production, and distribution costs. It does, however, stimulate customer loyalty and development of friendly customer-supplier relations.

A **cash discount** is a reduction in the purchase price when a bill is paid on time. Cash discounts are usually offered to customers in addition to any trade or quantity discounts. For example, a manufacturer may quote "2/30, net 60" terms to a customer. This means that the customer can deduct 2 percent of the purchase price if the invoice is paid within 30 days from the issue date. Otherwise, the full price must be paid within 60 days. Although 2 percent may appear insignificant at first, cash discounts should not be disregarded. If the invoice is paid within 60 days, this results in borrowing an amount equal to the purchase price at: (60 days $-$ 30 days) $\times$ 2 percent $\times$ 12 months = 24 percent per year.

It is advisable, therefore, for management to take full advantage of cash discounts, since they may help reduce the overall cost of purchases. Sellers, on the other hand, are also encouraged to offer significant cash discounts to customers in order to improve their cash flow.

A **promotional discount** is an allowance to customers for promoting new products or services. Manufacturers, for example, may use promotional discounts when launching new products in the marketplace. This gives wholesalers and retailers an additional incentive to market new products. Promotional discounts may also be offered in other forms, such as additional price reduction, free samples, or display materials. The magnitude of these discounts is normally determined by a marketing manager well in advance, according to promotional strategy.

Exhibit 5–15

Cumulative Quantity Discount

Annual purchase volume ($ 000)	Discount Percentage
10– 50	0.5
50–100	1.0
100–150	1.5
150–200	2.0

5.09 Promotional Strategy

One of the important functions of the marketing manager is to develop an effective promotional strategy and to inform the market about products or services offered by a company. **Promotional strategy** is that portion of an organization's overall marketing strategy designed to communicate the nature of the organization and its market offerings to the marketplace, usually through a set of activities.[20]

Promotional strategy helps management educate the market about the company's product or service, its purpose, qualities, and price. This information is usually introduced to target customers by advertising, personal selling, packaging, public relations, and sales promotion. The main purpose of these elements, known as the **communication** or **promotional mix**, is to develop a clear corporate identity for the company and to gain additional confidence and goodwill from the particular segment of the market. The overall development of a promotional strategy entails eight important tasks, which are summarized in Exhibit 5–16.

Several factors should be considered during the promotional strategy development process. These factors are:

- *Promotional resources.* These resources are usually allocated during the regular budgeting process and their size strongly depends upon the company's overall financial capabilities.
- *Nature of products.* All products have been classified earlier as consumer goods and industrial goods. Consumer goods are offered for sale to the general public and their promotion requires heavy advertising in the marketplace. These goods are usually low-priced and thus represent a lower risk to customers. Industrial goods, conversely, are generally high-priced and require more personal selling than consumer ones.
- *Product life-cycle stage.* All products undergo different stages during their life-cycle period. These stages include product introduction, growth, maturity, and decline in the marketplace. Each stage, in turn, requires development of a particular marketing mix as described in Exhibit 5–17.
- *Nature of the market.* Various characteristics of the market influence the development of a particular promotional strategy. Consumer markets, for example, are usually spread in different geographic locations and require a strong advertising and publicity campaign. Industrial markets, on the other hand, are generally concentrated in specially-allocated areas, thus making personal selling easier.

The marketing manager must evaluate the influence of the aforementioned factors and establish the overall direction of the promotional strategy as follows:

- **Push strategy.** The prime purpose of this strategy is to stimulate each member of the distribution network to carry and promote the product. Push strategy requires heavy personal selling in the marketplace and is frequently used by industrial and commercial organizations.
- **Pull strategy.** The prime purpose of this strategy is to stimulate the consumers' demand for the product, thereby creating a profitable environment for resellers. Pull strategy is based on heavy advertising in selected market segments to promote consumer goods.

Exhibit 5–16

Development of a Promotional Strategy

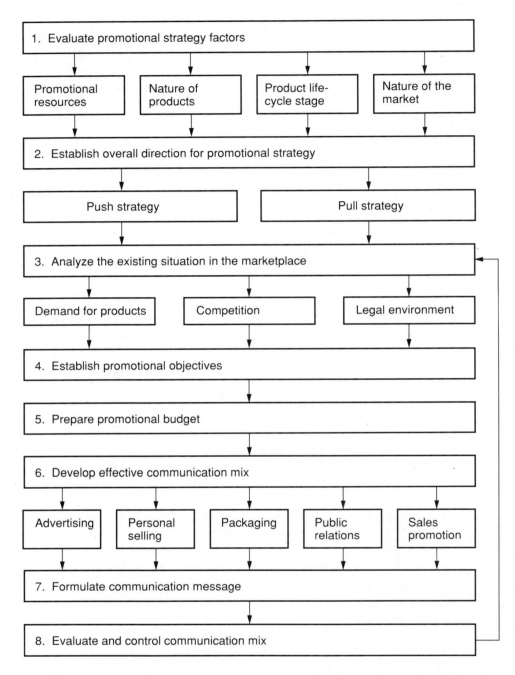

The next stage of promotional strategy development requires a detailed examination of the existing situation in the marketplace. The three prime elements of situation analysis are:

- Demand for products in the marketplace
- Existing and potential competition
- Legal environment

Situation analysis helps the marketing manager establish suitable promotional objectives that should be pursued by the company in the marketplace. Naturally, such objectives must be established in conjunction with the company's overall

Exhibit 5–17

Promotional Strategy During the Product Life Cycle

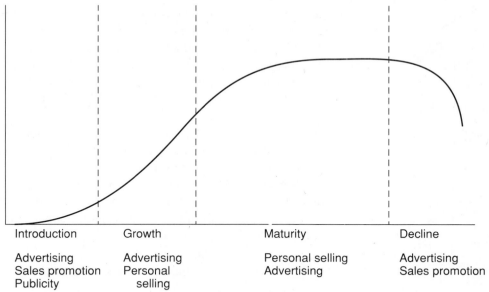

Introduction	Growth	Maturity	Decline
Advertising	Advertising	Personal selling	Advertising
Sales promotion	Personal	Advertising	Sales promotion
Publicity	selling		

SOURCE: Paul S. Busch and Michael J. Houston, *Marketing: Strategic Foundations* (Homewood, IL: Richard D. Irwin, 1985), p. 635. Reprinted with permission.

corporate strategy for a specific trading period. Examples of specific promotional objectives may include penetrating five additional market segments within six months or doubling market awareness for existing product lines within one year.

The ultimate effectiveness of a promotional strategy developed by the company depends upon its existing financial capabilities. This in turn imposes certain limitations on a preliminary promotional budget prepared by a marketing manager. There are several practical methods commonly used to decide on the suitable size of a particular budget. Some of these methods are:

- **Percentage of sales method.** The amount of promotional expenditure is budgeted at a specified percentage rate of total planned volume of sales.
- **Competition matching method.** The value of the promotional expenditure is determined in accordance with similar dollar amounts spent by the company's competitors.
- **Affordable value method.** The value of the promotional expenditure is established in accordance with specific financial abilities of the company.
- **Objective and task method.** Promotional expenditure is budgeted in accordance with the specific tasks that promotion is to perform.

Once the promotional budget is prepared, the development of an effective communication mix may begin. This process is influenced by the overall objectives of the organization, the features of the product or service, the type and size of the target market, the type and size of the company, and by its competition.

Advertising, an integral element of the communication mix, plays an important role in the process of promoting the company's offerings and its corporate image. It is used to inform the market media of availability of specific products and services, their application, features, price, and conditions of purchase. One important task of the marketing manager is to develop a suitable advertising program in selected target markets. Preparation of the advertising program requires a detailed examination of the following issues known as the **five M's of advertising**:

1. *M—Money.* How much should be spent for complete advertising program?
2. *M—Message.* What should be said by the advertiser?
3. *M—Media.* What advertising media should be used?
4. *M—Motion.* How should the advertising be introduced?
5. *M—Measurement.* What results should be expected from the advertisement and how should they be measured?

It is important to ensure that the company's advertising efforts are effectively introduced to the selected market media and the appropriate results are timely measured by the marketing manager.

Personal selling, in contrast to advertising, entails face-to-face communication of promotional information from a seller to a potential customer. Personal selling is a key feature of a push promotional strategy and it offers several important advantages to the company. Some of these advantages are:

- High flexibility of the personal selling effort is possible in selected market segments.
- Immediate feedback is provided by potential customers.
- Target markets can be approached with a greater degree of accuracy.
- Instant sales and cash receipts can be generated.
- Additional services may be provided by salespeople during routine sales calls.
- Flexible time is available to salespeople during face-to-face communication with potential customers.

Personal selling is an integral part of the overall sales management process and is discussed in detail later in this part.

Packaging is another important element of the communication mix. Packaging is often viewed as an extension of the physical product. The promotional impact of packaging comes mainly from the use of special wrapping materials, lettering, coloring, and illustrations. The prime purpose of an effective package design is to transmit a persuasive and informational message to generate interest and convince potential customers to buy. The packaging method has particular promotional significance in consumer goods marketing. As a result of effective packaging, consumer goods are expected to generate a better shelf impact and thus attract more potential buyers. Packaging is also used to symbolize a **brand**—a unique name, sign, symbol, or design of a particular product.

Public relations (PR) is also an important element of the marketing mix. PR is an essential management function designed to promote the image of the company and its products in the marketplace. PR duties in small and medium-sized organizations are usually performed by several executive managers as part of their ordinary functional responsibilities. In addition to developing PR activities, management should attempt whenever possible to obtain publicity in the marketplace. **Publicity** is a free message about an organization and appears in the mass media (e.g., newspaper, TV, or radio). Publicity is of particular importance to any organization because it helps to promote its image and products in a more believable way in the marketplace. It centers around newsworthy developments or activities in the company.

Sales promotion is the last important element of the marketing mix. American Marketing Association has defined sales promotion as:

> Those activities other than personal selling, advertising, and publicity that stimulate consumer purchasing and dealer effectiveness, such as displays, shows and exhibitions, demonstrations, and various nonrecurrent selling efforts not in the ordinary routine.[21]

The prime purpose of most promotions is to provide additional support to the company's products in the marketplace. Sales promotion is particularly important when new products are being introduced to potential customers or when failing products are being supported. Various types of sales promotion methods are used by manufacturers, wholesalers, and retailers. These types, summarized in Exhibit 5–18, differ by source and target.

Once all elements of an effective communication mix have been developed, the marketing manager should formulate a suitable communication message. The primary purpose of the **communication message** is to summarize the promotional information concerning a company and its products and to transmit this information to the marketplace. Since various messages can be transmitted through different elements of the communication mix, such messages should be properly coordinated by the marketing manager.

Finally, it is necessary to evaluate the effect of promotional strategy adopted by the company and to ensure continuous control over all elements of the communication mix. **Information feedback** related to advertising, personal selling, packaging, public relations, and sales promotion should be incorporated into the management of promotion.

The ultimate measure for judging success or failure of the promotional strategy is sales. However, it is often difficult to identify the individual contributors toward the overall promotional effort. It is important, therefore, that the marketing manager constantly monitors the effect of the promotional program on the company's performance and accumulates relevant experience.

Exhibit 5–18

Type of Sales Promotion Categorized by Source and Target

		Target		
Source	**Consumer**	**Organizational Users**	**Wholesalers**	**Retailers**
Manufacturers	Free samples Coupons Introducing low price Cash rebates Premiums Contests and sweepstakes	User brochures Design guides Product premiums Gifts Trade shows	Buying allowances Contests Trade shows	Buying allowances Contests Advertising and display allowances Trade shows
Wholesalers		Buying allowances		Buying allowances
Retailers	Coupons Contests Gifts Trading stamps			

SOURCE: Paul S. Busch and Michael J. Houston, *Marketing: Strategic Foundations* (Homewood, IL: Richard D. Irwin, 1985), p.631. Reprinted with permission.

5.10 Distribution Strategy

Development of a suitable **distribution strategy** is another important function of the marketing manager.[22] Every organization uses a number of alternative methods to distribute products in the marketplace. The channels of distribution vary from direct selling to consumers to utilizing one or more intermediaries. A **channel of distribution** is a set of interdependent organizations involved in the process of making a product or service available for use or consumption.[23]

Different types of organizations are involved in the distribution of products in the marketplace. These organizations, known as **intermediaries,** include wholesalers, distributors, agents, and retailers. Characteristics of these organizations are summarized in Exhibit 5–19. Intermediaries are used in the distribution process for several reasons, the most important of which is that they facilitate bringing the products into the marketplace. Without intermediaries, this function would have been performed by manufacturers, imposing additional difficulty on the distribution process.

Intermediaries play a highly visible role in an effective distribution process. These include organizations or individuals specializing in particular lines of products or operating in well-defined market segments. Throughout the process of their work, intermediaries establish strong personal contacts in the marketplace and learn to understand specific market requirements. This in turn facilitates a

Exhibit 5–19

Definitions and Characteristics of Common Intermediaries

Intermediary	Definition	Distinguishing Characteristics
Retailer	Merchant, or occasionally an agent, whose main business is selling directly to ultimate consumer	Size of units in which retailer sells is incidental rather than a primary element in character; sells typically to ultimate consumer
Wholesaler	Business unit that buys and resells merchandise to retailers and other merchants or to industrial, institutional, and commercial users	Many operate on a very small scale and in small lots; habitually sell for resale; do not sell in significant amounts to ultimate consumers; significant portion of sales to industrial users
Industrial Distributor	Merchant engaged primarily in selling industrial goods	Specialized types include metal warehouses, which handle about 20 percent of total steel tonnage; operates on the differential between mill prices for standard lots and smaller quantities and mill supply houses that handle as many as 20,000 items in 600 product lines
Manufacturer's Agent	An agent who generally operates on an extended contractual basis; often sells within an exclusive territory; handles noncompeting but related lines	May be authorized to sell a definite portion of the output of principals represented; also known as manufacturer's representative
Sales Agent	Intermediary in title-passing process, characterized by responsibility for disposing of principal's entire output on an extended contractual basis	The only functional intermediary frequently involved in financing the principal
Rack Jobber	A limited-function wholesaler who supplies merchandise and sets up displays	Receives payment only for items sold; usually puts merchandise in retail stores on a consignment basis; provides special services of selective brand and item merchandising; most prevalent in food business
Facilitating Agent	Performs or assists in performance of one or several marketing functions	Neither takes title to goods nor negotiates purchase of sales; includes bankers, graders, inspectors, advertisers, marketing researchers, packers, shippers

SOURCES: Irving J. Shapiro, *Marketing Terms*, 3rd ed. (West Long Branch, NJ: S-M-C Publishing, 1969); Reprinted with permission, *Marketing Definitions: A Glossary of Marketing Terms*, compiled by the Committee on Definitions of the American Marketing Association, 1960, American Marketing Association, Chicago, IL.

more efficient exchange process between manufacturers and consumers. In addition, intermediaries perform sorting and searching functions for manufacturers. The **sorting function** includes the following activities:

1. *Sorting out* is breaking down a heterogeneous supply into separate stocks that are more homogeneous, as in the grading of agricultural products.
2. *Accumulation* is the bringing of similar stocks together into a larger homogeneous supply.
3. *Allocation* is breaking a homogeneous supply into smaller lots. At the wholesaler level, this allocation process is known as "breaking bulk": wholesalers take carload lots and then break them down into smaller units to be sold to retailers.
4. *Assorting* is building up an array of products for use in association with each other. Wholesalers build assortments of goods for retailers. Retailers build assortments for their customers.[24]

The **searching function** entails constant movement of intermediaries in the marketplace with the objective of identifying and qualifying the exact requirements of prospective customers. This results in an improved customer-market intelligence level and facilitates a more effective process of distributing goods and services.

Different types of marketing channels are used by producers of goods or services for distribution purposes. These channels are usually categorized as:

- Consumer channels
- Industrial channels

Consumer channels include all channels of distribution that can be used by producers in making goods or services available to the consumer market. Four commonly used types of consumer channels, (A, B, C, and D), are illustrated in Exhibit 5–20.

The first type, *Channel A (producer-consumer)*, represents the simplest way of distributing goods or services to consumers. This is a direct marketing method and does not require intermediaries at all. This method is particularly useful when producers distribute highly perishable products (e.g., food stuffs,

Exhibit 5–20

Basic Channels of Distribution for Consumer Products

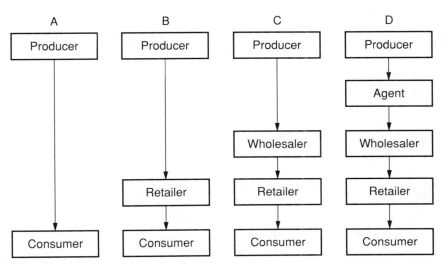

SOURCE: Paul S. Busch and Michael J. Houston, *Marketing: Strategic Foundations* (Homewood, IL: Richard D. Irwin, 1985), p. 458. Reprinted with permission.

flowers) or provide services that require personal attention (e.g., plumbers, accountants, lawyers). Probably one of the best-known direct marketing methods is offering products to prospective customers through mail. This method has become particularly popular in recent years.

The second type, *Channel B (producer-retailer-consumer)*, entails distribution of products to consumers through specialized retailers. This is the shortest indirect marketing method and requires only one intermediary. Different manufacturers, for example, use retailers to supply their products directly to consumers. Some manufacturers go even further and develop their own network of retail outlets in a particular geographic area.

The third type, *Channel C (producer-wholesaler-retailer-consumer)*, represents one of the most popular methods of distribution in the marketplace. This method enables manufacturers to sell their products to wholesalers in large quantities at a minimal promotional and distribution expense. Manufacturers can expect prompt settlement of accounts by wholesalers who finance, in part, the entire distribution process. Wholesalers usually specialize in particular product lines (e.g., furniture, appliances, jewelry) and obtain the merchandise from different manufacturers. Retailers also rely on wholesalers that can provide them with products that can be purchased in small quantities, with transportation, and with favorable credit terms.

The fourth type, *Channel D (producer-agent-wholesaler-retailer-consumer)*, represents an expensive method of product distribution. Nevertheless, this method is frequently used by producers that have a narrow product line and target a widely-dispersed market. For example, if a manufacturer from the East Coast wants to sell goods in California, he should look for a local agent that may have all the necessary contacts.

Industrial channels include all channels of distribution that can be used by producers in making goods and services available to the industrial market. Three types of industrial channels, (E, F, G), illustrated in Exhibit 5–21, are commonly used.

The first type, *Channel E (producer-industrial user)*, enables producers to distribute their goods or services directly to industrial users. Many manufacturers, for example, employ salespeople who serve specific market segments and maintain contacts with customers. The direct distribution approach is particularly effective for small and medium-sized manufacturers that wish to maintain a

Exhibit 5–21

Basic Channels of Distribution for Industrial Products

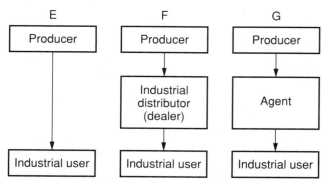

SOURCE: Paul S. Busch and Michael J. Houston, *Marketing: Strategic Foundations* (Homewood, IL: Richard D. Irwin, 1985), p. 459. Reprinted with permission.

strong presence in a defined market area and generate an additional volume of business. Customers may also benefit from a direct marketing approach, particularly when purchasing technical products or services.

The second type, *Channel F (producer-industrial-distributor/dealer-industrial user),* is similar to type C (producer-wholesaler-retailer-consumer) discussed earlier. This type of distribution is particularly useful for larger manufacturers that produce a narrow range of products on a flow production basis (e.g., steel, timber, chemicals, or textile). Industrial distributors act as wholesalers, purchase large quantities of industrial products from manufacturers, and promptly settle the outstanding accounts. Since distributors purchase materials from several manufacturers, they are able to offer a broad range of specialized product lines to their customers. In addition, industrial distributors provide warehousing, transportation, distribution, and credit facilities. Customers, on the other hand, are in a position to purchase all required materials in small quantities and at short notice. This in turn allows industrial buyers to minimize investment in inventory and to reduce storage space requirements.

The third type, *Channel G (producer-agent-industrial user),* is also frequently used by producers. This method is particularly useful for small and medium-sized manufacturers that wish to introduce new products into the market. Agents may provide several advantages to manufacturers since they already have established contacts in the marketplace. In contrast to industrial distributors, agents do not take title to merchandise nor do they offer warehousing, transportation, or credit facilities to customers. Agents merely link the manufacturers with customers and charge a commission for their services. One advantage of working with agents is that manufacturers can offer their products to customers at a lower price. Since agents usually handle a limited number of product lines on behalf of several manufacturers, they put substantial effort into the promotional activity. Sometimes, however, manufacturers are not able to maintain effective control over their agents' promotional activities. This in turn may result in poor coordination in the overall marketing and sales efforts and can subsequently force manufacturers to switch to the Channel E distribution method.

It is apparent that a variety of distribution channels are available for selection by the marketing manager. In order to develop the most suitable channel of distribution, it is necessary to examine the existing situation regarding the company's products, consumers' needs, competition, and legal requirement. Basic questions regarding consumer or industrial buying behavior must be answered:

1. How many buyers are there in the target market and where are they located?
2. What changes are occurring in purchasing patterns for the product?
3. When and where is the product purchased?
4. Where and how is the product consumed or used?
5. How much effort will the consumer expend in the search for the product?
6. What are the buyer's needs before, during and after the sale for technical and product information?[25]

Once all relevant questions have been answered, the marketing manager must select the most suitable channel of distribution and develop appropriate marketing objectives. The next step entails assessment of all relevant costs and preparation of a distribution budget. Finally, the selected method of product distribution should be implemented as an integral part of the company's activities and its performance should be monitored on a continuous basis.

5.11 Marketing Plan

One of the most important functions of the marketing manager is to formulate a suitable **marketing plan** to promote the company's products or services. Such a plan is particularly important for several reasons:

- It serves as a road map and helps management to progress from one point to another in the process of implementing planned actions and achieving desired results.
- It helps management to monitor and control planned activities and measure achieved results.
- It informs each member of the marketing team of individual responsibilities in various areas of marketing and sales management.
- It helps to allocate company resources to all elements of the marketing mix to obtain the most effective results.
- It helps to identify opportunities for new products or services, existing and potential problems in the marketplace, and threats created by competition.

William A. Cohen suggests that knowledge of marketing plans is not an option for marketing managers, but a requirement. Every marketing manager must not only understand and have working knowledge of marketing plans, but must also be able to develop and implement them.[26] Operational marketing plans are usually classified as:

- The new product plan
- Annual marketing plan

It is necessary to develop a **new product plan** when the company intends to introduce new products or services into the market. In fact, such a plan must be completed even before the development of a product plan is undertaken. A new product plan usually presents numerous difficulties to marketing managers since historical information is unavailable. This plan, therefore, is based on logical assumptions and common knowledge related to similar products and their performance in the marketplace.

The **annual marketing plan**, on the other hand, usually represents an easier task because previous information related to product performance is available to the marketing manager. The annual marketing plan normally starts with a comprehensive evaluation of past results and examination of appropriate trends in the marketplace. A detailed situation analysis enables the marketing manager to examine the performance of a particular product or service, to understand customer requirements, to evaluate competitors' threats, and to identify new opportunities in the marketplace.

Marketing plans must be prepared and summarized in accordance with the particular requirements and objectives of the organization. The structure of such a plan may include a number of issues that are outlined in Exhibit 5–22. The marketing plan development process requires strong cooperation among all members of the company management team. This is particularly important since the marketing plan provides the foundation for the company's overall planning and budgeting activities. Some of these activities have been discussed earlier in Part 3 (Volume I). A typical marketing planning procedure entails a number of steps which are summarized in Exhibit 5–23.

Exhibit 5–22

Marketing Plan Outline

Marketing Plan Outline

Executive Summary: *Overview of the entire plan, including a description of the product or service, the differential advantage, the required investment, and the anticipated sales and profits*

Table of contents

I. *Introduction:* What is the product and why will it be successful at this time?

II. *Situation Analysis*

1. The Situational Environment

1.01 Demand and demand trends: What is the forecast demand for the product? Is it growing or declining? Who are the decision makers, the purchase agents? How, when, where, what, and why do they buy?

1.02 Social and cultural factors

1.03 Demographics

1.04 Economic and business conditions for this product at this time in the geographical area selected

1.05 State of technology for this class of product: Is it high-tech state of the art? Are newer products succeeding older ones frequently (very short life cycle)? In short, how is technology affecting this product or service?

1.06 Politics: Do politics, current or otherwise, in any way affect the situation for marketing this product?

1.07 Laws and regulations: What laws or regulations are applicable here?

2. The Neutral Environment

2.01 Financial environment: How does the availability or nonavailability of funds affect the situation?

2.02 Government environment: Will legislative action or anything else currently going on in state, federal, or local government be likely to affect marketing of this product or service?

2.03 Media environment: What's happening in the media? Does current publicity favor or disfavor this project?

2.04 Special interest environment: Aside from direct competitors, are any influential groups likely to affect the plans?

3. The Competitor Environment

3.01 Describe the main competitors and their products, plans, experience, know-how, financial, human and capital resources, suppliers, and strategy. Do they enjoy any favor or disfavor with the customer? If so, why? What marketing channels do competitors use? What are the compeitors' strengths and weaknesses?

4. The Company Environment

4.01 Describe the product, experience, know-how, financial, human and capital resources, and suppliers. Does it enjoy any favor or disfavor with the customer? If so, why? What are its strengths and weaknesses?

III. *The Target Market*

1. Describe the target market segment in detail using demographics, psychographics, geographics, life style, or whatever segmentation is appropriate.

IV. *Problems and Opportunities*

1. State or restate each opportunity and indicate why it is, in fact, an opportunity. State or restate every problem and indicate what can be done about each problem.

V. *Marketing Objectives and Goals*

1. Precisely state marketing objectives in terms of sales volume, market share, return on investment, or other objectives for the marketing plan.

VI. *Marketing Strategy*

1. Consider alternatives for overall strategy. Further describe the strategy and how it is being employed. Note what the main competitors are likely to do when this strategy is implemented and what can be done to take advantage of the opportunities created and to avoid the threats.

VII. *Marketing Tactics*

1. State how the chosen marketing strategy(ies) will be implemented in terms of product, price, promotion, distribution, and other tactical or environmental variables.

VIII. *Control and Implementation*

1. Calculate break-even and accomplish a break-even chart for your project. Compute sales projections on a monthly basis for a one-year period. Compute cash flows on a monthly basis for a one-year period. Indicate start-up costs and monthly budget for this period.

IX. *Summary*

1. Summarize advantages, costs, and profits, and clearly state the differential advantages that your plan for this product or service offers over the competition and why the plan will succeed.

X. *Appendices*

1. Include all supporting information that you consider relevant.

SOURCE: Reprinted with permission of Macmillan Publishing Company from *The Practice of Marketing Management: Analysis, Planning and Implementation* by William A. Cohen. Copyright ©1988 by Macmillan Publishing Company.

Exhibit 5–23
The Strategic Marketing Planning Process

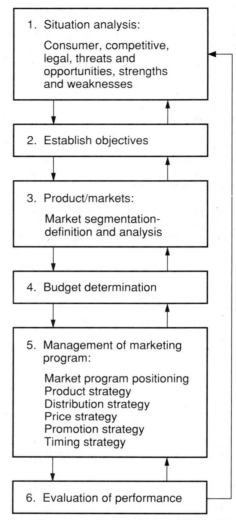

1. Situation analysis:

   Consumer, competitive, legal, threats and opportunities, strengths and weaknesses

2. Establish objectives

3. Product/markets:

   Market segmentation-definition and analysis

4. Budget determination

5. Management of marketing program:

   Market program positioning
   Product strategy
   Distribution strategy
   Price strategy
   Promotion strategy
   Timing strategy

6. Evaluation of performance

SOURCE: Paul S. Busch and Michael J. Houston, *Marketing: Strategic Foundations* (Homewood, IL: Richard D. Irwin, 1985), p. 765. Reprinted with permission.

Since the development of a marketing plan represents a critical element of overall planning activities, it is essential to make such plans as effective as possible. Some of the factors that should be considered at this stage are summarized as follows:[27]

1. Senior managers should participate in all stages of planning, especially the early stages.
2. Product managers and others who have the ultimate responsibility for the marketing plans should be kept informed and should be continually guided by top management and top management staff planners.
3. Individuals ultimately responsible for the marketing plan should be required to get the best inputs from all feasible sources, both internal and external.
4. Line managers responsible for planning should be encouraged to suggest new ideas at the beginning of the planning period before the plan is fixed.
5. Line managers responsible for planning should communicate both horizon-

tally to other organizations as well as up the organization to senior top management.

6. Planning procedures should include methods in which marketing plan development is channeled in directions desired by top management. These may include guidance documents, presentations, and so forth.

7. Marketing plans must be joined with the overall business strategy of the corporation; otherwise, it may contradict this strategy and result in "suboptimization." That is, although the marketing plan in itself is excellent and may succeed, this "success" may harm overall corporate strategy.

8. Marketing plans must reflect the fact of a product's life cycle and not an assumption of arithmetical increase in sales growth.[28,29]

9. Marketing plans must contain contingency provisions and evidence of recognition of multiple scenarios.

Preparation of effective marketing plans represents an ultimate challenge for the marketing manager. The immediate use of these plans starts within the marketing department and helps direct the overall activity of the organization. Successful implementation of marketing plans strongly depends upon the performance of the company's employees, particularly the sales force. This in turn necessitates regular planning of sales activities, effective motivation of sales force, and continuous monitoring of achieved results.

5.12 The Sales Management Process

Implementation of marketing mix strategies regarding product development, pricing, promotion, and distribution represents a central part of a sound marketing plan. This plan requires further development of promotional strategy and control of communication mix. The communication mix components, in turn, consist of advertising, personal selling, packaging, public relations, and sales promotions, as discussed earlier in this part.

Personal selling and sales promotion, the two components of the communication mix, create an underlying need for establishing a sales organization to meet the company's marketing objectives. This, in fact, is the beginning of the **sales management process.** This process entails a number of steps, that are outlined in Exhibit 5–24.

The sales management process starts with the preparation of detailed sales plans and budgets for the forthcoming fiscal period. These must be carefully prepared by the sales manager in accordance with the company's overall marketing objectives, strategies, and plans. Accurate sales plans and budgets provide the company with a key to effective guidance of the sales force and control of their performance.

Once the sales plans and budgets are approved, the sales manager must begin or continue with the process of building an efficient sales organization. The prime purpose of such an organization is to attain the company's objectives by selling its products or services, and thus satisfy customer needs. Since the sales organization is geared to meet customer requirements, it is essential to understand their buying behavior. This in turn helps the sales manager to utilize the sales force in the most effective manner.

Sales force recruitment and selection is the next step in the sales management process. This step is initiated by a thorough analysis of each sales job and preparation of a suitable job description and specification. Next, the sales manager must examine short-term personnel requirements in the sales department and

Exhibit 5–24

Position of Sales Management Process in the Marketing Mix

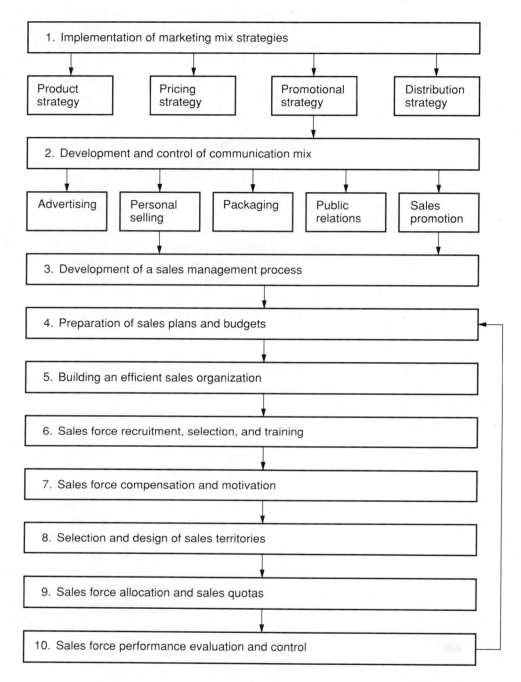

initiate the recruitment of suitable applicants. All applicants should be carefully evaluated in terms of the company's requirements and suitable individuals should be selected. Subsequent to their selection, all new employees must undergo a process of orientation and training. One of the prime objectives of sales force training is to ensure effective implementation of personal selling techniques and sound understanding of industrial buying behavior.

Sales force compensation and motivation represents another important element in the sales management process. Compensation is one of the most important factors that motivate an employee. It is important, therefore, to design a suitable compensation plan that may consist of straight salary or sales commission, or a combination of both. The prime purpose of such a plan is to ensure maximum motivation of the sales force to satisfy the customers' needs in the most efficient manner.

The next step in the sales management process entails evaluation of target markets selected by the company and design of appropriate sales territories. This step is particularly significant because it will enable the sales manager to develop an effective and economical method of servicing all target markets with the existing sales force. All sales territories should be subdivided in the most suitable manner and allocated to individual sales people. Subsequently, the sales manager must prepare sales quotas in accordance with the company's sales budget and allocate them to each member of the sales team. Salespeople in turn will be able to plan their individual activities in pursuing the company's commercial interests.

Sales force performance evaluation represents another important element in the sales management process. The sales manager is required to analyze and evaluate performance of the sales force, the level of sales achieved by various product groups in the marketplace, and the volume of sales generated by various customers. Finally, it is necessary to maintain constant control over sales force performance to ensure that customers receive all required products and services on time and in an acceptable condition.

All information pertaining to company sales performance must be collated on a continuous basis and used as feedback for future sales plans and budgets. This feedback helps management to adjust the planning and budgeting process and ensure maximum flexibility of operational activities. In addition, this information is instrumental in reviewing and modifying the overall marketing strategy, thus contributing to improved future organizational performance.

5.13 Sales Planning and Budgeting

The first important function of the sales manager is to initiate the **sales planning and budgeting process**. This process normally starts with appropriate market analysis, measurement of sales potential, and sales forecasting. All plans should be established in accordance with realistic estimates of the sales volume likely to be achieved during the forthcoming fiscal period.

The process of estimating the **sales potential** for various products has been described earlier in this part. This process represents a part of the market measurement and forecasting procedure, as illustrated in Exhibit 5–11, and can be accomplished by applying one of the following methods:

- Chain-ratio method
- Market-buildup method
- Buying-power-index method

Evaluation of the company's sales potential in selected market segments helps management in preparing more accurate **sales forecasts.** These forecasts provide quantitative estimates of the level of actual sales, expressed in monetary terms, or of units of product to be sold during a specified period of time. The sales forecast is usually prepared on an annual basis, taking into consideration past sales performance, existing market conditions, seasonal fluctuations of the product demand, competition, and other relevant factors.

From this forecast, the financial, production, and personnel departments plan their work and ascertain their needs for the budgeted period. If the sales forecast is too optimistic, the company can sustain substantial losses as a result of an overexpenditure of funds in anticipation of an income level that has not been achieved. If the sales forecast is too low, the company may not be in a position to accommodate all market needs and may subsequently forgo profits and present its competitors with additional sales opportunities.

There are several methods commonly used by managers in preparing sales forecasts. Among these methods are:

• Sales force composite opinion
• Jury of executive opinion
• Survey of buying intentions.

Sales force composite opinion is a popular forecasting method frequently used by sales managers. In accordance with this method, each salesperson is required to prepare individual sales projections for the forthcoming fiscal year and to submit a **detailed sales forecast** to the sales manager. These projections, illustrated in Exhibit 5–25, must be based on realistic sales estimates, taking into consideration past results and future expectations.

Subsequently, all sales projections must be added up in a **summarized sales forecast** to obtain the final forecast of sales volume. This is illustrated in Exhibit

Exhibit 5–25

Detailed Sales Forecast Form

Detailed Sales Forecast										
Period: 1990		Number of calls per year	Previous year sales ($)	Projected increase in sales (%)	Annual sales forecast ($)	Product group breakdown				
Customer	Type of industry					Type A	Type B	Type C	Type D	Type E
ABC, Inc.	1	12	100,000	10	110,000	20,000	40,000	30,000	----	20,000
XYZ, Inc.	2	24	150,000	20	180,000	40,000	60,000	40,000	40,000	----
Total			600,000	15	690,000	120,000	180,000	200,000	100,000	90,000
Salesperson: A.Brown				Approved: C. White					Date: 1.1.90	

5–26. Active participation by each member of the sales team and preparation of the sales forecast by customer, product, and sales territory represent the major advantages of this method.

Jury of executive opinion is another forecasting method commonly used by sales managers. This method is based on sales forecasts prepared by several members of the company's management team. All participating executives prepare a sales forecast using their own judgment. Several factors that are usually considered during this procedure include the nature of the company's products or services, customer requirements, competition, and overall economic conditions in the marketplace. Subsequently, all individual sales projections are evaluated and finally added up. Active participation by the company's executives has proven to be useful in preparing accurate short-term forecasts. This method, however, demands substantial experience and understanding of overall requirements in the marketplace.

Survey of buying intentions can be used as an alternative or an addition to the aforementioned sales forecasting methods. This method entails surveying a sample of customers to determine the types and quantities of products they are likely to buy in the future. These surveys are usually conducted via personal interviews, by phone, or by mail questionnaires. Customer responses are subsequently evaluated and added up to determine the total demand for each product. This method has proven to be useful in preparing sales forecasts for industrial goods in well-defined small market segments. However, it is often a time consuming and expensive method that does not guarantee that interviewed customers will always act according to their original intentions.

Exhibit 5–26

Summarized Sales Forecast Form

Summarized Sales Forecast										
Period: 1990		Number of calls per year	Previous year sales ($)	Projected increase in sales (%)	Annual sales forecast ($)	Product group breakdown				
Salesperson	Number of years in service					Type A	Type B	Type C	Type D	Type E
A. Brown	4	2,000	400,000	15	460,000	60,000	80,000	90,000	140,000	90,000
B. Gray	2	1,700	300,000	15	345,000	40,000	70,000	80,000	70,000	85,000
Total			2,000,000	15	2,300,000	400,000	500,000	600,000	500,000	300,000
Salesperson: C. White				Approved: A. Boss					Date: 1.1.90	

Since most organizations offer a variety of products or services to different customers in a constantly changing market environment, it is often impractical to use only one sales forecasting method. For this reason, sales managers often use a combination of methods and utilize the input from salespeople, executive managers, and customers at the same time.

Once the sales forecasts are prepared and overall sales objectives established, it is necessary to develop a set of appropriate **sales strategies** for the forthcoming fiscal year. These strategies represent the continuation of the marketing strategy previously discussed in this part. Some examples of sales strategies that could be adopted by a sales manager are outlined in Exhibit 5–27.

The next step in the sales planning effort entails evaluation of sales force requirements to meet the company **sales objectives.** The sales manager must assess the overall **sales plan** and decide whether to reduce, maintain, or increase the present number of salespeople. If the number of salespeople must be increased, it is necessary to determine whether to hire new ones or to use outside agents or independent representatives (reps). The use of agents has several advantages:

• Agents already have a network of well-established contacts.
• Agents usually have good experience in their product lines and maintain high standards of work.

Exhibit 5–27

Examples of Sales Strategies

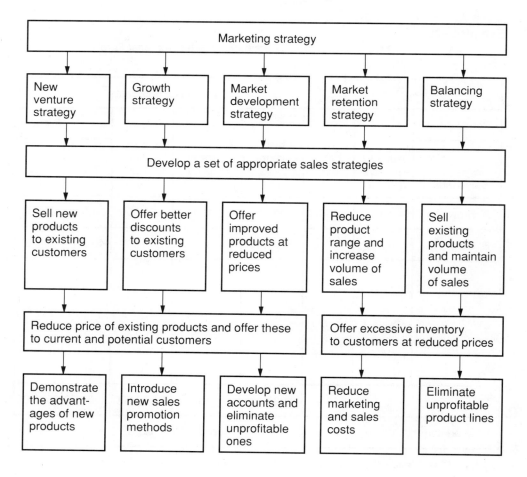

- Agents do not incur administrative costs for a company.
- Agents get paid only if they are successful in selling company products.

One of the prime disadvantages in dealing with agents is that their activities cannot be always effectively controlled by the sales manager. This represents a particular problem since agents plan their own movements in the marketplace. Another option that can be exercised by the sales manager is to hire new salespeople. This option may also present certain benefits which can be summarized as follows:

- Salespeople can be trained according to the company's specific requirements.
- Salespeople can be allocated to defined sales territories, customers, and product lines.
- The performance of salespeople can be planned as part of the overall sales effort.
- The performance of salespeople can be controlled on a regular basis.

Employment of salespeople usually represents a costly exercise. It is essential, therefore, to assess the need for additional sales employees and to estimate the total cost of their employment. Estimation of sales force size entails a number of considerations and may be carried out in several ways. Two methods commonly used by sales managers are:

- "How much can a company afford" method
- "Number of sales calls" method

The **"how much can a company afford" method** is based on matching the number of salespeople at a predetermined average cost-per-employee to a specific sales budget allocation. Consider, for example, a medium-sized company that projects $10 million in sales for the forthcoming fiscal year and allocates 5 percent of its revenue toward sales activities. Assuming that sales supervision requires 20 percent of the sales budget and the total cost of each salesperson is $40,000 per year (including straight salary, commission, and travel allowance), the total number of salespeople can be determined as follows:

Total budgeted revenue from sales	=	$10,000,000
Total sales budget allocation (x 0.05)	=	500,000
Total cost of sales supervision (x 0.2)	=	100,000
Total cost allocated to the sales force		
($500,000 − $100,000)	=	400,000
Total number of salespeople		
(at $40,000 per person per year)	=	10 people

This method has an advantage since all sales costs will remain in line with the company's projected revenues. The main disadvantage, however, is that this method does not account for real needs of customers in the marketplace.

The **"number of sales calls" method,** on the other hand, is designed to develop a sales force in accordance with specific customer needs. This method takes into account the number of existing and potential customers, the average number of sales calls per year required by each customer, the length of each sales call, and the selling time available per salesperson. The size of the sales force can be determined as follows:[30]

$$\text{Number of salespeople} = \frac{\left[\begin{array}{c} \text{Number of} \\ \text{existing} \\ \text{customers} \end{array} + \begin{array}{c} \text{Number of} \\ \text{potential} \\ \text{customers} \end{array}\right] \times \begin{array}{c} \text{Required} \\ \text{sales call} \\ \text{frequency} \end{array} \times \begin{array}{c} \text{Average} \\ \text{length of a} \\ \text{sales call} \end{array}}{\text{Selling time available per salesperson}}$$

Consider, for example, a medium-sized company that has 200 existing customers and plans to open 50 additional new accounts. Assuming that each customer should ideally be called at least once every two months (six times a year), that each sales call requires an average of two hours (including travel time), and that the selling time available per sales person is 1500 hours per year, the size of the sales force can be determined as follows:

$$\text{Number of salespeople} = \frac{(200 + 50) \times 6 \times 2}{1500} = 2 \text{ salespersons}$$

In reality, however, the company's customers usually vary in size and subsequently have different needs. This, in turn, should be translated into an ideal frequency of sales calls per year for each customer. Consider, for example, that the company has 40 large present and potential customers that require 18 calls per year, 100 medium-sized customers that require 12 calls per year, and 110 small customers that require 3 calls per year. Assuming that the average length of each sales call and the selling time per salesperson remain unchanged, the size of the sales force can be determined as follows:

$$\text{Number of salespeople} = \frac{[(40 \times 18) + (100 \times 12) + (110 \times 3)] \times 2}{1500}$$

$$= 3 \text{ salespersons}$$

The "number of sales calls" method enables the sales manager to determine the required size of the company's sales force well in advance in accordance with specific customer needs. One of the drawbacks of this method, however, is its failure to account for income and expenditure associated with different aspects of customer service. Thus, it becomes difficult to establish whether the current frequency of sales calls enables the company to maximize its profits through servicing customers.

Once the size of the sales force is determined, it becomes necessary to decide whether to hire experienced or inexperienced salespeople. Hiring experienced sales personnel enables the company to respond to immediate market demands and to provide better service to customers. However, the high compensation package often required by experienced salespeople may be a deterrent. Inexperienced salespeople, conversely, are usually satisfied with moderate compensation and generally demonstrate substantial flexibility for training purposes. Thus, the final decision regarding the choice of suitable salespeople remains with the sales manager.

The ultimate task of the sales planning process is development of a sound **sales budget**. This budget summarizes all details related to the projected level of company sales throughout the budgeted period; the selling expenditure budget, including salaries and commissions of sales personnel; the advertising budget; and the sales administration budget. All components of the sales budget must be prepared on an annual basis and thereafter divided into monthly targets in accordance with relevant sales projections. The main purpose of the budgetary procedure is to enable the management team to lead its organization toward a predetermined goal and to achieve the desired level of the company's profitability. A typical sales budgeting process is outlined in Exhibit 5–28.

Exhibit 5–28

The Sales Budgeting Process (Steps 1–5)

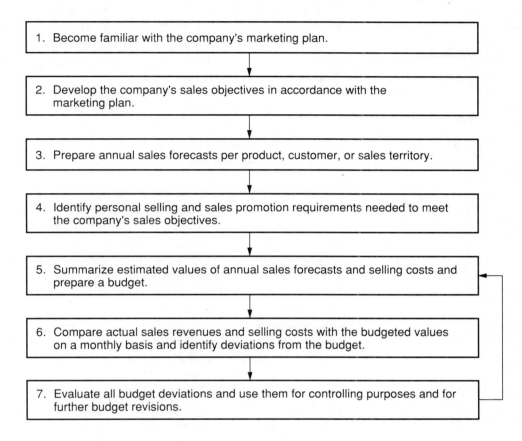

1. Become familiar with the company's marketing plan.

2. Develop the company's sales objectives in accordance with the marketing plan.

3. Prepare annual sales forecasts per product, customer, or sales territory.

4. Identify personal selling and sales promotion requirements needed to meet the company's sales objectives.

5. Summarize estimated values of annual sales forecasts and selling costs and prepare a budget.

6. Compare actual sales revenues and selling costs with the budgeted values on a monthly basis and identify deviations from the budget.

7. Evaluate all budget deviations and use them for controlling purposes and for further budget revisions.

5.14 Sales Organization

The implementation of marketing plans and promotion programs is effected by active selling of products and services in the marketplace. It is essential, therefore, to establish a suitable **sales organization** to meet the relevant marketing objectives of the company. This, in turn, necessitates thorough understanding of fundamental organizational principles in order to obtain desired results for the company.

The sales function does not stand in isolation from other organizational responsibilities. On the contrary, it represents a part of a well-integrated system of functions such as administration, personnel, finance, production, and marketing. In fact, sales represents an integral part of the marketing function. The sales manager, therefore, is responsible for developing an effective sales organization in order to implement all aspects of the company's marketing plan.

The sales organization development process entails creation of a specific pattern of work in which human and material resources can be utilized in the most efficient manner. Thus, the prime task of the sales manager is to develop a suitable organizational structure that will stimulate all employees toward effective performance. Since the development process represents a continuous task that is carried out in a constantly changing environment, it is essential to ensure high flexibility of the sales organization's structure. This is particularly important when a company plans to introduce new products or services into the market, to develop new sales territories, or to establish another branch.

Several basic issues must be considered throughout the sales organization development process. These issues, which have been discussed earlier in Part 1 (Volume I), include the following:

- Delegation of responsibility, authority, and accountability
- Reporting procedure
- Centralization and decentralization of control over sales activities
- Organizational specialization.[31]

All three elements of the organizational structure—**responsibility, authority,** and **accountability**—must be defined, implemented, and properly balanced to ensure effective functioning of the sales organization. The basic elements of the sales organization development process are outlined in Exhibit 5–29.

One important consideration of the sales organization development process is the **unity of command principle**. This principle, discussed earlier in Part 1, suggests that each employee should report to only one person within the organization. It is a general principle that is particularly useful in the sales management environment. When employees report to more than one individual, they may be given contradicting instructions that can, in turn, cause ineffective performance. It is essential, therefore, to prevent such a condition to avoid confusion among sales personnel.

Another issue that should be considered by the sales manager relates to the **span of control**, or the number of subordinates that can be effectively supervised by one manager. The importance of this issue depends upon the size of the sales organization and is particularly critical for larger companies. Small and medium-sized organizations usually employ a moderate number of salespeople and seldom experience problems caused by an excessive span of control.

The sales manager should also consider the issue of **centralization** or **decentralization** of control over the company's sales activities. A small organization normally starts its operations from one office, and management exercises cen-

Exhibit 5–29

Sales Organization Development

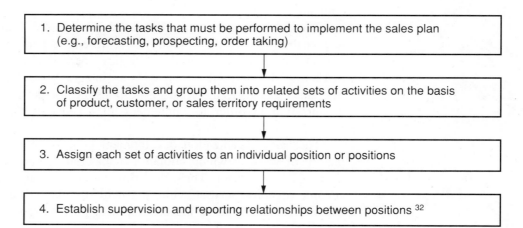

1. Determine the tasks that must be performed to implement the sales plan (e.g., forecasting, prospecting, order taking)

2. Classify the tasks and group them into related sets of activities on the basis of product, customer, or sales territory requirements

3. Assign each set of activities to an individual position or positions

4. Establish supervision and reporting relationships between positions [32]

tralized control over sales force activities. When the organization grows and develops business relations with customers in different geographic locations, however, it may be useful to decentralize control over the sales force activities. This may require a branch to be opened in a suitable geographic location in order to ensure effective service of local customers. Decentralization of sales activities helps minimize the travel time and expenses incurred by salespeople and maximize the quality of sales service provided by customers.

Finally, important consideration should be given by the sales manager to the issue of **organizational specialization**. Since companies build their activities around customer requirements, it is essential to develop a sales organization that will provide the most effective service in the marketplace. Several types of organizational specializations could be considered by the sales manager. These include the following:

- Geographic specialization
- Product specialization
- Customer specialization
- Functional specialization

Geographic specialization is particularly suitable for an organization that operates in widespread geographic markets. In this type of organization, each salesperson is assigned to sell all products to all customers within a specified geographic location. One of the advantages of this structure, illustrated in Exhibit 5–30, is that it stimulates development of strong ties between salespeople and their customers. In addition, travel time and selling costs can be substantially reduced because each salesperson covers limited sales territory. One disadvantage of this structure, however, is that a particular salesperson can handle only a limited number of uncomplicated products or product lines.

Product specialization is generally used by industrial organizations that offer various lines of products to the market. This type of structure is effective in the distribution of different highly-technical products. In this type of organization, each salesperson is trained to handle a particular product or product line. Thus, the number of salespeople depends upon the variety of products handled by the organization. One advantage of this structure, illustrated in Exhibit 5–31, is that it stimulates development of sound product knowledge by salespeople. This, in turn, enables the company to provide an effective product and technical support to their customers. One of the disadvantages of this structure, however,

Exhibit 5–30

Geographically-Specialized Sales Organization

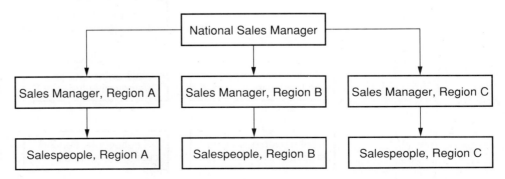

Exhibit 5–31

Product-Specialized Sales Organization

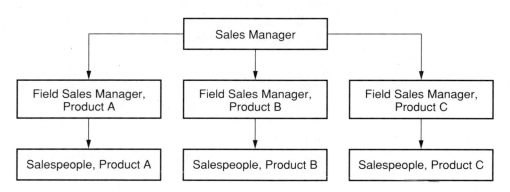

is that each salesperson must cover a much larger territory, which increases traveling time and selling expenses.

Customer specialization is frequently used by organizations that offer their products to different industries. In this type of an organization, each salesperson is assigned to a particular industry or individual customer. One of the advantages of this structure, illustrated in Exhibit 5–32, is that it allows the salesperson to become an expert on the customers' operations and stimulates the development of strong company-customer relations. However, the disadvantages of this structure, similar to the disadvantages of product specialization, are that each salesperson must cover a wide territory, spend more time on the road, and incur high selling expenses.

Functional specialization is most appropriate for organizations that offer relatively narrow product lines to nonsegmented and geographically concentrated markets. In this type of an organization, each salesperson is assigned particular functional responsibilities for the entire range of customers. Two basic responsibilities are usually assigned to salespeople in functional organizations: developing new accounts and maintaining existing ones. New accounts are generally developed by sales executives, and existing accounts are maintained by specially trained sales personnel. Functional specialization has limited application for small and medium-sized organizations, and is used infrequently.

It is essential that a sales manager understands the different types of specialization that can be used in the sales organization development process. Companies

Exhibit 5–32

Customer-Specialized Sales Organization

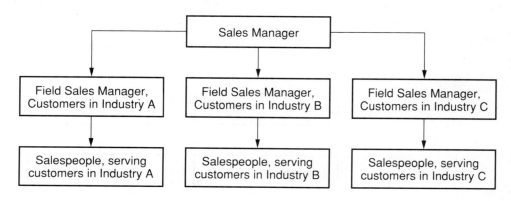

with widespread markets usually use geographic specialization, and those with diverse product lines find product specialization effective. If customers have highly-specialized needs, customer specialization is frequently used, and functional specialization is applied when team selling is more appropriate.

5.15 Sales Force Recruitment and Training

Effective implementation of marketing and sales plans depends substantially upon the type and quality of sales personnel employed by a company. It is essential, therefore, that the sales manager develops and implements a sound **sales force recruitment and training process.** This process entails a number of important steps which should be undertaken in accordance with a sequence outlined in Exhibit 5–33.

The basic principles of job analysis and employee recruitment and training have been discussed in detail in Part 2 (Volume I). **A job analysis** of sales positions generally entails evaluation of specific characteristics that should be demonstrated by each member of the sales force. Some of the major considerations pertinent to such an analysis include experience in personal selling, knowledge of the company's offerings in the marketplace, understanding of buyers' behavior, and ability to recognize customer needs.

Properly conducted job analyses provide basic information and help in preparing an accurate **job description** for each sales position. The prime purpose of a job description is to summarize major parameters of a particular job and to outline its relevant duties, responsibilities, authority, and accountability as follows:

- *Position title.* This is a descriptive title, like account representative, salesperson, or sales engineer.

Exhibit 5–33
Sales Force Recruitment, Selection, and Training Process

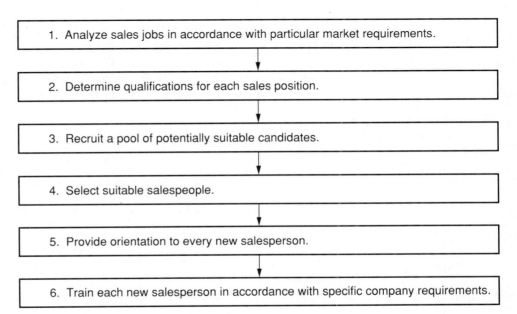

1. Analyze sales jobs in accordance with particular market requirements.

2. Determine qualifications for each sales position.

3. Recruit a pool of potentially suitable candidates.

4. Select suitable salespeople.

5. Provide orientation to every new salesperson.

6. Train each new salesperson in accordance with specific company requirements.

- *Job summary.* This is a summarized outline of a particular sales position.
- *Details of accountability.* These specify the reporting procedure in the sales department.
- *Details of responsibility and duties.* These describe the salesperson's principal activities—sales territories covered, industries involved, or customers to be served and product lines to be handled.

There are different types of job descriptions that could be prepared for the sales personnel. These types are based on five basic categories of salespeople identified by *Sales & Marketing Management* publication:

- **Account representative.** This salesperson calls on a large number of already established customers in, for example, the food, textiles, apparel, and wholesaling industries. Much of this selling is low key, and there is minimal pressure to develop new business.
- **Detail salesperson.** Instead of directly soliciting an order, this type of salesperson concentrates on performing promotional activities and introducing products. The medical detail salesperson, for example, seeks to persuade doctors, the indirect customers, to specify the pharmaceutical company's trade name product for prescriptions. The firm's actual sales are either made through wholesalers or directly to pharmacists who fill prescriptions.
- **Sales engineer.** This is a salesperson who sells products for which technical know-how and the ability to discuss technical aspects of the product are extremely important. The salesperson's expertise in identifying, analyzing, and solving customer problems is another critical factor. This type of selling is common in the chemical, machinery, and heavy equipment industries.
- **Industrial products salesperson, nontechnical.** This salesperson sells a tangible product to industrial or commercial purchasers, but is not required to have a high degree of technical knowledge. Industries that manufacture products such as packaging materials or standard office equipment use this type.
- **Service salesperson.** This type of salesperson sells intangibles, such as insurance and advertising. Unlike the four preceding types, those who sell service must be able to sell the benefits of intangibles.[33]

A well-designed job description is an important tool in the sales force recruitment and selection process because it helps to clarify various details relevant to a particular position and to summarize the necessary characteristics and qualifications of prospective employees. Furthermore, several additional factors should be considered by the sales manager during the sales force recruitment and selection process. These are:

- The experience factor
- The personality factor
- The matching factor

The **experience factor** suggests that buyers expect each salesperson to demonstrate the following:

- Understanding of the buyer's needs
- Product knowledge
- Company knowledge

- Competitors' products knowledge
- Understanding of trends in the marketplace

The **personality factor** includes several personal qualities which are essential for effective salesmanship:

- Sincerity, honesty, and integrity
- Pleasant conversational habits
- Enthusiasm and persistence
- Self-organization and self-analysis

The **matching factor** implies that buyers prefer to deal with salespeople who possess certain character traits similar to their own, such as:

- Effective communication skills
- Reliability and credibility
- Professionalism and commitment to the job
- Dependability and loyalty to customers
- Initiative and innovation in problem solving

Depending upon particular job requirements, each applicant should be evaluated by the sales manager in terms of the aforementioned factors. In addition, it is important to be aware of how buyers view salespeople and grade their qualities. This is illustrated in Exhibit 5–34.

Several laws and regulations must be complied with throughout the recruitment, selection, and hiring of new salespeople. These laws, such as the Civil Rights Act of 1964, Age Discrimination in Employment Act of 1967, and Vocational Rehabilitation Act of 1973 have also been discussed in detail in Part 2. It is the sales manager's responsibility to be fully familiar with appropriate employment laws and regulations and to apply them accordingly.

The prime purpose of the **recruitment process** is to attract a number of potentially qualified candidates to fill open positions within the organization. Sales managers use a variety of sources to find and attract new recruits. Some of these sources are schools and colleges, employment agencies, newspaper advertising, business associates, and present customers. The popularity of each source, presented in Exhibit 5–35, depends upon the specific requirements of the organization.

Exhibit 5–34

Buyer Comments about Salespeople

Good	Bad	Ugly
"Honesty"	"Poor listening skills"	"Pushy"
"Patience"	"Wastes my time"	"Smokes in my office"
"Dependable"	"Begins by talking sports"	"Whiners"
"Adaptability"	"Puts down competitor's products"	"Gets personal"
"Admits mistakes"	"Too many phone calls"	"Calls me dear or sweetheart"
"Loses a sale graciously"	"Walks in without an appointment"	"Plays one company
"Problem-solving capabilities"	"Lousy presentation"	against another"
"Knows my business"	"Fails to ask about needs"	"Wines and dines me"
"Well-prepared"	"Lacks product knowledge"	

SOURCE: *Sales & Marketing Management*, November 11, 1985, p.39. Reprinted with permission.

Exhibit 5–35

Popularity of Various Sources for Recruitment of Salespeople

Recruitment Source	Percentage Using Source to Recruit Sales Trainees	Percentage Using Source to Recruit Experienced Salespeople
Schools and colleges	57.9	21.1
Employment agencies	50.0	61.9
Present employees	45.8	46.3
Newspaper advertising	36.4	50.7
Business associates	32.2	56.3
Present customers	32.2	43.1
Sales executive clubs	22.4	19.6
Trade publications advertising	20.1	28.7

SOURCE: Reprinted by permission of the publisher from "How Industry Finds and Hires Salesmen," by H. Jay Bullen, *Industrial Marketing Management*. (March 1964), p. 68.

In addition, it is common practice to search for suitable salespeople among people already employed by the organization. These employees are expected to have good knowledge about the company's products and procedures, and would generally require less training than new recruits. Moreover, present employees have an established job history and their suitability for various sales positions could be effectively assessed. The transfer of suitable employees to the sales department is often considered a promotion, which helps to build morale within the organization.

Once a pool of applicants is recruited from the appropriate sources, each applicant must undergo a comprehensive **screening procedure**. All information obtained through job application forms, personal interviews, and tests must be examined, checked, and compared with the general hiring criteria pertaining to a specific sales position. Additional details about screening procedure, evaluation of job application forms, conduct of interviews, and pre-employment tests have been provided earlier in Part 2.

After completing the screening procedure, the sales manager is expected to make a decision regarding selection of suitable applicants. Each applicant should be informed of the appropriate decision as soon as possible in order to conclude the **selection process.**

Once the selection process is completed, every new employee must undergo a process of orientation and training. The prime purpose of the **orientation process** is to allow the new employee to familiarize himself with the company, its people, its products, and its relevant working procedures. After an initial introduction to the company, the sales manager must assess individual training requirements of each new employee and set appropriate training objectives. Some of the most important training objectives are:

- To provide sufficient knowledge about the company's product or service mix
- To provide updated information about the company's policies, rules, and regulations
- To provide updated information about the company's customers and their needs
- To provide updated information about competitors and governmental, legal and other uncontrollable factors
- To equip salespeople with effective personal selling techniques

There are several good reasons for training sales personnel. First, a well-trained employee will be better able to contribute to the company's overall volume of business and profitability. Second, an effective training program helps to reduce supervision costs and personnel turnover. Finally, a sound training program helps to improve morale, motivation, and company-customer relations.

The amount of time allocated to a particular training program depends on the nature of products or services offered by the company in the marketplace. The information presented in Exhibit 5–36 reflects a recent national breakdown of training time allocation across the prime areas of knowledge described earlier.

Different types of training methods are commonly used by management in small and medium-sized companies.[34] These methods include lectures (82 percent), videotapes (81 percent), one-on-one instruction (62 percent), role playing (45 percent), and case studies (41 percent).

Sales lectures may represent a cost-effective training method if a sufficient number of trainees attend them. This method is therefore particularly useful for larger organizations. The use of **videotapes** for training purposes has increased dramatically during recent years. This method can be effectively used for teaching product knowledge and basic techniques of personal selling. The cost effectiveness of this method does not depend upon the company's size.

One-on-one instruction is another popular method frequently used for field sales training purposes. Here a trainee accompanies the sales manager on a number of routine visits to customers and gains practical experience in a real business environment. The **role playing** approach has also become popular during recent years. With this approach, one trainee plays the role of a salesperson while another plays the role of a customer. The prime purpose of this approach is to practice different selling techniques prior to starting active selling. Finally, **case study discussions** encourage two-way communication among sales trainees.

Training salespeople is a never-ending managerial task in every organization. Three basic reasons for the need for continuous training in the organization are as follows:

1. The firm's effort to keep salespeople up-to-date on changes, product features, changing company policies, changing industry conditions, and changes in the competitive environment
2. The dynamic nature of both marketing, generally, and personal selling, specifically
3. The need for increased productivity[35]

The ultimate responsibility for ongoing training of the sales force rests with the sales manager. A sound sales training program helps the company achieve increased volume of sales and an improved level of profitability.

Exhibit 5–36

Sales Training Time for New Sales Personnel: Allocation to Knowledge Areas

Subject Matter	Consumer Goods Firms	Industrial Goods Firms	Service-Type Firms	All Firms
Product knowledge	36%	47%	39%	42%
Selling techniques	27	21	30	24
Market/industry orientation	20	17	13	17
Company orientation	11	13	13	13
Other (miscellaneous)	6	2	3	4

SOURCE: Adapted from information presented in David S. Hopkins, *Training the Sales Force: A Progress Report* (Published by The Conference Board, Inc., 1978). Reprinted with permission.

5.16 Personal Selling

One prime objective of the sales force training program is to ensure that salespeople understand the basic principles of personal selling. D. Jackson and colleagues suggest that:

> **Personal selling** consists of finding people who require your product or service, studying their needs, presenting your offering in such a way that your potential customers are convinced of its benefit to them, answering any objections they may have, asking for a commitment to close, and following up to ensure that those who have bought from you are satisfied. Truly professional selling is a process that fosters the development of a mutually beneficial relationship in which buyer and seller alike both profit and benefit. This mutually beneficial arrangement leads to long-term relationships, repeat business, and favorable word-of-mouth communication with other customers or prospects.[36]

Personal selling can be described as a process consisting of several distinct stages.[37] These stages are summarized in Exhibit 5–37.

One of the fundamental issues that a salesperson has to understand is the nature of relations between purchasing and selling organizations. The personal selling process is based on continuous interaction between buyers and sellers. The ultimate objective of this process is to facilitate a continuous exchange of products and services for money in the marketplace.

Buyers, on one hand, act on behalf of companies that constantly generate the need for additional products and services. One of the major objectives of

Exhibit 5–37

Eight Stages in the Personal Selling Process

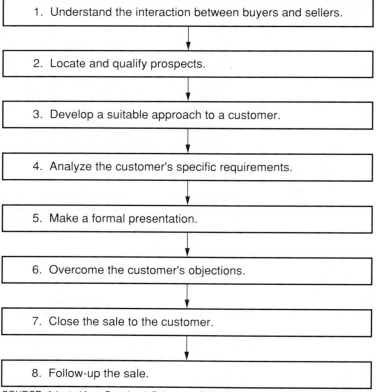

1. Understand the interaction between buyers and sellers.

2. Locate and qualify prospects.

3. Develop a suitable approach to a customer.

4. Analyze the customer's specific requirements.

5. Make a formal presentation.

6. Overcome the customer's objections.

7. Close the sale to the customer.

8. Follow-up the sale.

SOURCE: Adapted from Douglas J. Dalrymple, *Sales Management: Concepts and Cases* (New York: John Wiley & Sons, Inc., 1988), pp. 95-121. Reprinted with permission.

purchasing organizations is to acquire the necessary products and services at a minimal cost. Sellers, on the other hand, represent their companies and offer various products and services to customers at specific prices. The prime purpose of selling organizations is to sell as many products or services as possible and to make a sizeable profit. Each side, obviously, pursues its own interests and attempts to gain additional advantages throughout the interaction process. Normally, however, this process results in a mutually beneficial exchange where the buyers' needs for products and services are satisfied by sellers at prices acceptable to both parties.

Once the salesperson understands the basic mechanism of buyer-seller interaction, the active personal selling process may begin. The first task in personal selling is to **locate and qualify prospects.** Searching or "prospecting" for new customers is one of the most important and difficult sales tasks. This process usually requires a substantial investment in time, patience, and persistence on the part of the salesperson. A sale usually does not occur instantly or by accident. The salesperson must locate suitable prospects and identify their size, nature of business, and potential needs. The salesperson will subsequently have to make a number of sales calls, meet the prospective buyer, and cultivate a buyer-seller relationship to produce a sale.

There are numerous possibilities for locating new prospects. These often depend on whether the seller represents a new company or a well-established organization. New companies usually start from scratch and use all possible sources for locating new prospects. Well-established companies generally have an easier task since they are already known in the marketplace and have sound connections with buyers. Both types of companies, however, use similar methods, which include the following:

- Lead management
- Directories
- Referrals
- Opinion leaders
- Cold canvassing

Many companies receive direct inquiries about their products or services from existing customers or from people who have never bought from that company before. Such inquiries provide important leads to salespeople and must be attended to as soon as possible. Leads represent an excellent source for locating new customers who, in effect, invite the salesperson to call. **Lead management** is therefore an important method in initiating the personal selling process.

Additional leads may be generated by heavy advertising in appropriate newspapers and magazines, direct mailing to selected market segments, participating in trade shows, conducting introductory seminars, or using special computer programs. Some of these computer programs, such as Sales Manager, Sales Planner, or Prospecting, help salespeople to evaluate and locate suitable prospects.

Directories provide another important source of locating new prospects. Directories such as Dun & Bradstreet "Market Identifiers," The Survey of Industrial Purchasing Power, the Nielsen Retail Index, or the Thomas Register of American Manufacturers list the names and addresses of various companies according to their products or services, geographic location, number of employees, or assets. Depending upon a particular classification, the salesperson may estimate the size and potential requirements of the individual prospect in a required geographical location.

Referrals represent another important source of leads for a salesperson. With this method, an existing customer is asked to provide a recommendation about a particular product or service to another person or organization. The advantage of this method is that the recommendation is given by a customer who has already purchased the product or service and not by the salesperson who may express a biased opinion. Naturally, referrals can be expected only if existing customers are satisfied with products or services purchased from the company.

It may be extremely useful to have a good sales history with large organizations that are considered leaders in their particular areas of business. This way, if a successful sales history with an **opinion leader** can be produced, a salesperson may effectively use it as a recommendation for other companies. In addition, a successful sales history with an opinion leader may be effectively used in the advertising or direct marketing campaign.

Many direct sales organizations use a **cold canvassing** approach and initiate new contacts with prospective customers without prior appointments. Sometimes this approach can be effective in obtaining new prospects. However, there is no particular guarantee of success. Cold canvassing is often used by salespeople who may have a cancelled appointment in the middle of their schedule and need to fill the time until the next planned call.

Once a list of prospective customers is available, it is necessary to qualify each prospect on an individual basis. This entails evaluation of the company's possible purchasing requirements size, buying authority, and ability to pay. Possible purchasing requirements depend primarily upon the company's nature of business (e.g., plastic parts manufacturers need chemicals, furniture manufacturers need timber). A company's size may be judged by its total number of employees, annual volume of sales, or other suitable criteria. Furthermore, it is essential to understand the buying procedure and authority in a particular company. For example, a production manager may be interested in new equipment, but may not have authority to place a purchase order. In many instances, the selling begins with people who specify various products on the drawing board (e.g., architects, engineers, draftsmen).

Finally, it is important to establish the creditableness of a prospective customer. Dun & Bradstreet, for example, is one of the major sources of credit information used for this purpose. It is necessary to ascertain that the prospective customer does not represent a potential credit risk and will pay accounts promptly.

Once prospects are located and qualified, it is necessary to develop a suitable approach for each prospective customer. This means that salespeople must set specific objectives pertaining to their future calls, such as introducing a new product or promoting an existing service. Some methods commonly used by salespeople include the following:

- Personal letter
- Telephone contact
- Personal contact

Personal letters to prospective buyers are regularly used by salespeople as the first step in developing sound buyer-seller relations. Effectively drafted letters may help salespeople in introducing their companies and in forwarding the products or services that are offered to prospective customers. It is advisable to also include brochures or other descriptive material that could provide additional information about a particular product or service, and to list specific benefits which may interest a prospective buyer.

Telephone contacts are also frequently used by salespeople in initiating new buyer-seller relations. When approaching a new prospect by phone, the salesperson always has a better chance if a personal letter has been sent earlier. In this instance, the salesperson can refer to the letter and generate additional interest on the part of the prospective buyer. The prime purpose of the phone call is to follow up on the introductory letter and to sell the idea of a meeting with the buyer.

Personal contact is certainly the most effective approach in initiating buyer-seller relations. However, it is difficult to simply walk into the buyer's office without prior arrangement. Buyers, like other employees, are usually busy and follow their own work schedule. An additional barrier is created by receptionists who are instructed to obtain preliminary information from all visitors, particularly from salespeople. Thus, it is advisable to arrange a personal meeting with a prospective buyer well in advance by means of a preliminary telephone contact.

Once the interview with a prospective buyer is arranged, the salesperson must make final preparations for a meeting. Thorough preparation is particularly important since most salespeople do not get a second chance if the first meeting is a failure. In order to ensure a successful meeting, the salesperson must take the following steps:

- Develop a preliminary idea about the prospect's needs.
- Prepare promotional literature about the product or service.
- Summarize possible alternatives to solve the prospect's problems.
- Have a pleasant appearance.
- Be punctual.

At the outset of the meeting, the salesperson must hand a business card to the prospect and introduce him- or herself. The first few minutes of the face-to-face encounter with the prospect usually play a critical role in the success or failure of the meeting, so it is essential to establish a sense of trust between the salesperson and the prospective buyer. This, for example, may entail the following:

- Establish expectations and demonstrate dependability.
- Offer sources of proof to back up statements.
- Be honest and candid.
- Be businesslike and professional.
- Give pros and cons of product.
- Create an understanding of quality.
- Use technical knowledge.
- Demonstrate competence.
- Emphasize availability and ability to get the job done.
- Stress benefits.
- Stress ability to meet unique customer needs.
- Be friendly.
- Establish common ground.
- Be polite.[38]

Most face-to-face meetings start with a light, preliminary conversation about a particular topic of the day (e.g., weather, sports, politics). Sometimes it is appropriate to hand a small gift or novelty to a new prospect on behalf of the salesperson's organization. This may be a calendar, pen, or other suitable item.

Once rapport with the prospect is established, the salesperson must begin to analyze the customer's specific requirements. This is usually accomplished by questioning the prospect about the company's particular problems and then evaluating each answer in detail. The salesperson must have a clear understanding that the prospect does not really want to purchase products or services, but simply needs to solve a specific problem or satisfy a particular need. Hence, listening skills are the most critical at this stage.

After analyzing the customer's specific requirements, the salesperson can begin a **formal presentation**. The prime objective of such a presentation is to introduce certain products or services that may provide suitable solutions or satisfy the particular needs of the customer. The salesperson must provide a detailed description of the proposed product or service, and clarify all advantages and benefits offered to the customer. Salespeople generally use two different types of formal presentations to customers:

- Oral sales presentations
- Written sales presentations

An **oral sales presentation** encourages useful verbal exchange between the salesperson and the prospect. It enables the salesperson to explain all relevant details of the proposal and provides the customer with an opportunity to ask questions and receive immediate clarification. An oral sales presentation can be conducted in a canned, structured, or spontaneous manner. A **canned presentation** is a fully-automated approach in which the salesperson provides the customer with tightly-structured information prepared in advance. This may include movies, slides, and filmstrips. A **structured presentation**, on the other hand, is a more flexible approach that enables the salesperson to use his or her own wording while following a company-prepared presentation outline. This type of sales presentation is used most frequently and usually provides effective results. A **spontaneous presentation** does not impose any restrictions and enables the salesperson to conduct a meeting with a prospective customer without a particular plan. Such an unplanned presentation is often ineffective and fails to produce the desired results.

One of the critical issues that a salesperson has to face during a sales presentation is the flow of objections and excuses by prospective customers. A range of methods for handling typical **objections** and **excuses** are summarized in Exhibit 5–38.

Once the sales presentation is completed and various objections raised by a prospect are cleared, the salesperson should begin **closing the sale.** It is advisable to try to close the deal as early and as often as possible by asking appropriate **confirmation questions** during the **trial close.** Such questions provide direction to prospects in confirming their choice. For example:

- Do you prefer to pay cash or do you need terms?
- Do you want to purchase 10 or 20 items?
- Do you prefer the yellow or the brown?

There are several closing techniques frequently used by salespeople. Some of these techniques are:

- **Alternative choice.**   When the prospect is offered a variety of sizes, types, or colors, it is useful to ask confirmation questions that will help to narrow the choice for final selection.
- **Summary close.**   The salesperson should summarize benefits accepted by the prospect during the sales presentation and ask for a purchase order.
- **Assumption close.**   The salesperson should "assume" that the prospect is

Exhibit 5–38

How to Handle Objections and Excuses Raised by Prospects

Examples of Objections	Methods of Handling Objections
Simple Excuses from Prospects	
• I must speak to my partner. • Our budget is limited this year. • I am too busy during this week. • I will phone you back.	Recognize the excuse, try to ignore it and continue with the sales presentation. Determine what really bothers the prospect.
Source Objections Raised by Prospects	
• The last few deliveries from your company were too late. • Some of your products are defective. • You owe us a refund. • The previous salesperson was rude.	Do not argue with the prospect. Instead, recognize the problem, get all relevant details and promise to sort it out.
Need Objections Raised by Prospects	
• We do not need a new machine; our existing one performs well. • I am not interested.	Prospects are often unaware of what new products can do. Explain product's characteristics and benefits and ask for a "trial order."
Product Objections Raised by Prospects	
• I don't think your equipment will solve our problem. • I don't think our customers will like your products.	Stress additional benefits and advantages of your product against the one which is used by the prospect for comparison purposes.
Timing Objections Raised by Prospects	
• I will think about your proposal. • We will decide next month. • Contact us next year.	Stress additional cost and performance benefits if the prospect will consider the product now. Offer additional financial incentives.
Price Objections Raised by Prospects	
• Your product is too expensive. • I want a substantial discount. • I can't afford your product right now.	Compare the cost of your product with a similar one offered by competitors. Stress additional benefits against price difference. Offer flexible repayment conditions.

going to place an order. In this case the salesperson can start completing an order form or hand the prospect a pen and ask him or her to sign a purchase order.

- **Special concession close.** The salesperson should offer the prospect a special concession with a purchase order. This, for example, may include an additional bonus item, extended credit facility, or free delivery.
- **Last chance close.** The salesperson should tell the prospect that there are other interested parties and if the purchase order is not placed immediately, the item may be sold to others.
- **Confirmation close.** The salesperson should pose a number of questions that will force the prospect to agree and provide a "yes" answer. Subsequently these answers should be used as a confirmation of prospect's purchase order.

Finally, the salesperson must follow-up the sale and ensure that the customer is satisfied with the purchased product or service. **After-sales service** is particularly important if the company wishes to build strong business relations with customers and establish a sound reputation in the marketplace.

5.17 Sales Force Compensation

The development and implementation of an effective **sales force compensation plan** represents one of the major responsibilities of a sales manager. Basic principles of personnel compensation have been discussed earlier in Part 2 (Volume I). These principles provide guidance in developing a suitable compensation plan in accordance with specific organizational objectives. Development of a sales force compensation plan[39] requires a number of steps that are outlined in Exhibit 5–39.

Compensation objectives are commonly established in accordance with the overall organizational plans. The main objectives of an effective sales force compensation plan are:

- To attract and employ most qualified salespeople
- To encourage salespeople to maximize their efforts toward achievement of specific marketing and sales goals
- To enable the company to meet its overall organizational objectives

Once appropriate compensation objectives are established, the sales manager should select the most suitable method of sales force compensation. Several options can be considered at this stage. These options have been outlined in Exhibit 5–39 and include the following:

- Straight salary
- Straight commission
- Salary plus commission
- Salary plus bonus
- Combination plan

Straight salary represents fixed compensation that is payable to a salesperson on a regular basis, usually once a month. The level of compensation

Exhibit 5–39

Development and Implementation of a Sales Force Compensation Plan

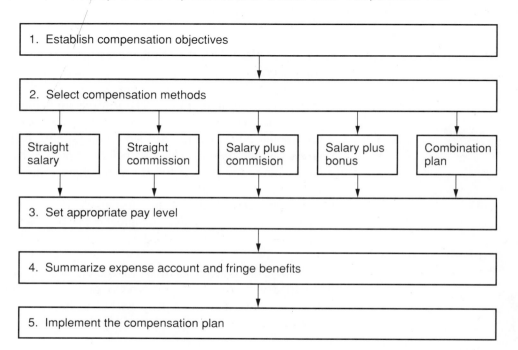

is determined in advance in accordance with the amount of time spent on the job. The salesperson is also compensated for any "out-of-pocket" expenses from promoting company interests and dealing with customers.

One of the major advantages of the straight salary method is that it provides better control over total salaries and wages expenditure. Since the amount of compensation is not tied to a specific volume of sales, it is easier to reassign salespeople to new territories or instruct them to perform nonselling tasks, like customer liaison or servicing old accounts. Salaried salespeople usually develop a strong sense of loyalty toward the company and maintain a high level of morale.

The straight salary method also has several limitations, however. First, this method does not allow the company to take advantage of the fluctuating business cycle. For example, during upswings salespeople are not sufficiently motivated to maximize their efforts in producing additional sales, and during downswings, fixed compensation to salespeople causes further increase of expenditure and reduction in profitability. For these reasons straight salary is not the most popular method and is used by approximately 17 percent of companies as Exhibit 5–40 shows.

The straight salary compensation is most appropriate when it is difficult to measure the contribution of an individual salesperson in achieving a particular sale. For this reason fixed salary is more common in industrial product selling than in consumer products. Straight salaries are also frequently paid to salespeople who work as a team and deal with products of a specialized or technical nature.

Straight commission represents a compensation plan that is the direct opposite of straight salary. A straight commission plan is based entirely on a salesperson's individual performance. The compensation is usually determined by applying a fixed or a sliding percentage rate to the value of sales or profit produced by the salesperson.

The design of a straight commission plan requires consideration of three important elements. First, it is necessary to establish a suitable **commission base** for measuring the performance and computing the commission—net sales, gross margin from sales, or net income. Second, it is necessary to determine the **commission rate** (percentage) and decide whether it is a *fixed* or *variable rate*. A special commission rate may be established for different types of products depending upon their profitability and demand in the marketplace. Third, it is necessary to specify whether the commission should be paid with the first sale or after achieving a predetermined level of sales.

The major advantage of the straight commission plan is that it provides a maximum incentive for salespeople. Management can use this method in focusing the selling effort on certain products or services in particular market

Exhibit 5–40

Percentage of Companies Using Different Compensation Plans, 1985

Method	All Industries	Industrial Products	Consumer Products
Straight salary	17.4%	14.1%	9.3%
Draw against commission	6.5	6.0	7.5
Salary plus commission	30.7	35.8	22.4
Salary plus individual bonus	33.7	32.5	45.8
Salary plus group bonus	2.7	2.1	4.7
Salary plus commission plus bonus	9.0	9.5	10.3
Total	100.0%	100.0%	100.0%

SOURCE: From the 1985/86 ECS Sales and Marketing Personnel Report. Published with permission from ECS/A Wyatt Data Services Company.

segments or developing new accounts. Since selling costs vary with the volume of sales, the company's cash flow is not affected by fluctuation in the business cycle. Moreover, straight commission is easily understood by salespeople and can be administered without difficulty.

One drawback of the straight commission plan is that management has less control and influence over the sales force. Since salespeople are motivated to maximize their earnings, many "not so profitable" product lines or accounts may become neglected. In addition, salespeople tend to promote their own interests rather than the company's and usually demonstrate little loyalty to their organization and its customers. Wide fluctuation in earnings also leads to low income security, poor morale, and high turnover rate among salespeople.

The straight commission plan is generally utilized in situations requiring high personal selling effort and minimal follow-up or after-sales service. Typical examples of such situations are door-to-door selling of consumer goods, and selling of automobiles, life insurance, or real estate.

Salary-plus-commission represents one of the widely used methods of compensating salespeople. This method enables management to combine the advantages of both plans discussed earlier. Basic salary provides salespeople with a secure minimal income while the additional commission creates the incentive to meet specific organizational objectives.

Salary-plus-commission plan, as recorded in Exhibit 5–40, is particularly popular in compensating industrial sales representatives. The main benefit of this plan is that it enables management to develop a tailor-made compensation program best suited for specific incentive needs. Thus, for example, if management wants to maintain an average incentive level among salespeople, the compensation package could consist of 80 percent salary and 20 percent commission. If a new product or service is being launched, however, the incentive level among salespeople must be raised. This can be accomplished by increasing the commission portion in the overall compensation package to 30 or 40 percent or more.

An additional advantage of the salary-plus-commission plan is that management can adjust the compensation level to achieve a variety of objectives. Thus, for example, some companies offer commission with the first sale, while others impose a certain minimal level of sales before commission can apply. Furthermore, the commission level may vary with the volume of sales on a progressive or regressive basis as follows:

- **Progressive commission rate.** This rate is used when the volume of sales depends upon the personal selling effort of each individual. In this case, for example, a salesperson may earn 3 percent on the first $20,000 of sales each month, 4 percent on the next $10,000, and 5 percent on anything above $30,000.
- **Regressive commission rate.** This rate is used when the volume of sales depends upon the company's advertising and promotion effort rather than on the personal selling effort of a particular individual. In this case, for example, a salesperson may earn 4 percent on the first $30,000 of sales each month, 3 percent on the next $10,000 and 2 percent on anything above $40,000.

Progressive commission rates are not always considered desirable because they cause a gradual increase of selling expenses with growth in the sales volume. Regressive commission rates, on the other hand, are frequently used by companies who presell their products or services through advertising and deal extensively with independent sales representatives.

The main disadvantages of the salary-plus-commission plan are that this plan is more expensive, more costly to administer, and more complicated to explain to salespeople. Nevertheless, this plan is widely used by various companies that specialize in industrial goods such as building materials, chemicals, paper, steel, machinery, and electrical supplies. Commissions are usually paid to salespeople on a monthly basis, ensuring immediate acknowledgment of their selling efforts. Sometimes the payment of commissions is spread out over a longer period of time, providing greater income stability to salespeople.

Salary-plus-bonus represents another widely-used method of compensating salespeople. This method enables management, who are concerned about expenses, to provide fair income security to employees in the form of a basic salary and to stimulate their motivation with a bonus payment. A **bonus** is a discretionary amount paid to an employee for reaching a specific goal. Bonuses are usually paid on an annual basis and vary from 5 to 20 percent of the salesperson's salary.

The main advantage of the salary-plus-bonus plan is that it helps management control expenses while providing income security and additional incentives to salespeople. According to information summarized in Exhibit 5–40, this plan is widely used by consumer goods companies and to a lesser extent by industrial goods companies. A typical compensation plan may entail a bonus payment based on individual sales achievement such as meeting a specific sales quota or opening a new account. This plan is more popular with consumer goods companies since they usually resell their products through heavy advertising and promotion. Therefore, it would not make sense to offer commission that may further increase selling expenses.

The size of the bonus is determined by the sales manager in accordance with the overall performance of a particular salesperson. Sometimes the bonus is paid to a group of salespeople who may be engaged in a team-selling effort. A **group bonus plan** often provides an effective method of stimulating team work and high morale among salespeople. Management usually computes the value of the group bonus by the overall performance of the sales department or by the company's profitability and then distributes appropriate amounts to each participant at the end of the year.

One of the drawbacks of the salary-plus-bonus plan is that salespeople are often disappointed with their bonus and suspect bias and favoritism on the part of management. Since bonuses are often paid long after the specific goals have been achieved, their motivating effect is minimized. Also, bonuses do not provide a long-lasting effect and may encourage some salespeople to leave the organization after the bonus is paid.

Salary-plus-bonus-plus-commission, also know as a **combination plan,** is another method of sales force compensation. This plan enables the sales manager to offer a broad range of benefits related to previous plans and to reward every accomplishment of the salesperson. A typical example of this plan may be illustrated as follows:

- Basic monthly salary—$1,500
- 4 percent commission on all sales above $30,000 per month
- 1 percent bonus if a sales quota of $180,000 is achieved every six months

According to Exhibit 5–40, this plan is not as popular as some of the other plans mentioned earlier. However, this plan is frequently adopted by companies using independent sales representatives and sales brokers. In this instance the main emphasis is placed on the selling activities irrespective of the nature of products or services.

Once the selection of suitable compensation methods is accomplished, it is necessary to set an appropriate pay level for salespeople. This should not present a particular problem since there are only three options available:

- *Compensation based on the average current rate.*   This option enables management to offer competitive compensation package to salespeople.
- *Compensation based on the above-average current rate.*   This option enables management to attract highly qualified salespeople.
- *Compensation based on the below-average current rate.*   This option enables management to reduce selling expenses.

The updated information pertinent to the compensation of salespeople is provided by sources such as ECS/A Wyatt Data Services Company, Sales & Marketing Management publication, and trade associations. A typical illustration of annual compensation for industrial salespeople in 1989 is presented in Exhibit 5–41.

In addition to setting an appropriate pay level, it is necessary to make a decision regarding the expense account and fringe benefits. This is particularly important if the selling activity entails frequent traveling, lodging, and entertaining of customers.

The prime purpose of an **expense account** is to reimburse salespeople for various "out-of-pocket" expenses incurred on company business, expenses such as food, telephone calls, gas, automobile hire, and hotel accommodation. Three basic types of expense plans are commonly used by sales managers. These are:

- **Unlimited repayment plan.** This plan is frequently used by small and medium-sized companies and it requires each salesperson to submit an itemized list of expenses incurred during each month. There is no limit imposed on a salesperson. However, management should watch that the expense allowance is not abused.
- **Per diem plan.**   This plan provides a fixed amount designed to cover a salesperson's out-of-pocket expenses for every day spent in the field. Although this plan is simple and inexpensive to control, it often motivates salespeople to reduce their out-of-pocket expenses to the detriment of the company's interests. Thus, instead of entertaining customers, some salespeople would prefer to "save" a part of the allowance for their own needs.
- **Limited repayment plan.**   This is another plan designed to cover salespersons' out-of-pocket expenses. With this plan, however, management imposes specific restrictions on such expenses, for example: 15 cents per mile, $30

Exhibit 5–41

Average Annual Compensation for Industrial Salespeople as of 3/1/89.

Job Title	Positions Paid Salary Only	Positions Paid Salary Plus Incentive	
		Salary	Incentive
Sales Trainee	$24,300	$24,800	$4,400
Sales Representative	31,200	31,900	9,500
Senior Sales Representative	39,600	40,500	14,300
Sales Supervisor	45,800	47,300	14,100

SOURCE: From the *1989/90 ECS Sales and Marketing Personnel Report.* Published with permission from ECS/A Wyatt Data Services Company.

Exhibit 5–42

List of Fringe Benefits Offered by Different Companies

Benefits	Percentage of Firms Offering
Hospital	99
Life insurance	92
Accident insurance	85
Moving expenses	65
Salary continuation plan	62
Educational assistance	60
Pension plan	56
Personal use of company car	52
Club or association membership	38
Profit sharing	36
Dental insurance	25
Stock purchase	18

SOURCE: Adapted from data in John Steinbrink's, "How to Pay Your Sales Force," *Harvard Business Review*, Vol. 56 (July–August, 1978), p. 121.

daily food allowance, or $60 hotel allowance. The prime purpose of this plan is to motivate the salesperson to control selling expenses.

Fringe benefits are another form of compensation and are frequently used to attract suitable salespeople. There are several types of benefits which can be offered to salespeople depending upon the seniority of their position and their overall importance to the organization. Some of these benefits are summarized in Exhibit 5–42.

Once all parameters of the sales force compensation package are established, the sales manager should evaluate the plan in terms of overall organizational objectives and its acceptance by salespeople. Finally, upon its approval, the compensation plan must be implemented and monitored consistently.

5.18 Sales Force Management and Motivation

The effective management and motivation of a sales force represents another major responsibility of a sales manager. This process entails evaluating, selecting, and designing sales territories; assigning salespeople and allocating sales quotas; implementing a territorial coverage plan; motivating salespeople; and conducting regular sales meetings. A typical **sales force management and motivation process** is illustrated in Exhibit 5–43.

The word "sales territory" is misleading because it does not relate to a specific geographic area alone. A **sales territory** represents a quantifiable and identifiable group of existing and potential buyers. A territory thus focuses upon sales potential from the company's point of view, and would be a slice of the total pie that the company hopes to obtain in sales.[40] There are several reasons for establishing sales territories:

- Ensuring thorough coverage of the existing and potential market
- Increasing motivation and efficiency of sales personnel
- Optimizing the level of selling costs
- Providing better control and evaluation of the sales force
- Facilitating improved customer relations

Prior to selecting and designing suitable sales territories, the sales manager must evaluate several **territorial planning factors** which include the following:[41]

Exhibit 5–43

Sales Force Management and Motivation Process

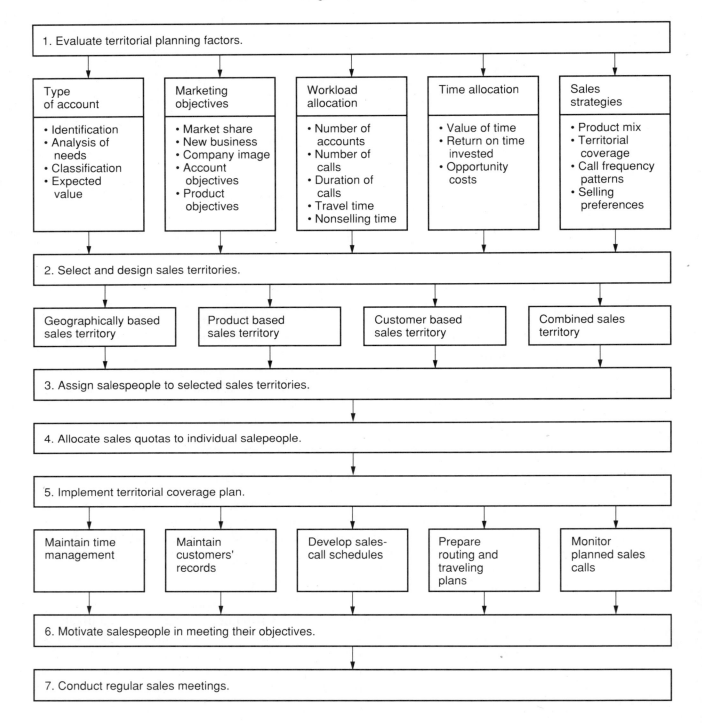

- *Type of account.* This entails identifying existing and potential customers, evaluating their needs, classifying customers into various categories, and estimating their business potential.
- *Marketing objectives.* This entails examining marketing plan requirements pertinent to market share, new business, company image, account, and product objectives.

- *Workload allocation.* This entails considering the number of accounts handled by a salesperson, the required frequency of calls, the average duration of each call, travel time, and nonselling time.
- *Time allocation.* This entails establishing the value of time for each salesperson, determining the required return on time invested, and summarizing opportunity costs such as the overall costs of the selling effort.
- *Sales strategies.* This entails examining relevant sales strategies regarding product mix, territorial coverage requirements, call frequency patterns and selling preferences. Several examples of sales strategies were presented earlier in Exhibit 5–27.

Upon completing the evaluation of the aforementioned factors, the sales manager should begin the selection and design of sales territories. There are four different types of sales territories that could be selected by the sales manager:

- Geographically-based sales territory
- Product-based sales territory
- Customer-based sales territory
- Combined sales territory

A **geographically-based sales territory** provides a method of assigning the sales force to specified sales territories or regions in which each salesperson handles a full range of company products or services. This method represents an integral part of the company's geographic specialization as was discussed earlier in this part and illustrated in Exhibit 5–30.

A **product-based sales territory** provides a method whereby salespeople are allocated in accordance with a specific product or service range and cover the marketplace without geographic limitation. This method enables the sales manager to build a product-specialized sales organization as was described earlier in this part and presented in Exhibit 5–31.

A **customer-based sales territory** provides a method whereby salespeople are assigned to individual customers or to a particular type of industry and cover the marketplace without geographic limitation. This method enables the sales manager to develop a customer-specialized sales organization as was discussed earlier in this part and illustrated in Exhibit 5–32.

Combined sales territory represents a method which enables the sales manager to utilize all three aforementioned methods on a selected basis. Thus, a certain number of salespeople may be allocated to geographically based sales territories, another group may be required to handle a limited number of products in the marketplace and the last group may be assigned to individual customers or industries. This method of sales force allocation enables the company to remain flexible and satisfy market demands at any given time.

If the sales manager selects the first type, geographically-based sales territory, the territory needs to be designed further. The sales territory design process consists of five steps, illustrated in Exhibit 5–44.

First, the sales manager must select suitable **geographic control units** in order to form and develop sales territories. Such units usually are zip code areas, cities, counties, or states. The first three types of geographic control units are used more frequently since their size provides sufficient flexibility in setting boundaries for sales territories. States are generally too large for sales territory design purposes. However, state-based geographic control may provide a sound overview for overall planning purposes. The choice of a suitable geographic

Exhibit 5–44

The Sales Territory Design Process

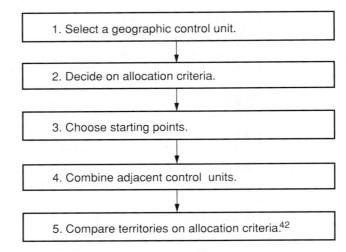

control unit also depends upon the availability of statistical information on population, number of companies, or volume of sales in each area.

Second, the sales manager must decide on **allocation criteria** for combining different control units into sales territories. This means that sales territories should be designed so that each salesperson has a fair opportunity to meet organizational and personal objectives. There are two selection factors frequently used by sales managers in designing sales territories. The first factor, based on the current number of customers, provides a realistic estimate of the workload in a particular sales territory. The second factor, based on the overall number of customers, may provide a good estimate of the workload potential in a specified territory.

Third, the sales manager must choose **starting points** for various sales territories. Probably the most practical approach is to identify the largest concentration of existing or potential customers and to use that as the starting point in developing a particular sales territory. From this point the sales manager may expand the territory in other directions to cover a larger area. Sometimes the salesperson's home may be used as the starting point. In this instance, each salesperson is required to develop a sales territory around his or her home as part of an overall selling effort.

Fourth, the sales manager must combine **adjacent control units** in order to complete the design of new sales territories. Thus, for example, if the potential number of customers per county is used as the selection factor, it is necessary to determine the total required number of customers and develop sales territories accordingly. A typical illustration of this procedure is presented in Exhibit 5–45.

The final stage of the sales territories design process entails the comparison of individual territories using different criteria. For example, a set of territories can be compared on the basis of square mileage, or number of customers in each territory. Such a comparison enables the sales manager to ensure a balanced allocation of workload and provide fair opportunity to each salesperson in meeting sales objectives.

Once the territories are designed, it is necessary to allocate suitable sales personnel and to proceed with implementation of the overall sales program.

Effective utilization of sales personnel cannot be accomplished without establishing detailed **sales volume quotas**. The type of quotas selected by the sales manager depends upon the nature of the product or service provided by the company, defined sales territories, type and number of customers, and the existing structure of the sales force. A sales volume quota represents a basic sales performance goal that is assigned to a salesperson, agent, or customer during a specific period of time. It assists in the process of planning, controlling, and evaluating the overall selling effort of the organization. Some of the major objectives of establishing sales volume quotas are:

- To indicate strengths and weaknesses of the selling structure
- To provide quantified objectives and incentives for the sales force
- To provide management with a tool for measuring and controlling sales performance
- To facilitate effective compensation of the sales personnel

Sales volume quotas are usually set in conjunction with the estimated territorial potential of the market, or, alternatively, in accordance with the company's

Exhibit 5–45

Design of Sales Territories

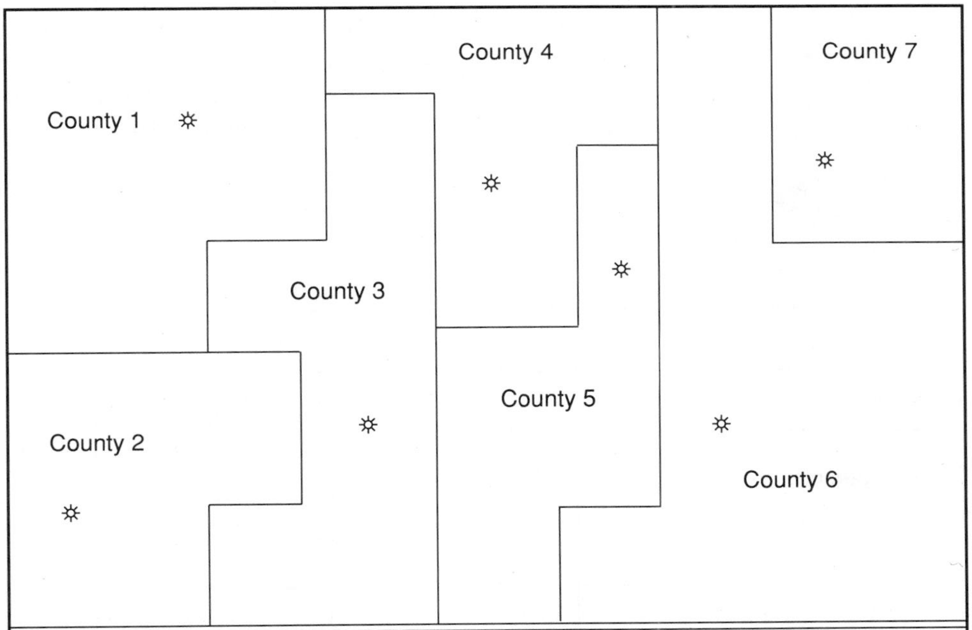

Geographic Control Unit	Number of Customers		Allocation
	At Present	Potential	
County 1	- -	30	Sales territory "A" with 140
County 2	30	60	potential customers
County 3	20	50	
County 4	40	70	Sales territory "B" with 120
County 5	20	50	potential customers
County 6	30	80	Sales territory "C" with 130
County 7	10	50	potential customers
Total	150	390	☼ — Starting point

sales forecasts. Quotas are frequently set on the basis of past sales experience and may also be related to a specific compensation plan designed to motivate the sales force of the organization. The effectiveness of the sales volume quota system usually depends upon its acceptance by the sales force and cooperation among the sales personnel. All sales volume quotas should be recorded in the **annual sales volume quota report** as illustrated in Exhibit 5–46.

Once sales volume quotas are allocated to individual salespeople, the implementation of a territorial coverage plan can begin. The sales manager should provide continuous guidance to each salesperson in an effort to produce the desired results. This entails guidance in such areas as:

- Time management
- Maintenance of customers' records
- Development of sales-call schedules
- Selection of sales routes

Effective **time management** is a critical element of successful selling performance. It is therefore essential that the sales manager guides each salesperson in time management. This is particularly important since salespeople are involved in a variety of activities such as prospecting, traveling, face-to-face selling, and preparing reports. A typical time allocation by a field salesperson is illustrated in Exhibit 5–47.

In order to ensure that the time allocated to each salesperson is spent in the most productive manner, it is necessary to minimize or eliminate various time-wasting habits. Continuous reduction or elimination of these habits helps salespeople develop effective sales-call schedules and produce excellent results. Some common time-wasters are summarized in Exhibit 5–48.

Exhibit 5–46

Annual Sales Volume Quota Report

Annual Sales Volume Quota Report						
Period: 1990	Sales quota (in $)			Commission allowance (%)	Product group breakdown	Sales territory
Salesperson	Total annual	Monthly average	Minimum level			
A. Brown	456,000	38,000	70%	5.0	A,B,C,D	1,2, and 3
B. Gray	360,000	30,000	80%	3.5	B,C,D,E	4 and 5
Total	1,920,000	160,000	80%	- - -	A,B,C,D,E	1,2,3,4,5,6,7
Prepared: C. White			Approved: A. Boss			Date: 1.1.90

Exhibit 5–47

Sales Force Time Allocation (1986)

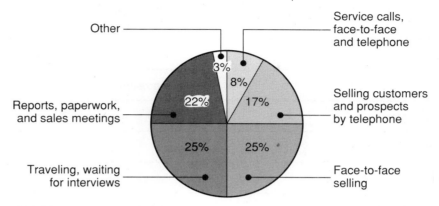

Other — 3%

Service calls, face-to-face and telephone — 8%

Reports, paperwork, and sales meetings — 22%

Selling customers and prospects by telephone — 17%

Traveling, waiting for interviews — 25%

Face-to-face selling — 25%

SOURCE: Adapted from data from *Sales & Marketing Management* (July 1986), p. 29. Reprinted with permission.

Maintenance of detailed customer records is another critical element of successful selling. The sales manager should guide each salesperson in gathering and recording updated information on each customer in a **customer record sheet**. A typical customer record sheet is illustrated in Exhibit 5–49.

Continuous updating of customer records helps salespeople identify immediate customer requirements and develop appropriate **sales-call schedules**. These schedules are usually prepared in advance on a weekly basis and include names of various individuals and organizations. A typical sales-call schedule is illustrated in Exhibit 5–50.

Selection of **sales routes** is another important area where salespeople often require guidance. Careful selection of sales routes may be useful in minimizing the travel time and expenses, increasing the number of sales calls, and producing better results. Several rules are frequently used to select the most suitable sales routes. These rules are:

- Sales routes should be circular.
- Sales routes should never cross.
- The same sales route should not be used more than once during one day.

Exhibit 5–48

Common Time-Wasters

General Problem Areas	Unique to Field Sales
Visitors	Waiting for customers
Telephone	Travel delays
Meetings	Broken appointments
Procrastination	Person contacted does not have authority to buy
Lack of planning	
Lack of priorities	Person contacted does not need your product
Overcommitment	
Lack of delegation	Chitchat about the weather or sports
Routine correspondence	Phoning in while on the road to check on prices and problems
	Adjusting call schedule on the road to fill broken appointments and put out fires

SOURCE: Douglas J. Dalrymple, *Sales Management: Concepts and Cases* (New York: John Wiley & Sons, Inc., 1988), p. 484. Reprinted with permission.

Exhibit 5–49

Customer Record Sheet

Customer Record Sheet			
Customer name:		Code No.:	
Phone No.:		Sales representative:	
Street address:			
Postal address:			
Sales territory allocation:			
Type of business:			
Number of employees:		Estimated annual sales:	
Materials/products used:			
Volume of business:		Paying behavior:	Days
Competition:			
Contact name		Position	Time to contact
1.			
2.			
3.			
Date	Contact	Current business activity	Future action

Once a routine is established, the sales manager must ensure that salespeople are constantly motivated to meet their individual objectives. The basic principles of personnel motivation have been discussed in detail in Part 2. Additional types of motivation which are particularly useful in sales management may include contests, recognition awards, or prizes.

The final important element in the sales force management and motivation process is a **sales meeting.** The prime purpose of a sales meeting is to develop

Exhibit 5–50

Sales-Call Schedule

Sales-Call Schedule					
Salesperson: A. Brown				For period: 10.2.89 – 10.7.89	
Time	Monday	Tuesday	Wednesday	Thursday	Friday
8:00	Customer A				
9:00	Customer B				
10:00	Customer C				
16:00					
17:00					
18:00					

and maintain effective communication between the sales manager and each member of the sales team. In order to ensure meaningful results each sales meeting must be planned in advance. This entails preparation of a **sales meeting agenda** that may include several topics as illustrated in Exhibit 5–51.

Sales meetings must be conducted on a regular weekly or biweekly basis to ensure continuous communication within the sales department. Sales meetings also provide an opportunity for sales personnel to report their individual progress and introduce relevant details concerning customers. The reporting procedure involves completion of a **sales progress report**, and enables the sales manager to monitor current results and evaluate business potential. A typical sales progress report is presented in Exhibit 5–52.

Exhibit 5–51

Common Topics of Sales Meetings

Subject	How Often Included		
	Always	**Sometimes**	**Never**
Sales force feedback	77	22	1
Sales progress reports	76	23	1
Sales training	60	35	5
Information on competitors' efforts	56	41	3
Product introductions	55	44	1
Product promotions	52	44	3
Recognition awards for salespeople	39	51	10
Motivational talks	36	53	11
Announcement of incentive programs	22	61	17

SOURCE: *Sales & Marketing Management,* (November 14, 1983), p. 67. Reprinted with permission.

Exhibit 5–52

Sales Progress Report

Sales Progress Report				
Period: 10.2.89 - 10.7.89		Result (in $)		Product description
Date	Customer	Quotation required	Order	
			Secured	Received	
10.2	Customer A	10,000	- - -	5,000	Product line 1
10.2	Customer B	- - -	20,000		Product line 2
10.2	Customer C	- - -	5,000	15,000	Product line 3
Total monthly		Sales quota	30,000	Final comments
		Actual	20,000	Additional orders valued at
		Variance	-10,000	$50,000 can be expected next week.
Total year-to-date		Sales quota	300,000	
		Actual	260,000	
		Variance	-40,000	
Prepared: A. Brown		Approved: C. White		Date: 10.9.89

All actual results achieved by each salesperson and recorded in the sales progress report must be summarized on a monthly and year-to-date basis. Subsequently, these results need to be compared with the corresponding sales quotas in order to determine respective variances. The aforementioned procedure provides the foundation for sales performance evaluation and control discussed next in this part.

5.19 Sales Performance Evaluation and Control

Evaluation and subsequent control of performance are critical elements of the sales management process. **Sales performance evaluation** is essentially a comparison between projected sales objectives and actual results achieved by the company. The most common sales objectives include a predetermined level of sales by a salesperson, by sales territory, by a product or service line, and by a customer. These objectives are set during the planning stage and facilitate effective **sales performance control.** In addition, performance standards are set for each salesperson, thus providing a yardstick for measuring individual results. The differences between planned objectives and actual results are identified and subsequent corrective action is taken accordingly. The sales performance evaluation and control process is outlined in Exhibit 5–53.

Evaluation of sales performance is based on detailed analysis of sales revenues attained by the company during a particular operating period. It is common, for example, to find that the bulk of business can be attributed to a small number of customers. This is known as an **80–20 principle**, which states that 80 percent of sales revenue is generated by 20 percent of the customers, or products, or sales territories. Thus, it is necessary to analyze the sales data and to identify major sources of sales revenue.

The first step in the sales performance analysis entails condensation of individual sales progress reports described earlier and preparation of **summarized sales reports.** Such reports provide *monthly* and *year-to-date* information based on the following breakdown:

- Sales by a salesperson
- Sales by sales territory
- Sales by product or service line
- Sales by a customer or industry

Exhibit 5–53

Sales Performance Evaluation and Control

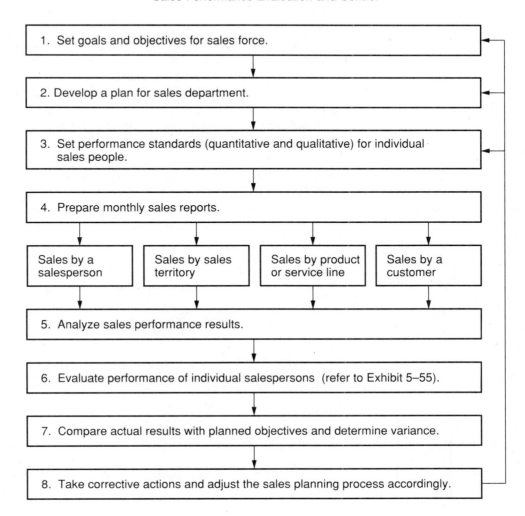

Exhibit 5–54

Sales-by-a-Salesperson Report

Sales-by-a-Salesperson Report									
Name of salesperson	Month: October 1989				Year-to-date: 1989				Percentage of plan achieved
	Sales quota	Actual result	Variance (F/U)		Sales quota	Actual result	Variance (F/U)		
Salesperson 1	$40,000	$47,000	$7,000	F	$400,000	$360,000	$40,000	U	90.0
Salesperson 2	40,000	32,000	8,000	U	400,000	410,000	10,000	F	102.5
Salesperson 3	40,000	28,000	12,000	U	400,000	300,000	100,000	U	75.0
Total	120,000	107,000	13,000	U	1,200,000	1,070,000	130,000	U	89.2

Note: *F* signifies a *favorable* result and *U* signifies an *unfavorable* result.

A **sales-by-a-salesperson report** enables the sales manager to monitor individual performance and examine results achieved by each salesperson. This report, presented in Exhibit 5–54 compares relevant sales volume quotas with appropriate monthly and year-to-date results produced and determines variances accordingly.

It appears from Exhibit 5–54 that Salesperson 1 exceeded monthly sales quota by $7,000, though he or she is still behind on a year-to-date basis by $40,000. Salesperson 2 is $8,000 short of meeting the monthly sales quota. However, on a year-to-date basis, this salesperson is still well ahead by $10,000. Salesperson 3 is behind by $12,000 and $100,000 respectively in meeting monthly and year-to-date sales quotas. The final conclusion derived from this report is expressed in *percentages of plan achieved* by each salesperson. Thus, Salesperson 2 appears on the top of the list with 102.5 percent, Salesperson 1 is 10 percent (100–90) below the plan, and Salesperson 3 is 25 percent (100–75) below the plan.

A **sales-by-a-sales-territory report** provides information about sales revenues generated by different sales territories. This report, presented in Exhibit 5–55, summarizes sales volumes per territory on a monthly and year-to-date basis and produces variances in a manner similar to the previous example.

The examination of Exhibit 5–55 leads to the conclusion that Territory 3 generates the best results by producing $15,000 and $80,000 in excess of

Exhibit 5–55

Sales-by-a-Sales-Territory Report

Sales-by-a-Sales-Territory Report									
Sales territory	Month: October 1989				Year-to-date: 1989				Percentage of plan achieved
	Budget sales	Actual sales	Variance (F/U)		Budget sales	Actual sales	Variance (F/U)		
Territory 1	$50,000	$80,000	$30,000	F	$500,000	$450,000	$50,000	U	90.0
Territory 2	70,000	60,000	10,000	U	700,000	720,000	20,000	F	102.9
Territory 3	60,000	75,000	15,000	F	600,000	680,000	80,000	F	113.3
Total	180,000	215,000	35,000	F	1,800,000	1,850,000	50,000	F	102.8

the sales budget on a monthly and year-to-date basis, respectively. Territory 2 generates second-best results by producing an excess of $20,000 on a year-to-date basis despite the fact that monthly actual sales were short by $10,000. Territory 3 generates the worst results by being short of $50,000 on a year-to-date basis, although actual monthly sales exceeded the budget by $30,000. The final conclusions are expressed in percentages of plan achieved by the company in each sales territory, i.e., Territory 3—113.3 percent, Territory 2—102.9 percent, and Territory 1—90 percent.

A sales-by-a-product-line report contains information about sales revenues generated by different product or service lines. This report, presented in Exhibit 5–56, summarizes sales volumes per product or service line on a monthly and year-to-date basis and computes variances in a manner similar to the previous examples.

Exhibit 5–56 shows that Product line C, the bestseller, achieved 108.9 percent of the plan with $80,000 excess in the year-to-date sales against the budget despite a $10,000 shortage in monthly sales. The second-best performer is Product line A. This line achieved 96.7 percent of the plan with a $20,000 shortage in the year-to-date sales, although monthly sales exceeded the budget by $15,000. Finally, the worst performer is Product line B at 75 percent of the plan achieved with a $200,000 shortage in the year-to-date sales. Its monthly sales, however, were $10,000 in excess of the budget.

A **sales-by-a-customer report** enables the sales manager to examine sales revenues generated by individual customers or industries. This report, presented in Exhibit 5–57, summarizes sales volumes per customer or industry on a monthly and year-to-date basis and produces variances similar to the previous examples.

Examination of Exhibit 5–57 enables the sales manager to identify Customer A as the best customer. This customer "achieved" 125 percent of the plan with $100,000 excess in the year-to-date sales against the budget. Customer B appears to be second best with 113.3 percent of the plan achieved with $80,000 excess in the year-to-date sales against the budget. Finally, the only poor results were derived from Customer C. Here the company achieved only 87.5 percent of the plan with $100,000 below the year-to-date sales budget.

Evaluation of monthly and year-to-date results enables the sales manager to monitor and control the overall performance of the sales organization. Although monthly results reflect the most recent sales performance, special attention should be drawn to the year-to-date values. This is particularly important because

Exhibit 5–56

Sales-by-a-Product-Line Report

Sales-by-a-Product-Line Report								
Description of a product or service line	Month: October 1989				Year-to-date: 1989				Percentage of plan achieved
	Budget sales	Actual sales	Variance (F/U)		Budget sales	Actual sales	Variance (F/U)		
Product line A	$60,000	$75,000	$15,000	F	$600,000	$580,000	$20,000	U	96.7
Product line B	80,000	90,000	10,000	F	800,000	600,000	200,000	U	75.0
Product line C	90,000	80,000	10,000	U	900,000	980,000	80,000	F	108.9
Total	230,000	245,000	15,000	F	2,300,000	2,160,000	140,000	U	93.9

Exhibit 5–57

Sales-by-a-Customer Report

	Month: October 1989			Year-to-date: 1989			Percentage of plan achieved
Name of customer	Budget sales	Actual sales	Variance (F/U)		Budget sales	Actual sales	Variance (F/U)	
Customer A	$40,000	$50,000	$10,000	F	$400,000	$500,000	$100,000	F	125.0
Customer B	60,000	50,000	10,000	U	600,000	680,000	80,000	F	113.3
Customer C	80,000	50,000	30,000	U	800,000	700,000	100,000	U	87.5
Total	180,000	150,000	30,000	U	1,800,000	1,880,000	80,000	F	104.4

year-to-date results may indicate favorable performance despite unfavorable monthly results or vice versa. By evaluating performance results the sales manager can identify company strengths and weaknesses in relation to individual sales territories, product or service lines, customers, or industries. The subsequent comparison of actual results with the planned objectives and determination of variances enables the sales manager to take corrective action and adjust the sales planning process.

Although sales volume analysis provides useful information, it does not indicate the profitability of sales territories, products and services, or customer groups. The answer to this issue can be obtained by conducting a detailed **marketing cost analysis.** This analysis accounts for all relevant cost factors involved in the production and distribution of a particular range of products or services supplied by the company. One of the major problems with the marketing cost analysis is the degree of accuracy in allocating various production and distribution costs to individual sales territories, product lines, or customer groups. Despite its potential inaccuracy, such an analysis may be a useful guideline for the level of profitability of various products and services and may facilitate improved decision-making on the part of the sales manager.

In addition to evaluating the company's sales efforts in the marketplace, it is essential to review the efforts of each salesperson. Performance evaluation by individual salesperson entails examination of several factors as illustrated in Exhibit 5–58.

The first step entails evaluation of the **quantitative factors** that relate to the "quantity" of the sales force effort (input) and results (output) during a specified operating period. The *input factors* include such elements as number of calls per day, number of working days, selling time versus nonselling time, direct selling expenses, and indirect selling activities. The *output factors,* on the other hand, include sales volume per product, customer, territory, or as a percentage of quota and market potential; and gross margin contribution by product, customer, or territory.

The second step is an examination of the **qualitative factors** that relate to the quality of the sales force effort during a specified operating period. Some of these factors are the salesperson's knowledge about products, company, competitors and customers; personal selling abilities; customer relations; and personality.

A thorough evaluation of the sales force performance and timely identification of problematic areas represent important sales management activities. These tasks enable the sales manager to monitor results produced by each salesperson and to provide effective guidance on a continuous basis.

Exhibit 5–58

Sales Force Performance Evaluation

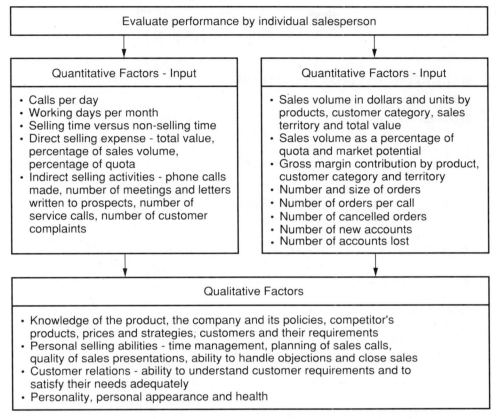

Evaluate performance by individual salesperson

Quantitative Factors - Input	Quantitative Factors - Input
• Calls per day • Working days per month • Selling time versus non-selling time • Direct selling expense - total value, percentage of sales volume, percentage of quota • Indirect selling activities - phone calls made, number of meetings and letters written to prospects, number of service calls, number of customer complaints	• Sales volume in dollars and units by products, customer category, sales territory and total value • Sales volume as a percentage of quota and market potential • Gross margin contribution by product, customer category and territory • Number and size of orders • Number of orders per call • Number of cancelled orders • Number of new accounts • Number of accounts lost

Qualitative Factors
• Knowledge of the product, the company and its policies, competitor's products, prices and strategies, customers and their requirements • Personal selling abilities - time management, planning of sales calls, quality of sales presentations, ability to handle objections and close sales • Customer relations - ability to understand customer requirements and to satisfy their needs adequately • Personality, personal appearance and health

SOURCE: Adapted from William J. Stanton and Richard H. Buskirk, *Management of the Sales Force,* 5th ed., (Homewood, IL: Richard D. Irwin, 1978), pp. 596–598. Reprinted with permission.

5.20 Marketing Audit

One of the most effective tools available to the marketing manager in evaluating the company's marketing and sales practice is a **marketing audit**.

A marketing audit is a systematic, critical, and unbiased review and appraisal of the basic objectives and policies of the marketing function and of the organization, methods, procedures, and personnel used to implement those policies and to achieve those objectives.[43]

A typical marketing audit is conducted in the same way as an accounting audit and has four basic characteristics:

- It covers the entire scope of marketing and sales activities described earlier in this part.
- It does not depend upon the operation being evaluated.
- It provides a systematic methodology for evaluating company performance in the area of marketing and sales management.
- It is conducted on a regular basis, not just when the company is experiencing problems.[44]

Marketing audits in larger companies are usually conducted by company executives who are not directly involved in the marketing and sales management

Exhibit 5–59

Major Areas of a Marketing Audit

Major Areas of a Marketing Audit

MARKETING ENVIRONMENT AUDIT

I. Macro-Environment

Economic-Demographic

1. What does the company expect in the way of inflation, material shortages, unemployment, and credit availability in the short run, intermediate run, and long run?
2. What effect will forecast trends in the size, age distribution, and regional distribution of population have on the business?

Technology

1. What major changes are occurring in product technology? In process technology?
2. What are the major generic substitutes that might replace this product?

Political-Legal

1. What laws are being proposed that may affect marketing strategy and tactics?
2. What federal, state, and local agency actions should be watched? What is happening in the areas of pollution control, equal employment opportunity, product safety, advertising, price control, etc., that is relevant to marketing planning?

Social-Cultural

1. What attitudes is the public taking toward business and toward products such as those produced by the company?
2. What changes are occurring in consumer life styles and values that have a bearing on the company's target markets and marketing methods?

II. Task Environment

Markets

1. What is happening to market size, growth, geographical distribution, and profits?
2. What are the major market segments? What are their expected rates of growth? Which are high opportunity and low opportunity segments?

Customers

1. How do current customers and prospects rate the company and its competitors, particularly with respect to reputation, product quality, service, sales force, and price?
2. How do different classes of customers make their buying decisions?
3. What are the evolving needs and satisfactions being sought by the buyers in this market?

Competitors

1. Who are the major competitors? What are the objectives and strategy of each major competitor? What are their strengths and weaknesses? What are the sizes and trends in market shares?

2. What trends can be foreseen in future competition and substitutes for this product?

Distribution and Dealers

1. What are the main trade channels bringing products to customers?
2. What are the efficiency levels and growth potentials of the different trade channels?

Suppliers

1. What is the outlook for the availability of different key resources used in production?
2. What trends are occurring among suppliers in their pattern of selling?

Facilitators

1. What is the outlook for the cost and availability of transportation services?
2. What is the outlook for the cost and availability of warehousing facilities?
3. What is the outlook for the cost and availability of financial resources?
4. How effectively is the advertising agency performing? What trends are occurring in advertising agency services?

MARKETING STRATEGY AUDIT

Marketing Objectives

1. Are the corporate objectives clearly stated and do they lead logically to the marketing objectives?
2. Are the marketing objectives stated in a clear form to guide marketing planning and subsequent performance measurement?
3. Are the marketing objectives appropriate, given the company's competitive position, resources, and opportunities? Is the appropriate strategic objective to build, hold, harvest, or terminate this business?

Strategy

1. What is the core marketing strategy for achieving the objectives? Is it a sound marketing strategy?
2. Are enough resources (or too many resources) budgeted to accomplish the marketing objectives?
3. Are the marketing resources allocated optimally to prime market segments, territories, and products of the organization?
4. Are the marketing resources allocated optimally to the major elements of the marketing mix, i.e., product quality, service, sales force, advertising, promotion, and distribution?

MARKETING ORGANIZATION AUDIT

Formal Structure

1. Is there a high level marketing officer with adequate authority and responsibility over those company activities that affect the customer's satisfaction?

Exhibit 5–59

Major Areas of a Marketing Audit (Concluded)

2. Are the marketing responsibilities optimally structured along functional product, end user, and territorial lines?

Functional Efficiency

1. Are there good communication and working relations between marketing and sales?
2. Is the product management system working effectively? Are the product managers able to plan profits or only sales volume?
3. Are there any groups in marketing that need more training, motivation, supervision, or evaluation?

Interface Efficiency

1. Are there any problems between marketing and manufacturing that need attention?
2. What about marketing and R&D?
3. What about marketing and financial management?
4. What about marketing and purchasing?

MARKETING SYSTEMS AUDIT

Marketing Information System

1. Is the marketing intelligence system producing accurate, sufficient, and timely information about developments in the marketplace?
2. Is marketing research being adequately used by company decision makers?

Marketing Planning System

1. Is the marketing planning system well-conceived and effective?
2. Is sales forecasting and market potential measurement soundly carried out?
3. Are sales quotas set on a proper basis?

Marketing Control System

1. Are the control procedures (monthly, quarterly, etc.) adequate to insure that the annual plan objectives are being achieved?
2. Is provision made to analyze periodically the profitability of different products, markets, territories, and channels of distribution?
3. Is provision made to examine and validate periodically various marketing costs?

New-Product Development System

1. Is the company well-organized to gather, generate, and screen new product ideas?
2. Does the company do adequate concept research and business analysis before investing heavily in a new idea?
3. Does the company carry out adequate product and market testing before launching a new product?

MARKETING PRODUCTIVITY AUDIT

Profitability Analysis

1. What is the profitability of the company's different products, served markets, territories, and channels of distribution?

2. Should the company enter, expand, contract, or withdraw from any business segments and what would be the short- and long-run profit consequences?

Cost-Effectiveness Analysis

1. Do any marketing activities seem to have excessive costs? Are these costs vaild? Can cost-reducing steps be taken?

MARKETING FUNCTION AUDIT

Products

1. What are the product line objectives? Are these objectives sound? Is the current product line meeting these objectives?
2. Are there particular products that should be phased out?
3. Are there new products that are worth adding?
4. Are any products able to benefit from quality, feature, or style improvements?

Price

1. What are the pricing objectives, policies, strategies, and procedures? To what extent are prices set on sound cost, demand, and competitive criteria?
2. Do the customers see the company's prices as being in line or out of line with the perceived value of its offer?
3. Does the company use price promotions effectively?

Distribution

1. What are the distribution objectives and strategies?
2. Is there adequate market coverage and service?
3. Should the company consider changing its degree of reliance on distributors, sales reps, and direct selling?

Sales Force

1. What are the organization's sales force objectives?
2. Is the sales force large enough to accomplish the company's objectives?
3. Is the sales force organized along the proper principle(s) of specialization (territory, market, product)?
4. Does the sales force show high morale, ability, and effort? Are they sufficiently trained and incentivized?
5. Are the procedures adequate for setting quotas and evaluating performances?
6. How is the company's sales force perceived in relation to competitors' sales forces?

Advertising, Promotion, and Publicity

1. What are the organization's advertising objectives? Are they sound?
2. Is the right amount being spent on advertising? How is the budget determined?
3. Are the ad themes and copy effective? What do customers and the public think about the advertising?
4. Are the advertising media well chosen?
5. Is sales promotion used effectively?
6. Is there a well-conceived publicity program?

process. Alternatively, such an audit can be conducted by an outside consultant, or in the case of smaller companies, it may be conducted as a self-audit by the marketing manager. Self-audit, however, may be biased and produce less accurate results. The marketing audit process consists of three steps:

1. Management and the auditor agree on the audit objectives, areas to be covered, depth of the investigation, sources of information, report format, and the time period of the audit.
2. Auditor collects relevant information, and conducts interviews with appropriate company employees and customers.
3. Auditor prepares final report and presents it to management.

The marketing audit, presented in Exhibit 5–59, covers six major areas:

- **Marketing environment audit.** This includes examination of broad economic, technological, political, legal, and social factors as well as consideration of customers, competitors, and other factors which may have a direct effect on the company.
- **Marketing strategy audit.** This examines the company's marketing objectives and strategies in terms of the existing situation in the marketplace.
- **Marketing organization audit.** This is an analysis of the company's ability to meet the necessary objectives through the existing formal structure and its overall organizational efficiency.
- **Marketing systems audit.** This examines the marketing information systems employed by the company and methods of marketing planning, control, and new product development.
- **Marketing productivity audit.** This includes profitability and cost-effectiveness analysis of various products, sales territories, customer groups, and other relevant units of evaluation.
- **Marketing function audit.** This includes a detailed examination of various elements of the marketing mix such as product, price, distribution, sales force, advertising, promotion, and publicity.

Once the marketing audit is completed, it provides an objective opinion pertinent to the company's current strategies and its ability to meet planned objectives within a specified period of time. It is essential, therefore, that management take a closer look at the results and adjust the marketing planning process.

5.21 Working Instructions and Forms

All information related to marketing and sales management principles has been presented in Sections 5.01–5.20. It is essential to understand this information and to proceed with the compilation of forms provided at the end of Part 5. Working instructions for completing these forms follow immediately. These instructions require that management rate its knowledge of marketing and sales management principles and evaluate company performance in the area of marketing and sales management. Aggregate scores will help to identify possible problems and to assign priorities for implementing the most effective solutions. The sequence of activities pertinent to completion of working forms is presented in Exhibit 5-60.

Exhibit 5–60

Summary of Forms for Part 5

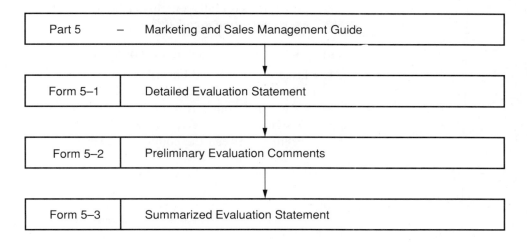

| Part 5 | – | Marketing and Sales Management Guide |

| Form 5–1 | Detailed Evaluation Statement |

| Form 5–2 | Preliminary Evaluation Comments |

| Form 5–3 | Summarized Evaluation Statement |

Form 5–1 Detailed Evaluation Statement

29. Study the description of all checkpoints related to *marketing and sales management principles* as outlined in Part 5.

30. Evaluate your personal knowledge in the area of marketing and sales management and score your *personal knowledge level* of each checkpoint. Scores should be based on the scale shown below:

0–20(%)   Very poor level of knowledge
21–40(%)   Poor level of knowledge
41–60(%)   Fair level of knowledge
61–80(%)   Good level of knowledge
81–100(%)   Very good level of knowledge

31. Evaluate your company's performance in the area of marketing and sales management and score your *company's performance level* on each checkpoint. Scores should be based on the scale shown below:

0–20(%)   Very poor level of performance (the checkpoint has never been implemented)
21–40(%)   Poor level of performance (the checkpoint is implemented sometimes)
41–60(%)   Fair level of performance (the checkpoint is implemented, but not managed well)
61–80(%)   Good level of performance (the checkpoint is implemented and managed well)
81–100(%)   Very good level of performance (the checkpoint is constantly implemented and managed very well)

32. Determine the *average evaluation level* pertaining to your personal knowledge and the company's performance within each area of marketing and sales management as follows:

$$\text{Average Evaluation Level}(\%) = \frac{\text{Total Score}}{\text{Number of Applicable Checkpoints}}$$

Form 5–2   Preliminary Evaluation Comments

33.   State your personal opinion related to marketing and sales management principles currently employed by your company and summarize *preliminary evaluation comments*.

Form 5–3   Summarized Evaluation Statement

34.   Issue Form 5–1 and Form 5–2 to key executives within your company who are actively involved in the *marketing and sales management activities* and ensure that both forms are completed in accordance with instructions.

35.   Designate a *final evaluation level*[a] for each checkpoint as a result of a meeting between the company's executives.

See continuation of working instructions on page 226 (Part 6)

---

[a]The final evaluation level may not represent an average value of the individual results and should be determined by mutual consent.

MARKETING AND SALES MANAGEMENT ANALYSIS
DETAILED EVALUATION STATEMENT

No.	DESCRIPTION	PERSONAL KNOWLEDGE LEVEL (%)	COMPANY'S PERFORMANCE LEVEL (%)				
			VERY POOR	POOR	FAIR	GOOD	VERY GOOD
		0 - 100	0 - 20	21 - 40	41 - 60	61 - 80	81 - 100
5.01	The Marketing Management Process						
5.02	Buying Behavior						
5.03	Marketing Information and Research						
5.04	Market Segmentation						
5.05	Market Measurement and Forecasting						
5.06	Marketing Strategy						
5.07	Product Strategy						
5.08	Pricing Strategy						
5.09	Promotional Strategy						
5.10	Distribution Strategy						
5.11	Marketing Plan						
5.12	The Sales Management Process						
5.13	Sales Planning and Budgeting						
5.14	Sales Organization						
5.15	Sales Force Recruitment and Training						
5.16	Personal Selling						
5.17	Sales Force Compensation						
5.18	Sales Force Management and Motivation						
5.19	Sales Performance Evaluation and Control						
5.20	Marketing Audit						
➡	AVERAGE EVALUATION LEVEL						

NAME:	POSITION:	DATE:

MARKETING AND SALES MANAGEMENT ANALYSIS
PRELIMINARY EVALUATION COMMENTS

No.	DESCRIPTION	PRELIMINARY EVALUATION COMMENTS
5.01	The Marketing Management Process	
5.02	Buying Behavior	
5.03	Marketing Information and Research	
5.04	Market Segmentation	
5.05	Marketing Measurement and Forecasting	
5.06	Marketing Process	
5.07	Product Strategy	
5.08	Pricing Strategy	
5.09	Promotional Stratgey	
5.10	Distribution Strategy	
5.11	Marketing Plan	
5.12	The Sales Management Process	
5.13	Sales Planning and Budgeting	
5.14	Sales Organization	
5.15	Sales Force Recruitment and Training	
5.16	Personal Selling	
5.17	Sales Force Compensation	
5.18	Sales Force Management and Motivation	
5.19	Sales Performance Evaluation and Control	
5.20	Marketing Audit	

| NAME: | POSITION: | DATE: |

NAME OF COMPANY:

MARKETING AND SALES MANAGEMENT ANALYSIS
SUMMARIZED EVALUATION STATEMENT

No.	DESCRIPTION	COMPANY'S PERFORMANCE LEVEL (%)				
		ASSESSED BY PRESIDENT	ASSESSED BY MARKETING EXECUTIVE	ASSESSED BY	ASSESSED BY	FINAL EVALUATION LEVEL
5.01	The Marketing Management Process					
5.02	Buying Behavior					
5.03	Marketing Information and Research					
5.04	Market Segmentation					
5.05	Market Measurement and Forecasting					
5.06	Marketing Strategy					
5.07	Product Strategy					
5.08	Pricing Strategy					
5.09	Promotional Strategy					
5.10	Distribution Strategy					
5.11	Marketing Plan					
5.12	The Sales Management Process					
5.13	Sales Planning and Budgeting					
5.14	Sales Organization					
5.15	Sales Force Recruitment and Training					
5.16	Personal Selling					
5.17	Sales Force Compensation					
5.18	Sales Force Management and Motivation					
5.19	Sales Performance Evaluation and Control					
5.20	Marketing Audit					
➝	AVERAGE EVALUATION LEVEL					

NAME:	POSITION:	DATE:

5.22 References

1. AMA Board Approves New Marketing Definition, *Marketing News*, Vol. 19 (March 1, 1985), p. 1.
2. Theodore Levitt, "Marketing Myopia," *Harvard Business Review* (July-August 1960).
3. Peter F. Drucker, *Management Tasks, Responsibilities, Practices* (New York: Harper & Row Publishers, 1974), p. 64.
4. This section is based on Paul S. Busch and Michael J. Houston, *Marketing: Strategic Foundations* (Homewood, IL: Richard D. Irwin, 1985) pp. 138, 206–207, 236–241, 255.
5. Adapted from James H. Meyers and Richard R. Mead, *The Management of Marketing Research* (Scranton, PA: International Textbook Company, 1969), pp. 27–46. Reprinted in Busch and Houston, p. 781.
6. Donald F. Cox and Robert E. Good, "How to Build a Marketing Information System," *Harvard Business Review*, Vol. 45 (May-June 1967), p. 146.
7. Richard H. Brien and James E. Stafford, "Marketing Information Systems: A New Dimension for Marketing Research," *Journal of Marketing*, Vol. 32 (July 1968), p. 20.
8. Busch and Houston, p. 807.
9. William A. Cohen, *The Practice of Marketing Management: Analysis, Planning and Implementation* (New York: Macmillan Publishing Company, 1988), p. 108.
10. Adapted from Gilbert A. Churchill, Jr., *Marketing Research: Methodological Foundations*, 3rd edition, (Hinsdale, IL: Dryden Press, 1983), pp. 145–148; Reprinted in Busch and Houston, p. 793.
11. Adapted from Busch and Houston, pp. 294–295, 309–312.
12. Spyros Makridakis and Steven C. Wheelwright, "Forecasting: Issues and Challenges for Marketing Management," *Journal of Marketing*, Vol. 41 (October 1977), p. 24. Reprinted in Cohen, p. 199. Reprinted with permission.
13. Adapted from Busch and Houston, pp. 316–317, 321–327.
14. "1983 Survey of Buying Power," *Sales & Marketing Management* (October 31, 1983); Busch and Houston, pp. 325–327. Reprinted with permission.
15. Adapted from Philip Kotler, *Marketing Management-Analysis, Planning and Control* (Englewood Cliffs, NJ: Prentice Hall, Inc., 1980).
16. Committee on Definitions of American Marketing Association, *Marketing Definitions: A Glossary of Marketing Terms* (Chicago: American Marketing Association, 1960).
17. Tom W. White, "Use Variety of Internal, External Sources to Gather and Screen New Product Ideas," *Marketing News* (September 16, 1983), p. 12. Reprinted with permission.
18. Adapted from Kent B. Monroe, *Pricing: Making Profitable Decisions* (New York: McGraw Hill, 1979), p. 5.
19. Adapted from Busch and Houston, pp. 558–570. Reprinted with permission.
20. Ibid., pp. 625–655.
21. *Marketing Definitions: A Glossary of Marketing Terms* (Chicago: American Marketing Association, 1960), p.20.
22. Adapted from Busch and Houston, p. 454–487.
23. Louis W. Stern and Adel I. El-Ansary, *Marketing Channels* (Englewood Cliffs, NJ: Prentice Hall, Inc., 1982), p. 3.
24. Busch and Houston, p. 457.
25. Ibid., pp. 467–468.
26. Adapted from William A. Cohen, pp. 44–68.
27. Ibid., pp. 66–67.
28. Stasch and Lanktree, *Can Your Marketing Planning Procedures Be Improved*, pp. 88–89.
29. Daniel T. Carroll, "How to Make Marketing Plans More Effective," *Management Review*, Vol. 68, (October 1979), pp. 60–61.

30. Adapted from Douglas J. Dalrymple, *Sales Management: Concepts and Cases* (New York: John Wiley & Sons, Inc., 1988), pp. 54–67.
31. Adapted from J. Hodge and H. J. Johnson, *Manpower and Organizational Behavior*, (New York: John Wiley & Sons, Inc., 1970), pp. 158–159.
32. Adapted from Dan H. Robertson and Danny N. Bellinger, *Sales Management: Decision Making For Improved Profitability* (New York: Macmillan Publishing Co., 1980), p. 395.
33. "Cost Per Call Up Sharply in 1977," *Sales & Marketing Management* (February 27, 1978), p. 21. Reprinted with permission.
34. The Wall Street Journal (December 1, 1986), p. 14.
35. Thomas F. Stroh, *Training and Developing the Professional Salesman* (New York: Amacom Publishing Company, 1972), p. 208.
36. Donald W. Jackson, Jr., William H. Cunningham, and Isabella C. M. Cunningham, *Selling: The Personal Force in Marketing* (New York: John Wiley & Sons, Inc., 1988), p. 2.
37. Adapted from Douglas J. Dalrymple, pp. 95–121.
38. John E. Swan, I. Frederick Trawick, and David W. Silva, "How Industrial Salespeople Gain Customer Trust," *Industrial Marketing Management*, Vol. 14, No. 1 (April 1985), pp. 203–211. Copyright 1985, by Elsevier Science Publishing Co., Inc.
39. Adapted from Douglas J. Dalrymple, pp. 376–393.
40. Adapted from Dan H. Robertson and Danny N. Bellinger, pp. 297–298.
41. Adapted from Robert F. Vizza and Thomas E. Chambers, *Time and Territorial Management for Salesmen* (New York: The Sales Executives Club, 1971), pp. 8–20.
42. Adapted from Dalrymple, pp. 474–483.
43. Abraham Schuchman, "The Marketing Audit: Its Nature, Purpose, and Problems," *Analyzing and Improving Marketing Performance*, Report no. 32 (New York: American Management Association, 1959), p. 13.
44. Philip Kotler, William Gregor, and William Rodgers, "The Marketing Audit Comes of Age," *Sloan Management Review*, Vol. 18 (Winter, 1977), p. 276.

Part 6

Business Analysis and Action Guide

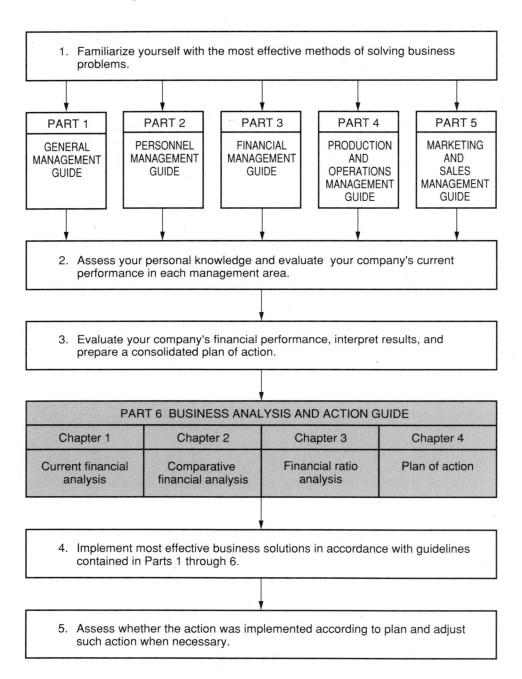

1. Familiarize yourself with the most effective methods of solving business problems.

PART 1	PART 2	PART 3	PART 4	PART 5
GENERAL MANAGEMENT GUIDE	PERSONNEL MANAGEMENT GUIDE	FINANCIAL MANAGEMENT GUIDE	PRODUCTION AND OPERATIONS MANAGEMENT GUIDE	MARKETING AND SALES MANAGEMENT GUIDE

2. Assess your personal knowledge and evaluate your company's current performance in each management area.

3. Evaluate your company's financial performance, interpret results, and prepare a consolidated plan of action.

PART 6 BUSINESS ANALYSIS AND ACTION GUIDE			
Chapter 1	Chapter 2	Chapter 3	Chapter 4
Current financial analysis	Comparative financial analysis	Financial ratio analysis	Plan of action

4. Implement most effective business solutions in accordance with guidelines contained in Parts 1 through 6.

5. Assess whether the action was implemented according to plan and adjust such action when necessary.

- *The basic elements of practical business analysis and plan of action*
- *Guidelines for evaluating your company's financial condition and performance*
- *Guidelines for developing an effective plan of action*
- *Working instructions and forms for consolidating business analysis and plan of action*

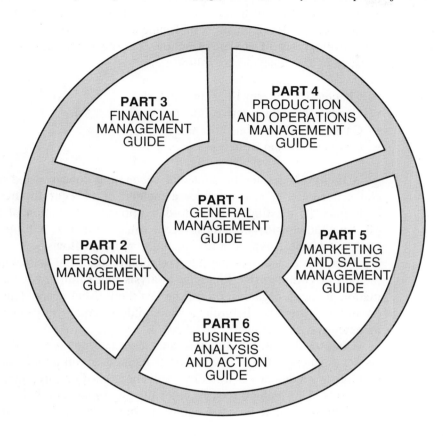

Contents

6.00 Introduction

The prime purposes of the **business analysis and action guide** are to provide effective methods of evaluating the financial condition and performance of an organization, to interpret results, and to prepare a consolidated plan of action. These methods entail a study of fundamental concepts of financial accounting system, detailed examination of financial statements, consolidation of results and development of a plan of action. The business analysis and action guide consists of four chapters as follows:

- Chapter 1—Current financial analysis
- Chapter 2—Comparative financial analysis
- Chapter 3—Financial ratio analysis
- Chapter 4—Plan of action

Chapter 1 defines fundamental accounting concepts and introduces financial statements. It also provides a method of **current financial analysis** that highlights the existing, or year-to-date, financial condition of an organization. This method considers the most recent values of assets, liabilities, shareholders' equity, revenues, expenditures, income, and cash flows.

Chapter 2 discusses the interpretation of financial statements. It presents a method of **comparative financial analysis** that summarizes the financial information about an organization for the last three fiscal years. This method focuses on trends in assets, liabilities, shareholders' equity, revenues, expenditures, income, and cash flows.

Chapter 3 continues financial statement interpretation with a special emphasis on financial ratios. It contains a method of **financial ratio analysis** that highlights a company's liquidity, solvency, profitability, and ability to manage assets. This method focuses on evaluating financial relationships between assets, liabilities, shareholders' equity, revenues, expenditures, income, and cash flows.

Chapter 4 provides a practical method for summarizing final evaluation results pertaining to a company's performance and for developing an effective **plan of action**. This method entails consolidation of information obtained during the evaluation process as discussed earlier in Parts 1 through 6. The actual implementation of a plan of action is discussed at the end of Chapter 4. In addition, this part provides details pertinent to the objectives and activities of Business Management Club, Inc.

A company's economic potential should become clearer as a result of a comprehensive financial performance evaluation. Such an evaluation will help to identify the company's existing and potential problems. This in turn will play a critical role in formulating a sound plan of action and implementing the most effective solutions to help secure a company's future.

Chapter 1

Current Financial Analysis

Contents

6.01 Introduction to Current Financial Analysis

Managers and owners need to have current financial information on the company's performance available. This information can be provided by various financial statements and should be examined on a regular basis.

Current financial analysis requires management to understand, compile, and evaluate financial information on the company's performance for the present fiscal year. This analysis will provide answers to a broad range of questions such as

- Can the company pay its current debts?
- Is the company solvent and what is its net worth?
- Is the company profitable?
- Does the company generate a positive cash flow?
- Is the company's inventory managed effectively and how does this affect profitability?
- Are the company's assets financed mainly by debt or by shareholders' equity?

The current financial analysis entails an examination of all assets, liabilities, shareholders' equity, revenues, expenses, income, cash flows, and the relationships between items of the various financial statements. It is concerned only with the most recent financial statements as the basis of evaluation.

The company's current financial analysis is divided into three tasks and includes evaluation of the following financial statements:

- Balance sheet
- Income statement (including statement of cost of goods manufactured)
- Statement of cash flows

Evaluation of the company's financial statements requires a thorough understanding of accounting terminology. In this chapter, many basic terms are presented and defined in accordance with the *generally accepted accounting principles (GAAP)*. Working instructions and forms pertinent to the current financial analysis are provided at the end of Chapter 1. Both are designed to help management complete the most recent financial statements in accordance with the **work program** presented in Exhibit 6–1.

Exhibit 6–1

Work Program for Chapter 1 of Part 6

Work Program	
Planned Action	**Objective**
1. Study of information about various components of financial statements	To attain an adequate level of knowledge pertaining to the current financial analysis method
2. Preparation of the company's latest balance sheet	To identify, summarize, and examine the year-to-date values of assets, liabilities, working capital, and shareholders' equity
3. Preparation of the company's latest income statement (including the statement of cost of goods manufactured)	To identify, summarize, and examine the year-to-date values of revenues, expenses, and income
4. Preparation of the company's latest statement of cash flows	To identify, summarize, and examine the year-to-date values of cash flows from operating, investing, and financing activities

Note: Please familiarize yourself with relevant working instructions prior to completing forms at the end of this chapter. Additional information on these forms is available from Business Management Club, Inc. upon request

6.02 Balance Sheet

The first task of the company's current financial analysis is to identify, summarize, and evaluate all components of the latest available **balance sheet.** The purposes of this statement are:

- To illustrate the financial condition of the company as of a specific date.
- To disclose all assets and liabilities of the company.
- To determine the values of working capital and shareholders' equity.

Sections 6.02.1 through 6.02.4 define the components of the balance sheet: assets, liabilities, working capital, and shareholders' equity.

6.02.1 Classification of Assets

Assets are "probable future economic benefits obtained or controlled by a particular entity as a result of past transactions or events."[1] In other words, assets represent economic resources controlled by a company and are expected to provide benefits in its future business activities. All assets, presented in Exhibit 6–2, may be classified as follows:

- Current assets
- Capital assets
- Long-term investments
- Intangible assets

Current Assets.   Current assets are " . . . cash or other assets that are reasonably expected to be. realized in cash or sold during a normal operating cycle of a business or within one year if the operating cycle is shorter than one year."[2] Such assets include cash, accounts receivable (less an allowance for uncollectible amounts), inventory, notes receivable, payments in advance, refundable deposits, short-term investments, and other assets expected to be realized in cash or utilized in operations during the normal trading cycle or within a year.

Cash includes currency, checks, money orders, certificates of deposit, and funds deposited in banks in the name of the company. This also includes cash on hand and petty cash.

Accounts receivable are short-term liquid assets that arise from the sale of materials and supply of services to customers on a credit basis. Such credit is usually termed trade credit.

Allowance for bad debt is a provision for all potentially uncollectible accounts—that portion of accounts receivable from customers who are not expected to pay.

Inventory includes all goods stored within a company or issued to its customers on a consignment basis. The classification of inventory depends upon the nature of the company's operations, for example:

- All inventory for a merchandising company is termed *merchandise inventory*.
- All inventory for a manufacturing company is categorized as *direct materials inventory*, *work-in-process inventory*, and *finished goods inventory*.

Notes receivable include all promissory notes received by the company from its debtors during the ordinary course of operating activities. These notes represent an unconditional promise to pay a specific sum of money on demand

Exhibit 6–2

A Summary of Company Assets

Current Assets:

(+)   Cash
(+)   Accounts Receivable
(−)   Allowance for Bad Debt
(+)   Merchandise Inventory
(+)   Direct Materials Inventory
(+)   Work-In-Process Inventory
(+)   Finished Goods Inventory
(+)   Notes Receivable
(+)   Prepaid Expenses
(+)   Refundable Deposits
(+)   Short-Term Investments

(+)   (=)   Total Current Assets

Capital Assets:

(+)   Land
(+)   Buildings
(−)   Accumulated Depreciation, Buildings
(+)   Production Equipment
(−)   Accumulated Depreciation, Production Equipment
(+)   Office Equipment and Furniture
(−)   Accumulated Depreciation, Office Equipment and Furniture
(+)   Vehicles
(−)   Accumulated Depreciation, Vehicles

(+)   (=)   Total Capital Assets

Long-Term Investments:

(+)   (=)   Total Long-Term Investments

Intangible Assets:

(+)   Patents, Copyrights and Trademarks (Net)
(+)   Goodwill and Other Intangible Assets (Net)

(+)   (=)   Total Intangible Assets

(=)   **Total Assets**

or during a period which usually does not exceed one year. Such notes, for example, may be issued by the company's customers for materials and services received or by the company's officers and associated organizations for short-term loans obtained.

Prepaid expenses include all payments in advance made by the company. These expenses usually include payments for rent, insurance, and certain supplies.

Refundable deposits include all company funds placed temporarily in the custody of other organizations and repayable during a period not exceeding one year.

Short-term investments include all of the company's marketable securities such as stocks and U.S. Treasury Bills intended to be realized during a period not exceeding one year.

Capital Assets.   Capital assets, alternatively known as **fixed assets** or **long-term assets**, are those resources of the company that are expected to provide service for more than one year. Such assets include land and buildings, production equipment and machinery, office equipment, furniture, and vehicles. None of these assets is intended for resale. Capital assets do not last forever, except for land. The value of these assets declines continuously because of their physical deterioration and possible obsolescence. This decline in usefulness is called **depreciation**. The total amount by which any capital asset (except land) depreciates is termed **accumulated depreciation**, and the difference between the asset's original cost and its accumulated depreciation is termed as **book value** or **carrying value**.

Land and buildings include all properties registered in the company's name. These assets, however, are often excluded from a trading company's asset list. Instead, they are assigned to a property-holding organization in order to protect them from creditors.

Production equipment is defined as all machinery and equipment within the production facility. This also includes all capitalized tools, dies, and other production accessories.

Office equipment and furniture are those capital assets utilized in the company's offices such as computers, copiers, word processors, typewriters, furniture, and other office accessories.

Vehicles include all cars and trucks owned by the company and used by the senior management, sales personnel, drivers, and other employees.

Long-Term Investments.   Long-term investments are all types of capital assets purchased by the company and held during a certain period for speculative reasons. These assets are not acquired for use in the ordinary business operations, but for resale at a suitable time for a profit. Such assets may include land, buildings, equipment, and machinery.

Intangible Assets.   Intangible assets include all types of assets which do not possess a physical substance. These assets usually relate to a range of legal rights and other trading advantages held by the company such as patents, copyrights, trademarks, and goodwill. The cost of intangible assets is allocated to a period in which the company benefits from their use. This is known as **amortization**.

6.02.2 Classification of Liabilities

Liabilities are debts. In accounting terms, liabilities are "probable future sacrifices of economic benefits arising from present obligations of a particular entity to transfer assets or provide services to other entities in the future as a result of past transactions or events."[3] All liabilities, presented in Exhibit 6–3, may be classified as follows:

- Current liabilities
- Long-term liabilities

Current Liabilities.   Current liabilities are debts and commitments that the company expects to meet either by the use of current assets or by creation of additional liabilities during the current operating cycle not exceeding one year. Such liabilities include accounts payable, bank overdraft, current portion of long-term debt, deferred revenues, dividends payable, notes payable, payroll liabilities, sales and excise taxes payable, income and property taxes payable, product warranty liability, and other obligations expected to be paid within a year.

Accounts payable are amounts owed to creditors on a short-term basis. These amounts normally arise as a result of purchasing materials and services by a company on credit.

Exhibit 6–3

A Summary of Company Liabilities

Current Liabilities:

(+)		Accounts Payable
(+)		Bank Overdraft
(+)		Current Portion of Long-Term Debt
(+)		Deferred Revenues
(+)		Dividends Payable
(+)		Notes Payable
(+)		Payroll Liabilities
(+)		Sales and Excise Taxes Payable
(+)		Income Taxes Payable
(+)		Property Taxes Payable
(+)		Product Warranty Liability
(+)		Accrued Liabilities
(+)	(=)	Total Current Liabilities

Long-Term Liabilities:

(+)		Bonds Payable
(+)		Capital Leases
(+)		Mortgages Payable
(+)		Pension Liability
(+)	(=)	Total Long-Term Liabilities
	(=)	**Total Liabilities**

Bank overdraft is a short-term financial obligation to a bank for advancing cash to the company in order to enable it to continue normal operating activities.

Current portion of long-term debt includes those parts of the long-term liabilities which are payable by the company to its creditors during the current fiscal period.

Deferred revenues include all of a company's commitments to supply materials and provide services to its customers in return for a payment received in advance. This short-term liability is also known as **unearned revenues**.

Dividends payable become a current liability only upon a decision by the company's board of directors to distribute a certain portion of earnings to shareholders. This liability does not exist until the board declares such dividends.

Notes payable include all promissory notes issued by the company to its creditors during the ordinary course of operating activities. These notes may have been issued to lenders for short-term loans received or to trade creditors for materials and services supplied.

Payroll liabilities include all of a company's liabilities associated with payroll accounting. These may include the following:

- Liabilities for employee compensation
- Liabilities for employee payroll withholdings
- Liabilities for employer payroll taxes
- Vacation pay liability

Liabilities for employee compensation include the net amount of all salaries and wages due, payable by the company to its employees at any given point in time. Wages are usually paid on a weekly or biweekly basis, and salaries are normally paid on a biweekly or monthly basis.

Liabilities for employee payroll withholdings are all of the deductions that the company is required by law to withhold from its employees and send to relevant government agencies. Such liabilities include Federal Insurance Contribution Act (FICA) taxes, and federal and state income taxes. Additional withholdings made by the company for the benefit of its employees may include medical insurance premiums, payments for pension and life insurance, union dues, and other deductions.

Liabilities for employer payroll taxes include the total amounts of all contributions that are required by law to be paid by the employer and sent directly to relevant government agencies. Such liabilities include FICA taxes (an amount of contribution paid by the employer equal to the one deducted from the employee), a federal unemployment insurance tax that is payable in accordance with the Federal Unemployment Tax Act (FUTA), and state unemployment insurance tax. All these contributions are considered operating expenses.

Vacation pay liability includes the total amount of additional compensation payable by the company to its employees on account of annual leave. The exact amount of this liability cannot be established until a later date and has to be estimated for the anticipated employment period. This liability, therefore, is termed **estimated liability** and its final value must be adjusted at a later time.

Sales and excise taxes payable are the total amount of sales and excise taxes collected by the company from its customers during a specific fiscal period in accordance with particular federal, state, and municipal requirements.

Income taxes payable represent another estimated liability and are imposed by the federal government, most state governments, and several cities. The final amount of this liability depends on the company's profitability. It must be estimated before the year's end in accordance with the anticipated results.

Property taxes payable include all property taxes levied on land, buildings, equipment, and other capital assets. These taxes are assessed by local governments on an annual basis and usually represent an additional estimated liability for the company. The exact amount of such liability can be determined only upon receiving the final account from authorities.

Product warranty liability is another example of an estimated liability. The estimated value of such liability is the projected total cost of repair and replacement of the company's products and services under guarantee. Such projection is based on past experience. This liability lasts for the life of the warranty on its products or services supplied to customers.

Accrued liabilities are all liabilities that are not already specified in accounting records. These include, for example, the interest payable on the borrowed capital and additional discounts offered to customers for a prompt settlement of accounts. The actual value of accrued liabilities can be accurately established only at the end of the accounting period.

Long-Term Liabilities.   Long-term liabilities are those commitments that the company expects to meet during a period of time exceeding one year. These include bonds payable, capital leases, mortgages payable, pensions, and other long-term financial obligations.

Bonds payable are the total value of long-term funds borrowed by the company. Repayment of these bonds is carried out in accordance with the prearranged conditions. However, the interest on the outstanding balance is normally paid every six months. Interest is an operating expense, and is not included in the amount owed on the bond.

Capital lease is a method in which one company (the *lessee*) acquires use of a capital asset over a certain period from another company (the *lessor*). The capital lease is essentially the purchase of an asset with payments on a deferred basis, but the title might not pass to the user until the final payment is made.

Each payment is regarded as a debt reduction, *not* as an operating expense. The leased asset is depreciated over the period of its useful life by the lessee, however, producing an additional tax advantage. It is important not to confuse the capital lease with an **operating lease**, which represents a short-term method of renting a capital asset. Operating lease payments are shown as **rental expense** among the operating expenses on the income statement.

Mortgages payable are long-term debts incurred by the company and secured by real estate. This liability is the principal amount of debt owed at a certain date. Payments include principal reduction and interest expense and are usually repaid on a monthly basis over a certain period ranging from 10 to 30 years or longer.

Pension liability includes the total amount payable by the company to its employees in accordance with a prearranged pension plan. This liability includes all contributions paid by the company into the pension fund and also includes amounts deducted from employees' salaries and wages.

6.02.3 Working Capital

Working capital is the difference between the values of total current assets and total current liabilities of the company. As the term suggests, it provides a working capital for day-to-day running of the business and is financed by long-term capital sources.

Working Capital = Total Current Assets − Total Current Liabilities

Working capital is frequently referred to as **net working capital** or **net current assets** of the organization. If the company's current liabilities exceed its current assets, this represents a **working capital deficit** or **net current liability**. Management should appreciate the importance of working capital and its influence on the daily running of the organization. A sufficient level of working capital will enable the company to meet its current liabilities as they mature; insufficient working capital, on the other hand, is the prime reason for slow payments to creditors and may cause financial embarrassment to management. It is essential, therefore, to evaluate the company's current financial needs and to calculate the required amount of working capital, taking into account the following:

- The value of operating and manufacturing expenses such as salaries, wages, materials, rent, and utilities
- The length of the sales or manufacturing cycle—the period from the time when the operating and manufacturing expenses are incurred to the time when the services and finished goods are paid for
- The amount of credit obtained from suppliers and other creditors and the length of such a credit

6.02.4 Shareholders' Equity

Shareholders' equity, also known as **stockholders' equity** or **owners' equity**, represents the **net worth** of the corporation, "the residual interest in the assets of an entity that remains after deducting its liabilities."[4] In other words, it is the difference between the values of total assets and total liabilities as reflected in the balance sheet presented in Exhibit 6–4.

Exhibit 6–4
Balance Sheet (Simplified)

(+)	Total Current Assets	
(−)	Total Current Liabilities	
(=)	Working Capital	
(+)	Total Capital Assets	
(+)	Total Long-Term Investments	
(+)	Total Intangible Assets	
(−)	Total Long-Term Liabilities	
(=)	Shareholders' Equity	

The value of shareholders' equity consists of two prime components:

- Contributed capital
- Retained earnings

The first component of the shareholders' equity, the **contributed capital**, represents total stock investment made by the corporations' shareholders and includes the following:

- **Preferred stock.**   This type of stock provides the most favorable conditions for distribution of assets, that is, *payment of dividends* to shareholders.
- **Common stock.**   This type of stock provides the basic rights of ownership of the company to shareholders and usually is the only stock that carries *voting rights*.
- **Paid-in capital.**   Every share of stock can be classified as "par stock" or "no-par stock." The **par stock** is a capital stock which has certain "par value," while the **no-par stock** is a capital stock which does not have a "par value." **Par value** represents a nominal amount per share that is entered into the *capital stock account* of the corporation, making up its *legal capital* structure. Legal capital represents the minimal amount which may be reported as the *contributed capital* of the corporation. Any additional amount received in excess of the minimal value of legal capital is identified and recorded as *Paid-in Capital in Excess of Par Value.*

The second component of the shareholders' equity, the **retained earnings**, represents the total net income (less adjustments) accumulated by the company since the beginning of its operating activities. Adjustments include losses, payments of dividends, and transfers to contributed capital. A typical example of both elements of the shareholders' equity is presented in Exhibit 6–5.

Exhibit 6–5

Shareholders' Equity (Example)

Contributed Capital:

(+)	Preferred Stock—$100 par value, 600 shares authorized and issued		$ 60,000
(+)	Common Stock—$10 par value, 20,000 shares authorized, 15,000 shares issued	$150,000	
(+)	Paid-in Capital in Excess of Par Value, Common	50,000	200,000
(=)	Total Contributed Capital		260,000
(+)	Retained Earnings		100,000
(=)	Total Shareholders' Equity		360,000

6.03 Income Statement

The second task of the company's current financial analysis is to identify, summarize, and evaluate all components of the latest available **income statement.** The purposes of this statement are:

- To illustrate the financial performance of the company during a certain period of time
- To establish the total values of net revenues from rendition of services or sale of goods, manufacturing costs, and operating expenses incurred during the accounting period
- To determine the values of gross margin from sales, income before taxes, and net income

The format of the income statement depends upon the nature of the company's activities. There are three general formats:

- Income statement for a service company
- Income statement for a merchandising company
- Income statement for a manufacturing company

The basic differences between the aforementioned types of business have been described earlier in Parts 3 (Volume I) and 4. Some of these differences are summarized below.

A **service company** provides a broad range of *custom* and *standard services* to its customers at regular or prearranged fees. These companies, for example, may include a beauty shop, an auto repair shop, or a painting contractor. Services are also provided by professional people, such as accountants, dentists, doctors, engineers, management consultants, and lawyers. A special feature of this type of business is that a service company does not purchase goods for resale, and has no need to carry inventory except for a minimal volume of consumable items. The cost of these items represents a part of the company's operating expenses and becomes an integral component of rendering services to customers.

A **merchandising company**, conversely, is engaged in a business of purchasing various types of merchandise for resale to customers at a profit. The merchandising operation can be carried out on two levels:

- Wholesale merchandising
- Retail merchandising

Wholesalers purchase merchandise directly from local or foreign manufacturers and usually sell their goods to individual retailers. Wholesalers normally purchase the merchandise in large quantities and are in position to enjoy the benefits of bulk buying and to obtain goods at the lowest possible prices. The process of wholesaling requires that wholesale merchants finance their operations and extend credit to customers. Wholesalers tend to specialize in certain product lines and carry substantial quantities of merchandise inventory to meet their customers' requirements.

Retailers usually purchase merchandise for resale from the wholesale trade and sometimes directly from manufacturers. They sell their goods to the general public and carry a much broader range of merchandise inventory to satisfy customers' needs. Most of the retail trade is done on a cash basis, though there is a tendency initiated by larger departmental stores to offer credit to approved customers.

Finally, a **manufacturing company** converts raw materials into a range of finished products in *job shop, batch,* or *flow production* environments. This conversion is known as the manufacturing process and it requires the input of direct materials and labor and the utilization of equipment, tools, and other production facilities. A manufacturing company carries three different types of inventories: direct materials, work-in-process, and finished goods.

The following sections describe the terminology for income calculation by defining revenues and expenses. These sections also present different formats for reporting income by service, merchandising, and manufacturing companies. Section 6.04 details the calculation of cost of goods manufactured and Section 6.05 focuses on cash flow determination.

6.03.1 Classification of Revenues

Revenue from services includes all fees charged by the company to its customers for services rendered during a specified accounting period. Sales discounts allowed to customers during this period should be deducted from the gross revenue. The balance is termed **net revenue from services**.

Revenue from sales includes all fees charged by the company to its customers for supply of merchandise or finished goods during a specified accounting period. The total value of sales returns, allowances, and discounts passed to customers during such a period should be deducted from the gross value and the balance is termed **net sales**.

Miscellaneous revenue includes total incidental revenue generated by the company during a specified accounting period—bad debt recovered, commission received, income from renting out assets, funds recovered from insurance claims, interest received, profit (loss) on disposal of capital assets, and rent received. Miscellaneous revenue is *not* added to net revenue from services nor to net sales. Rather, it should be reported after the normal income from operations has been calculated, as illustrated in Exhibit 6–6.

6.03.2 Classification of Costs

Every organization incurs expenses during a specific accounting period. **Expenses** are the **costs** of goods and services used by a company in the process of obtaining revenue. All costs have been discussed in detail in Part 3 and summarized in this section as follows:

- Costs in a service company
- Costs in a merchandising company
- Costs in a manufacturing company

Exhibit 6–6
Income Statement for a
Service Company (Simplified)

(+)	Net Revenue from Services
(−)	Total Operating Expenses
(=)	Income from Operations
(−)	Interest Expense
(+)	Net Miscellaneous Revenue
(=)	Income before Taxes
(−)	Income Taxes Expense
(=)	Net Income

Classification of Costs in a Service Company.   All costs incurred by a service company during a specified accounting period are classified as follows:

- Direct service costs
- Indirect service costs

   Direct service costs include all operating expenses that can be physically traced to a supply of services such as the salary of a consultant or the wages of a mechanic. **Indirect service costs**, or **service overheads**, conversely, include all operating expenses that cannot be directly traced to the supply of services, such as administrative, general, and selling expenses. The values of interest expense and income taxes expense are excluded from the total operating expenses and are shown separately on the income statement, as illustrated in Exhibit 6–6.

Classification of Costs in a Merchandising Company.   All costs incurred by a merchandising company during a specified accounting period are classified as follows:

- Direct merchandising costs
- Indirect merchandising costs

   Direct merchandising costs include the cost of merchandise sold by the company during a specific accounting period. This merchandise is withdrawn from the stock of goods available for sale. Such stock comprises a *beginning merchandise inventory*—merchandise inventory at the start of the accounting period plus net purchases. Stock left at the end of the accounting period becomes the *ending merchandise inventory*. The merchandise inventory level fluctuates during the accounting period and this is reflected in the values of **cost of goods available for sale** and the **cost of goods sold**.

   Indirect merchandising costs, or **merchandising overheads**, include all operating expenses such as administrative, general, and selling expenses incurred during a specific accounting period. The values of interest expense and income taxes expense are excluded from the total operating expenses and are shown separately on the income statement as illustrated in Exhibit 6–7.

Exhibit 6–7
Income Statement for a
Merchandising Company (Simplified)

(+)	Net Sales	
	(+)	Merchandise Inventory (Beginning)
	(+)	Net Purchases
	(=)	Cost of Goods Available for Sale
	(−)	Merchandise Inventory (Ending)
(−)	(=)	Cost of Goods Sold
(=)	Gross Margin from Sales	
(−)	Total Operating Expenses	
(=)	Income from Operations	
(−)	Interest Expense	
(+)	Net Miscellaneous Revenue	
(=)	Income before Taxes	
(−)	Income Taxes Expense	
(=)	Net Income	

Exhibit 6–8
Income Statement for a
Manufacturing Company (Simplified)

```
( + )   Net Sales
        ( + )   Finished Goods Inventory (Beginning)
        ( + )   Cost of Goods Manufactured
        ( = )   Cost of Goods Available for Sale
        ( − )   Finished Goods Inventory (Ending)
( − )   ( = )   Cost of Goods Sold
( = )   Gross Margin from Sales
( − )   Total Operating Expenses
( = )   Income from Operations
( − )   Interest Expense
( + )   Net Miscellaneous Revenue
( = )   Income before Taxes
( − )   Income Taxes Expense
( = )   Net Income
```

Classification of Costs in a Manufacturing Company. All costs incurred by a manufacturing company during a specified accounting period are classified as follows:

- Direct manufacturing costs
- Indirect manufacturing costs

Direct manufacturing costs include all manufacturing expenses that can be physically traced to a particular product. These costs include the net costs of all direct materials, direct labor, and direct subcontracting services.

Indirect manufacturing costs include plant overhead costs and operating expenses that cannot be physically traced to a particular product. Plant overhead costs, in turn, consist of the costs of indirect materials, indirect labor and supervision, indirect subcontracting service, production equipment depreciation, maintenance, insurance, rent, and utilities. Operating expenses, on the other hand, include all administrative, general, and selling expenses incurred during a specific accounting period. The values of interest expense and income taxes expense are excluded from the total operating expenses and are shown separately on the income statement as illustrated in Exhibit 6–8.

All direct manufacturing costs and plant overhead costs are included in the **cost of goods manufactured**. This cost is determined in the statement of cost of goods manufactured and discussed next in this chapter. The final value of this cost depends upon the utilization of *finished goods inventory,* or products ready for sale and delivery to customers. The level of finished goods inventory fluctuates during the accounting period and this is reflected in the values of **cost of goods available for sale** and **cost of goods sold**.

6.04 Statement of Cost of Goods Manufactured

This statement relates exclusively to a manufacturing company and provides a detailed breakdown of **cost of goods manufactured.** This cost has been identified earlier as the sum of all direct manufacturing costs and plant overhead costs. Additional details pertaining to these costs have been provided in Part 3.

Exhibit 6–9
Statement of Cost of Goods Manufactured (Simplified)

	(+)	Direct Materials Inventory (Beginning)
	(+)	Direct Materials Purchases (Net)
	(=)	Cost of Direct Materials Available for Use
	(−)	Direct Materials Inventory (Ending)
(+)	(=)	Cost of Direct Materials Used
(+)		Direct Labor Costs
(+)		Direct Subcontracting Service Costs
(+)		Total Plant Overhead Costs
(=)		Total Manufacturing Costs
(+)		Work-in-Process Inventory (Beginning)
(=)		Total Cost of Work-in-Process
(−)		Work-in-Process Inventory (Ending)
(=)		Cost of Goods Manufactured

The cost of goods manufactured depends upon the value of direct materials used (raw materials purchased and kept within the company's stores) and *work-in-process inventory* (raw materials used in the manufacturing process and not yet completed as finished goods). The level of *raw materials inventory* fluctuates during the accounting period, and this is reflected in the values of **cost of direct materials available for use** and **cost of direct materials used**. The level of work-in-process inventory also fluctuates during the accounting period, and this in turn is reflected in the values of **total cost of work-in-process** and **cost of goods manufactured**. All costs are summarized in the statement of cost of goods manufactured as illustrated in Exhibit 6–9.

6.05 Statement of Cash Flows

The third task of the company's current financial analysis is to identify, summarize, and evaluate all components of the latest available **statement of cash flows.**[5] The purposes of this statement are:

- To provide information about the company's **cash receipts** and **cash payments** during a specified accounting period
- To identify the company's cash flows resulting from operating, investing, and financing activities during a specified accounting period

The statement of cash flows represents an important tool that enables management to evaluate the company's liquidity; to assess the effects of major policy decisions in relation to the company's operating, investing, and financing activities, and to determine the company's dividend policy.

6.05.1 Classification of Cash Flows

The statement of cash flows includes all **cash receipts** and **cash payments** related to the company's activities during a specified accounting period. These activities are categorized as:

- Operating activities
- Investing activities
- Financing activities

Cash Flows from Operating Activities. Operating activities include all trans-actions that are neither investing nor financing. Generally, these transactions determine the company's net income, except gain or loss on the sale of capi-tal assets or retirement of debt. These activities include all operating expenses incurred during the regular running of the business. Typical cash flows from operating activities are listed below.

Cash Inflows from Operating Activities:
- Receipts from sales of goods and services to cash and credit customers
- Receipts from miscellaneous revenue—administrative fees received, bad debt recovered, commissions received, receipts of dividends or interest on investments or loans, funds recovered from insurance and legal claims, refunds from suppliers

Cash Outflows from Operating Activities:
- Payments to suppliers of goods and services
- Payments to employees for salaries and wages
- Payments for other manufacturing expenses
- Payments for other operating expenses
- Payments for interest expenses
- Payments for income taxes and penalties
- Refunds to customers

The difference between total cash inflows and total cash outflows specified above is termed **net cash flow from operating activities**.

Cash Flows from Investing Activities. Investing activities include only trans-actions relating to the acquisition or sale of capital assets, purchase or sale of short- and long-term marketable securities, and advance or collection of princi-pal amounts of loans. Typical cash flows from investing activities are illustrated below.

Cash Inflows from Investing Activities:
- Proceeds from sales of capital assets such as land, buildings, production equipment, office equipment, furniture, and vehicles
- Proceeds from sales of marketable securities and other short- and long-term investments
- Proceeds from collecting the principal amounts of loans

Cash Outflows from Investing Activities:
- Payments to purchase capital assets such as land, buildings, production equipment, office equipment, furniture, and vehicles
- Payments to purchase marketable securities and other short- and long-term investments
- Advances or loans to borrowers

The difference between total cash inflows and total cash outflows specified above is termed **net cash flow from investing activities**.

Cash Flows from Financing Activities. Financing activities include only transactions that relate to obtaining and repaying resources from or to share-holders and short- and long-term creditors. Typical cash flows from financing activities are illustrated below.

Exhibit 6–10

A Statement of Cash Flows (Simplified)

	(+)	Total Cash Inflow from Operating Activities
	(−)	Total Cash Outflow from Operating Activities
(+)	(=)	Net Cash Flow from Operating Activities
	(+)	Total Cash Inflow from Investing Activities
	(−)	Total Cash Outflow from Investing Activities
(+)	(=)	Net Cash Flow from Investing Activities
	(+)	Total Cash Inflow from Financing Activities
	(−)	Total Cash Outflow from Financing Activities
(+)	(=)	Net Cash Flow from Financing Activities
(=)		Net Increase (Decrease) in Cash
(+)		Cash Balance at the Start of the Period
(=)		Cash Balance at the End of the Period

Cash Inflows from Financing Activities:

- Proceeds from the issuance of common and preferred stock to shareholders, that is, funds received from shareholders
- Proceeds from the issuance of notes payable for short-term borrowing from creditors, that is, short-term loans received from creditors
- Proceeds from the issuance of bonds payable for long-term borrowing from creditors, such as long-term loans received from creditors

Cash Outflows from Financing Activities:

- Payments of dividends and distribution of company's reserves to shareholders
- Repayment of short-term borrowing to creditors, excluding interest
- Repayment of long-term borrowing to creditors, excluding interest
- Payments to purchase treasury stock

The difference between total cash inflows and total cash outflows specified above is termed **net cash flow from financing activities**.

6.05.2 Format of the Statement of Cash Flows

The general format of the statement of cash flows includes three basic parts that relate to operating, investing, and financing activities of the company. Each part has been previously described in detail and the whole statement requires a thorough examination. A simplified statement of cash flows is illustrated in Exhibit 6–10.

6.06 Working Instructions and Forms for Chapter 1

All information related to the company's current financial analysis has been presented in Sections 6.01–6.05. It is essential to understand this information and to proceed with the completion of the appropriate forms provided at the end of Chapter 1. Working instructions for completing these forms follow immediately. These instructions require that management compile the most recent financial statements in accordance with the sequence of activities presented in Exhibit 6–11.

Exhibit 6–11

Summary of Forms for Current Financial Analysis

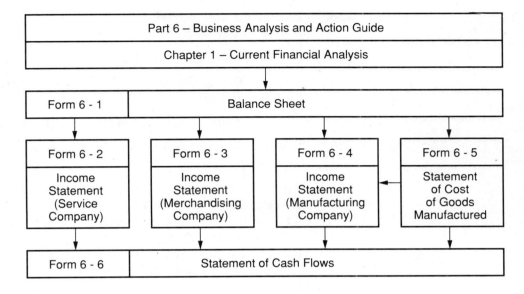

Form 6–1 Balance Sheet

36. Select an appropriate balance sheet date. This date is usually accepted as the previous month-end date, or earlier, depending upon the availability of financial information. Enter the following values at this date:

36.1 Current assets should be recorded in accordance with information contained in the general ledger. The value of inventory should be calculated on the basis of cost values and determined by physical inventory count.

36.2 Capital assets should be recorded according to their respective book values (i.e., cost minus accumulated depreciation), as reflected in the general ledger. Alternatively, they may be recorded as shown in the latest balance sheet, making due allowance for depreciation for time elapsed since the balance sheet date and taking into account any subsequent acquisition or sale of capital assets.

36.3 Long-term investments should be recorded according to their respective costs as reflected in the general ledger, or alternatively, as shown in the latest balance sheet.

36.4 Intangible assets should be recorded according to their respective book values (i.e., cost minus accumulated amortization) as reflected in the general ledger. Alternatively, they may be recorded as shown in the latest balance sheet, making due allowance for amortization for time elapsed since the balance sheet date and taking into account any subsequent acquisition or sale of intangible assets.

36.5 Current liabilities should be recorded in accordance with information contained in the general ledger.

36.6 Long-term liabilities should be recorded in accordance with information contained in the general ledger. The value shown is the principal amount owed and does not include interest.

37. Sum all assets and liabilities under their appropriate headings and compute the total assets and total liabilities respectively.

$$\text{Total Assets} = \text{Current Assets} + \text{Capital Assets} + \text{Long-Term Investments} + \text{Intangible Assets}$$

and

$$\text{Total Liabilities} = \text{Current Liabilities} + \text{Long-Term Liabilites}$$

38. Compute the working capital by deducting the total current liabilities from the total current assets.

$$\text{Working Capital} = \text{Total Current Assets} - \text{Total Current Liabilities}$$

39. Compute shareholders' equity, or net worth, by deducting the total liabilities from the total assets.

$$\text{Shareholders' Equity} = \text{Net Worth} = \text{Total Assets} - \text{Total Liabilities}$$

40. Compute the percentages that represent each aforementioned value against total assets.[a]

41. Prepare the income statement appropriate for your company's operations, and select one of the following:
- **41.1** Form 6–2—Income Statement for a Service Company (refer to instructions 42–48)
- **41.2** Form 6–3—Income Statement for a Merchandising Company (refer to instructions 49–58)
- **41.3** Form 6–4—Income Statement for a Manufacturing Company (refer to instructions 59–68)

Form 6–2 Income Statement (Service Company)

42. Select an appropriate income statement period. This period should start with the beginning of your company's current fiscal year and should end with the previously selected balance sheet date.

43. Enter the gross revenue from services generated during the period, deduct the sales discounts allowed to customers, and compute the net revenue from services.

$$\frac{\text{Net Revenue}}{\text{from Services}} = \frac{\text{Gross Revenue}}{\text{from Services}} - \frac{\text{Sales}}{\text{Discounts}}$$

44. Enter all operating expenses incurred during the period and sum these to total operating expenses.

45. Compute the income from operations for the period by deducting total operating expenses from the net revenue from services.

$$\frac{\text{Income from}}{\text{Operations}} = \frac{\text{Net Revenue}}{\text{from Services}} - \frac{\text{Total}}{\text{Operating Expenses}}$$

46. Compute the income before taxes for the period by deducting interest expense from the income from operations and adding to this the net miscellaneous revenue.

$$\frac{\text{Income before}}{\text{Taxes}} = \frac{\text{Income from}}{\text{Operations}} - \frac{\text{Interest}}{\text{Expense}} + \frac{\text{Net Miscellaneous}}{\text{Revenue}}$$

47. Compute the net income for the period by deducting the income taxes expense from the income before taxes.

$$\text{Net Income} = \frac{\text{Income}}{\text{before Taxes}} - \frac{\text{Income}}{\text{Taxes Expense}}$$

---

[a]The value of total assets is used as a reference and represents 100.0% for calculating purposes.

48. Compute the percentages that represent each aforementioned value against net revenue from services[a] and proceed with the completion of the statement of cash flows (refer to instructions 78–88).

Form 6–3 Income Statement (Merchandising Company)

49. Select an appropriate income statement period. This period should start with the beginning of your company's current fiscal year and should end with the previously selected balance sheet date.

50. Enter the gross sales generated during the period, deduct sales returns, allowances, and discounts passed to customers and compute net sales.

$$\text{Net Sales} = \text{Gross Sales} - \begin{array}{c}\text{Sales Returns,}\\\text{Allowances, and Discounts}\end{array}$$

51. Compute the cost of goods available for sale during the period by adding the cost of merchandise inventory at the start of the period to net purchases of merchandise during the same period, that is, gross purchases less purchase returns, allowances, and discounts received from suppliers.

$$\begin{array}{c}\text{Cost of Goods Available}\\\text{for Sale}\end{array} = \begin{array}{c}\text{Merchandise Inventory}\\\text{(Beginning)}\end{array} + \text{Net Purchases}$$

and

$$\begin{array}{c}\text{Net}\\\text{Purchases}\end{array} = \begin{array}{c}\text{Gross}\\\text{Purchases}\end{array} - \begin{array}{c}\text{Purchase Returns, Allowances, and}\\\text{Discounts}\end{array}$$

52. Compute the cost of goods sold during the period by deducting the cost of merchandise inventory at the end of the period from the cost of goods available for sale.

$$\begin{array}{c}\text{Cost of Goods}\\\text{Sold}\end{array} = \begin{array}{c}\text{Cost of Goods}\\\text{Available for Sale}\end{array} - \begin{array}{c}\text{Merchandise Inventory}\\\text{(Ending)}\end{array}$$

53. Compute the gross margin from sales for the period by deducting the cost of goods sold from the net sales.

$$\text{Gross Margin from Sales} = \text{Net Sales} - \text{Cost of Goods Sold}$$

54. Enter all operating expenses incurred during the period and sum these to total operating expenses.

55. Compute income from operations for the period by deducting total operating expenses from the gross margin from sales.

$$\begin{array}{c}\text{Income}\\\text{from Operations}\end{array} = \begin{array}{c}\text{Gross Margin}\\\text{from Sales}\end{array} - \begin{array}{c}\text{Total}\\\text{Operating Expenses}\end{array}$$

56. Compute the income before taxes for the period by deducting the interest expense from the income from operations and adding to this the net miscellaneous revenue.

$$\begin{array}{c}\text{Income}\\\text{Before Taxes}\end{array} = \begin{array}{c}\text{Income}\\\text{from Operations}\end{array} - \begin{array}{c}\text{Interest}\\\text{Expense}\end{array} + \begin{array}{c}\text{Net Miscellaneous}\\\text{Revenue}\end{array}$$

57. Compute the net income for the period by deducting the income taxes expense from the income before taxes.

$$\text{Net Income} = \text{Income before Taxes} - \text{Income Tax Expense}$$

---

[a]Net revenue from services is used as a reference and represents 100.0% for calculating purposes.

58. Compute the percentages that represent each aforementioned value against net sales[a] and proceed with the completion of the statement of cash flows (refer to instructions 78–88).

Form 6–4 Income Statement (Manufacturing Company)

59. Select an appropriate income statement period. This period should start with the beginning of your company's current fiscal year and should end with the previously selected balance sheet date.

60. Enter the gross sales during the selected period, deduct sales returns, allowances, and discounts passed to customers and compute the net sales.

$$\text{Net Sales} = \text{Gross Sales} - \begin{array}{c} \text{Sales Returns,} \\ \text{Allowances, and Discounts} \end{array}$$

61. Compute the cost of goods available for sale during the period by adding the cost of finished goods inventory at the start of the period and the cost of goods manufactured[b] during the same period.

$$\begin{array}{c} \text{Cost of Goods} \\ \text{Available for Sale} \end{array} = \begin{array}{c} \text{Finished Goods Inventory} \\ \text{(Beginning)} \end{array} + \begin{array}{c} \text{Cost of Goods} \\ \text{Manufactured} \end{array}$$

62. Compute the cost of goods sold during the period by deducting the cost of finished goods inventory at the end of the period from the cost of goods available for sale.

$$\begin{array}{c} \text{Cost of Goods} \\ \text{Sold} \end{array} = \begin{array}{c} \text{Cost of Goods} \\ \text{Available for Sale} \end{array} - \begin{array}{c} \text{Finished Goods Inventory} \\ \text{(Ending)} \end{array}$$

63. Compute the gross margin from sales for the period by deducting the cost of goods sold from net sales.

$$\text{Gross Margin from Sales} = \text{Net Sales} - \text{Cost of Goods Sold}$$

64. Enter all operating expenses incurred during the period and sum these to total operating expenses.

65. Compute the income from operations for the period by deducting the total operating expenses from the gross margin from sales.

$$\text{Income from Operations} = \begin{array}{c} \text{Gross Margin} \\ \text{from Sales} \end{array} - \begin{array}{c} \text{Total Operating} \\ \text{Expenses} \end{array}$$

66. Compute the income before taxes for the period by deducting the interest expense from the income from operations and adding to this the net miscellaneous revenue.

$$\begin{array}{c} \text{Income} \\ \text{before Taxes} \end{array} = \begin{array}{c} \text{Income from} \\ \text{Operations} \end{array} - \begin{array}{c} \text{Interest} \\ \text{Expense} \end{array} + \begin{array}{c} \text{Net Miscellaneous} \\ \text{Revenue} \end{array}$$

67. Compute the net income for the period by deducting the income taxes expense from the income before taxes.

$$\text{Net Income} = \text{Income before Taxes} - \text{Income Taxes Expense}$$

68. Compute the percentages that represent each aforementioned value against net sales[a] and proceed with the completion of the statement of cash flows (refer to instructions 78–88).

---

[a]Net sales is used as a reference and represents 100.0% for calculating purposes.

[b]The cost of goods manufactured is computed in Form 6–5 (refer to instructions 69–77).

Form 6–5 Statement of Cost of Goods Manufactured

69. Enter the income statement period as specified in Form 6–4 (refer to instruction 59).

70. Compute the cost of direct materials available for use during the period by adding the cost of direct materials inventory at the start of the period to direct materials purchases (net) during the same period.

$$\text{Cost of Direct Materials Available for Use} = \text{Direct Materials Inventory (Beginning)} + \text{Direct Materials Purchases (Net)}$$

and

$$\text{Direct Materials Purchases (Net)} = \text{Direct Materials Purchases (Gross)} - \text{Purchase Returns, Allowances, and Discounts}$$

71. Compute the cost of direct materials used during the period by deducting the cost of direct materials inventory at the end of the period from the cost of direct materials available for use.

$$\text{Cost of Direct Materials Used} = \text{Cost of Direct Materials Available for Use} - \text{Direct Materials Inventory (Ending)}$$

72. Enter the direct labor costs and direct subcontracting service costs incurred during the period.

73. Enter all plant overhead costs incurred during the period and sum these to total plant overhead costs.

74. Compute the total manufacturing costs incurred during the period by adding the cost of direct materials used, direct labor costs, direct subcontracting service costs and total plant overhead costs.

$$\text{Total Manufacturing Costs} = \text{Cost of Direct Materials Used} + \text{Direct Labor Costs} + \text{Direct Sub-Contracting Service Costs} + \text{Total Plant Overhead Costs}$$

75. Compute the total cost of work-in-process during the period by adding the total manufacturing costs to the work-in-process inventory at the start of the same period.

$$\text{Total Cost of Work-in-Process} = \text{Total Manufacturing Costs} + \text{Work-in-Process Inventory (Beginning)}$$

76. Compute the cost of goods manufactured during the period by deducting the cost of work-in-process inventory at the end of the same period from the total cost of work-in-process. Transfer this cost to Form 6-4.

$$\text{Cost of Goods Manufactured} = \text{Total Cost of Work-in-Process} - \text{Work-in-Process Inventory (Ending)}$$

77. Compute the percentages that represent each aforementioned value against net sales specified in Form 6–5.

Form 6–6 Statement of Cash Flows

78. Select an appropriate statement of cash flows period. This period should start with the beginning of your company's current fiscal year and should end with the previously selected balance sheet date.

79. Enter all cash receipts and payments related to the operating activities during the period and compute the net cash flow from operating activities.

80. Enter all cash receipts and payments related to the investing activities during the period and compute the net cash flow from investing activities.

81. Enter all cash receipts and payments related to the financing activities during the period and compute the net cash flow from financing activities.

82. Sum all cash receipts from operating, investing, and financing activities and compute total increases in cash during the period.

83. Sum all cash payments for operating, investing, and financing activities and compute total decreases in cash during the period.

84. Compute the net increase (decrease) in cash during the period by adding the net cash flows from operating, investing, and financing activities.

$$\begin{matrix} \text{Net Increase} \\ \text{(Decrease)} \\ \text{in Cash} \end{matrix} = \begin{matrix} \text{Net Cash Flow} \\ \text{from Operating} \\ \text{Activities} \end{matrix} + \begin{matrix} \text{Net Cash Flow} \\ \text{from Investing} \\ \text{Activities} \end{matrix} + \begin{matrix} \text{Net Cash Flow} \\ \text{from Financing} \\ \text{Activities} \end{matrix}$$

85. Enter the cash balance at the start of the period from in Form 6–1—Balance Sheet.

86. Compute the cash balance at the end of the period by adding the net increase (decrease) in cash during the period and cash balance at the start of the period.

$$\begin{matrix} \text{Cash Balance} \\ \text{at the End} \\ \text{of the Period} \end{matrix} = \begin{matrix} \text{Cash Balance} \\ \text{at the Start} \\ \text{of the Period} \end{matrix} + \begin{matrix} \text{Net Increase} \\ \text{(Decrease) in Cash} \\ \text{During the Period} \end{matrix}$$

87. Compute the percentages that represent each aforementioned cash receipt and net cash inflow against the total increases in cash during the period.[a]

88. Compute the percentages that represent each aforementioned cash payment and net cash outflow against the total decreases in cash during the period.[b]

See continuation of working instructions on page 254 (Chapter 2, Part 6)

---

[a]Total increases in cash during the period are used as a reference for evaluating individual contributors of cash increase and represent 100.0% for calculating purposes.

[b]Total decreases in cash during the period are used as reference for evaluating individual contributors of cash decrease and represent 100.0% for calculating purposes.

CURRENT FINANCIAL ANALYSIS
BALANCE SHEET

	ACTION			BALANCE SHEET DATE:		
1	2	3	CODE	ACCOUNT DESCRIPTION	VALUE	%
*			⟶	CURRENT ASSETS:		
+			101	Cash		
+			102	Accounts Receivable		
−			103	Allowance for Bad Debt		
+			104	Merchandise Inventory		
+			105	Direct Materials Inventory		
+			106	Work-in-Process Inventory		
+			107	Finished Goods Inventory		
+			108	Notes Receivable		
+			109	Prepaid Expenses		
+			110	Refundable Deposits		
+			111	Short-Term Investments		
+			112			
+			113			
=	+		100	TOTAL CURRENT ASSETS		
*			⟶	CAPITAL ASSETS:		
+			121	Land		
+			122	Buildings		
−			123	Accumulated Depreciation, Buildings		
+			124	Production Equipment		
−			125	Accumulated Depreciation, Production Equipment		
+			126	Office Equipment and Furniture		
−			127	Accumulated Depreciation, Office Equipment and Furniture		
+			128	Vehicles		
−			129	Accumulated Depreciation, Vehicles		
=	+		120	TOTAL CAPITAL ASSETS		
*			⟶	LONG-TERM INVESTMENTS:		
+			131			
+			132			
=	+		130	TOTAL LONG-TERM INVESTMENTS		
*			⟶	INTANGIBLE ASSETS:		
+			141	Patents, Copyrights and Trademarks (Net)		
+			142	Goodwill and Other Intangible Assets (Net)		
=	+		140	TOTAL INTANGIBLE ASSETS		
	=		150	TOTAL ASSETS		100.0

CURRENT FINANCIAL ANALYSIS
BALANCE SHEET

BALANCE SHEET DATE:

	ACTION					
1	2	3	CODE	ACCOUNT DESCRIPTION	VALUE	%
*			⟶	CURRENT LIABILITES:		
+			161	Accounts Payable		
+			162	Bank Overdraft		
+			163	Current Portion of Long-Term Debt		
+			164	Deferred Revenues		
+			165	Dividends Payable		
+			166	Notes Payable		
+			167	Payroll Liabilities		
+			168	Sales and Excise Taxes Payable		
+			169	Income Taxes Payable		
+			170	Property Taxes Payable		
+			171	Product Warranty Liability		
+			172	Accrued Liabilities		
+			173			
+			174			
=	+		160	TOTAL CURRENT LIABILITIES		
*			⟶	LONG-TERM LIABILITIES		
+			181	Bonds Payable		
+			182	Capital Leases		
+			183	Mortgages Payable		
+			184	Pension Liability		
+			185			
=	+		180	TOTAL LONG-TERM LIABILITIES		
	=		190	TOTAL LIABILITIES		
*	*	*	⟶	SUMMARY:		
+			100	TOTAL CURRENT ASSETS		
−	+		160	TOTAL CURRENT LIABILITIES		
=			200	WORKING CAPITAL		
+			120	TOTAL CAPITAL ASSETS		
+			130	TOTAL LONG-TERM INVESTMENTS		
+			140	TOTAL INTANGIBLE ASSETS		
−	+		180	TOTAL LONG-TERM LIABILITIES		
=	+		300	SHAREHOLDERS' EQUITY		
	=		400	SHAREHOLDERS' EQUITY AND TOTAL LIABILITIES		100.0

CURRENT FINANCIAL ANALYSIS
INCOME STATEMENT (SERVICE COMPANY)

ACTION				INCOME STATEMENT PERIOD:		
1	2	3	CODE	ACCOUNT DESCRIPTION	VALUE	%
*			➤	REVENUE FROM SERVICES:		
+			501	Gross Revenue from Services		
−			502	Sales Discounts		
=			500	NET REVENUE FROM SERVICES		100.0
	*		➤	OPERATING EXPENSES:		
	+		601	Advertising Expenses		
	+		602	Audit and Secretarial Fees		
	+		603	Bad Debt Expenses		
	+		604	Commission Fees		
	+		605	Communication Expenses		
	+		606	Depreciation and Amortization		
	+		607	Insurance Expenses		
	+		608	Legal Fees		
	+		609	Management Consulting Fees		
	+		610	Maintenance Expenses		
	+		611	Materials Purchases (Net)		
	+		612	Office Supplies and Expenses		
	+		613	Personnel Recruitment and Training Fees		
	+		614	Property Taxes		
	+		615	Rent		
	+		616	Royalties		
	+		617	Salaries and Wages, Administration and Sales		
	+		618	Salaries, Officers		
	+		619	Travelling and Entertainment		
	+		620	Utilities		
	+		621			
	+		622			
	+		623			
	+		624			
	+		625			
	+		626			
	+		627			
	+		628			
	+		629			
	=		➤	SUB-TOTAL OPERATING EXPENSES		

| | | | NAME OF COMPANY: |

CURRENT FINANCIAL ANALYSIS
INCOME STATEMENT (SERVICE COMPANY)

	ACTION			INCOME STATEMENT PERIOD:		
1	2	3	CODE	ACCOUNT DESCRIPTION	VALUE	%
		+	500	NET REVENUE FROM SERVICES (From Page 1)		100.0
	+		→	SUB-TOTAL OPERATING EXPENSES (From Page 1)		
	+		630			
	+		631			
	+		632			
	+		633			
	+		634			
	+		635			
	+		636			
	+		637			
	+		638			
	+		639			
	+		640			
	+		641			
	+		642			
	+		643			
	+		644			
	+		645			
	+		646			
	+		647			
	+		648			
	+		649			
	+		650			
	+		651			
	+		652			
	+		653			
	+		654			
	+		655			
	=	−	600	TOTAL OPERATING EXPENSES		
		=	700	INCOME FROM OPERATIONS		
		−	698	Interest Expense		
		+	580	Net Miscellaneous Revenue		
		=	800	INCOME BEFORE TAXES		
		−	699	Income Taxes Expense		
		=	900	NET INCOME		

© BUSINESS MANAGEMENT CLUB, INC. 1989

CURRENT FINANCIAL ANALYSIS
INCOME STATEMENT (MERCHANDISING COMPANY)

ACTION				INCOME STATEMENT PERIOD:		
1	2	3	CODE	ACCOUNT DESCRIPTION	VALUE	%
*			⟶	REVENUE FROM SALES:		
+			501	Gross Sales		
−			502	Sales Returns and Allowances		
−			503	Sales Discounts		
=	+		500	NET SALES		100.0
*			⟶	COST OF GOODS SOLD:		
+			601	Merchandise Inventory (Beginning)		
+			610	Net Purchases		
=			620	COST OF GOODS AVAILABLE FOR SALE		
−			621	Merchandise Inventory (Ending)		
=	−		630	COST OF GOODS SOLD		
	=		640	GROSS MARGIN FROM SALES		
	*		⟶	OPERATING EXPENSES:		
	+		651	Advertising Expenses		
	+		652	Audit and Secretarial Fees		
	+		653	Bad Debt Expenses		
	+		654	Commission Fees		
	+		655	Communication Expenses		
	+		656	Depreciation and Amortization		
	+		657	Freight Out Expenses		
	+		658	Insurance Expenses		
	+		659	Legal Fees		
	+		660	Management Consulting Fees		
	+		661	Maintenance Expenses		
	+		662	Office Supplies and Expenses		
	+		663	Personnel Recruitment and Training Fees		
	+		664	Property Taxes		
	+		665	Rent		
	+		666	Royalties		
	+		667	Salaries and Wages, Administration and Sales		
	+		668	Salaries, Officers		
	+		669	Travelling and Entertainment		
	+		670	Utilities		
	+		671			
	=		⟶	SUB-TOTAL OPERATING EXPENSES		

NAME OF COMPANY:	FORM 6 – 3 PAGE 2 OF 2

CURRENT FINANCIAL ANALYSIS

INCOME STATEMENT (MERCHANDISING COMPANY)

ACTION				INCOME STATEMENT PERIOD:		
1	2	3	CODE	ACCOUNT DESCRIPTION	VALUE	%
		+	640	GROSS MARGIN FROM SALES (From Page 1)		
	*		→	SUB-TOTAL OPERATING EXPENSES (From Page 1)		
	+		672			
	+		673			
	+		674			
	+		675			
	+		676			
	+		677			
	+		678			
	+		679			
	+		680			
	+		681			
	+		682			
	+		683			
	+		684			
	+		685			
	+		686			
	+		687			
	+		688			
	+		689			
	+		690			
	+		691			
	+		692			
	+		693			
	+		694			
	+		695			
	+		696			
	+		697			
	=	–	650	TOTAL OPERATING EXPENSES		
		=	700	INCOME FROM OPERATIONS		
		–	698	Interest Expense		
		+	580	Net Miscellaneous Revenue		
		=	800	INCOME BEFORE TAXES		
		–	699	Income Taxes Expense		
		=	900	NET INCOME		

CURRENT FINANCIAL ANALYSIS
INCOME STATEMENT (MANUFACTURING COMPANY)

NAME OF COMPANY:

ACTION				INCOME STATEMENT PERIOD:		
1	2	3	CODE	ACCOUNT DESCRIPTION	VALUE	%
*			→	REVENUE FROM SALES:		
+			501	Gross Sales		
–			502	Sales Returns and Allowances		
–			503	Sales Discounts		
=	+		500	NET SALES		100.0
*			→	COST OF GOODS SOLD:		
+			601	Finished Goods Inventory (Beginning)		
+			700	COST OF GOODS MANUFACTURED (REFER TO FORM 6–5)		
=			610	COST OF GOODS AVAILABLE FOR SALE		
–			611	Finished Goods Inventory (Ending)		
=	–		620	COST OF GOODS SOLD		
	=		630	GROSS MARGIN FROM SALES		
	*		→	OPERATING EXPENSES:		
	+		641	Advertising Expenses		
	+		642	Amortization		
	+		643	Audit and Secretarial Fees		
	+		644	Bad Debt Expenses		
	+		645	Commission Fees		
	+		646	Communication Expenses		
	+		647	Depreciation, Office Equipment and Vehicles		
	+		648	Freight Out Expenses		
	+		649	Insurance, Vehicles		
	+		650	Legal Fees		
	+		651	Management Consulting Fees		
	+		652	Maintenance, Office Equipment and Vehicles		
	+		653	Office Supplies and Expenses		
	+		654	Personnel Recruitment and Training Fees		
	+		655	Royalties		
	+		656	Salaries and Wages, Administration and Sales		
	+		657	Salaries, Officers		
	+		658	Travelling and Entertainment		
	+		659			
	+		660			
	+		661			
	=		→	SUB-TOTAL OPERATING EXPENSES		

NAME OF COMPANY:

CURRENT FINANCIAL ANALYSIS
INCOME STATEMENT (MANUFACTURING COMPANY)

ACTION				INCOME STATEMENT PERIOD:		
1	2	3	CODE	ACCOUNT DESCRIPTION	VALUE	%
		+	630	GROSS MARGIN FROM SALES (From Page 1)		
	*		⟶	SUB-TOTAL OPERATING EXPENSES (From Page 1)		
	+		662			
	+		663			
	+		664			
	+		665			
	+		666			
	+		667			
	+		668			
	+		669			
	+		670			
	+		671			
	+		672			
	+		673			
	+		674			
	+		675			
	+		676			
	+		677			
	+		678			
	+		679			
	+		680			
	+		681			
	+		682			
	+		683			
	+		684			
	+		685			
	+		686			
	+		687			
=	−		640	TOTAL OPERATING EXPENSES		
	=		800	INCOME FROM OPERATIONS		
	−		698	Interest Expense		
	+		580	Net Miscellaneous Revenue		
	=		900	INCOME BEFORE TAXES		
	−		699	Income Taxes Expense		
	=		999	NET INCOME		

CURRENT FINANCIAL ANALYSIS
STATEMENT OF COST OF GOODS MANFACTURED

ACTION			CODE	INCOME STATEMENT PERIOD (**):	VALUE	%
1	2	3	CODE	ACCOUNT DESCRIPTION	VALUE	%
*			⟶	DIRECT MATERIALS USED:		
+			701	Direct Materials Inventory (Beginning)		
+			710	Direct Materials Purchases (Net)		
=			720	COST OF DIRECT MATERIALS AVAILABLE FOR USE		
−			721	Direct Materials Inventory (Ending)		
=		+	730	COST OF DIRECT MATERIALS USED		
		+	740	DIRECT LABOR COSTS		
		+	750	DIRECT SUBCONTRACTING SERVICE COSTS		
	*		⟶	PLANT OVERHEAD COSTS:		
	+		761	Depreciation, Production Equipment		
	+		762	Indirect Labor and Supervision Costs		
	+		763	Indirect Materials Purchases (Net)		
	+		764	Insurance, Production Equipment		
	+		765	Maintenance, Production Equipment		
	+		766	Property Taxes		
	+		767	Rent		
	+		768	Rental Expense, Production Equipment		
	+		769	Utilities		
	+		770			
	+		771			
	+		772			
	+		773			
	+		774			
	+		775			
	+		776			
	+		777			
	+		778			
	+		779			
	=	+	760	TOTAL PLANT OVERHEAD COSTS		
		=	780	TOTAL MANUFACTURING COSTS		
		+	781	Work-in-Process Inventory (Beginning)		
		=	790	TOTAL COST OF WORK-IN-PROCESS		
		−	791	Work-in-Process Inventory (Ending)		
		=	700	COST OF GOODS MANUFACTURED (**)		
(**)				REFER TO INCOME STATEMENT (FORM 6 - 4)		

NAME OF COMPANY:						

CURRENT FINANCIAL ANALYSIS
STATEMENT OF CASH FLOWS

ACTION				STATEMENT OF CASH FLOWS PERIOD:		(%) OF CASH	
1	2	3	4	ACCOUNT DESCRIPTION	VALUE	INCREASE	DECREASE
*				CASH FLOWS FROM OPERATING ACTIVITIES:		–	–
+	+			Receipts from Sales of Goods and Services			–
+	+			Receipts from Miscellaneous Income			–
–		+		Payments to Suppliers of Goods and Services		–	
–		+		Payments to Employees for Salaries and Wages		–	
–		+		Payments for Other Manufacturing Expenses		–	
–		+		Payments for Other Operating Expenses		–	
–		+		Payments for Interest Expenses		–	
–		+		Payments for Income Taxes and Penalties		–	
–		+		Refunds to Customers		–	
=				NET CASH FLOW FROM OPERATING ACTIVITIES			
*				CASH FLOWS FROM INVESTING ACTIVITIES:		–	–
+	+			Proceeds from Sales of Capital Assets			–
+	+			Proceeds from Sales of Marketable Securities			–
+	+			Proceeds from Collecting Notes Receivable			–
–		+		Payments to Purchase Capital Assets		–	
–		+		Payments to Purchase Marketable Securities		–	
–		+		Advances of Loans to Borrowers		–	
=				NET CASH FLOW FROM INVESTING ACTIVITIES			
*				CASH FLOWS FROM FINANCING ACTIVITIES:		–	–
+	+			Proceeds from Issuance of Stock			–
+	+			Proceeds from Issuance of Notes Payable			–
+	+			Proceeds from Issuance of Bonds Payable			–
–		+		Payments of Dividends and Reserves to Shareholders		–	
–		+		Repayment of Short-Term Borrowings		–	
–		+		Repayment of Long-Term Borrowings		–	
–		+		Payments for Repurchase of Stock		–	
=				NET CASH FLOW FROM FINANCING ACTIVITIES			
				SUMMARY:			
	=		+	TOTAL INCREASES IN CASH DURING THE PERIOD		100.0	–
		=	–	TOTAL DECREASES IN CASH DURING THE PERIOD		–	100.0
			=	NET INCREASE (DECREASE) IN CASH			
			+	CASH BALANCE AT THE START OF THE PERIOD		–	–
			=	CASH BALANCE AT THE END OF THE PERIOD		–	–

Chapter 2

Comparative Financial Analysis

Contents

6.07 Introduction to Comparative Financial Analysis

To avoid short-sided conclusions from current financial analysis, managers need to evaluate the trend of the company's past financial performance. The latest financial statements may indicate that the company has performed well recently, but prior financial statements may reflect deteriorating conditions. Conversely, the latest financial statements may reflect bleak financial conditions and poor operating results, although the overall direction of performance may show consistent improvement.

Comparative financial analysis requires management to understand, compile, and evaluate financial information on the company's performance over a period of at least three fiscal years. This analysis should provide answers to a broad range of questions, such as:

- Is the business progressing (operating profitably) or failing (operating unprofitably)?
- Are the capital assets expanding to the detriment of working capital and, if so, is it justifiable?
- Are current and long-term liabilities causing a burdensome increase of the interest expense?
- Is shareholders' equity increasing in a proportion similar to the increase in assets?
- Is net income increasing in proportion to the increase in sales?
- Is cash flow increasing as a result of the company's operating, investing, and financing activities?

Comparative financial analysis is a detailed study of various trends reflected in a comparison of successive financial statements. In order to ease the comparison of such statements, dollar values are converted into percentages. These percentages show relative size of a particular item to the whole. The resulting statements are called **comparative** or **common-size financial statements.** For example, assets, liabilities, working capital, and shareholders' equity are expressed as percentages of total assets in the comparative (common-size) balance sheet. Revenues, expenses, and income are expressed as percentages of net revenue in the comparative (common-size) income statement. Cash receipts and cash payments associated with operating, investing, and financing activities are expressed as percentages of total increases and decreases in cash in the comparative (common-size) statement of cash flows.

The company's comparative financial analysis is divided into three tasks and includes evaluation of the following financial statements:

- Comparative balance sheet
- Comparative income statement (including comparative statement of cost of goods manufactured)
- Comparative statement of cash flows

Working instructions and forms pertinent to the comparative financial analysis are provided at the end of Chapter 2. Both are designed to help management complete comparative financial statements in accordance with the **work program** presented in Exhibit 6–12.

Exhibit 6–12

Work Program for Chapter 2 of Part 6

Work Program

Planned Action	Objective
1. Study of information about the interpretation of financial statements	To attain an adequate level of knowledge pertaining to the comparative financial analysis method
2. Preparation of the company's comparative balance sheet	To summarize the values and to examine the trends of assets, liabilities, working capital, and shareholders' equity for the last three fiscal years
3. Preparation of the company's comparative income statement (including the statement of cost of goods manufactured)	To summarize the values and to examine the trends of revenues, expenses, and income generated during the last three fiscal years
4. Preparation of the company's comparative statement of cash flows	To summarize the values and to examine the trends of cash flows from operating, investing and financing activities during the last three fiscal years

Note: Please familiarize yourself with relevant working instructions prior to completing forms at the end of this chapter. Additional information on these forms is available from Business Management Club, Inc. upon request

6.08 Comparative Balance Sheet

The first task of the company's comparative financial analysis is to identify, summarize, and evaluate trends of all balance sheet items during the last three fiscal years. The purposes of the **comparative balance sheet** are:

- To evaluate changes in the company's financial position.
- To examine changes in assets and liabilities.
- To examine changes in working capital and shareholders' equity.

6.08.1 Composition and Trend of Current Assets

Current assets generally include cash, accounts receivable, allowance for bad debts, inventory (merchandise, direct materials, work-in-process, and finished goods), notes receivable, prepaid expenses, refundable deposits, and short-term investments. These assets are discussed below and their fluctuation in value should be monitored and evaluated on a regular basis.

Cash provides the first indication of a company's liquidity, or its ability to access cash quickly. The amount and fluctuation of cash, therefore, should be monitored on a continuous basis. Cash fluctuations from one year to another should be explained if the reasons are not clear. It is important, however, to ensure that the cash position is strong during periods of sales decline, at the end of the trading season, or at the start of a long holiday. The cash balance is usually affected by management's financial policies and actions. By increasing or reducing the amount of bank overdraft and other loans on the balance sheet date, the amount of cash balance can be altered substantially although the financial condition of the company will remain unchanged. Management frequently tries to minimize the amount of the bank overdraft and other loans prior to the accounting date. Such reduction of debt by paying down with available cash resources will obviously improve certain important financial ratios. However, it may also weaken the company's liquidity.

Accounts receivable usually vary with fluctuations in sales. If the amount of accounts receivable increases at a rate faster than the increase in sales, this reflects a weakening financial condition. It may be because of poor collection efforts, an inappropriate policy of extending credit, or adverse economic conditions. Management should evaluate changes in receivables balance in conjunction with the aforementioned factors.

Allowance for bad debt should fluctuate with the potential for nonpayments by the company's customers. Slow collection may result from the poor financial condition of some customers, an unresolved dispute between the company and a particular customer, or at the onset of difficult economic times. It is essential to maintain a strict credit control policy to minimize the effect of bad debts on the company's performance.

Inventory consists of merchandise for merchandising companies or direct materials, work-in-process, and finished goods for manufacturing companies. Obviously, a larger inventory is needed as the volume of sales rises. However, it is important to keep the inventory at the lowest acceptable level because overstocking merchandise requires additional financing and results in an increased expenditure. With a reduction in sales activity, inventory should be reduced to maintain a steady level of the company's liquidity.

Notes receivable may fluctuate depending upon the financial condition of the organization. With excess cash the company may extend credit to customers or advance short-term loans to shareholders and associated organizations. As liquidity declines, the notes should be collected and not renewed. It is important to ensure that the cash loaned does not become a burden to the company's ability to pay its own accounts on time.

Prepaid expenses often depend upon the requirements imposed by the company's suppliers. Management therefore should search for alternative sources of materials and services which do not insist on payments in advance and offer favorable credit to customers. Prepayments should be kept to a minimum to avoid tying up cash.

Refundable deposits are usually required if the company is purchasing merchandise or raw materials in which the packaging must be returned to the supplier. These deposits also take place in a form of special financial guarantees provided as a part of the contractual obligation. Refundable deposits and securities should be constantly monitored and kept to a minimum to improve the liquidity of the company.

Short-term investments may fluctuate depending upon the level of available cash within the company. A highly liquid company should increase its short-term investments to get some yield from its excess cash. However, the ratio of short-term investments to the total current assets should not be too large, unless, of course, it is an investment organization.

6.08.2 Composition and Trend of Capital Assets

Capital assets normally include land and buildings, production equipment, office equipment, furniture, and vehicles. The book value of capital assets is expected to decline over a period of their useful life because of depreciation and obsolescence. These assets, however, should be evaluated on an individual basis and in conjunction with a company's overall profitability.

Land and buildings are generally the largest portion of the company's capital assets, unless they are assigned to a separate property organization. Small and medium-sized firms often form a holding company to protect land and buildings from creditors. If land and buildings belong to the primary company, their value should not exceed a certain percentage of total assets. Capital assets should support profitable operations and not be an idle investment.

Production equipment is one of the most important capital investments of any organization. Such equipment is integral to the manufacturing and operational processes and contributes toward the overall growth of the company. An increased investment in production equipment is generally needed to sustain such growth in sales and profits. Expansion should be financed by surplus cash from prior operations, by sale of stock (shareholders' equity financing), or by long-term debt financing. These methods of financing are the most suitable in acquiring capital assets. A simple withdrawal of funds from the company's working capital should not be used.

Office equipment and furniture usually represent a small percentage of the company's total capital assets and should not require special attention. It is important, however, to ensure that the amount of capital committed to such assets remains relatively low and in accordance with the overall company requirements.

Vehicles can be one of the more expensive items among the company's capital assets. The value of motor vehicles may vary depending upon the requirements of the organization and modesty of its management. It is essential to limit the company's financial resources committed to this category and to ensure that funds are employed in the most productive manner.

6.08.3 Composition and Trend of Long-Term Investments

Long-term investments usually provide the first indication of the company's solvency and its trend. A financially-strong company is expected to generate excess income from its operations. This income could be used to reduce debt, to expand production facilities, or to establish a long-term investment. The trend should show whether the company is able to maintain long-term investments for an extended period of time. Stable investments tend to indicate financial strength, but variations indicate weakness and managerial inconsistency.

6.08.4 Composition and Trend of Intangible Assets

Intangible assets are usually a minor percentage of total assets in small or medium-sized organizations. However, their importance may be great. A franchise may be the most valuable asset of a fast-food restaurant, for example, though its cost may be less than that of buildings and equipment. Only when management sells the company will such value become known. Meanwhile, intangible assets change little. They are reported only at their original cost after amortization, and amortization may be as low as 2.5% per year.

6.08.5 Composition and Trend of Current Liabilities

Current liabilities generally include accounts payable, bank overdraft, current portion of long-term debt, deferred revenues, dividends payable, notes payable, payroll liabilities, sales and excise taxes payable, income and property taxes payable, product warranty liability, and accrued liabilities. These liabilities are discussed below and their fluctuation in value should be monitored and evaluated on a continuous basis.

Accounts payable normally vary in direct proportion to purchases supporting the company's sales. If the accounts payable remain high as sales decline, this indicates a lack of cash to pay debts or poor management of purchasing merchandise. It may also result from purchasing a substantial volume of materials at a lower cost. The extension of the accounts payable period is probably one of the cheapest methods of financing operations (inventory financing). However, it is essential to ensure that such action will not affect the continuance of a sound customer-supplier relationship.

The **bank overdraft,** or **credit line,** is probably the most popular source of short-term finance for many organizations. The amount of overdraft can fluctuate continuously within the limits established by the bank. The bank expects the overdraft to be self-liquidating, that is, funds are borrowed for a limited period and should be repaid at a specified date. A sound relationship exists when sales and profits increase, and the overdraft is maintained at a prearranged level. If, however, the bank overdraft increases while the company's performance deteriorates, this should cause a concern for both parties. The bank manager may in this instance ask for additional security such as a pledge of company's assets or a guarantee of personal assets from shareholders. The bank manager will normally maintain sufficient asset security from the company in order not to be dependent upon its future sales for repayment of the overdraft.

The **current portion of long-term debt** will fluctuate in accordance with financial provisions between the company and its long-term creditors: bondholders, capital lessors, mortgagors, and note-holders. All back-payments (arrears) are also included in this liability. All payments must be met on the due date or the company's credit rating may decline rapidly. The trend of the current portion of long-term debt should not exceed the trend of cash from operations during a specific accounting period.

Deferred revenues are a cash advance received by a company for a future supply of goods or services. The amount of deferred revenues depends upon a specific agreement between the company and a particular customer. An increase of deferred revenues reflects a favorable trend and provides an effective form of financing the company's activities.

Dividends payable depend upon the decisions undertaken by the company's board of directors in accordance with the overall profitability of the organization. Small and medium-sized companies usually do not declare substantial dividends and often prefer to reinvest the bulk of their profits into the business.

Notes payable tend to fluctuate with the financial condition of the organization. An increasing trend of notes payable usually represents an unfavorable situation. It indicates that the company does not generate sufficient cash to meet operating needs and is forced subsequently to increase borrowing. However, these notes must generally be repaid within one year. It is essential to monitor the level of notes payable on a continuous basis and to limit short-term borrowing. Any additional deficiency in working capital should be funded by long-term borrowing to relieve pressure from short-term creditors. The fluctuation of notes payable should also be viewed in conjunction with the overall profitability of the organization. If notes payable increase during a period of improved profitability, this indicates effective management and an opportunity to refinance the notes with long-term debt or stock. The long-term financing can be repaid after a lengthy period of the company's expansion.

Payroll liability usually varies in direct proportion to the fluctuation of sales. An increased payroll liability can be expected during the largest sales season, but management should ensure that all payroll liabilities are discharged in time in view of high penalties imposed by various governmental institutions for late payments.

Sales and excise taxes payable depend upon the volume of the company's sales. Sales and excise taxes are collected by the company from its customers, and should be paid strictly in accordance with the regulations to avoid interest for late payments. Companies that delay prompt payment may incur penalties in addition to interest and suffer unnecessary legal problems.

Income taxes payable normally fluctuate in direct proportion to the overall profitability of the organization unless recent profits are offset by previous losses. An increased tax liability should be based on a favorable trend of the company's profits rather than poor tax management. It is essential to plan for income taxes well in advance in order to minimize the tax burden. Because of the Tax Reform Act of 1986, a small corporation may consider reverting to Subchapter S corporation, partnership, or sole proprietorship, in order to avoid both personal and corporate taxation, or double taxation. This decision should be made in collaboration with a professional tax advisor and should consider managerial benefits such as a retirement plan.

Property taxes payable change with the assessed values of the company's capital assets. This liability also depends upon the specific governmental regulations and is imposed on all organizations in a similar manner. It cannot, therefore, be regulated by the company's management and should be duly paid to avoid any penalties.

Product warranty liability depends primarily upon the quality of products and services supplied by the company to its customers. An increasing trend of product warranty liability reflects a negative situation in which management estimates that more funds will be needed in the future to accommodate possible product defects. However, no cash needs to be set aside immediately. Cash payments will be made as defects are corrected in the future.

Accrued liabilities usually vary with the fluctuation of sales. These liabilities represent a small portion of total current liabilities, but should be kept under control and reviewed on a continuous basis.

6.08.6 Composition and Trend of Long-Term Liabilities

Long-term liabilities usually include bonds payable, capital leases, mortgages payable, and pension liability. These liabilities may fluctuate from one year to the next and their values should be examined on a regular basis.

Bonds payable vary in accordance with the long-term financial requirements of the organization and its ability to generate surplus cash flow. The fluctuation of bonds payable should be examined in conjunction with an assessment of the company's profitability and a need for permanent working capital or capital assets. A favorable situation exists when a trend of increased bonds payable is accompanied by a constantly improving return on investment. If bonds payable increase while the return on investment falls, however, management has cause for concern.

Capital leases may fluctuate with the company's development plans and requirements for capital assets. These assets are usually very costly and are paid for by the organization over a period of several years. An increasing trend of capital leases indicates a purchase of additional equipment, furniture, vehicles, and other capital assets. Such a trend is favorable, provided the company expands its operational activities. If, however, the company commits itself to purchasing additional capital assets while there is inadequate growth of sales, this may subsequently lead to weakened liquidity and cash flow problems.

Mortgages payable depend upon the overall long-term commitments of the organization pertaining to the ownership of real estate. Every new acquisition of land and buildings results in a sizeable increase of mortgages payable. This often imposes an additional burden on the company's liquidity, but it may result in a lucrative long-term investment and subsequently strengthen the overall financial condition of the organization.

Pension liability varies according to the number and tenure of employees within the organization, and hence, this liability is expected to increase during a period of growth. The percentage of such a liability should always remain small in relation to the total amount of long-term liabilities.

6.08.7 Composition and Trend of Working Capital

Working capital requirements fluctuate widely from one accounting period to another depending upon the volume of business transacted by the company. The level and quality of current assets require careful examination, particularly accounts receivable and inventory. When the company's volume of sales is decreasing, working capital requirements are usually reduced in a similar proportion. Accounts receivable should decline and the level of inventory should be reduced in line with the decreased volume of sales. Current liabilities should also decline. Unfortunately, these reductions are not automatic. Receivables collection slows in recession, and a decreased volume of sales causes accumulation of inventory. Extra managerial action is needed to avoid the financial strains of excessive working capital.

As the company's volume of sales increases, working capital requirements normally grow in a similar proportion. Accounts receivable will increase and the level of inventory should rise in proportion with the increased volume of sales. Indeed, inventory accumulation may lead the rise of sales in an expansion. This growth of current assets must be properly funded. Accounts receivable from customers are an inadequate and very temporary source of funds, and bank overdraft and other forms of short-term finance are also generally insufficient for such needs. Hence, long-term financing is required for a "permanent" expansion of working capital. Without extended financing the company's liquidity will be threatened and insolvency could ensue.

The fluctuation of working capital may be influenced by various sources as follows:

- Working capital may be increased as a result of improved profits that are not paid as dividends, by sales of stock to shareholders, by an increase in long-term liabilities, and finally by the sale of certain capital assets with the reinvestment of cash received into additional current assets.
- Working capital may be reduced as a result of decreasing profit, excessive dividend payout, the retirement of long-term liabilities, or the purchase of additional capital assets using short-term funds.

If sales grow but the company does not produce increased earnings, the working capital requirements will continue to grow. The company must either reduce expenses or find new sources of finance to continue the sales expansion.

This can be achieved by raising additional short-term or long-term funds in which:

- Short-term funds should be utilized if the increase in sales is of a temporary nature.
- Long-term funds should be utilized if the increase in sales is permanent.

6.08.8 Composition and Trend of Shareholders' Equity

Shareholders' equity represents the **net worth**, or **residual value**, of the company to owners. This is the amount left for shareholders after assets are sold and debts paid. Shareholders' equity can be valued in two ways: book value and market value. Both measures will be discussed below.

Book value represents the value of shareholders' equity according to accounting rules used to compile the balance sheet. This is the amount that shareholders would theoretically receive in a liquidation if assets were sold at the amount shown on the books after paying off all liabilities. Book value does not represent the "true" value of the shareholders' interest in the company.

The **market value,** on the other hand, is the fair price that shareholders could obtain by selling their interest. The difference between book value and market value can be substantial, depending primarily upon the variance between the book value and market price of the company's assets, including its goodwill.

Shareholders' equity on the books is changed by earnings, dividends, and stock issuance. The most common factor influencing the value of shareholders' equity is the profitability of the organization. Earnings cause a direct increase in the book value of shareholders' equity, and losses reduce the value by a similar amount.

The payment of dividends also reduces shareholders' equity. The amount of these payments depends upon the company's financial policy and its level of profitability during a specific accounting period. Retaining the bulk of the company's earnings and reinvesting them into the business represents a sound practice commonly used in commerce. Retained earnings may provide sufficient working capital for expanding the business or financing an increased investment in capital assets. Retained earnings usually represent the largest single source of capital available to small and medium-sized organizations.

Shareholders' equity may also be increased by the sale of stock. These sales provide additional capital needed to offset losses or to expand the company's operations. The sale of stock obviously increases the shareholders' equity and the redemption of shares decreases shareholders' equity. If the company's board of directors decides to declare a bonus issue of stock, or **stock dividend,** this will have no effect on the total value of shareholders' equity. A stock dividend represents the investment of retained earnings to issued shares. No assets, however, are affected by such a transaction.

6.09 Comparative Income Statement

The second task of the company's comparative financial analysis is to identify, summarize, and evaluate trends of all income statement items during the last three fiscal years. The primary purposes of the **comparative income statement** are:

- To evaluate changes in the company's financial performance
- To examine the composition of revenues generated and expenses incurred
- To examine the gross margin from sales and net income

6.09.1 Composition and Trend of Revenues

Revenue is one of the most important parameters of a company's performance. It is essential to monitor the trend of revenues from services rendered or goods sold in order to ascertain whether there is a positive or negative growth in business activity. An increasing trend in revenues does not necessarily mean that the company's profitability increases: on the contrary, an increase in revenues may sometimes cause a loss if the selling price has not kept pace with costs. Hence, the trend in revenues should be viewed in conjunction with expenses.

6.09.2 Composition and Trend of Expenditure

Expenditure is another important parameter that reflects the performance of an organization. The nature of the company's expenses has been previously described in Chapter 1. How expenses behave will be revealed in their relationship to sales revenue over several accounting periods. Each expense should be expressed as a percentage of net revenue generated during the same period. A particular cost may increase steadily although the trend of percentages may decrease continuously. This suggests that management of such expenditure is increasingly efficient. When the growth rate of net revenue is slower than the growth rate of a given cost, however, the reverse situation will occur. It is essential not only to examine the values of the company's expenditure, but also to compute the percentages relative to net revenue. It is important, therefore, to establish the trend for each cost and to compare it with the industry average if possible.

6.09.3 Composition and Trend of Net Income

Net income summarizes organizational performance for a specific accounting period. All economic consequences to shareholders are included in net income, except for the appreciation of inventory, capital assets, and long-term investments. The trend of net income should be monitored on a continuous basis, particularly in relation to the shareholders' equity and in relation to investment opportunities.

The company's trend of net income, similar to the trend of revenues, should be compared to that of the particular industry. Net income and revenue trends are usually comparable with one another, but several observations have been made about net income:

- Net income of most successful organizations tends to increase at a faster rate than the growth in sales volume.
- Net income of most unsuccessful organizations tends to decrease at a faster rate than the decrease in sales volume.

Most manufacturing companies, for example, have substantial plant overhead costs, so a certain volume of sales must be obtained before the manufacturing operations become profitable. When the company reaches the **break-even point,** no profit is earned and no loss is incurred. As the sales volume exceeds the break-even level, the company's earnings will rise more rapidly than the growth in sales volume. This indicates a more efficient utilization of capital assets.

The company's level of earnings may not increase at the start of growth in sales, however. This may happen because of increased costs of materials, labor, and other expenses. A capacity expansion of capital assets may also add costs and reduce earnings.

The company's level of earnings is an important item for comparative analysis. It is essential not only to identify the trend of net income but also to establish reasons for a particular trend. There are three general reasons for trends: price, volume, and costs. Price should be competitive for the value of product sold. There are occasions when additional sales are generated only through substantial price reductions, but under such conditions, an increase in sales may be accompanied by deteriorating profitability. Often advertising and marketing costs may be necessary to boost sales, but these increased costs may prevent net income from changing.

Volume may be inadequate despite pricing below competition, perhaps because the company's products or services are not of sufficient quality. Deficient quality may result from obsolete equipment, ineffective management, or both. Volume may also be low if the company does not employ suitable personnel or has a poor marketing plan. The comparative analysis of company costs should indicate the deficiency.

6.10 Comparative Statement of Cash Flows

The third task of the company's comparative financial analysis is to identify, summarize, and evaluate trends of all statement of cash flow items during the last three fiscal years. The primary purposes of the **comparative statement of cash flows** are:

- To evaluate the effects on the company's cash flows as a result of its operating, investing, and financing activities
- To examine the cash receipts and cash payments
- To examine the net cash flows from operating, investing, and financing activities
- To examine the net increase or decrease in cash

6.10.1 Composition and Trend of Cash Flows from Operating Activities

The **net cash flow from operating activities** represents one of the most significant parameters of the company's liquidity. It is important, therefore, to monitor the trend of net cash flow from such activities and to ensure that the company will not have difficulties in meeting its short-term financial obligations.

The company's liquidity can be evaluated by observing the trend of cash from operations and the net balance of accounts receivable minus accounts payable. If the trend of the net cash flows declines, it may be offset by a positive difference between accounts receivable and accounts payable. Cash should be available shortly from the receivables. However, if the trend of the net cash flow is declining while the difference between accounts receivable and accounts payable is negative, the company's liquidity is threatened. Payments are due soon, but operations are not expected to provide adequate cash. A positive net cash flow from operating activities enhances the company's ability to meet its short-term financial commitments and allows investment of excess funds.

6.10.2 Composition and Trend of Cash Flows from Investing Activities

The **net cash flow from investing activities** provides information about the expansion or contraction of the company's capacity. It also includes information about the accumulation or liquidation of reserves available to retire long-term debt. This value relates primarily to the purchase and sale of capital assets and marketable securities. Hence, the trend of net cash flow from investing activities indicates whether management is carrying out its strategic plans in the preparation for a long-term future.

6.10.3 Composition and Trend of Cash Flows from Financing Activities

The **net cash flow from financing activities** describes the financial condition of the organization. This value summarizes the short- and long-term financial transactions between the company and its creditors and shareholders. Greater debt indicates greater risk and higher interest rates in the future. Thus, the trend of net cash flow from financing activities and determination of its influence on the overall trend of cash flows may provide a useful information.

6.10.4 Composition and Trend of Net Increase or Decrease in Cash

The **net increase or decrease in cash** is an important consequence of management's operating, investing, and financing activities. This value provides a critical parameter in evaluating the overall liquidity of the organization and is useful in assessing the company's ability to generate positive cash flow in the future. It is essential to examine the net increase or decrease in cash, taking into account the effect of operating, investing, and financing activities on an individual basis. This will provide the company's management with the following:

- Contribution of net cash flow from operating activities to the cash balance at the end of the accounting period
- Contribution of net cash flow from investing activities to the cash balance at the end of the accounting period
- Contribution of net cash flow from financing activities to the cash balance at the end of the accounting period

6.11 Working Instructions and Forms for Chapter 2

All information related to the company's comparative financial analysis has been presented in Sections 6.07–6.10. It is essential to understand this information and to proceed with the completion of the appropriate forms provided at the end of Chapter 2. Working instructions for completing these forms follow immediately. These instructions require that management summarize information contained in the relevant financial statements in accordance with the sequence of activities presented in Exhibit 6–13.

Exhibit 6–13

Summary of Forms for Comparative Financial Analysis

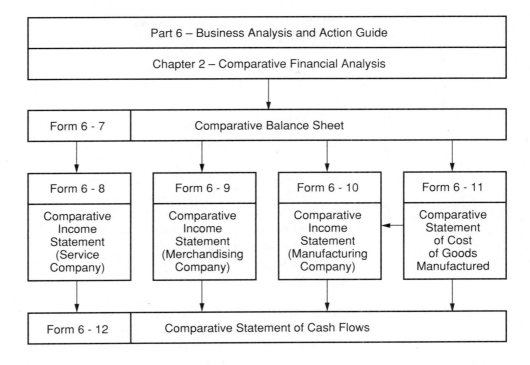

Form 6–7 Comparative Balance Sheet

89. Select appropriate comparative balance sheet dates that represent the closing dates of three previous fiscal years and enter the following values pertinent to each date:

    89.1 Current assets should be recorded in accordance with information contained in relevant balance sheets.

    89.2 Capital assets should be recorded in accordance with information contained in relevant balance sheets.

    89.3 Long-term investments should be recorded in accordance with information contained in relevant balance sheets.

    89.4 Intangible assets should be recorded in accordance with information contained in relevant balance sheets.

    89.5 Current liabilities should be recorded in accordance with information contained in relevant balance sheets

    89.6 Long-term liabilities should be recorded in accordance with information contained in relevant balance sheets.

90. Sum all assets and liabilities under their appropriate headings and compute the total assets and total liabilities respectively.

91. Compute the working capital by deducting total current liabilities from the corresponding total current assets.

92. Compute shareholders' equity, or net worth, by deducting the total liabilities from the corresponding total assets.

93. Compute the percentages that represent each aforementioned value against the corresponding total assets.[a]

---

[a]The values of total assets for each period are used as a reference and represent 100.0% for calculating purposes.

94.   Prepare the comparative income statement appropriate for your company's operations, and select one of the following:

    94.1   Form 6–8—Comparative Income Statement for a Service Company (refer to instructions 95–101).

    94.2   Form 6–9—Comparative Income Statement for a Merchandising Company (refer to instructions 102–111).

    94.3   Form 6–10—Comparative Income Statement for a Manufacturing Company (refer to instructions 112–121).

Form 6–8 Income Statement (Service Company)

95.   Select appropriate comparative income statement periods that represent three previous fiscal years.

96.   Enter the gross revenue from services generated during each period, deduct the appropriate sales discounts passed to customers, and compute the net revenue from services.

97.   Enter all operating expenses incurred during each period and sum these to total operating expenses.

98.   Compute the income from operations for each period by deducting the total operating expenses from the corresponding net revenue from services.

99.   Compute the income before taxes for each period by deducting interest expense from the corresponding income from operations and adding to this the net miscellaneous revenue.

100.   Compute the net income for each period by deducting the income taxes expense from the corresponding income before taxes.

101.   Compute the percentages that represent each aforementioned value against net revenue[a] from services and proceed with the completion of the comparative statement of cash flows (refer to instructions 131–141).

Form 6–9 Income Statement (Merchandising Company)

102.   Select appropriate comparative income statement periods that represent three previous fiscal years.

103.   Enter the gross sales generated during each period, deduct the appropriate sales returns, allowances, and discounts passed to customers, and compute the net sales.

104.   Compute the cost of goods available for sale during each period by adding the cost of merchandise inventory at the start of the period to the corresponding net purchases of merchandise during the period, i.e., gross purchases less purchase returns, allowances and discounts received from suppliers.

105.   Compute the cost of goods sold during each period by deducting the cost of merchandise inventory at the end of the period from the corresponding cost of goods available for sale.

106.   Compute the gross margin from sales for each period by deducting the cost of goods sold from the corresponding net sales.

107.   Enter all operating expenses incurred during each period and sum these to total operating expenses.

---

[a]Net revenue from services for each period is used as a reference and represents 100.0% for calculating purposes.

108. Compute income from operations for each period by deducting the total operating expenses from the corresponding gross margin from sales.

109. Compute the income before taxes for each period by deducting interest expense from the corresponding income from operations and adding to this the net miscellaneous revenue.

110. Compute the net income for each period by deducting the income taxes expense from the corresponding income before taxes.

111. Compute the percentages that represent each aforementioned value against net sales[a] and proceed with the completion of the comparative statement of cash flows (refer to instructions 131–141).

Form 6–10 Income Statement (Manufacturing Company)

112. Select appropriate comparative income statement periods that represent three previous fiscal years.

113. Enter the gross sales generated during each period, deduct the appropriate sales returns, allowances, and discounts passed to customers, and compute the net sales.

114. Compute the cost of goods available for sale during each period by adding the cost of finished goods inventory at the start of each period to the corresponding cost of goods manufactured during the period.[b]

115. Compute the cost of goods sold during each period by deducting the cost of finished goods inventory at the end of the period from the corresponding cost of goods available for sale.

116. Compute the gross margin from sales for each period by deducting the cost of goods sold from the corresponding net sales.

117. Enter all operating expenses incurred during each period and sum these to total operating expenses.

118. Compute the income from operations for each period by deducting the total operating expenses from the corresponding gross margin from sales.

119. Compute the income before taxes for each period by deducting interest expense from the corresponding income from operations and adding to this the net miscellaneous revenue.

120. Compute the net income for each period by deducting the income taxes expense from the corresponding income before taxes.

121. Compute the percentages that represent each aforementioned value against net sales[a] and proceed with the completion of the comparative statement of cash flows (refer to instructions 131–141).

Form 6–11 Comparative Statement of Cost of Goods Manufactured

122. Enter the comparative income statement periods as specified in Form 6–10, (refer to instruction 112).

123. Compute the cost of direct materials available for use during each period by adding the cost of direct materials inventory at the start of the period to the corresponding direct materials purchases (net).

124. Compute the cost of direct materials used during each period by deducting the cost of direct materials inventory at the end of the period from the corresponding cost of direct materials available for use.

125. Enter direct labor costs and direct subcontracting service costs incurred during each period.

---

[a]Net sales for each period is used as a reference and represents 100.0% for calculating purposes.

[b]The cost of goods manufactured during each period is computed in Form 6–11 (refer to instructions 122–130).

126. Enter all plant overhead costs incurred during each period and sum these to the total plant overhead costs.

127. Compute the total manufacturing costs incurred during each period by adding the cost of direct materials used, direct labor costs, direct subcontracting service costs, and total plant overhead costs.

128. Compute the total cost of work-in-process during each period by adding total manufacturing costs incurred to the corresponding cost of work-in-process inventory at the start of the period.

129. Compute the cost of goods manufactured during each period by deducting the cost of work-in-process inventory at the end of the period from the corresponding total cost of work-in-process.

130. Compute the percentages that represent each aforementioned cost against net sales.[a]

Form 6–12 Comparative Statement of Cash Flows

131. Select appropriate comparative statement of cash flows periods that represent the three previous fiscal years.

132. Enter all cash receipts and payments related to the operating activities during each period and compute the net cash flow from operating activities.

133. Enter all cash receipts and payments related to the investing activities during each period and compute the net cash flow from investing activities.

134. Enter all cash receipts and payments related to the financing activities during each period and compute the net cash flow from financing activities.

135. Sum all cash receipts from the operating, investing, and financing activities for each period into total increases in cash during the period.

136. Sum all cash payments for the operating, investing, and financing activities for each period into total decreases in cash during the period.

137. Compute the net increase (decrease) in cash during each period by adding the corresponding values of net cash flow from operating, investing, and financing activities.

138. Enter the cash balance at the start of the period for each period as reflected in Form 6–7—Comparative Balance Sheet.

139. Compute the cash balance at the end of the period for each period by adding the net increase (decrease) in cash during the period and corresponding cash balance at the start of the period.

140. Compute the percentages that represent each aforementioned cash receipt and net cash flow increases against the total increases in cash during each period.[b]

141. Compute the percentages that represent each aforementioned cash payment and net cash flow decrease against the total decreases in cash during each period.[c]

See continuation of working instructions on page 292 (Chapter 3, Part 6)

---

[a] Net sales for each period is used as a reference and represents 100.0% for calculating purposes.

[b] Total increases in cash during each period are used as a reference for evaluating individual contributors of cash increase and represent 100.0% for calculating purposes.

[c] Total decreases in cash during each period are used as a reference for evaluating individual contributors of cash decrease and represent 100.0% for calculating purposes.

COMPARATIVE FINANCIAL ANALYSIS
COMPARATIVE BALANCE SHEET

ACTION				ACCOUNT DESCRIPTION	A		
1	2	3	CODE			VALUE	%
*			⟶	CURRENT ASSETS:			
+			101	Cash			
+			102	Accounts Receivable			
–			103	Allowance for Bad Debt			
+			104	Merchandise Inventory			
+			105	Direct Materials Inventory			
+			106	Work-in-Process Inventory			
+			107	Finished Goods Inventory			
+			108	Notes Receivable			
+			109	Prepaid Expenses			
+			110	Refundable Deposits			
+			111	Short-Term Investments			
+			112				
+			113				
=	+		100	TOTAL CURRENT ASSETS			
*			⟶	CAPITAL ASSETS:			
+			121	Land			
+			122	Buildings			
–			123	Accumulated Depreciation, Buildings			
+			124	Production Equipment			
–			125	Accumulated Depreciation, Production Equipment			
+			126	Office Equipment and Furniture			
–			127	Accumulated Depreciation, Office Equipment and Furniture			
+			128	Vehicles			
–			129	Accumulated Depreciation, Vehicles			
=	+		120	TOTAL CAPITAL ASSETS			
*			⟶	LONG TERM-INVESTMENTS:			
+			131				
+			132				
=	+		130	TOTAL LONG-TERM INVESTMENTS			
*			⟶	INTANGIBLE ASSETS:			
+			141	Patents, Copyrights and Trademarks (Net)			
+			142	Goodwill and Other Intangible Assets (Net)			
=	+		140	TOTAL INTANGIBLE ASSETS			
	=		150	TOTAL ASSETS			100.0

COMPARATIVE FINANCIAL ANALYSIS
COMPARATIVE BALANCE SHEET

1	2	3	CODE	ACCOUNT DESCRIPTION	A	VALUE	%
*			——►	CURRENT LIABILITES:			
+			161	Accounts Payable			
+			162	Bank Overdraft			
+			163	Current Portion of Long-Term Debt			
+			164	Deferred Revenues			
+			165	Dividends Payable			
+			166	Notes Payable			
+			167	Payroll Liabilities			
+			168	Sales and Excise Taxes Payable			
+			169	Income Taxes Payble			
+			170	Property Taxes Payble			
+			171	Product Warranty Liability			
+			172	Accrued Liabilities			
+			173				
+			174				
–	+		160	TOTAL CURRENT LIABILITIES			
*			——►	LONG-TERM LIABILITIES:			
+			181	Bonds Payable			
+			182	Capital Leases			
+			183	Mortgages Payable			
-			184	Pension Liability			
+			185				
–	+		180	TOTAL LONG-TERM LIABILITIES			
	=		190	TOTAL LIABILITIES			
*	*	*	——►	SUMMARY:			
+			100	TOTAL CURRENT ASSETS			
–	+		160	TOTAL CURRENT LIABILITIES			
=			200	WORKING CAPITAL			
+			120	TOTAL CAPITAL ASSETS			
+			130	TOTAL LONG-TERM INVESTMENTS			
+			140	TOTAL INTANGIBLE ASSETS			
–	+		180	TOTAL LONG-TERM LIABILITIES			
=	+		300	SHAREHOLDERS' EQUITY			
	=		400	SHAREHOLDERS' EQUITY AND TOTAL LIABILITIES			100.0

COMPARATIVE FINANCIAL ANALYSIS
COMPARATIVE BALANCE SHEET

1	2	3	CODE	ACCOUNT DESCRIPTION	A VALUE	%
*			⟶	CURRENT LIABILITES:		
+			161	Accounts Payable		
+			162	Bank Overdraft		
+			163	Current Portion of Long-Term Debt		
+			164	Deferred Revenues		
+			165	Dividends Payable		
+			166	Notes Payable		
+			167	Payroll Liabilities		
+			168	Sales and Excise Taxes Payable		
+			169	Income Taxes Payble		
+			170	Property Taxes Payble		
+			171	Product Warranty Liability		
+			172	Accrued Liabilities		
+			173			
+			174			
–	+		160	TOTAL CURRENT LIABILITIES		
*			⟶	LONG-TERM LIABILITIES:		
+			181	Bonds Payable		
+			182	Capital Leases		
+			183	Mortgages Payable		
-			184	Pension Liability		
+			185			
–	+		180	TOTAL LONG-TERM LIABILITIES		
	=		190	TOTAL LIABILITIES		
*	*	*	⟶	SUMMARY:		
+			100	TOTAL CURRENT ASSETS		
–	+		160	TOTAL CURRENT LIABILITIES		
=			200	WORKING CAPITAL		
+			120	TOTAL CAPITAL ASSETS		
+			130	TOTAL LONG-TERM INVESTMENTS		
+			140	TOTAL INTANGIBLE ASSETS		
–	+		180	TOTAL LONG-TERM LIABILITIES		
=	+		300	SHAREHOLDERS' EQUITY		
	=		400	SHAREHOLDERS' EQUITY AND TOTAL LIBILITIES		100.0

INFORMATION CONTAINED HEREIN RELATES TO THE FOLLOWING FISCAL PERIODS:							
COLUMNS A, B, C				COLUMN D		COLUMN E	
COMPARATIVE ANALYSIS RESULTS				CURRENT YEAR BUDGET		NEXT YEAR BUDGET	
B		C		D		E	
VALUE	%	VALUE	%	VALUE	%	VALUE	%
	100.0		100.0		100.0		100.0

COMPARATIVE FINANCIAL ANALYSIS
COMPARATIVE INCOME STATEMENT (SERVICE COMPANY)

ACTION				ACCOUNT DESCRIPTION	A		
1	2	3	CODE			VALUE	%
*			→	REVENUE FROM SERVICES:			
+			501	Gross Revenue from Services			
−			502	Sales Discounts			
=		+	500	NET REVENUE FROM SERVICES			100.0
	*		→	OPERATING EXPENSES:			
	+		601	Advertising Expenses			
	+		602	Audit and Secretarial Fees			
	+		603	Bad Debt Expenses			
	+		604	Commission Fees			
	+		605	Communication Expenses			
	+		606	Depreciation and Amortization			
	+		607	Insurance Expenses			
	+		608	Legal Fees			
	+		609	Management Consulting Fees			
	+		610	Maintenance Expenses			
	+		611	Materials Purchases (Net)			
	+		612	Office Supplies and Expenses			
	+		613	Personnel Recruitment and Training Fees			
	+		614	Property Taxes			
	+		615	Rent			
	+		616	Royalties			
	+		617	Salaries and Wages, Administration and Sales			
	+		618	Salaries, Officers			
	+		619	Travelling and Entertainment			
	+		620	Utilities			
	+		621				
	+		622				
	+		623				
	+		624				
	+		625				
	+		626				
	+		627				
	+		628				
	+		629				
	=		→	SUB-TOTAL OPERATING EXPENSES			

INFORMATION CONTAINED HEREIN RELATES TO THE FOLLOWING FISCAL PERIODS:							
COLUMNS A, B, C				COLUMN D		COLUMN E	
COMPARATIVE ANALYSIS RESULTS				CURRENT YEAR BUDGET		NEXT YEAR BUDGET	
B		C		D		E	
VALUE	%	VALUE	%	VALUE	%	VALUE	%
	100.0		100.0		100.0		100.0

COMPARATIVE FINANCIAL ANALYSIS
COMPARATIVE INCOME STATEMENT (SERVICE COMPANY)

ACTION			CODE	ACCOUNT DESCRIPTION	A	VALUE	%
1	2	3					
		+	500	NET REVENUE FROM SERVICES (From Page 1)			100.0
	+		→	SUB-TOTAL OPERATING EXPENSES (From Page 1)			
	+		630				
	+		631				
	+		632				
	+		633				
	+		634				
	+		635				
	+		636				
	+		637				
	+		638				
	+		639				
	+		640				
	+		641				
	+		642				
	+		643				
	+		644				
	+		645				
	+		646				
	+		647				
	+		648				
	+		649				
	+		650				
	+		651				
	+		652				
	+		653				
	+		654				
	+		655				
=	−		600	TOTAL OPERATING EXPENSES			
	=		700	INCOME FROM OPERATIONS			
	−		698	Interest Expense			
	+		580	Net Miscellaneous Revenue			
	=		800	INCOME BEFORE TAXES			
	−		699	Income Taxes Expense			
	=		900	NET INCOME			

INFORMATION CONTAINED HEREIN RELATES TO THE FOLLOWING FISCAL PERIODS:								
COLUMNS A, B, C				COLUMN D		COLUMN E		
COMPARATIVE ANALYSIS RESULTS				CURRENT YEAR BUDGET		NEXT YEAR BUDGET		
B		C		D		E		
VALUE	%	VALUE	%	VALUE	%	VALUE	%	
	100.0		100.0		100.0		100.0	

COMPARATIVE FINANCIAL ANALYSIS
COMPARATIVE INCOME STATEMENT (MERCHANDISING COMPANY)

ACTION 1	ACTION 2	ACTION 3	CODE	ACCOUNT DESCRIPTION	A VALUE	%
*			→	REVENUE FROM SALES:		
+			501	Gross Sales		
−			502	Sales Returns and Allowances		
−			503	Sales Discounts		
=	+		500	NET SALES		100.0
*			→	COST OF GOODS SOLD:		
+			601	Merchandise Inventory (Beginning)		
+			610	Net Purchases		
=			620	COST OF GOODS AVAILABLE FOR SALE		
−			621	Merchandise Inventory (Ending)		
=	−		630	COST OF GOODS SOLD		
	=		640	GROSS MARGIN FROM SALES		
	*		→	OPERATING EXPENSES:		
	+		651	Advertising Expenses		
	+		652	Audit and Secretarial Fees		
	+		653	Bad Debt Expenses		
	+		654	Commission Fees		
	+		655	Communication Expenses		
	+		656	Depreciation and Amortization		
	+		657	Freight Out Expenses		
	+		658	Insurance Expenses		
	+		659	Legal Fees		
	+		660	Management Consulting Fees		
	+		661	Maintenance Expenses		
	+		662	Office Supplies and Expenses		
	+		663	Personnel Recruitment and Training Fees		
	+		664	Property Taxes		
	+		665	Rent		
	+		666	Royalties		
	+		667	Salaries and Wages, Administration and Sales		
	+		668	Salaries, Officers		
	+		669	Travelling and Entertainment		
	+		670	Utilities		
	+		671			
	=		→	SUB-TOTAL OPERATING EXPENSES		

INFORMATION CONTAINED HEREIN RELATES TO THE FOLLOWING FISCAL PERIODS:							
COLUMNS A,B,C				COLUMN D		COLUMN E	
COMPARATIVE ANALYSIS RESULTS				CURRENT YEAR BUDGET		NEXT YEAR BUDGET	
B		C		D		E	
VALUE	%	VALUE	%	VALUE	%	VALUE	%
	100.0		100.0		100.0		100.0

COMPARATIVE FINANCIAL ANALYSIS
COMPARATIVE INCOME STATEMENT (MERCHANDISING COMPANY)

	ACTION				A	
1	2	3	CODE	ACCOUNT DESCRIPTION	VALUE	%
		+	640	GROSS MARGIN FROM SALES (From Page 1)		
	*		→	SUB-TOTAL OPERATING EXPENSES (From Page 1)		
	+		672			
	+		673			
	+		674			
	+		675			
	+		676			
	+		677			
	+		678			
	+		679			
	+		680			
	+		681			
	+		682			
	+		683			
	+		684			
	+		685			
	+		686			
	+		687			
	+		688			
	+		689			
	+		690			
	+		691			
	+		692			
	+		693			
	+		694			
	+		695			
	+		696			
	+		697			
=	−		650	TOTAL OPERATING EXPENSES		
		=	700	INCOME FROM OPERATIONS		
		−	698	Interest Expense		
		+	580	Net Miscellaneous Revenue		
		=	800	INCOME BEFORE TAXES		
		−	699	Income Taxes Expense		
		=	900	NET INCOME		

INFORMATION CONTAINED HEREIN RELATES TO THE FOLLOWING FISCAL PERIODS:							
COLUMNS A, B, C				COLUMN D		COLUMN E	
COMPARATIVE ANALYSIS RESULTS				CURRENT YEAR BUDGET		NEXT YEAR BUDGET	
B		C		D		E	
VALUE	%	VALUE	%	VALUE	%	VALUE	%

COMPARATIVE FINANCIAL ANALYSIS
COMPARATIVE INCOME STATEMENT (MANUFACTURING COMPANY)

	ACTION				A		
1	2	3	CODE	ACCOUNT DESCRIPTION		VALUE	%
*			⟶	REVENUE FROM SALES:			
+			501	Gross Sales			
−			502	Sales Returns and Allowances			
−			503	Sales Discounts			
=	+		500	NET SALES			100.0
*			⟶	COST OF GOODS SOLD:			
+			601	Finished Goods Inventory (Beginning)			
+			700	COST OF GOODS MANUFACTURED (REFER TO FORM 6 -11)			
=			610	COST OF GOODS AVAILABLE FOR SALE			
−			611	Finished Goods Inventory (Ending)			
=	−		620	COST OF GOODS SOLD			
	=		630	GROSS MARGIN FROM SALES			
	*		⟶	OPERATING EXPENSES:			
	+		641	Advertising Expenses			
	+		642	Amortization			
	+		643	Audit and Secretarial Fees			
	+		644	Bad Debt Expenses			
	+		645	Commission Fees			
	+		646	Communication Expenses			
	+		647	Depreciation, Office Equipment and Vehicles			
	+		648	Freight Out Expenses			
	+		649	Insurance, Vehicles			
	+		650	Legal Fees			
	+		651	Management Consulting Fees			
	+		652	Maintenance, Office Equipment and Vehicles			
	+		653	Office Supplies and Expenses			
	+		654	Personnel Recruitment and Training Fees			
	+		655	Royalties			
	+		656	Salaries and Wages, Administration and Sales			
	+		657	Salaries, Officers			
	+		658	Travelling and Entertainment			
	+		659				
	+		660				
	+		661				
	=		⟶	SUB-TOTAL OPERATING EXPENSES			

INFORMATION CONTAINED HEREIN RELATES TO THE FOLLOWING FISCAL PERIODS:							
COLUMNS A,B,C				COLUMN D		COLUMN E	
COMPARATIVE ANALYSIS RESULTS				CURRENT YEAR BUDGET		NEXT YEAR BUDGET	
B		C		D		E	
VALUE	%	VALUE	%	VALUE	%	VALUE	%
	100.0		100.0		100.0		100.0

COMPARATIVE FINANCIAL ANALYSIS
COMPARATIVE INCOME STATEMENT (MANUFACTURING COMPANY)

	ACTION					A	
1	2	3	CODE	ACCOUNT DESCRIPTION		VALUE	%
		+	630	GROSS MARGIN FROM SALES (From Page 1)			
	*		→	SUB-TOTAL OPERATING EXPENSES (From Page 1)			
	+		662				
	+		663				
	+		664				
	+		665				
	+		666				
	+		667				
	+		668				
	+		669				
	+		670				
	+		671				
	+		672				
	+		673				
	+		674				
	+		675				
	+		676				
	+		677				
	+		678				
	+		679				
	+		680				
	+		681				
	+		682				
	+		683				
	+		684				
	+		685				
	+		686				
	+		687				
=	−		640	TOTAL OPERATING EXPENSES			
	=		800	INCOME FROM OPERATIONS			
	−		698	Interest Expense			
	+		580	Net Miscellaneous Revenue			
	=		900	INCOME BEFORE TAXES			
	−		699	Income Taxes Expense			
	=		999	NET INCOME			

INFORMATION CONTAINED HEREIN RELATES TO THE FOLLOWING FISCAL PERIODS:							
COLUMNS A,B,C				COLUMN D		COLUMN E	
COMPARATIVE ANALYSIS RESULTS				CURRENT YEAR BUDGET		NEXT YEAR BUDGET	
B		C		D		E	
VALUE	%	VALUE	%	VALUE	%	VALUE	%

NAME OF COMPANY:	FORM 6 – 11
	PAGE 1 OF 1

COMPARATIVE FINANCIAL ANALYSIS

COMPARATIVE STATEMENT OF COST OF GOODS MANUFACTURED

ACTION				ACCOUNT DESCRIPTION	A	
1	2	3	CODE		VALUE	%
*			→	DIRECT MATERIALS USED:		
+			701	Direct Materials Inventory (Beginning)		
+			710	Direct Materials Purchases (Net)		
=			720	COST OF DIRECT MATERIALS AVAILABLE FOR USE		
–			721	Direct Materials Inventory (Ending)		
=		+	730	COST OF DIRECT MATERIALS USED		
		+	740	DIRECT LABOR COSTS		
		+	750	DIRECT SUBCONTRACTING SERVICE COSTS		
	*		→	PLANT OVERHEAD COSTS:		
	+		761	Depreciation, Production Equipment		
	+		762	Indirect Labor and Supervision Costs		
	+		763	Indirect Materials Purchases (Net)		
	+		764	Insurance, Production Equipment		
	+		765	Maintenance, Production Equipment		
	+		766	Property Taxes		
	+		767	Rent		
	+		768	Rental Expense, Production Equipment		
	+		769	Utilities		
	+		770			
	+		771			
	+		772			
	+		773			
	+		774			
	+		775			
	+		776			
	+		777			
	+		778			
	+		779			
	=	+	760	TOTAL PLANT OVERHEAD COSTS		
		=	780	TOTAL MANUFACTURING COSTS		
		+	781	Work-in-Process Inventory (Beginning)		
		+	790	TOTAL COST OF WORK-IN-PROCESS		
		–	791	Work-in-Process Inventory (Ending)		
		=	700	COST OF GOODS MANUFACTURED (**)		

(**) REFER TO COMPARATIVE INCOME STATEMENT (FORM 6 - 10)

INFORMATION CONTAINED HEREIN RELATES TO THE FOLLOWING FISCAL PERIODS:							
COLUMNS A,B,C				COLUMN D		COLUMN E	
COMPARATIVE ANALYSIS RESULTS				CURRENT YEAR BUDGET		NEXT YEAR BUDGET	
B		C		D		E	
VALUE	%	VALUE	%	VALUE	%	VALUE	%

CURRENT FINANCIAL ANALYSIS
COMPARATIVE STATEMENT OF CASH FLOWS

ACTION				ACCOUNT DESCRIPTION	A		(%) OF CASH	
1	2	3	4			VALUE	INCREASE	DECREASE
*				CASH FLOWS FROM OPERATING ACTIVITIES:			–	–
+	+			Receipts from Sales of Goods and Services				–
+	+			Receipts from Miscellaneous Income				–
–		+		Payments to Suppliers of Goods and Services			–	
–		+		Payments to Employees for Salaries and Wages			–	
–		+		Payments for Other Manufacturing Expenses			–	
–		+		Payments for Other Operating Expenses			–	
–		+		Payments for Interest Expenses			–	
–		+		Payments for Income Taxes and Penalties			–	
–		+		Refunds to Customers			–	
=				NET CASH FLOW FROM OPERATING ACTIVITIES				
*				CASH FLOWS FROM INVESTING ACTIVITIES:			–	–
+	+			Proceeds from Sales of Captial Assets				–
+	+			Proceeds from Sales of Marketable Securities				–
+	+			Proceeds from Collecting Notes Receivable				–
–		+		Payments to Purchase Capital Assets			–	
–		+		Payments to Purchase Marketable Securities			–	
–		+		Advances of Loans to Borrowers			–	
=				NET CASH FLOW FROM INVESTING ACTIVITIES				
*				CASH FLOWS FROM FINANCING ACTIVITIES:			–	–
+	+			Proceeds from Issuance of Stock				–
+	+			Proceeds from Issuance of Notes Payable				–
+	+			Proceeds from Issuance of Bonds Payable				–
–		+		Payments of Dividends and Reserves to Shareholders			–	
–		+		Repayment of Short-Term Borrowings			–	
–		+		Repayment of Long-Term Borrowings			–	
–		+		Payments for Repurchase of Stock			–	
=				NET CASH FLOW FROM FINANCING ACTIVITIES				
				SUMMARY:				
	=		+	TOTAL INCREASES IN CASH DURING THE PERIOD			100.0	–
		=	–	TOTAL DECREASES IN CASH DURING THE PERIOD			–	100.0
			=	NET INCREASE (DECREASE) IN CASH				
			+	CASH BALANCE AT THE START OF THE PERIOD			–	–
			=	CASH BALANCE AT THE END OF THE PERIOD			–	–

INFORMATION CONTAINED HEREIN RELATES TO THE FOLLOWING FISCAL PERIODS:								
COLUMNS A,B,C						COLUMN D		
COMPARATIVE ANALYSIS RESULTS						CURRENT YEAR BUDGET		
B	(%) OF CASH		C	(%) OF CASH		D	(%) OF CASH	
VALUE	INCREASE	DECREASE	VALUE	INCREASE	DECREASE	VALUE	INCREASE	DECREASE
	–	–		–	–		–	–
		–			–			–
		–			–			–
	–			–			–	
	–			–			–	
	–			–			–	
	–			–			–	
	–			–			–	
	–			–			–	
	–			–			–	
	–	–		–	–		–	–
		–			–			–
		–			–			–
		–			–			–
	–			–			–	
	–			–			–	
	–			–			–	
	–	–		–	–		–	–
		–			–			–
		–			–			–
		–			–			–
	–			–			–	
	–			–			–	
	–			–			–	
	–			–			–	
	100.0	–		100.0	–		100.0	–
	–	100.0		–	100.0		–	100.0
	–	–		–	–		–	–
	–	–		–	–		–	–

Chapter 3

Financial Ratio Analysis

Contents

6.12 Introduction to Financial Ratio Analysis

Management is responsible for understanding the financial condition and performance of the organization. Such an understanding can be enhanced by interpreting a set of ratios from the existing financial statements. The evaluation of ratios should minimize the amount of time spent on interpreting the financial statements. This evaluation can provide answers to a broad range of questions, such as:

- How many times may the company's current liabilities be paid with its current assets?
- What is the average number of days for collecting accounts receivable?
- What is the average number of days for paying accounts payable?
- What portion of the company's assets is financed by its shareholders?
- What is the return on assets employed by the company?
- What is the return on shareholders' equity?

Financial ratio analysis is a process of identifying, measuring, and evaluating financial relationships, or ratios, in the financial position and performance of the company. The advantage of the financial ratio is twofold. First, each ratio shows the relative size of two items, such as the amount of assets available to pay debts. Second, each ratio minimizes the effect of inflation when comparing results from one year with the next. For example, operating expenses may remain a constant percentage of sales even as total expenses increase during inflation. Throughout the financial ratio analysis a number of significant ratios will be presented. Some financial ratios will be individually evaluated as acceptable and others as poor, but each will provide essential information about the company's condition and performance.

Financial ratio analysis enables management to evaluate the following attributes of the company:

- Liquidity
- Solvency
- Profitability
- Ability to manage assets

These attributes are described by **20 financial ratios** discussed in this chapter. These ratios should be computed and subsequently compared with the prescribed industry norms. Working instructions and forms pertinent to financial ratio analysis are provided at the end of Chapter 3. Both are designed to help management compute the relevant financial ratios in accordance with the **work program** presented in Exhibit 6–14.

Exhibit 6–14

Work Program for Chapter 3 of Part 6

Work Program

Planned Action	Objective
1. Study of information about financial ratios	To attain an adequate level of knowledge pertaining to the financial ratio analysis method
2. Computation of the company's financial ratios	To determine the financial ratios for the last three fiscal years and the year-to-date
3. Preparation of the company's comparative financial ratio statement	To summarize the values of financial ratios for the last three fiscal periods and the year-to-date

Note: Please familiarize yourself with relevant working instructions prior to completing forms at the end of this chapter. Additional information on these forms is available from Business Management Club, Inc. upon request

6.13 Evaluation of the Company's Liquidity

The **liquidity** of a company is its ability to pay all short-term debts upon their maturity by liquidating current assets. These assets are expected to be converted into cash, which in turn will be used to pay current liabilities. Liquidity analysis entails the calculation of the following financial ratios:

- Current ratio
- Quick ratio
- Receivables collection period
- Payment period to creditors

6.13.1 Current Ratio

The **current ratio** measures the number of times that the current liabilities could be paid from the proceeds of current assets. Current assets are resources that are, or will become, available as cash within one fiscal year. These assets generally include cash, accounts receivable, inventory, notes receivable, prepaid expenses, refundable deposits, and short-term investments. Current liabilities, on the other hand, include all debts that require cash payment within one fiscal year.

$$(1) \quad \text{Current Ratio} = \frac{\text{Current Assets} \times 100\%}{\text{Current Liabilities}}$$

Normally a current ratio of 200% or more is a favorable indication of the company's liquidity. Such a ratio suggests that the existing current assets may repay twice the amount of current liabilities. Alternatively stated, current liabilities could be paid even if current assets are liquidated at 50% of their book value. If the ratio is considerably smaller, say 120%, sufficient cash may not be available to pay all current liabilities if current assets are liquidated for less than book value. Conversely, if the current ratio is large, say 300%, this may indicate that the company has an excessive investment in current assets. Holding these assets does not produce a significant return. It is essential, therefore, to monitor the current ratio and to ensure that it will not be dangerously low or excessively high.

6.13.2 Quick Ratio (Liquid Ratio or Acid Test Ratio)

The current ratio has one particular shortcoming. It does not take into account the different degrees of liquidity of various current assets. It may be useful, therefore, to divide current assets into two categories:

- **Liquid assets.** These assets, which do not have to be sold in order to obtain cash, are cash, accounts receivable, notes receivable, refundable deposits, and short-term investments.
- **Other current assets.** These assets, which have to be sold or used in order to obtain cash, are inventory including merchandise, direct materials, work-in-process and finished goods, and prepaid expenses.

This subdivision of current assets enables computation of the **quick ratio**, commonly known as the **liquid ratio** or **acid test**. This ratio is one of the most significant measures of liquidity of the business enterprise.

$$(2) \quad \text{Quick Ratio} = \frac{\text{Liquid Assets} \times 100\%}{\text{Current Liabilities}}$$

Normally a quick ratio of 100% or more is considered to be a favorable indication of the company's liquidity. A quick ratio of 100% indicates that the company has sufficient liquid assets to pay off all current liabilities on demand by creditors.

The quick ratio in conjunction with current ratio may provide a more complete evaluation of liquidity. For instance, the current and quick ratios of 220% and 150% respectively reflect a much stronger liquidity than, say, 220% and 80%, but whether the former or latter projects a more favorable financial condition depends on many other factors. When evaluating the company's liquidity it may be necessary to account for special characteristics of the industry in which the business operates and the conditions of credit it grants to customers and receives from suppliers.

Furthermore, a comparison between the current and quick ratios may indicate the influence of the inventory on the company's liquidity. If the current ratio is favorable but the quick ratio is below the acceptable norm, it usually indicates an excessive level of inventory held by the company. Equally undesirable is high liquidity because it reflects poor management of the cash. Idle funds could be employed more profitably elsewhere in the business.

6.13.3 Receivables Collection Period

The turnover rate of accounts receivable is another important measure of the company's liquidity. The **receivables collection period** is the average period of time required to collect cash after a sale on credit. The receivables collection period depends directly upon the value of credit sales and credit terms granted by the company to its customers. It does not depend upon the volume of cash sales.

Receivables collection period reflects the quality of customer accounts arising from credit sales. These accounts are usually summarized in a debtors age analysis report reflecting the amount and age, or the outstanding period, of such accounts.

$$(3) \qquad \frac{\text{Receivables}}{\text{Collection Period}} = \frac{\text{Average Accounts Receivable} \times 365 \text{ Days}}{\text{Net Sales}}$$

Calculation of the receivables collection period on an annual basis uses the average value of accounts receivable between the first and the last dates of the fiscal period. Sometimes, however, this method may not provide the most accurate results. It is advisable to determine the receivables collection period on a monthly or quarterly basis by substituting 30 days or 120 days into the above formula for 365 days.

The average receivables collection period should not be excessive when compared with the usual credit sales terms offered by the company. If the value of accounts receivable appears disproportionately large on the balance sheet, this may be a direct result of one of the following factors:

- Credit sales volume increases sharply toward the end of the fiscal year.
- Certain finished goods and services are sold by the company on a seasonable basis.
- A substantial credit sale is made to a particular customer toward the end of the fiscal year.
- Slow-paying accounts or even potential bad debts are being carried.
- Credit sales are made on installment basis or other special terms offered to select customers.

- Credit terms are extended to some customers during unfavorable trading conditions.
- A poor collection of accounts receivable is made and inadequate accounting control methods are used.

If, conversely, the amount of accounts receivable appears disproportionately small on the balance sheet, this may be a direct result of one of the following reasons:

- Most sales are carried out on a cash basis.
- Credit is offered only for short collection periods.
- Sales fluctuate seasonally, declining sharply toward the end of the fiscal year.
- Customers promptly settle outstanding accounts due to the favorable discount structure offered by the company.
- An effective credit collection policy is maintained by the company.

6.13.4 Payment Period to Creditors

The **payment period to creditors** represents an additional measure of the company's liquidity. This ratio reflects the average period of time taken to pay suppliers once materials or services have been acquired. Payment period to creditors depends primarily upon the credit conditions stipulated by suppliers and followed by the company. It does not depend upon the company's volume of cash purchases. Payment period to creditors reflects the quality of managing cash, considering the discounts and conditions within a specific type of industry. Accounts payable to suppliers are normally summarized in the creditors age analysis report reflecting the amount and age of such accounts.

$$(4) \qquad \frac{\text{Payment Period}}{\text{to Creditors}} = \frac{\text{Average Accounts Payable} \times 365 \text{ Days}}{\text{Cost of Goods Sold}}$$

The payment period to creditors on an annual basis uses the average value of accounts payable between the first and the last dates of the fiscal period. This method, however, may not always provide the most accurate results. It is useful, therefore, to calculate the payment period on a monthly or quarterly basis by substituting 30 or 120 days into the above formula for 365 days.

The cost of goods sold is applicable to merchandising and manufacturing companies only and is reflected in their income statements. It is assumed that the company's selling, administrative, and general expenses are paid shortly after incurrence. The average payment period to creditors should not exceed the credit terms and conditions offered by suppliers. If the average payment period increases, this may result from one of the following factors:

- Seasonal purchasing of materials and services
- A sharp increase of credit purchases by the company toward the end of the fiscal year.
- A substantial credit purchase from a particular supplier toward the end of the fiscal year or excessive use of credit offered by certain suppliers
- Credit purchases on an installment basis or other special terms of repayment
- Extending credit from certain suppliers due to unfavorable trading conditions
- Poor handling of accounts payable and ineffective accounting controls

However, if the value of accounts payable appears disproportionately small on the balance sheet, this may be a direct result of one of the following reasons:

- A large proportion of the company's purchases made on a cash basis
- Suppliers offering credit only for short repayment periods
- Seasonal fluctuation of the company's purchasing requirements
- Reduction of the company's credit purchases toward the end of the fiscal year
- Prompt settlement of outstanding accounts by the company because of suppliers' discounts

6.14 Evaluation of the Company's Solvency

The **solvency** of a company reflects its ability to pay off debts when they become due irrespective of the particular repayment period. Debt payments may be made by liquidating assets or by using cash generated from operations. Preferably, debt should be retired with cash provided by current operations rather then by selling assets. Solvency analysis entails calculation of the following financial ratios:

- Current liability ratio
- Long-term liability ratio
- Equity ratio
- Debt-to-equity ratio
- Interest coverage ratio

6.14.1 Current Liability Ratio

The **current liability ratio** is the portion of total assets that has been provided by current liabilities. Because these liabilities are current, they have to be paid during the current fiscal year. These liabilities include accounts payable, bank overdraft, current portion of a long-term debt, deferred revenues, notes payable, payroll liabilities, taxes payable, and other accrued current liabilities.

$$(5) \qquad \text{Current Liability Ratio} = \frac{\text{Current Liabilities} \times 100\%}{\text{Total Assets}}$$

Normally, a current liability ratio ranging from 20% to 40% is an acceptable level of solvency. This ratio indicates that between 20% to 40% of all assets are financed by short-term creditors. The specific percentage of the current liability ratio should vary in direct proportion to the amount of current assets needed to support sales activity. Some current assets should be financed by short-term liabilities so as to not to burden the company with long-term commitments. On the other hand, long-term debt should provide financing for the "permanent" portion of current assets, such as working capital.

6.14.2 Long–Term Liability Ratio

The **long-term liability ratio** is the percentage of assets provided by creditors who will be repaid sometime after the current fiscal year. Such liabilities are generally due from one to ten years in the future. Long-term liabilities include bonds payable, capital leases, mortgages payable, and pension liability.

$$(6) \qquad \text{Long-Term Liability Ratio} = \frac{\text{Long-Term Liabilities} \times 100\%}{\text{Total Assets}}$$

A long-term liability ratio ranging from 20% to 40% is generally an acceptable level of solvency. The specific percentage tends to vary in direct proportion to the consistency of sales and net income. Greater long-term debt is granted when sales and net income are consistent. In addition, management should ensure that capital assets are financed strictly by long-term obligations, not by increasing the level of short-term liabilities. The repayment of a large debt is possible only after several periods of successful operation and accumulation of assets.

6.14.3 Equity Ratio

The **equity ratio** measures the level of financing provided by shareholders. The equity ratio indicates the extent of shareholders' contribution in the process of acquiring all assets. Shareholders' equity represents the sum of total investment contributed by the owners to their business through acquisition of the company's stock plus the net earnings that have not been distributed to shareholders.

$$(7) \qquad \text{Equity Ratio} = \frac{\text{Shareholders' Equity} \times 100\%}{\text{Total Assets}}$$

Normally, an equity ratio of 50% is considered an adequate reflection of solvency. Small and new companies, however, may require greater equity financing. This arises particularly in the first three years of operation. Banks will often not lend to companies with fewer than three years of operating results. Creditors generally require more assets to be financed by equity than liabilities of any sort, yet managers get lower rates of return on investment until more debt is used in financing. A continuing management task is therefore to maintain an advantageous portion of debt versus equity financing.

6.14.4 Debt-to-Equity Ratio

As previously discussed in Part 3, there are two basic sources of funds available to the organization: shareholders' funds and creditors' funds. The utilization of these funds depends upon several factors, such as the financial policy and objectives of the company, immediate and long-term requirements, and financial resources available from shareholders. The specific contribution provided by each source will determine the level of the company's debt and shareholders' equity in relation to the total value of assets employed by the organization.

A comparison between these two sources of funds is shown by the **debt-to-equity ratio**. This ratio measures the proportion of financing provided to the company by outside creditors to the funds introduced by its shareholders:

$$(8) \qquad \text{Debt-to-Equity Ratio} = \frac{\text{Total Liabilities} \times 100\%}{\text{Shareholders' Equity}}$$

Normally, a debt-to-equity ratio of 100% is an acceptable reflection of solvency for a small or medium-sized company after several years of operation. When the debt-to-equity ratio is below 100%, this signifies an excess of shareholders' funds over the funds provided by outside creditors. If such a ratio exceeds 100%, however, this means that the larger portion of financing is provided to the company by creditors' sources. As the debt-to-equity ratio increases above 100%, the amount of risk accepted by creditors increases. Such a ratio would indicate a decreasing creditableness of the organization and may result in the weakening of the company's abilities to obtain new credit or raise additional finance. The increasing trend of the debt-to-equity ratio over 100% is therefore considered to be a negative one.

6.14.5 Interest Coverage Ratio

The main purpose of borrowing funds from outside sources is to employ these funds in such a manner that they will generate sufficient revenue to service the interest and to produce a sizeable income to repay the borrowed capital. The **interest coverage ratio**, or **times interest earned**, reflects the company's ability to meet various financial commitments to outside creditors.

$$(9) \qquad \text{Interest Coverage Ratio} = \frac{\text{Income before Taxes} + \text{Interest Expense}}{\text{Interest Expense}}$$

In determining this ratio, the interest expense is added to the value of income before taxes. This is done to determine the amount earned from operating activities that is available to pay the interest burden. The income before taxes is used because it is the maximum amount available to pay interest. A multiple of at least 6.0 is often taken as adequate coverage for solvency. An increasing trend of the interest coverage ratio reflects an improvement of the company's solvency.

6.15 Evaluation of the Company's Profitability

The **profitability** of the company is a measure of its ability to generate revenue to meet all operating expenses and to produce a net income sufficient to provide a favorable return on the shareholders' equity. The profitability analysis entails calculation of the following financial ratios:

- Gross margin from sales
- Return on sales
- Return on assets
- Return on shareholders' equity

6.15.1 Gross Margin from Sales

Gross margin from sales measures the cost of goods sold in relation to net sales generated by the company during a specific accounting period. The ratio applies solely to the merchandising and manufacturing organizations and it indicates the relationship between the cost of goods sold and their selling price through operating activities.

$$(10) \qquad \frac{\text{Gross Margin}}{\text{From Sales}} = \frac{\text{Gross Margin From Sales} \times 100\%}{\text{Net Sales}}$$

Normally, if a gross margin from sales range is between 30% and 40%, it is a favorable reflection of the company's profitability. The level of gross margin from sales fluctuates depending upon the nature of the specific operating activity of the organization and the contribution of cost of goods sold to the overall expenditure of the company. An increasing trend of the gross margin from sales signifies an improvement of the company's profitability.

6.15.2 Return on Sales

The **return on sales** ratio compares the company's net income against net sales during a specific accounting period. Since all expenses are deducted, this ratio summarizes the efficiency of operations and financing.

$$(11) \quad \text{Return on Sales} = \frac{\text{Net Income} \times 100\%}{\text{Net Sales}}$$

A return on sales ratio of 3% to 5% is typical of large manufacturing and merchandising companies. Small and medium-sized companies normally attain returns between 5% and 10%. The level of the return on sales ratio usually fluctuates depending upon the nature of the company's business activities. An increasing trend of return on sales ratio indicates an improvement of the company's profitability.

6.15.3 Return on Assets

The **return on assets** ratio is one of the most important criterions of the company's profitability. This ratio measures the efficiency of investment within the organization. The main purpose of such an analysis is to assist management in deciding whether to increase the level of investment within the company or to invest the capital elsewhere.

$$(12) \quad \text{Return on Assets} = \frac{\text{Net Income} \times 100\%}{\text{Average Total Assets}}$$

The rate of return on assets can be compared with the prime bank lending rate at a particular time. If the rate of return on assets exceeds the specific bank lending rate, this reflects a favorable level of company profitability. There is no upper limit for the rate of return on assets within the business and it is obvious that an increased trend in such a rate represents the most desirable indication of the company's profitability. However, the return on assets percentage should be at least as great as tax-free interest available to investors by reliable financial institutions.

6.15.4 Return on Shareholders' Equity

Return on shareholders' equity represents another essential ratio of the company's profitability. The return on shareholders' equity is the ultimate criterion of the company's viability as far as its shareholders are concerned because it measures the results of management's use of shareholders' funds. The main objective of such an analysis is to identify the rate of return on the shareholders' investment.

$$(13) \quad \text{Return on Shareholders' Equity} = \frac{\text{Net Income} \times 100\%}{\text{Average Shareholders' Equity}}$$

The rate of return on shareholders' equity can be compared with the prime bank lending rate or the best rate at which the firm may borrow from its bank. The minimum rate of return on shareholders' funds, however, should be at least as great as the tax-free interest available to shareholders' investment of funds. Furthermore, shareholders who are actively engaged in the management of their businesses usually derive additional fringe benefits. Thus, the value of such benefits may compensate for a presumed deficiency in the rate of return on shareholders' equity.

Finally, for a given rate of return on assets, the rate of return on shareholders' equity will decrease as the equity ratio increases. The reverse situation also applies. The rate of return on shareholders' equity will increase as the equity ratio decreases. This condition, described in detail in Part 3, is known as **financial leveraging**. It shows the efficiency of using creditors' money to maximize the return on shareholders' equity. The greater the difference between the company's rate of return on assets and the average cost of interest payable on the debt, the more effective the financial leveraging of the company's performance.

6.16 Evaluation of the Company's Ability to Manage Assets

It is essential to establish how effectively the company is managing its assets during a particular accounting period. Assets include working capital, inventory, capital assets, and other investments. The **evaluation of assets management** entails calculation of the following financial ratios:

- Working capital turnover
- Inventory turnover rate
- Inventory turnover period
- Inventory-to-working capital ratio
- Capital assets turnover
- Total assets turnover
- Income taxes payment ratio

6.16.1 Working Capital Turnover

Working capital is the net of current assets minus current liabilities employed in day-to-day operating activities. The company may employ too much or too little working capital. Too much working capital is costly because it has to be financed by interest-charging creditors or return-expecting shareholders. Too little working capital may cause the company to lose an opportunity to earn additional profit elsewhere.

The **working capital turnover** is the ratio of net sales achieved by the company during a specific accounting period to working capital. This ratio is useful in showing whether the company is trading normally, overtrading, or undertrading through the process of utilizing existing working capital:

- **Trading normally.** This means that the company generates sufficient volume of sales in relation to available working capital.
- **Overtrading.** This means that the company generates an excessive volume of sales in relation to available working capital. This condition normally results when the company generates an inadequate cash flow from operations and cannot obtain additional financing.
- **Undertrading.** This, conversely, means that the level of sales is not sufficient to justify the value of working capital employed by the company. Generally, the company has too much inventory or a large amount of accounts receivable.

$$(14) \qquad \text{Working Capital Turnover} = \frac{\text{Net Sales} \times 100\%}{\text{Average Working Capital}}$$

A company's norm for working capital turnover depends upon the nature of the company's operating activities. When appraising the adequacy of the working capital, particular attention should be given to the degree of short-term financing used by the company. For example, when the working capital turnover is extremely high, this may signify that working capital is financed mainly on a short-term basis. This may result in a high cost of interest and excessive time devoted to paying or refinancing the short-term debts.

6.16.2 Inventory Turnover Rate

Merchandising and manufacturing companies must maintain a certain level of inventory to ensure a continuity of operations. Inventory usually fluctuates directly with the variation of the company's sales. This variation should be monitored continuously. The **inventory turnover rate** is an important ratio that reflects the company's ability to manage assets. This ratio compares the cost of goods sold with the average value of inventory kept by the company during a specified accounting period.

$$(15) \qquad \text{Inventory Turnover Rate} = \frac{\text{Cost of Goods Sold}}{\text{Average Inventory}}$$

Each time the company's product is sold, some profit should be realized. It is evident that a high inventory turnover rate is desirable, but an excessively high rate may indicate that the company does not have sufficient merchandise to satisfy customers. The company may be losing sales from not having sufficient inventory. A low inventory turnover rate, conversely, may indicate that merchandise, raw materials, or finished goods are lying idle, and this shows inefficient utilization of company resources.

The inventory turnover rate usually depends upon the nature of operating activities and the particular type of products offered by the organization. If the company sells durable or expensive products, a low inventory turnover rate may be expected. This rate is usually matched with a high gross margin from sales to ensure an acceptable level of profitability. If, however, the company sells perishable products, a high inventory turnover rate is expected with a lower gross margin from sales.

6.16.3 Inventory Turnover Period

The **inventory turnover period** is the average number of days during which the company undergoes a complete cycle of replacing its inventory. For merchandisers, this is the period from purchase to the sale of merchandise. For manufacturers, this is the period from raw materials acquisition through conversion to the sale of finished goods.

Upon the completion of one cycle, inventory is converted into cash. New inventory will subsequently create the next cycle. The inventory turnover period depends upon the nature of the company's business and specific type of products sold by the organization.

$$(16) \qquad \text{Inventory Turnover Period} = \frac{365 \text{ Days}}{\text{Inventory Turnover Rate}}$$

An annual calculation may not provide the most accurate results. It may be preferable to monitor the inventory turnover period on a monthly basis by substituting the monthly cost of goods sold into the equation for the yearly cost of goods sold, and substituting 30 days for 365 days.

6.16.4 Inventory-to-Working Capital Ratio

The **inventory-to-working capital ratio** is an important parameter of assets management. This ratio indicates whether inventory is too large or too small in relation to the working capital employed by the company. Normally, the inventory-to-working capital ratio is less than 100%. If this ratio exceeds 100%, the level of inventory may be too high or the accounts payable too low.

$$(17) \quad \text{Inventory-to-Working Capital Ratio} = \frac{\text{Average Inventory} \times 100\%}{\text{Average Working Capital}}$$

There are two particular situations where the inventory-to-working capital ratio may be substantially higher than 100%, both of which are undesirable:

- The company is undercapitalized for the volume of business being transacted because it has insufficient working capital. This situation is described as overtrading and is characterized by a favorable inventory turnover rate but a poor current ratio.
- The company may have on hand a considerable amount of slow-moving or obsolete inventory. In this situation the company may show a favorable current ratio but will have a low inventory turnover rate.

The inventory-to-working capital ratio is usually affected by either excessive or low levels of inventory within the company. When inventory appears disproportionately large in relation to working capital or has a very slow turnover rate it should be thoroughly examined to establish the specific reason. Some possible reasons that may cause such a situation within the company are:

- Inventory may include a high level of raw materials purchased either in anticipation of drastic price increases or for speculation.
- Inventory may include slow-moving or obsolete merchandise, raw materials, and finished goods.
- Inventory may have been built-up to assist in meeting various manufacturing requirements.
- Inventory may have been built-up either to avoid possible shortages in the market place or because of a lengthy lead time period.
- Inventory may have been accumulated because of the seasonal nature of the business activities or the operational method of the company.

When inventory appears disproportionately small in relation to working capital or has a very high turnover rate, it should also be investigated to determine the reason. Some possible reasons that may cause a low level of inventory are:

- A conservative method of inventory evaluation is used during the accounting period.
- The company's policy demands inventory to be kept at minimum levels.
- Shortage of merchandise or raw materials in the marketplace.
- A substantial portion of finished goods may have been counted as consignment stock or may be in transit.
- Inventory has not been properly accounted for during the inventory counting process.

6.16.5 Capital Assets Turnover

Capital assets turnover is another important yardstick for evaluating a company's efficiency in utilizing capital assets to generate revenue. This ratio compares net sales against the average value of capital assets employed.

$$(18) \quad \text{Capital Assets Turnover} = \frac{\text{Net Sales}}{\text{Average Capital Assets}}$$

The recommended capital assets turnover depends upon the type of industry and the nature of the company's operation (service, merchandising, or manufacturing). In evaluating this ratio, it is essential to take into account that the book value of most capital assets does not usually represent their true market value. The value of capital assets is particularly understated if accelerated depreciation methods are applied. Hence, a young company with recently acquired capital assets will have a more favorable capital assets turnover ratio than an older organization.

In order to obtain a valid result, it may be useful to substitute the average book value of capital assets, that is, cost minus accumulated depreciation, with a realistic market value. This method may result in a more qualified evaluation of capital assets utilization by the company. This is particularly important to manufacturing organizations that employ expensive production equipment.

If the capital assets turnover is below the industry average, it indicates that the company has not generated sufficient sales or that some of its capital assets are underutilized. It is essential to either increase the volume of business or to dispose of the least utilized capital assets. An increasing trend of capital assets turnover generally represents a desirable condition and should be maintained.

6.16.6 Total Assets Turnover

The **total assets turnover** is another important parameter for evaluating the efficiency of assets management by the organization. This ratio compares net sales generated by the company during a particular accounting period with the average value of total assets employed.

$$(19) \quad \text{Total Assets Turnover} = \frac{\text{Net Sales}}{\text{Average Total Assets}}$$

The recommended total assets turnover depends upon the type of industry and nature of the company's business but generally ranges between 1.0 and 2.0. This ratio indicates how many times the company's assets are "turned over" in sales during a specific accounting period. A total assets turnover of 2.0, for example, means that every dollar invested in the company's assets produces two dollars in sales. It is obvious that a higher ratio represents a more efficient utilization of assets and is a desirable trend.

6.16.7 Income Taxes Payment Ratio

Every company is liable to pay income taxes in accordance with its taxable income. The payment of income taxes (local, state, and federal) may create a burden on the cash flow available to management. Hence, the level of income taxes paid by the company may be interpreted as a part of assets management.

Income taxes payable by the company can be affected by:

- The choice of organizational form: corporation, subchapter S corporation, partnership, or sole proprietorship
- Recording an expenditure as an operating expense or as capital expense
- Applying accelerated methods of depreciation and amortization
- Paying allowable personal expenses, such as vehicles, travel, and pension through the business

The **income taxes payment** ratio expresses the amount of income taxes paid as a percentage of net sales.

$$(20)\ \text{Income Taxes Payment Ratio} = \frac{\text{Income Taxes Expense} \times 100\%}{\text{Net Sales}}$$

It is useful to examine this ratio in conjunction with the overall evaluation of assets management efficiency. If the income taxes payment ratio is too high it may be necessary to implement a more effective tax-planning strategy. This strategy represents a part of the budgeting process and may minimize the company's tax liability if successful. In this case, additional funds may be utilized to purchase new capital assets, thereby contributing to a further expansion of the company's operations.

6.17 Working Instructions and Forms for Chapter 3

All information related to the company's financial ratio analysis has been presented in Sections 6.12–6.16. It is essential to understand this information and to proceed with the completion of the appropriate forms provided at the end of Chapter 3. Working instructions for completing these forms follow immediately. These instructions require that management compute the relevant financial ratios in accordance with the sequence of activities presented in Exhibit 6–15.

Exhibit 6–15

Summary of Forms for Financial Ratio Analysis

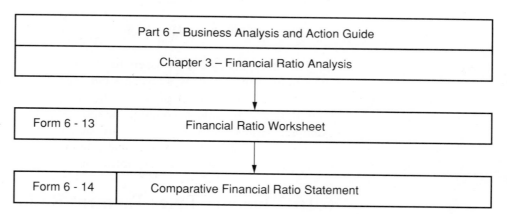

Form 6–13   Financial Ratio Worksheet

142.   Make four copies of this form and select appropriate financial ratio analysis periods as follows:

142.1   The last three fiscal years that represent the comparative financial analysis period.

142.2   Current fiscal year (or portion thereof) that represents the current financial analysis period.

143.   Enter appropriate values specified in financial statements and compute financial ratios as prescribed by the financial ratio chart presented in Exhibit 6–16 below.

Exhibit 6–16

Financial Ratio Chart

Financial Ratio Chart		
No.	**Description**	**Method of Calculation**
1	Current Ratio	$= \dfrac{\text{Current Assets} \times 100\%}{\text{Current Liabilities}}$ (%)
2	Quick Ratio	$= \dfrac{\text{Liquid Assets} \times 100\%}{\text{Current Liabilities}}$ (%)
3	Receivables Collection Period	$= \dfrac{\text{Average Accounts Receivable} \times 365 \text{ Days}}{\text{Net Sales}}$ (Days)
4	Payment Period to Creditors	$= \dfrac{\text{Average Accounts Payable} \times 365 \text{ Days}}{\text{Cost of Goods Sold}}$ (Days)
5	Current Liability Ratio	$= \dfrac{\text{Current Liabilities} \times 100\%}{\text{Total Assets}}$ (%)
6	Long-Term Liability Ratio	$= \dfrac{\text{Long-Term Liabilities} \times 100\%}{\text{Total Assets}}$ (%)
7	Equity Ratio	$= \dfrac{\text{Shareholders' Equity} \times 100\%}{\text{Total Assets}}$ (%)
8	Debt-to-Equity Ratio	$= \dfrac{\text{Total Liabilities} \times 100\%}{\text{Shareholders' Equity}}$ (%)
9	Interest Coverage Ratio	$= \dfrac{\text{Income before Taxes} + \text{Interest Expense}}{\text{Interest Expense}}$ (Times)
10	Gross Margin from Sales	$= \dfrac{\text{Gross Margin from Sales} \times 100\%}{\text{Net Sales}}$ (%)
11	Return on Sales	$= \dfrac{\text{Net Income} \times 100\%}{\text{Net Sales}}$ (%)
12	Return on Assets	$= \dfrac{\text{Net Income} \times 100\%}{\text{Average Total Assets}}$ (%)
13	Return on Shareholders' Equity	$= \dfrac{\text{Net Income} \times 100\%}{\text{Average Shareholders' Equity}}$ (%)
14	Working Capital Turnover	$= \dfrac{\text{Net Sales}}{\text{Average Working Capital}}$ (Times)
15	Inventory Turnover Rate	$= \dfrac{\text{Cost of Goods Sold}}{\text{Average Inventory}}$ (Times)
16	Inventory Turnover Period	$= \dfrac{365 \text{ Days}}{\text{Inventory Turnover Rate}}$ (Days)
17	Inventory-to-Working Capital Ratio	$= \dfrac{\text{Average Inventory} \times 100\%}{\text{Average Working Capital}}$ (%)
18	Capital Assets Turnover	$= \dfrac{\text{Net Sales}}{\text{Average Capital Assets}}$ (Times)
19	Total Assets Turnover	$= \dfrac{\text{Net Sales}}{\text{Average Total Assets}}$ (Times)
20	Income Taxes Payment Ratio	$= \dfrac{\text{Income Taxes Expense} \times 100\%}{\text{Net Sales}}$ (%)

Form 6–14   Comparative Financial Ratio Statement

144. Enter the appropriate financial ratio analysis periods as specified in Form 6–13 (refer to instruction 142).

145. Enter the financial ratio values into their appropriate columns.

146. Examine the financial ratio trends starting with the earliest period of financial ratio analysis.

See continuation of working instructions on page 306 (Chapter 4, Part 6)

FINANCIAL RATIO ANALYSIS
FINANCIAL RATIO WORKSHEET

NO.	DESCRIPTION	FINANCIAL RATIO CALCULATION
		PERIOD:
1	Current Ratio	———————————— = %
2	Quick Ratio	———————————— = %
3	Receivables Collection Period	———————————— = Days
4	Payment Period to Creditors	———————————— = Days
5	Current Liability Ratio	———————————— = %
6	Long-Term Liability Ratio	———————————— = %
7	Equity Ratio	———————————— = %
8	Debt-to-Equity Ratio	———————————— = %
9	Interest Coverage Ratio	———————————— = Times
10	Gross Margin from Sales	———————————— = %
11	Return on Sales	———————————— = %
12	Return on Assets	———————————— = %
13	Return on Shareholders' Equity	———————————— = %
14	Working Capital Turnover	———————————— = Times
15	Inventory Turnover Rate	———————————— = Times
16	Inventory Turnover Period	———————————— = Days
17	Inventory-to-Working Capital Ratio	———————————— = %
18	Capital Assets Turnover	———————————— = Times
19	Total Assets Turnover	———————————— = Times
20	Income Taxes Payment Ratio	———————————— = %

| NAME: | POSITION: | DATE: |

FINANCIAL RATIO ANALYSIS
COMPARATIVE FINANCIAL RATIO STATEMENT

No.	DESCRIPTION		THE LAST THREE FISCAL YEARS			CURRENT FISCAL YEAR
1	Current Ratio	%				
2	Quick Ratio	%				
3	Receivables Collection Period	Days				
4	Payment Period to Creditors	Days				
5	Current Liability Ratio	%				
6	Long-Term Liability Ratio	%				
7	Equity Ratio	%				
8	Debt-to-Equity Ratio	%				
9	Interest Coverage Ratio	Times				
10	Gross Margin from Sales	%				
11	Return on Sales	%				
12	Return on Assets	%				
13	Return on Shareholders' Equity	%				
14	Working Capital Turnover	Times				
15	Inventory Turnover Rate	Times				
16	Inventory Turnover Period	Days				
17	Inventory-to-Working Capital Ratio	%				
18	Capital Assets Turnover	Times				
19	Total Assets Turnover	Times				
20	Income Taxes Payment Ratio	%				

NAME:	POSITION:	DATE:

Chapter 4

Plan of Action

Contents

6.18 Introduction to Plan of Action

After attaining an adequate level of knowledge in various areas of business management and evaluating the company's performance, it is essential to develop a **plan of action** for the forthcoming fiscal period. The prime objective of such a plan is to rectify existing problems in various areas of the company's operational activities in order to secure its successful performance in the future.

A sound plan of action can provide management with an effective guidance in the following areas of the company's activities:

- General administration
- Personnel
- Finance and accounting
- Production and operations
- Marketing and sales

These activities have been discussed in detail in Parts 1 through 5. Managers need to apply the knowledge obtained by studying information contained in these parts and formulating an effective plan of action in accordance with the **work program** presented in Exhibit 6–17.

Exhibit 6–17

Work Program for Chapter 4 of Part 6

Work Program

Planned Action	Objective
1. Preparation of the company's consolidated plan of action in the areas of general administration, personnel, finance and accounting, production and operations, marketing and sales	To develop a comprehensive plan of work and establish a suitable work priority pertaining to all operational activities of the organization for the forthcoming fiscal period
2. Preparation of the company's consolidated management report	To summarize final evaluation results and the plan of action for the forthcoming fiscal period
3. Preparation of the company's consolidated financial statements—balance sheet, income statement (including statement of cost of goods manufactured), statement of cash flows, and financial ratios	To present a summary of results and to evaluate trends pertaining to the financial condition and performance of the organization (this information is subsequently used for budgeting)
4. Implementation of the company's consolidated plan of action in the areas of general administration, personnel, finance and accounting, production and operations, and marketing and sales	To secure implementation of effective management solutions in all areas of operating activities in accordance with the guidelines provided earlier

Note: Please familiarize yourself with relevant working instructions prior to completing forms at the end of this chapter. Additional information on these forms is available from Business Management Club, Inc. upon request.

6.19 Consolidated Plan of Action

The final evaluation results pertinent to the operational and financial performance of your organization must be summarized in the **consolidated plan of action**. This plan consists of five major elements as follows:

1. Plan of action in the area of general management
2. Plan of action in the area of personnel management
3. Plan of action in the area of financial management
4. Plan of action in the area of production and operations management
5. Plan of action in the area of marketing and sales management

The plan of action should be supported by a set of consolidated financial statements that summarize the company's condition and results during recent fiscal periods. These statements are described in detail in Section 6.20.

6.19.1 Plan of Action in the Area of General Management

The company's **plan of action in the area of general management** may concern the following issues, discussed in detail in Part 1:

1. The basic management process
2. Evolution of management theory
3. Business engineering method
4. Environment and organizational culture
5. Principles of decision making
6. The planning process
7. Strategic planning
8. Implementation of strategic plans
9. Management by objectives
10. Operational planning
11. Plan of management
12. The organizing process
13. Organizational departmentation
14. Management structure
15. Organizational development
16. The leading process
17. Principles of communication
18. The controlling process
19. Managerial ethics
20. Theory Z

Your company's plan of action in the area of general management should be outlined on Page 1 of Form 6–15. Thereafter, this plan should be summarized in the **consolidated management report**, presented in Form 6–16.

6.19.2 Plan of Action in the Area of Personnel Management

The company's **plan of action in the area of personnel management** may concern the following issues, discussed in detail in Part 2:

1. The personnel management process
2. Equal employment opportunity laws
3. Job analysis
4. Job descriptions and job specifications
5. Personnel planning and forecasting
6. Personnel recruitment and hiring
7. Screening and testing of applicants
8. Employment interviews
9. Personnel orientation
10. Personnel training
11. Management development
12. Personnel motivation
13. Basic job compensation
14. Financial incentives
15. Fringe benefits
16. Personnel performance appraisal
17. Personnel career management
18. Labor-management relations
19. Collective bargaining and conflict management
20. Personnel safety and health

Your company's plan of action in the area of personnel management should be outlined on Page 2 of Form 6–15. Thereafter, this plan should be summarized in the consolidated management report, presented in Form 6–16.

6.19.3 Plan of Action in the Area of Financial Management

The company's **plan of action in the area of financial management** may concern the following issues, discussed in detail in Part 3:

1. The financial management process
2. Accounting information
3. Bookkeeping system
4. Financial statements
5. Financial performance evaluation
6. Operating budget
7. Capital expenditure budget
8. Cash budget
9. Tax strategies
10. Sources of finance
11. Internal control and cash management
12. Control of purchases and disbursements
13. Credit control
14. Inventory management
15. Capital assets management

16. Payroll accounting system
17. Cost accounting system
18. Pricing methods
19. Management accounting system
20. Computerized system

Your company's plan of action in the area of financial management should be outlined on Page 3 of Form 6–15. Thereafter this plan should be summarized in the consolidated management report presented in Form 6–16.

6.19.4 Plan of Action in the Area of Production and Operations Management

The company's **plan of action in the area of production and operations management** may concern the following issues, discussed in detail in Part 4:

1. The production and operations management process
2. Classification of operational activities
3. Facility design, location, and organization
4. Product selection, design, and standardization
5. Process design
6. The drafting office
7. Equipment evaluation and selection
8. Plant layout
9. Equipment maintenance
10. Equipment replacement
11. Tool control
12. Cost estimating
13. Production planning
14. Material requirements planning
15. Production control
16. Planning and control of services and projects
17. Quality control
18. Materials purchasing
19. Materials control, storage, and dispatch
20. Just-in-time manufacturing philosophy

Your company's plan of action in the area of production and operations management should be outlined on Page 4 of Form 6–15. Thereafter this plan should be summarized in the consolidated management report, presented in Form 6–16.

6.19.5 Plan of Action in the Area of Marketing and Sales Management

The company's **plan of action in the area of marketing and sales management** may concern the following issues, discussed in detail in Part 5:

1. The marketing management process
2. Buying behavior
3. Marketing information and research

4. Market segmentation
5. Market measurement and forecasting
6. Marketing strategy
7. Product strategy
8. Pricing strategy
9. Promotional strategy
10. Distribution strategy
11. Marketing plan
12. The sales management process
13. Sales planning and budgeting
14. Sales organization
15. Sales force recruitment and training
16. Personal selling
17. Sales force compensation
18. Sales force management and motivation
19. Sales performance evaluation and control
20. Marketing audit

Your company's plan of action in the area of marketing and sales management should be outlined on Page 5 of Form 6–15. Thereafter this plan should be summarized in the consolidated management report, presented in Form 6–16.

6.20 Consolidated Financial Statements

An effective plan of action must be supported by a set of **consolidated financial statements** pertaining to your company's past and present financial condition and operating performance. These statements provide a condensed management report summarizing results, conclusions, and recommendations which arise from the following:

- Current financial analysis
- Comparative financial analysis
- Financial ratio analysis

Consolidated financial statements help management identify the existing trends of the company's assets, liabilities, working capital, shareholders' equity, revenues, expenditure, and income. This in turn is instrumental in formulating budgets for the forthcoming fiscal period.

Consolidated financial statements consist of the following:

- Consolidated balance sheet
- Consolidated income statement
- Consolidated statement of cash flows
- Consolidated financial ratio statement

The **consolidated balance sheet** of your company is presented in Form 6–17. This statement summarizes the comparison and determines the trend of assets, liabilities, working capital, and shareholders' equity at the current analysis date and at the last accounting dates of the three previous fiscal periods.

The **consolidated income statement** of your company is presented as follows:

- Form 6–18—Consolidated Income Statement for a Service Company
- Form 6–19—Consolidated Income Statement for a Merchandising Company
- Form 6–20—Consolidated Income Statement for a Manufacturing Company
- Form 6–21—Consolidated Statement of Cost of Goods Manufactured

Each aforementioned statement summarizes the comparison and determines the trend of revenues, expenditure, and income during the current analysis period and during three previous fiscal years.

The **consolidated statement of cash flows** of your company is presented in Form 6–22. This statement summarizes the comparison and determines the trend of cash flows arising from operating, investing, and financing activities during the current analysis period and during three previous fiscal years.

The **consolidated financial ratio statement** of your company is presented in Form 6–23 (pages 1–10). This statement summarizes the comparison and determines the trend of various financial ratios pertaining to the current analysis period and three previous fiscal years.

6.21 Implementation of Plan of Action

The main purpose of the final chapter of Part 6 is to ensure an effective utilization of results, conclusions, and recommendations pertinent to all operating activities and performance of your organization. Although the company may perform reasonably well in certain areas of its operating activities, the performance in other areas may require substantial and often immediate rectification.

Hence, the ultimate task of your company's management team concerns the implementation of the consolidated plan of action discussed earlier in this part. In order to ensure an effective implementation of this plan it is necessary to identify any problems which may be experienced by members of the management team. These problems may include:

- Difficulty in conducting self-evaluation of knowledge by members of the management team
- Difficulty in evaluating the company's operating and financial performance
- A management problem in a specific area of operating activities
- Difficulty in formulating a suitable plan of action in a specific area of operating activities
- Difficulty in implementing a suitable plan of action in a specific area of operating activities

The aforementioned problems may relate to various areas of the company's operating activities such as general administration, personnel, finance and accounting, production and operations, and marketing and sales. These problems need to be identified and summarized in the **statement of current management problems**. This statement is presented in Form 6–24 (pages 1 through 5). Once all relevant problems are identified, it is necessary to select the most suitable method of implementing effective management solutions. There are at least three options related to the process of development and subsequent implementation of management solutions within your company. These options are as follows:

- *First option.* This is a straightforward effort to solve the range of identified problems utilizing the skills and experience of the existing in-house management team.

- *Second option*. This calls for the engagement of skills of a professional management consultant in a particular area of operating activities.
- *Third option*. This is based on the utilization of management solutions developed by Business Management Club, Inc. and prescribed to its members.

In order to ensure selection of the most suitable method it is essential to examine the advantages and disadvantages of each option separately.

6.21.1 First Option—In-House Management Solutions

The process of solving company problems with an existing **in-house management team** has certain advantages:

- There is no need to engage a management consultant or any other specialist from outside.
- There is no additional expenditure incurred as a result of management consulting services.
- Avoidance of exposure and possible embarrassment as a result of any mismanagement in the past.
- The development and implementation of management solutions is constantly controlled by the company's executives.

Some disadvantages of the first option are:

- The abilities, skills, and experience of the in-house management team may not be sufficient to develop and implement the most suitable management solutions.
- The development and implementation of management solutions are often carried out without professional guidance. This restricts the effectiveness of the in-house management team, which might have caused previous mishandling of the company's affairs in the first place.
- The development and implementation of new management solutions usually requires a fresh approach and a substantial investment in time by the company's executives. These are not always available under normal circumstances.
- The ultimate cost of developing and implementing new management solutions by the in-house management team is often higher and less effective than the cost of engaging a professional management consultant, who is trained and experienced to solve specific problems.
- It causes excessive reliance on the company's accountants to obtain the necessary management advice. Accountants are not usually trained or experienced in rendering management consulting service to their clients.

6.21.2 Second Option—Engagement of a Management Consultant

The engagement of a **management consultant** has a number of advantages:

- The company's existing problems are identified, evaluated, and solved on a professional basis by a specialist who is trained and experienced in a particular area of business management.
- The management consulting service is usually provided on a contractual basis and lasts for a limited period in accordance with a prearranged program of work and predetermined management consulting fees.

- Although the initial cost of management consulting may be substantial, this may eventually turn into a highly effective investment that produces such tangible results as increased efficiency and profitability of the organization and improved morale of its employees.
- Conducting management consulting assignments does not usually disrupt the routine functional activities of the in-house management team.

Some of the disadvantages of the second option are:

- The engagement of a management consultant is usually restricted to a specific area of the company's operating activities, which leaves other areas to further possible mismanagement.
- The company's existing management team is often skeptical and sometimes even uncooperative during the management consulting assignment.
- There is normally a certain amount of inner resistance toward the examination of the current situation within the company and implementation of new management solutions.
- The reinforcement of revised management solutions sometimes lasts only while the consultant is engaged by the company.

6.21.3 Third Option—Business Management Club, Inc.

The final option specified in this section relates to the service offered by **Business Management Club, Inc.** The main objective of this organization is to provide a unique opportunity for small and medium-sized firms to obtain the necessary management information and assistance required to secure successful performance on a continuous basis.

The basic approach used by Business Management Club, Inc. is as follows:

- To accommodate the needs of small and medium-sized organizations that are usually managed by entrepreneurs who do not have formal training in business management.
- To provide the entrepreneurs with a wide range of practical management methods, systems, and solutions in all functional areas of their business activity and to enable them to act as management consultants to their own organizations.
- To provide the entrepreneurs with the ability to utilize their existing in-house management teams and to direct and control the development and implementation of relevant management solutions on a professional do-it-yourself basis.
- To provide the entrepreneurs with an opportunity to utilize the services of specially trained management consultants in accordance with the particular needs of their organizations.
- To minimize the cost of developing and implementing management solutions by means of ensuring high simplicity and practicability of do-it-yourself business systems and securing low cost management consulting services.
- To provide the entrepreneurs with a permanent source of business management information, methods, and systems and to keep them abreast of all the latest developments pertinent to their specific activities.
- To ensure that the entrepreneurs maintain their independence by securing the continuous successful performance of their organizations.

Since the service offered by Business Management Club, Inc. represents a combination of the first two options it provides the entrepreneurs with the distinct advantages pertinent to those options. Hence, entrepreneurs are given an opportunity to become management consultants to their own organizations by learning the basic principles of the business engineering methodology.

Membership in Business Management Club, Inc.   It is assumed at this stage that the strengths and weaknesses of the organization have been successfully identified and a suitable plan of action formulated. It is essential, therefore, to evaluate the relevant results, comments, and recommendations summarized previously and to select the most suitable method of solving existing management problems. The final choice of options is entirely in the hands of the company's management and hopefully the choice will be in the best interests of the organization. However, if management selects the last option and decides to utilize the broad range of management solutions developed and distributed by Business Management Club, it could be the beginning of a most productive and successful association.

It should be stressed that Business Management Club is totally committed to the progress and promotion of interests of all small and medium-sized organizations. This commitment remains the most important single factor in the process of development, distribution, and implementation of sound and effective management solutions on a do-it-yourself basis or through services of specially trained management consultants.

A wide range of management information and services are provided exclusively to members of the Business Management Club. The information and services provided by the Club's network relate to various aspects of the business engineering methodology including general administration, personnel, finance and accounting, production and operations, and marketing and sales.

Since management assistance is provided solely to members of the Business Management Club, small and medium-sized organizations are invited to apply for a *free membership*. In order to become a member of this Club, companies must complete a **Membership Application Form** (refer to Form 6–25) and mail it to Business Management Club, Inc.

Once the application for a free membership is approved the company will be contacted by the local representative of the Business Management Club's network who will provide additional details pertaining to management assistance that the company may expect in the future.

6.22 Working Instructions and Forms for Chapter 4

All information related to the company's operational and financial performance evaluation has been presented in Parts 1 through 6. It is essential to summarize this information and to proceed with the completion of appropriate forms provided at the end of Chapter 4. Working instructions for completing these forms follow immediately. These instructions require that management consolidates relevant information in accordance with the sequence of activities presented in Exhibit 6–18.

Form 6–15   Consolidated Plan of Action

147.   Enter the summary of final evaluation level results pertaining to your company's operational performance in the following areas:

Exhibit 6–18

Summary of Forms for Plan of Action

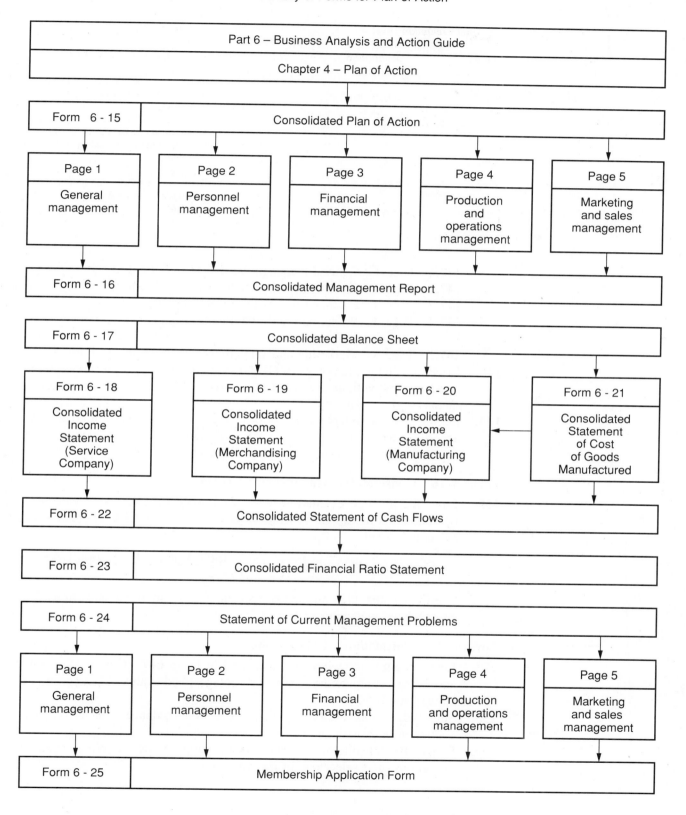

Exhibit 6–19

Summarized Operating Instructions for Implementing a Plan of Action

Final Evaluation Level		Plan of Work	
Range	Description	No.	Operating Instruction
0–20%	Very Poor	1	To introduce new methods or systems to substantially upgrade existing performance
21–40%	Poor	2	To introduce improved methods or systems to upgrade existing performance
41–60%	Fair		
61–80%	Good	3	To maintain performance on the existing level and improve if possible
81–100%	Very Good		

147.1 Page 1—General management (Refer to Form 1–3)

147.2 Page 2—Personnel management (Refer to Form 2–3)

147.3 Page 3—Financial management (Refer to Form 3–3)

147.4 Page 4—Production and operations management (Refer to Form 4–3)

147.5 Page 5—Marketing and sales management (Refer to Form 5–3)

148. Select a suitable plan of work (1/2/3) in accordance with the summarized operating instructions presented in Exhibit 6–19 and the specific requirements of your company.

149. Decide upon a suitable work priority (very urgent/urgent/not so urgent) according to the final evaluation results and specific considerations of your company's executive management team.

Form 6–16   Consolidated Management Report

150. Enter the average evaluation level results pertinent to your company's operational activities (refer to Form 6–15) and compute the consolidated evaluation level as follows:

$$\text{Consolidated Evaluation Level} = \frac{\text{Total Average Evaluation Level}}{5}$$

151. Summarize the plan of action specified in Form 6–15 and prepare a consolidated management report.

Form 6–17   Consolidated Balance Sheet

152. Enter the summarized values specified in Form 6–7—Comparative Balance Sheet, compute the relative percentages, and evaluate the appropriate annual trends.[a]

153. Summarize final results and conclusions in accordance with information contained in this statement.

154. Prepare the consolidated income statement appropriate for your company's operations, and select one of the following:

---

[a]For the purpose of annual trend evaluation, the respective values of the first fiscal year represent 100.0% in relation to the corresponding values of the second fiscal year, similar values of the second fiscal year represent 100.0% in relation to the corresponding values of the third fiscal year, and so on.

154.1   Form 6–18—Consolidated Income Statement for a Service Company (Refer to instructions 155–156)

154.2   Form 6–19—Consolidated Income Statement for a Merchandising Company (Refer to instructions 157–158)

154.3   Form 6–20—Consolidated Income Statement for a Manufacturing Company (Refer to instructions 159–160)

Form 6–18   Consolidated Income Statement (Service Company)

155.   Enter the summarized values specified in Form 6–8—Comparative Income Statement for a Service Company, compute the relative percentages, and evaluate the appropriate annual trends.[a]

156.   Summarize final results and conclusions in accordance with information contained in this statement.

Form 6–19   Consolidated Income Statement (Merchandising Company)

157.   Enter the summarized values specified in Form 6–9—Comparative Income Statement for a Merchandising Company, compute the relative percentages, and evaluate the appropriate annual trends.[a]

158.   Summarize final results and conclusions in accordance with information contained in this statement.

Form 6–20   Consolidated Income Statement (Manufacturing Company)

159.   Enter the summarized values specified in Form 6–10—Comparative Income Statement for a Manufacturing Company, compute the relative percentages, and evaluate the appropriate annual trends.[a]

160.   Summarize final results and conclusions in accordance with information contained in this statement.

Form 6–21   Consolidated Statement of Cost of Goods Manufactured

161.   Enter the summarized values specified in Form 6–11—Comparative Statement of Cost of Goods Manufactured, compute the relative percentages, and evaluate the appropriate annual trends.[a]

162.   Summarize final results and conclusions in accordance with information contained in this statement.

Form 6–22   Consolidated Statement of Cash Flows

163.   Enter the summarized values specified in Form 6–12—Comparative Statement of Cash Flows, compute the relative percentages, and evaluate the appropriate annual trends.[a]

162.   Summarize final results and conclusions in accordance with information contained in this statement.

Form 6–23   Consolidated Financial Ratio Statement

165.   Identify the suggested norm pertinent to each financial ratio in accordance with the nature of your company's operations and type of industry.[b]

166.   Enter the financial ratio values specified in Form 6–14—Comparative Financial Ratio Statement, compute relative percentages, and evaluate the appropriate annual trends.[a]

---

[a]Refer to instruction 152.

[b]A set of financial ratios appropriate to your type of business is available upon request from Business Management Club, Inc.

167. Compare the actual financial ratio values with the suggested norms and summarize final comments, conclusions, and recommendations in accordance with information contained in this statement.

Form 6–24   Statement of Current Management Problems

168. Identify current management problems in a specific area of operating activities and summarize these.

    168.1 Page 1—General management

    168.2 Page 2—Personnel management

    168.3 Page 3—Financial management

    168.4 Page 4—Production and operations management

    168.5 Page 5—Marketing and sales management

Form 6–25   Membership Application Form

169. Complete and mail the application for a free membership in Business Management Club, Inc. in order to qualify for additional management assistance.

This concludes the listing of working instructions pertaining to the evaluation of your company's performance and development of the plan of action.

FINAL EVALUATION RESULTS
CONSOLIDATED PLAN OF ACTION

NO.	DESCRIPTION	FINAL EVALUATION LEVEL (%)	PLAN OF WORK (1/2/3)	WORK PRIORITY		
				VERY URGENT	URGENT	NOT SO URGENT
1.00	GENERAL MANAGEMENT					
1.01	The Basic Management Process					
1.02	Evolution of Management Theory					
1.03	Business Engineering Method					
1.04	Environment and Organizational Culture					
1.05	Principles of Decision Making					
1.06	The Planning Process					
1.07	Strategic Planning					
1.08	Implementation of Strategic Plans					
1.09	Management by Objectives					
1.10	Operational Planning					
1.11	Plan of Management					
1.12	The Organizing Process					
1.13	Organizational Departmentation					
1.14	Management Structure					
1.15	Organizational Development					
1.16	The Leading Process					
1.17	Principles of Communication					
1.18	The Controlling Process					
1.19	Managerial Ethics					
1.20	Theory Z					
⟶	AVERAGE EVALUATION LEVEL		REFER TO FORM 1–3			

NAME:	POSITION:	DATE:

FINAL EVALUATION RESULTS
CONSOLIDATED PLAN OF ACTION

No.	DESCRIPTION	FINAL EVALUATION LEVEL (%)	PLAN OF WORK (1/2/3)	WORK PRIORITY		
2.00	PERSONNEL MANAGEMENT			VERY URGENT	URGENT	NOT SO URGENT
2.01	The Personnel Management Process					
2.02	Equal Employment Opportunity Laws					
2.03	Job Analysis					
2.04	Job Descriptions and Job Specifications					
2.05	Personnel Planning and Forecasting					
2.06	Personnel Recruitment and Hiring					
2.07	Screening and Testing of Applicants					
2.08	Employment Interviews					
2.09	Personnel Orientation					
2.10	Personnel Training					
2.11	Management Development					
2.12	Personnel Motivation					
2.13	Basic Job Compensation					
2.14	Financial Incentives					
2.15	Fringe Benefits					
2.16	Personnel Performance Appraisal					
2.17	Personnel Career Management					
2.18	Labor-Management Relations					
2.19	Collective Bargaining and Conflict Management					
2.20	Personnel Safety and Health					
→	AVERAGE EVALUATION LEVEL		REFER TO FORM 2–3			

NAME:	POSITION:	DATE:

FINAL EVALUATION RESULTS
CONSOLIDATED PLAN OF ACTION

NO.	DESCRIPTION	FINAL EVALUATION LEVEL (%)	PLAN OF WORK (1/2/3)	WORK PRIORITY		
				VERY URGENT	URGENT	NOT SO URGENT
3.00	FINANCIAL MANAGEMENT					
3.01	The Financial Management Process					
3.02	Accounting Information					
3.03	Bookkeeping System					
3.04	Financial Statements					
3.05	Financial Performance Evaluation					
3.06	Operating Budget					
3.07	Capital Expenditure Budget					
3.08	Cash Budget					
3.09	Tax Strategies					
3.10	Sources of Finance					
3.11	Internal Control and Cash Management					
3.12	Control of Purchases and Disbursements					
3.13	Credit Control					
3.14	Inventory Management					
3.15	Capital Assets Management					
3.16	Payroll Accounting System					
3.17	Cost Accounting System					
3.18	Pricing Methods					
3.19	Management Accounting System					
3.20	Computerized System					
→	AVERAGE EVALUATION LEVEL		REFER TO FORM 3–3			

| NAME: | POSITION: | DATE: |

FINAL EVALUATION RESULTS
CONSOLIDATED PLAN OF ACTION

NO.	DESCRIPTION	FINAL EVALUATION LEVEL (%)	PLAN OF WORK (1/2/3)	WORK PRIORITY		
				VERY URGENT	URGENT	NOT SO URGENT
4.00	PRODUCTION AND OPERATIONS MANAGEMENT					
4.01	The Production and Operations Management Process					
4.02	Classification of Operational Activities					
4.03	Facility Design, Location, and Organization					
4.04	Product Selection, Design, and Standardization					
4.05	Process Design					
4.06	The Drafting Office					
4.07	Equipment Evaluation and Selection					
4.08	Plant Layout					
4.09	Equipment Maintenance					
4.10	Equipment Replacement					
4.11	Tool Control					
4.12	Cost Estimating					
4.13	Production Planning					
4.14	Material Requirements Planning					
4.15	Production Control					
4.16	Planning and Control of Services and Projects					
4.17	Quality Control					
4.18	Materials Purchasing					
4.19	Materials Control, Storage, and Dispatch					
4.20	Just-In-Time Manufacturing Philosophy					
⟶	AVERAGE EVALUATION LEVEL		REFER TO FORM 4–3			

NAME:	POSITION:	DATE:

FINAL EVALUATION RESULTS

CONSOLIDATED PLAN OF ACTION

NO.	DESCRIPTION	FINAL EVALUATION LEVEL (%)	PLAN OF WORK (1/2/3)	WORK PRIORITY		
				VERY URGENT	URGENT	NOT SO URGENT
5.00	MARKETING AND SALES MANAGEMENT					
5.01	The Marketing Management Process					
5.02	Buying Behavior					
5.03	Marketing Information and Research					
5.04	Market Segmentation					
5.05	Market Measurement and Forecasting					
5.06	Marketing Strategy					
5.07	Product Strategy					
5.08	Pricing Strategy					
5.09	Promotional Strategy					
5.10	Distribution Strategy					
5.11	Marketing Plan					
5.12	The Sales Management Process					
5.13	Sales Planning and Budgeting					
5.14	Sales Organization					
5.15	Sales Force Recruitment and Training					
5.16	Personal Selling					
5.17	Sales Force Compensation					
5.18	Sales Force Management and Motivation					
5.19	Sales Performance Evaluation and Control					
5.20	Marketing Audit					
⟶	AVERAGE EVALUATION LEVEL		REFER TO FORM 5–3			

| NAME: | POSITION: | DATE: |

FINAL EVALUATION RESULTS
CONSOLIDATED MANAGEMENT REPORT

NO.	DESCRIPTION	AVERAGE EVALUATION LEVEL (%)				
		VERY POOR	POOR	FAIR	GOOD	VERY GOOD
		0-20	21-40	41-60	61-80	81-100
1	GENERAL MANAGEMENT					
2	PERSONNEL MANAGEMENT					
3	FINANCIAL MANAGEMENT					
4	PRODUCTION AND OPERATIONS MANAGEMENT					
5	MARKETING AND SALES MANAGEMENT					
→	CONSOLIDATED EVALUATION LEVEL					

CONSOLIDATED MANAGEMENT REPORT

	GENERAL MANAGEMENT:
1	

	PERSONNEL MANAGEMENT:
2	

SEE CONTINUATION OF THIS REPORT ON THE FOLLOWING PAGE

FINAL EVALUATION RESULTS
CONSOLIDATED MANAGEMENT REPORT

CONSOLIDATED MANAGEMENT REPORT (CONTINUATION)

3 — FINANCIAL MANAGEMENT:

4 — PRODUCTION AND OPERATIONS MANAGEMENT:

5 — MARKETING AND SALES MANAGEMENT:

| NAME: | POSITION: | DATE: |

FINAL EVALUATION RESULTS

CONSOLIDATED BALANCE SHEET

ACTION				ACCOUNT DESCRIPTION	A		
1	2	3	CODE			VALUE	%
+	+		100	TOTAL CURRENT ASSETS	$		
					%	100.0	⟶
–		+	160	TOTAL CURRENT LIABILITIES	$		
					%	100.0	⟶
=			200	WORKING CAPITAL	$		
					%	100.0	⟶
+	+		120	TOTAL CAPITAL ASSETS	$		
					%	100.0	⟶
+	+		130	TOTAL LONG-TERM INVESTMENTS	$		
					%	100.0	⟶
+	+		140	TOTAL INTANGIBLE ASSETS	$		
					%	100.0	⟶
–		+	180	TOTAL LONG-TERM LIABILITIES	$		
					%	100.0	⟶
=		+	300	SHAREHOLDERS' EQUITY	$		
					%	100.0	⟶
	=		150	TOTAL ASSETS =	$		100.0
		=	400	SHAREHOLDERS' EQUITY + TOTAL LIABILITIES	%	100.0	⟶

FINAL RESULTS AND CONCLUSIONS:

NAME:	POSITION:	DATE:

INFORMATION CONTAINED HEREIN RELATES TO THE FOLLOWING FISCAL PERIODS:							
COLUMNS A,B,C				COLUMN D		COLUMN E	
COMPARATIVE ANALYSIS RESULTS				CURRENT YEAR BUDGET		NEXT YEAR BUDGET	
B		C		D		E	
VALUE	%	VALUE	%	VALUE	%	VALUE	%
	⟶		⟶		⟶		⟶
	⟶		⟶		⟶		⟶
	⟶		⟶		⟶		⟶
	⟶		⟶		⟶		⟶
	⟶		⟶		⟶		⟶
	⟶		⟶		⟶		⟶
	⟶		⟶		⟶		⟶
	⟶		⟶		⟶		⟶
	100.0		100.0		100.0		100.0
	⟶		⟶		⟶		⟶

FINAL RESULTS AND CONCLUSIONS:

FINAL EVALUATION RESULTS
CONSOLIDATED INCOME STATEMENT (SERVICE COMPANY)

ACTION				ACCOUNT DESCRIPTION		A	VALUE	%
1	2	3	CODE					
+			500	NET REVENUE FROM SERVICES	$			100.0
					%		100.0	⟶
–			600	TOTAL OPERATING EXPENSES	$			
					%		100.0	⟶
=			700	INCOME FROM OPERATIONS	$			
					%		100.0	⟶
–			698	INTEREST EXPENSE	$			
					%		100.0	⟶
+			580	NET MISCELLANEOUS REVENUE	$			
					%		100.0	⟶
=			800	INCOME BEFORE TAXES	$			
					%		100.0	⟶
–			699	INCOME TAXES EXPENSE	$			
					%		100.0	⟶
=			900	NET INCOME	$			
					%		100.0	⟶

FINAL RESULTS AND CONCLUSIONS:

NAME:	POSITION:	DATE:

INFORMATION CONTAINED HEREIN RELATES TO THE FOLLOWING FISCAL PERIODS:							
COLUMNS A,B,C				COLUMN D		COLUMN E	
COMPARATIVE ANALYSIS RESULTS				CURRENT YEAR BUDGET		NEXT YEAR BUDGET	
B		C		D		E	
VALUE	%	VALUE	%	VALUE	%	VALUE	%
	100.0		100.0		100.0		100.0
	——→		——→		——→		——→
	——→		——→		——→		——→
	——→		——→		——→		——→
	——→		——→		——→		——→
	——→		——→		——→		——→
	——→		——→		——→		——→
	——→		——→		——→		——→
	——→		——→		——→		——→

FINAL RESULTS AND CONCLUSIONS:

NAME OF COMPANY:

FINAL EVALUATION RESULTS
CONSOLIDATED INCOME STATEMENT (MERCHANDISING COMPANY)

ACTION			CODE	ACCOUNT DESCRIPTION	A		
1	2	3				VALUE	%
	+		500	NET SALES	$		100.0
					%	100.0	⟶
+			601	MERCHANDISE INVENTORY (BEGINNING)	$		
					%	100.0	⟶
+			610	NET PURCHASES	$		
					%	100.0	⟶
=			620	COST OF GOODS AVAILABLE FOR SALE	$		
					%	100.0	⟶
−			621	MERCHANDISE INVENTORY (ENDING)	$		
					%	100.0	⟶
=	−		630	COST OF GOODS SOLD	$		
					%	100.0	⟶
	=		640	GROSS MARGIN FROM SALES	$		
					%	100.0	⟶
	−		650	TOTAL OPERATING EXPENSES	$		
					%	100.0	⟶
	=		700	INCOME FROM OPERATIONS	$		
					%	100.0	⟶
	−		698	INTEREST EXPENSE	$		
					%	100.0	⟶
	+		580	NET MISCELLANEOUS REVENUE	$		
					%	100.0	⟶
	=		800	INCOME BEFORE TAXES	$		
					%	100.0	⟶
	−		699	INCOME TAXES EXPENSE	$		
					%	100.0	⟶
	=		900	NET INCOME	$		
					%	100.0	⟶

FINAL RESULTS AND CONCLUSIONS:

NAME: | POSITION: | DATE:

INFORMATION CONTAINED HEREIN RELATES TO THE FOLLOWING FISCAL PERIODS:							
COLUMNS A,B,C				COLUMN D		COLUMN E	
COMPARATIVE ANALYSIS RESULTS				CURRENT YEAR BUDGET		NEXT YEAR BUDGET	
B		C		D		E	
VALUE	%	VALUE	%	VALUE	%	VALUE	%
	100.0		100.0		100.0		100.0
	→		→		→		→
	→		→		→		→
	→		→		→		→
	→		→		→		→
	→		→		→		→
	→		→		→		→
	→		→		→		→
	→		→		→		→
	→		→		→		→
	→		→		→		→
	→		→		→		→
	→		→		→		→
	→		→		→		→
	→		→		→		→
	→		→		→		→
FINAL RESULTS AND CONCLUSIONS:							

NAME OF COMPANY:

FINAL EVALUATION RESULTS
CONSOLIDATED INCOME STATEMENT (MANUFACTURING COMPANY)

ACTION				ACCOUNT DESCRIPTION	A		
1	2	3	CODE			VALUE	%
	+		500	NET SALES	$		100.0
					%	100.0	⟶
+			601	FINISHED GOODS INVENTORY (BEGINNING)	$		
					%	100.0	⟶
+			700	COST OF GOODS MANUFACTURED (REFER TO FORM 6-21)	$		
					%	100.0	⟶
=			610	COST OF GOODS AVAILABLE FOR SALE	$		
					%	100.0	⟶
−			611	FINISHED GOODS INVENTORY (ENDING)	$		
					%	100.0	⟶
=	−		620	COST OF GOODS SOLD	$		
					%	100.0	⟶
	=		630	GROSS MARGIN FROM SALES	$		
					%	100.0	⟶
	−		640	TOTAL OPERATING EXPENSES	$		
					%	100.0	⟶
	=		800	INCOME FROM OPERATIONS	$		
					%	100.0	⟶
	−		698	INTEREST EXPENSE	$		
					%	100.0	⟶
	+		580	NET MISCELLANEOUS REVENUE	$		
					%	100.0	⟶
	=		900	INCOME BEFORE TAXES	$		
					%	100.0	⟶
	−		699	INCOME TAXES EXPENSE	$		
					%	100.0	⟶
	=		999	NET INCOME	$		
					%	100.0	⟶

FINAL RESULTS AND CONCLUSIONS:

NAME:	POSITION:	DATE:

INFORMATION CONTAINED HEREIN RELATES TO THE FOLLOWING FISCAL PERIODS:							
COLUMNS A,B,C				COLUMN D		COLUMN E	
COMPARATIVE ANALYSIS RESULTS				CURRENT YEAR BUDGET		NEXT YEAR BUDGET	
B		C		D		E	
VALUE	%	VALUE	%	VALUE	%	VALUE	%
	100.0		100.0		100.0		100.0
	→		→		→		→
	→		→		→		→
	→		→		→		→
	→		→		→		→
	→		→		→		→
	→		→		→		→
	→		→		→		→
	→		→		→		→
	→		→		→		→
	→		→		→		→
	→		→		→		→
	→		→		→		→
	→		→		→		→
	→		→		→		→
	→		→		→		→
FINAL RESULTS AND CONCLUSIONS:							

FINAL EVALUATION RESULTS
CONSOLIDATED STATEMENT OF COST OF GOODS MANUFACTURED

ACTION				ACCOUNT DESCRIPTION	A		
1	2	3	CODE			VALUE	%
+			701	DIRECT MATERIALS INVENTORY (BEGINNING)	$		
					%	100.0	⟶
+			710	DIRECT MATERIALS PURCHASES (NET)	$		
					%	100.0	⟶
=			720	COST OF DIRECT MATERIALS AVAILABLE FOR USE	$		
					%	100.0	⟶
−			721	DIRECT MATERIALS INVENTORY (ENDING)	$		
					%	100.0	⟶
=	+		730	COST OF DIRECT MATERIALS USED	$		
					%	100.0	⟶
	+		740	DIRECT LABOR COSTS	$		
					%	100.0	⟶
	+		750	DIRECT SUBCONTRACTING SERVICE COSTS	$		
					%	100.0	⟶
	+		760	TOTAL PLANT OVERHEAD COSTS	$		
					%	100.0	⟶
	=		780	TOTAL MANUFACTURING COSTS	$		
					%	100.0	⟶
	+		781	WORK-IN-PROCESS INVENTORY (BEGINNING)	$		
					%	100.0	⟶
	=		790	TOTAL COST OF WORK-IN-PROCESS	$		
					%	100.0	⟶
	−		791	WORK-IN-PROCESS INVENTORY (ENDING)	$		
					%	100.0	⟶
	=		700	COST OF GOODS MANUFACTURED (REFER TO FORM 6-20)	$		
					%	100.0	⟶

FINAL RESULTS AND CONCLUSIONS:

NAME:	POSITION:	DATE:

INFORMATION CONTAINED HEREIN RELATES TO THE FOLLOWING FISCAL PERIODS:							
COLUMNS A, B, C				COLUMN D		COLUMN E	
COMPARATIVE ANALYSIS RESULTS				CURRENT YEAR BUDGET		NEXT YEAR BUDGET	
B		C		D		E	
VALUE	%	VALUE	%	VALUE	%	VALUE	%
	→		→		→		→
	→		→		→		→
	→		→		→		→
	→		→		→		→
	→		→		→		→
	→		→		→		→
	→		→		→		→
	→		→		→		→
	→		→		→		→
	→		→		→		→
	→		→		→		→
	→		→		→		→
FINAL RESULTS AND CONCLUSIONS:							

FINAL EVALUATION RESULTS
CONSOLIDATED STATEMENT OF CASH FLOWS

ACTION				ACCOUNT DESCRIPTION	A		(%) OF CASH	
1	2	3	4			VALUE	INCREASE	DECREASE
+				NET CASH FLOW FROM OPERATING ACTIVITIES	$			
					%	100.0	————————►	
+				NET CASH FLOW FROM INVESTING ACTIVITIES	$			
					%	100.0	————————►	
+				NET CASH FLOW FROM FINANCING ACTIVITIES	$			
					%	100.0	————————►	
	+			TOTAL INCREASES IN CASH DURING THE PERIOD	$		100.0	—
					%	100.0	————————►	
	–			TOTAL DECREASES IN CASH DURING THE PERIOD	$		—	100.0
					%	100.0	————————►	
=	=	+		NET INCREASE (DECREASE) IN CASH	$			
					%	100.0	————————►	
		+		CASH BALANCE AT THE START OF THE PERIOD	$		—	—
					%	100.0	————————►	
		=		CASH BALANCE AT THE END OF THE PERIOD	$		—	—
					%	100.0	————————►	

FINAL RESULTS AND CONCLUSIONS:

NAME:	POSITION:	DATE:

INFORMATION CONTAINED HEREIN RELATES TO THE FOLLOWING FISCAL PERIODS:								
COLUMNS A,B,C						COLUMN D		
COMPARATIVE ANALYSIS RESULTS						CURRENT YEAR BUDGET		
B		(%) OF CASH		C		(%) OF CASH		D		(%) OF CASH	
VALUE	INCREASE	DECREASE	VALUE	INCREASE	DECREASE	VALUE	INCREASE	DECREASE
	——→			——→			——→	
	——→			——→			——→	
	——→			——→			——→	
	100.0	—		100.0	—		100.0	—
	——→			——→			——→	
	—	100.0		—	100.0		—	100.0
	——→			——→			——→	
	——→			——→			——→	
	—	—		—	—		—	—
	——→			——→			——→	
	—	—		—	—		—	—
	——→			——→			——→	
FINAL RESULTS AND CONCLUSIONS:								

FINAL EVALUATION RESULTS
CONSOLIDATED FINANCIAL RATIO STATEMENT

1. CURRENT RATIO

SUGGESTED NORM		COMPARATIVE ANALYSIS RESULTS			CURRENT ANALYSIS RESULTS
RATIO	%				
TREND	%	100.0			

COMMENTS	
CONCLUSIONS	
RECOMMENDATIONS	

2. QUICK RATIO

SUGGESTED NORM		COMPARATIVE ANALYSIS RESULTS			CURRENT ANALYSIS RESULTS
RATIO	%				
TREND	%	100.0			

COMMENTS	
CONCLUSIONS	
RECOMMENDATIONS	

| NAME: | POSITION: | DATE: |

NAME OF COMPANY:		

FINAL EVALUATION RESULTS
CONSOLIDATED FINANCIAL RATIO STATEMENT

3. RECEIVABLES COLLECTION PERIOD

SUGGESTED NORM		COMPARATIVE ANALYSIS RESULTS			CURRENT ANALYSIS RESULTS
RATIO	Days				
TREND	%	100.0			
COMMENTS					
CONCLUSIONS					
RECOMMENDATIONS					

4. PAYMENT PERIOD TO CREDITORS

SUGGESTED NORM		COMPARATIVE ANALYSIS RESULTS			CURRENT ANALYSIS RESULTS
RATIO	Days				
TREND	%	100.0			
COMMENTS					
CONCLUSIONS					
RECOMMENDATIONS					

NAME:	POSITION:	DATE:

FINAL EVALUATION RESULTS
CONSOLIDATED FINANCIAL RATIO STATEMENT

5. CURRENT LIABILITY RATIO

SUGGESTED NORM		COMPARATIVE ANALYSIS RESULTS			CURRENT ANALYSIS RESULTS
RATIO	%				
TREND	%	100.0			

COMMENTS	
CONCLUSIONS	
RECOMMENDATIONS	

6. LONG-TERM LIABILITY RATIO

SUGGESTED NORM		COMPARATIVE ANALYSIS RESULTS			CURRENT ANALYSIS RESULTS
RATIO	%				
TREND	%	100.0			

COMMENTS	
CONCLUSIONS	
RECOMMENDATIONS	

NAME:	POSITION:	DATE:

FINAL EVALUATION RESULTS
CONSOLIDATED FINANCIAL RATIO STATEMENT

7. EQUITY RATIO

SUGGESTED NORM		COMPARATIVE ANALYSIS RESULTS			CURRENT ANALYSIS RESULTS
RATIO	%				
TREND	%	100.0			

COMMENTS	
CONCLUSIONS	
RECOMMENDATIONS	

8. DEBT-TO-EQUITY RATIO

SUGGESTED NORM		COMPARATIVE ANALYSIS RESULTS			CURRENT ANALYSIS RESULTS
RATIO	%				
TREND	%	100.0			

COMMENTS	
CONCLUSIONS	
RECOMMENDATIONS	

NAME:	POSITION:	DATE:

FINAL EVALUATION RESULTS
CONSOLIDATED FINANCIAL RATIO STATEMENT

9. INTEREST COVERAGE RATIO

SUGGESTED NORM		COMPARATIVE ANALYSIS RESULTS			CURRENT ANALYSIS RESULTS
RATIO	Times				
TREND	%	100.0			

COMMENTS	
CONCLUSIONS	
RECOMMENDATIONS	

10. GROSS MARGIN FROM SALES

SUGGESTED NORM		COMPARATIVE ANALYSIS RESULTS			CURRENT ANALYSIS RESULTS
RATIO	%				
TREND	%	100.0			

COMMENTS	
CONCLUSIONS	
RECOMMENDATIONS	

NAME:	POSITION:	DATE:

FINAL EVALUATION RESULTS
CONSOLIDATED FINANCIAL RATIO STATEMENT

11. RETURN ON SALES

SUGGESTED NORM		COMPARATIVE ANALYSIS RESULTS			CURRENT ANALYSIS RESULTS
RATIO	%				
TREND	%	100.0			

COMMENTS	

CONCLUSIONS	

RECOMMENDATIONS	

12. RETURN ON ASSETS

SUGGESTED NORM		COMPARATIVE ANALYSIS RESULTS			CURRENT ANALYSIS RESULTS
RATIO	%				
TREND	%	100.0			

COMMENTS	

CONCLUSIONS	

RECOMMENDATIONS	

NAME:	POSITION:	DATE:

FINAL EVALUATION RESULTS
CONSOLIDATED FINANCIAL RATIO STATEMENT

13. RETURN ON SHAREHOLDERS' EQUITY

SUGGESTED NORM		COMPARATIVE ANALYSIS RESULTS			CURRENT ANALYSIS RESULTS
RATIO	%				
TREND	%	100.0			

COMMENTS	
CONCLUSIONS	
RECOMMENDATIONS	

14. WORKING CAPITAL TURNOVER

SUGGESTED NORM		COMPARATIVE ANALYSIS RESULTS			CURRENT ANALYSIS RESULTS
RATIO	Times				
TREND	%	100.0			

COMMENTS	
CONCLUSIONS	
RECOMMENDATIONS	

NAME:	POSITION:	DATE:

FINAL EVALUATION RESULTS
CONSOLIDATED FINANCIAL RATIO STATEMENT

15. INVENTORY TURNOVER RATE

SUGGESTED NORM		COMPARATIVE ANALYSIS RESULTS			CURRENT ANALYSIS RESULTS
RATIO	Times				
TREND	%	100.0			

COMMENTS	
CONCLUSIONS	
RECOMMENDATIONS	

16. INVENTORY TURNOVER PERIOD

SUGGESTED NORM		COMPARATIVE ANALYSIS RESULTS			CURRENT ANALYSIS RESULTS
RATIO	Days				
TREND	%	100.0			

COMMENTS	
CONCLUSIONS	
RECOMMENDATIONS	

NAME:	POSITION:	DATE:

NAME OF COMPANY:

FINAL EVALUATION RESULTS
CONSOLIDATED FINANCIAL RATIO STATEMENT

17. INVENTORY-TO-WORKING CAPITAL RATIO

SUGGESTED NORM		COMPARATIVE ANALYSIS RESULTS			CURRENT ANALYSIS RESULTS
RATIO	%				
TREND	%	100.0			
COMMENTS					
CONCLUSIONS					
RECOMMENDATIONS					

18. CAPITAL ASSETS TURNOVER

SUGGESTED NORM		COMPARATIVE ANALYSIS RESULTS			CURRENT ANALYSIS RESULTS
RATIO	Times				
TREND	%	100.0			
COMMENTS					
CONCLUSIONS					
RECOMMENDATIONS					

NAME:	POSITION:	DATE:

FINAL EVALUATION RESULTS
CONSOLIDATED FINANCIAL RATIO STATEMENT

19. TOTAL ASSETS TURNOVER

SUGGESTED NORM		COMPARATIVE ANALYSIS RESULTS			CURRENT ANALYSIS RESULTS
RATIO	Times				
TREND	%	100.0			

COMMENTS	
CONCLUSIONS	
RECOMMENDATIONS	

20. INCOME TAXES PAYMENT RATIO

SUGGESTED NORM		COMPARATIVE ANALYSIS RESULTS			CURRENT ANALYSIS RESULTS
RATIO	%				
TREND	%	100.0			

COMMENTS	
CONCLUSIONS	
RECOMMENDATIONS	

NAME:	POSITION:	DATE:

STATEMENT OF CURRENT MANAGEMENT PROBLEMS
GENERAL MANAGEMENT

No.	DESCRIPTION	CURRENT MANAGEMENT PROBLEM
1.01	The Basic Management Process	
1.02	Evolution of Management Theory	
1.03	Business Engineering Method	
1.04	Environment and Organizational Culture	
1.05	Principles of Decision Making	
1.06	The Planning Process	
1.07	Strategic Planning	
1.08	Implementation of Strategic Plans	
1.09	Management by Objectives	
1.10	Operational Planning	
1.11	Plan of Management	
1.12	The Organizing Process	
1.13	Organizational Departmentation	
1.14	Management Structure	
1.15	Organizational Development	
1.16	The Leading Process	
1.17	Principles of Communication	
1.18	The Controlling Process	
1.19	Managerial Ethics	
1.20	Theory Z	

| NAME: | POSITION: | DATE: |

STATEMENT OF CURRENT MANAGEMENT PROBLEMS
PERSONNEL MANAGEMENT

No.	DESCRIPTION	CURRENT MANAGEMENT PROBLEM
2.01	The Personnel Management Process	
2.02	Equal Employment Opportunity Laws	
2.03	Job Analysis	
2.04	Job Descriptions and Job Specifications	
2.05	Personnel Planning and Forecasting	
2.06	Personnel Recruitment and Hiring	
2.07	Screening and Testing of Applicants	
2.08	Employment Interviews	
2.09	Personnel Orientation	
2.10	Personnel Training	
2.11	Management Development	
2.12	Personnel Motivation	
2.13	Basic Job Compensation	
2.14	Financial Incentives	
2.15	Fringe Benefits	
2.16	Personnel Performance Appraisal	
2.17	Personnel Career Management	
2.18	Labor-Management Relations	
2.19	Collective Bargaining and Conflict Management	
2.20	Personnel Safety and Health	

| NAME: | POSITION: | DATE: |

STATEMENT OF CURRENT MANAGEMENT PROBLEMS

FINANCIAL MANAGEMENT

No.	DESCRIPTION	CURRENT MANAGEMENT PROBLEMS
3.01	The Financial Management Process	
3.02	Accounting Information	
3.03	Bookkeeping System	
3.04	Financial Statements	
3.05	Financial Performance Evaluation	
3.06	Operating Budget	
3.07	Capital Expenditure Budget	
3.08	Cash Budget	
3.09	Tax Strategies	
3.10	Sources of Finance	
3.11	Internal Control and Cash Management	
3.12	Control of Purchases and Disbursements	
3.13	Credit Control	
3.14	Inventory Management	
3.15	Capital Assets Management	
3.16	Payroll Accounting System	
3.17	Cost Accounting System	
3.18	Pricing Methods	
3.19	Management Accounting System	
3.20	Computerized System	

NAME:	POSITION:	DATE:

STATEMENT OF CURRENT MANAGEMENT PROBLEMS

Note: If you experience a problem in a specific area, mark X accordingly

No.	DESCRIPTION	DIFFICULTY IN CONDUCTING SELF-EVALUATION OF KNOWLEDGE	DIFFICULTY IN EVALUATING THE COMPANY'S PERFORMANCE	MANAGEMENT PROBLEM IN A SPECIFIC AREA OF ACTIVITIES	DIFFICULTY IN FORMULATING A PLAN OF ACTION	DIFFICULTY IN IMPLEMENTING A PLAN OF ACTION
4.00	PRODUCTION AND OPERATIONS MANAGEMENT					
4.01	The Production and Operations Management Process					
4.02	Classification of Operational Activities					
4.03	Facility Design, Location, and Organization					
4.04	Product Selection, Design, and Standardization					
4.05	Process Design					
4.06	The Drafting Office					
4.07	Equipment Evaluation and Selection					
4.08	Plant Layout					
4.09	Equipment Maintenance					
4.10	Equipment Replacement					
4.11	Tool Control					
4.12	Cost Estimating					
4.13	Production Planning					
4.14	Materials Requirements Planning					
4.15	Production Control					
4.16	Planning and Control of Services and Projects					
4.17	Quality Control					
4.18	Materials Purchasing					
4.19	Materials Control, Storage, and Dispatch					
4.20	Just-In-Time Manufacturing Philosophy					

NAME:	POSITION:	DATE:

STATEMENT OF CURRENT MANAGEMENT PROBLEMS

MARKETING AND SALES MANAGEMENT

No.	DESCRIPTION	CURRENT MANAGEMENT PROBLEM
5.01	The Marketing Management Process	
5.02	Buying Behavior	
5.03	Marketing Information and Research	
5.04	Market Segmentation	
5.05	Market Measurement and Forecasting	
5.06	Marketing Strategy	
5.07	Product Strategy	
5.08	Pricing Strategy	
5.09	Promotional Strategy	
5.10	Distribution Strategy	
5.11	Marketing Plan	
5.12	The Sales Management Process	
5.13	Sales Planning and Budgeting	
5.14	Sales Organization	
5.15	Sales Force Recruitment and Training	
5.16	Personal Selling	
5.17	Sales Force Compensation	
5.18	Sales Force Management and Motivation	
5.19	Sales Performance Evaluation and Control	
5.20	Marketing Audit	

NAME:	POSITION:	DATE:

| NAME OF COMPANY: | FORM 6 – 25 |
| | PAGE 1 OF 1 |

BUSINESS MANAGEMENT CLUB, INC.
MEMBERSHIP APPLICATION FORM

To: Membership Section
Business Management Club, Inc.
1223 Wilshire Blvd.
Santa Monica
CA 90403
U.S.A.

APPLICATION FOR A FREE MEMBERSHIP IN THE BUSINESS MANAGEMENT CLUB

Please admit our company as a full member of the Business Management Club. We understand that the membership in your organization is free and does not oblige or restrict us in any way.

POSTAL ADDRESS:

| TELEPHONE No.: | FAX No.: |

TYPE OF BUSINESS   (mark X wherever appropriate):

☐ Service; ☐ Wholesale; ☐ Retail; ☐ Manufacturing; ☐ Construction;

☐ Special Projects; ☐ Other (please specify): _____

NATURE OF PRODUCTS OR SERVICES (please specify):

| NUMBER OF EMPLOYEES: | YEARS IN BUSINESS: |

Please enclose a copy of a completed Statement of Current Management Problems (Form 6-24) in order to obtain the most effective management assistance from the Business Management Club. All information provided by you will be treated with the utmost confidentiality.

Please specify any additional management problems which you may experience at present:

| NAME: | POSITION: | DATE: |

6.23 References

1. *Statement of Financial Accounting Concepts No. 6*, "Elements of Financial Statements" (Stamford, CT: Financial Accounting Standards Board, December, 1985), par. 25.

2. Accounting Principles Board, *Statement of the Accounting Principles Board, No. 4.* (New York: American Institute of Certified Public Accountants, 1970), par. 198.

3. *Financial Accounting Standards: Original Pronouncements as of July 1, 1977.* (Stamford, CT: Financial Accounting Standards Board, 1977), ARB No. 43, Ch. 9, Sec. C, par. 35.

4. Ibid., par 49.

5. *Statement of Financial Accounting Standards No. 95*, "Statement of Cash Flows", (Stamford, CT: Financial Accounting Standards Board, 1987).

Index

Page numbers in **bold print** represent entries in this volume; all others are from Volume I of *Maximum Performance*.